KAZUKI TAKAHASHI
LATELY I REALLY ENJOY DRAWING COLOR ILLUSTRATIONS AND STICKING THEM UP IN FRONT OF MY COMPUTER. I'LL WORK HARD AND SHOW THEM TO YOU SOON.

KAZUKI TAKAHASHI
Artist/author Kazuki Takahashi first tried to break into the manga business in 1982, but success eluded him until *Yu-Gi-Oh!* debuted in the Japanese *Weekly Shonen Jump* magazine in 1996. *Yu-Gi-Oh!*'s themes of friendship and fighting, together with Takahashi's weird and imaginative monsters, soon became enormously successful, spawning a real-world card game, video games, and four anime series (two Japanese *Yu-Gi-Oh!* series, *Yu-Gi-Oh! GX* and *Yu-Gi-Oh! 5D's*). A lifelong gamer, Takahashi enjoys shogi (Japanese chess), Mahjong, card games, and tabletop RPGs, among other games.

NAOYUKI KAGEYAMA
Naoyuki Kageyama was born April 12th, 1969, which makes him an Aries, and is originally from Tokyo, Japan. He is the recipient of an honorable mention for the 1990 *Weekly Shonen Jump* Hop Step Award for his work, *Mahou No Trump* (Magic Trump) and started drawing *Yu-Gi-Oh! GX* for *Monthly V Jump* in February 2006. Kageyama is a baseball fan and his favorite team is the Seibu Lions.

NAOYUKI KAGEYAMA
THE *YU-GI-OH! GX* CHAPTERS USED TO BE 21 PAGES LONG, BUT NOW THEY'RE 31 PAGES LONG. ALTHOUGH THE EXTRA PAGES MAKE IT HARDER TO FINISH ALL THE WORK, I CAN USE BIGGER PANELS NOW TO MAKE THE SCENES MORE ENERGETIC. I'LL DO MY BEST TO CONTINUE DRAWING MANGA THAT ENTERTAINS YOU.

YU-GI-OH! GX Volume 4
SHONEN JUMP Manga Edition

This manga contains material that was originally published in English in **SHONEN JUMP** #75-80.

ORIGINAL CONCEPT/SUPERVISED BY
KAZUKI TAKAHASHI

STORY AND ART BY
NAOYUKI KAGEYAMA

Translation & English Adaptation/Kinami Watabe & Ian Reid,
HC Language Solutions
Touch-up Art & Lettering/John Hunt
Designer/Ronnie Casson
Editors/Mike Montesa & Jason Thompson

VP, Production/Alvin Lu
VP, Sales & Product Marketing/Gonzalo Ferreyra
VP, Creative/Linda Espinosa
Publisher/Hyoe Narita

Printed in the U.S.A.

Published by VIZ Media, LLC
P.O. Box 77010
San Francisco, CA 94107

10 9 8 7 6 5 4 3 2 1
First printing, January 2010

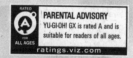

RATED **A** FOR ALL AGES | **PARENTAL ADVISORY**
YU-GI-OH! GX is rated A and is
suitable for readers of all ages.
ratings.viz.com

THE WORLD'S
MOST POPULAR MANGA

www.viz.com

www.shonenjump.com

Yu-Gi-Oh! GX

VOLUME
4
The Semifinals
Begin!!

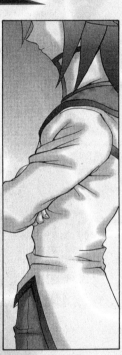

Original Concept/
Supervised by
**KAZUKI
TAKAHASHI**

Story & Art by
**NAOYUKI
KAGEYAMA**

THE STORY SO FAR

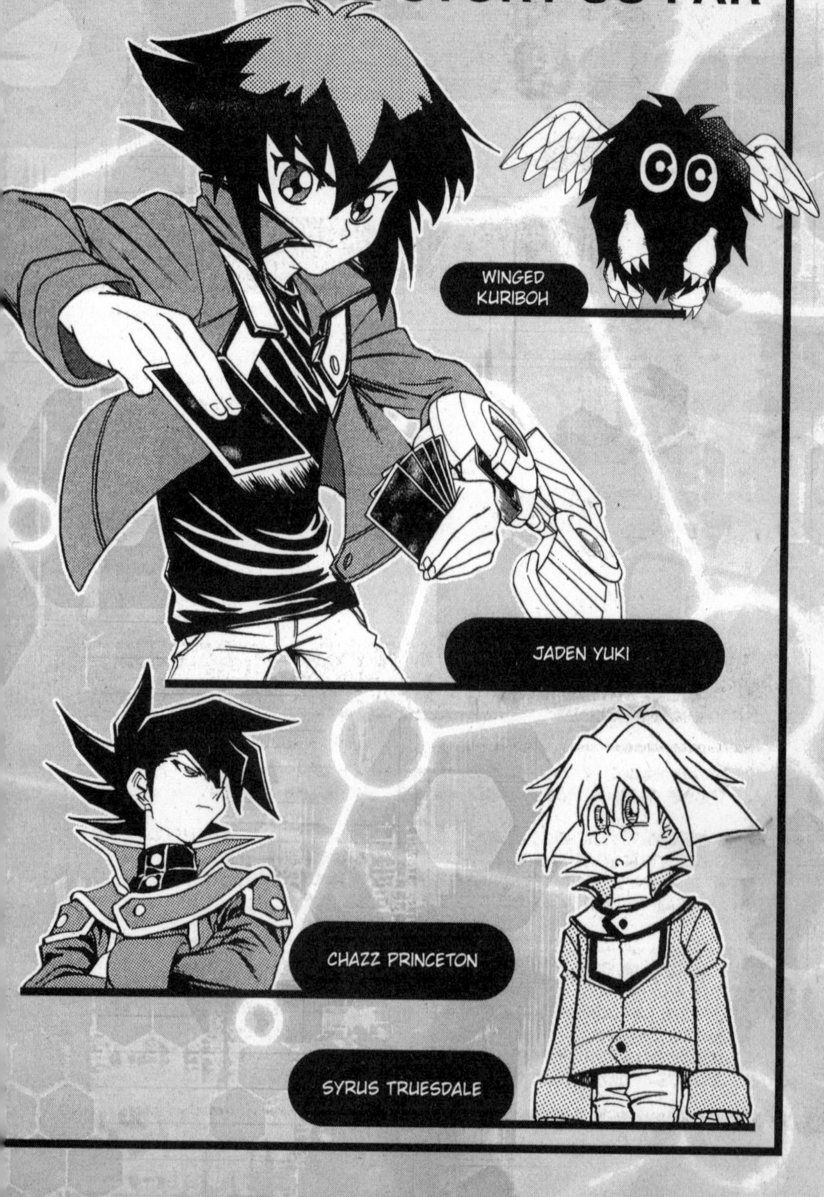
WINGED KURIBOH
JADEN YUKI
CHAZZ PRINCETON
SYRUS TRUESDALE

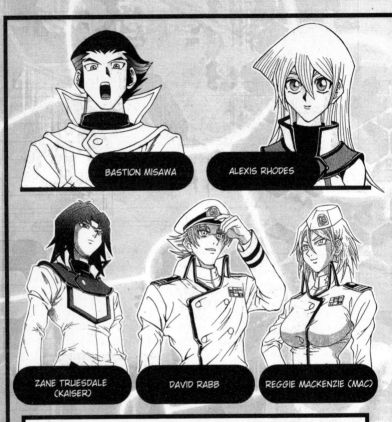

ALEXIS RHODES
BASTION MISAWA
REGGIE MACKENZIE (MAC)
DAVID RABB
ZANE TRUESDALE (KAISER)

ON AN ISLAND IN THE SOUTHERN SEA THERE IS AN ACADEMY THAT TRAINS THE NEXT GENERATION OF DUELISTS—DUEL ACADEMY!

JADEN YUKI LEARNED ABOUT THE EXCITEMENT OF DUELING THROUGH AN ENCOUNTER WITH THE DUEL WORLD CHAMPION, KOYO HIBIKI. ENTRUSTED WITH HIBIKI'S DECK, JADEN TAKES ON ALL CHALLENGERS AT THE ACADEMY IN ORDER TO BECOME A TRUE DUELIST!

SYRUS'S OLDER BROTHER ZANE, AKA KAISER, THE TOP-RANKED DUELIST, HAS RETURNED FROM AMERICA, AND A TOURNAMENT IS BEING HELD AT THE ACADEMY TO WIN THE RIGHT TO CHALLENGE HIM. JADEN AND THE OTHERS, INCLUDING SOME EXCHANGE STUDENTS FROM AMERICA, HAVE BATTLED THROUGH THE PRELIMINARIES, AND THE DUELISTS THAT WILL COMPETE IN THE SEMI-FINALS HAVE BEEN DECIDED. DAVID SECRETLY COVETS A CERTAIN CARD BELONGING TO ONE OF THEM...!

Volume 4: The Semifinals Begin!!

CONTENTS

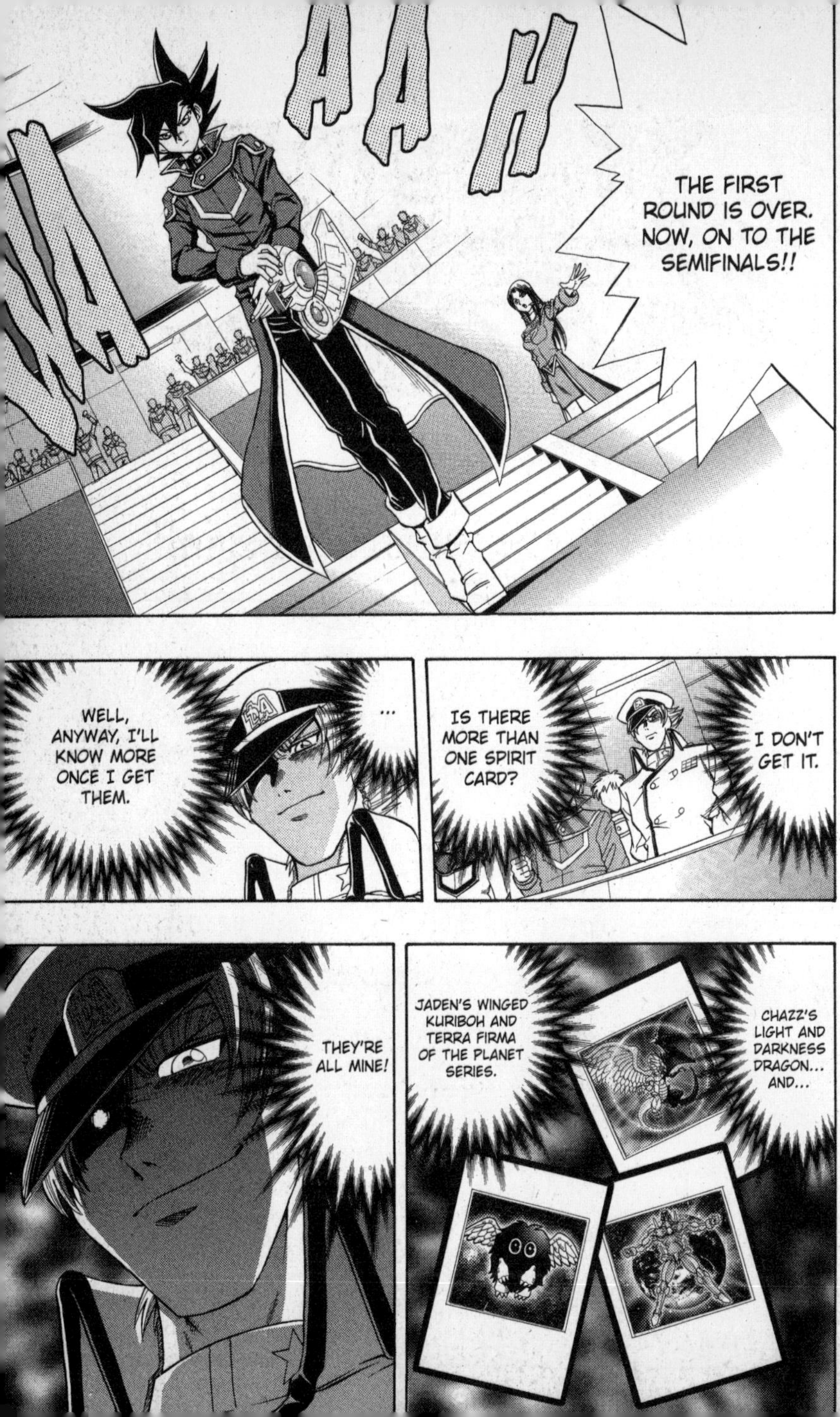
WAAAH
THE FIRST ROUND IS OVER. NOW, ON TO THE SEMIFINALS!!
I DON'T GET IT.
IS THERE MORE THAN ONE SPIRIT CARD?
...
WELL, ANYWAY, I'LL KNOW MORE ONCE I GET THEM.
CHAZZ'S LIGHT AND DARKNESS DRAGON... AND...
JADEN'S WINGED KURIBOH AND TERRA FIRMA OF THE PLANET SERIES.
THEY'RE ALL MINE!

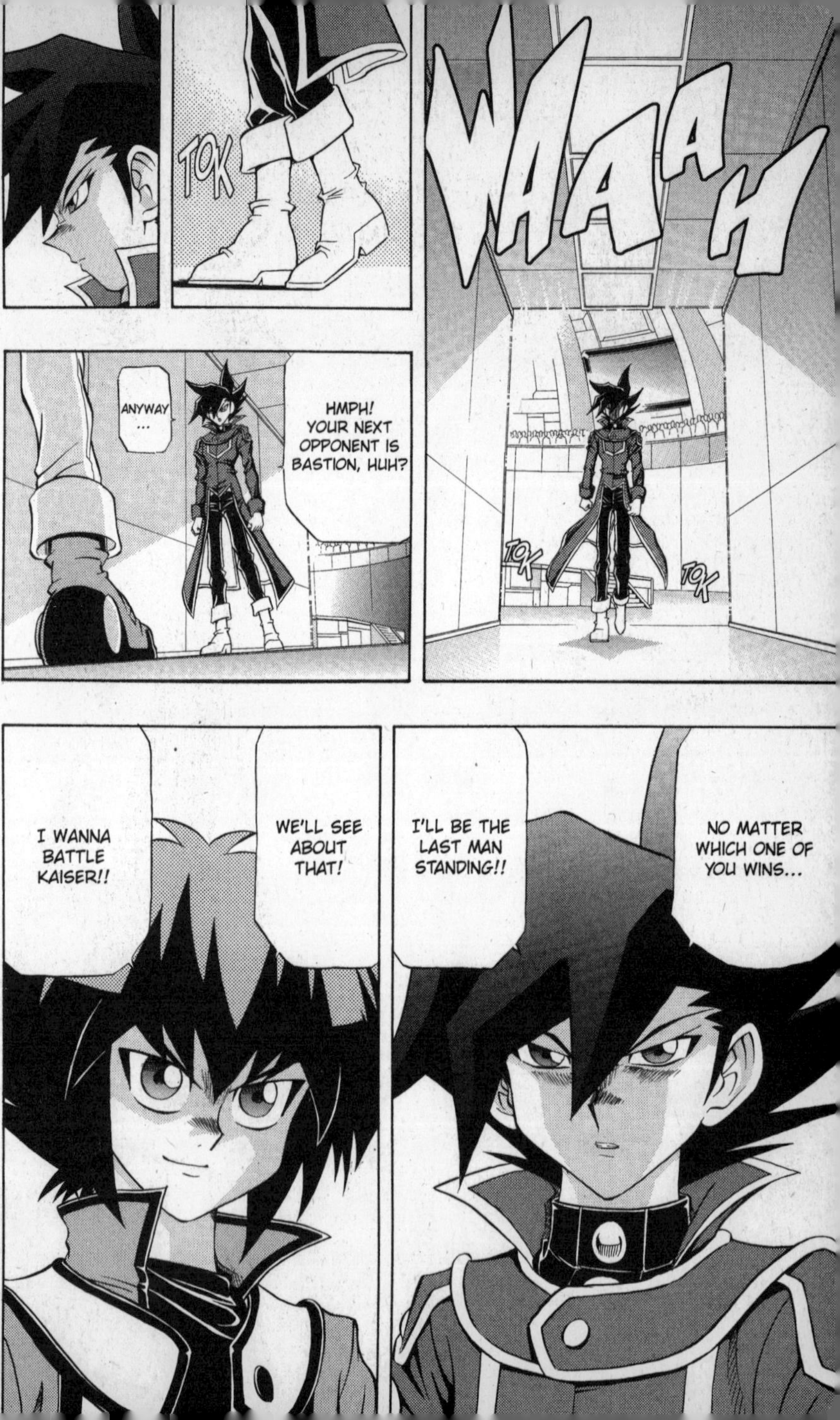
WAAAH
TOK
TOK
TOK
HMPH! YOUR NEXT OPPONENT IS BASTION, HUH?
ANYWAY...
NO MATTER WHICH ONE OF YOU WINS...
I'LL BE THE LAST MAN STANDING!!
WE'LL SEE ABOUT THAT!
I WANNA BATTLE KAISER!!

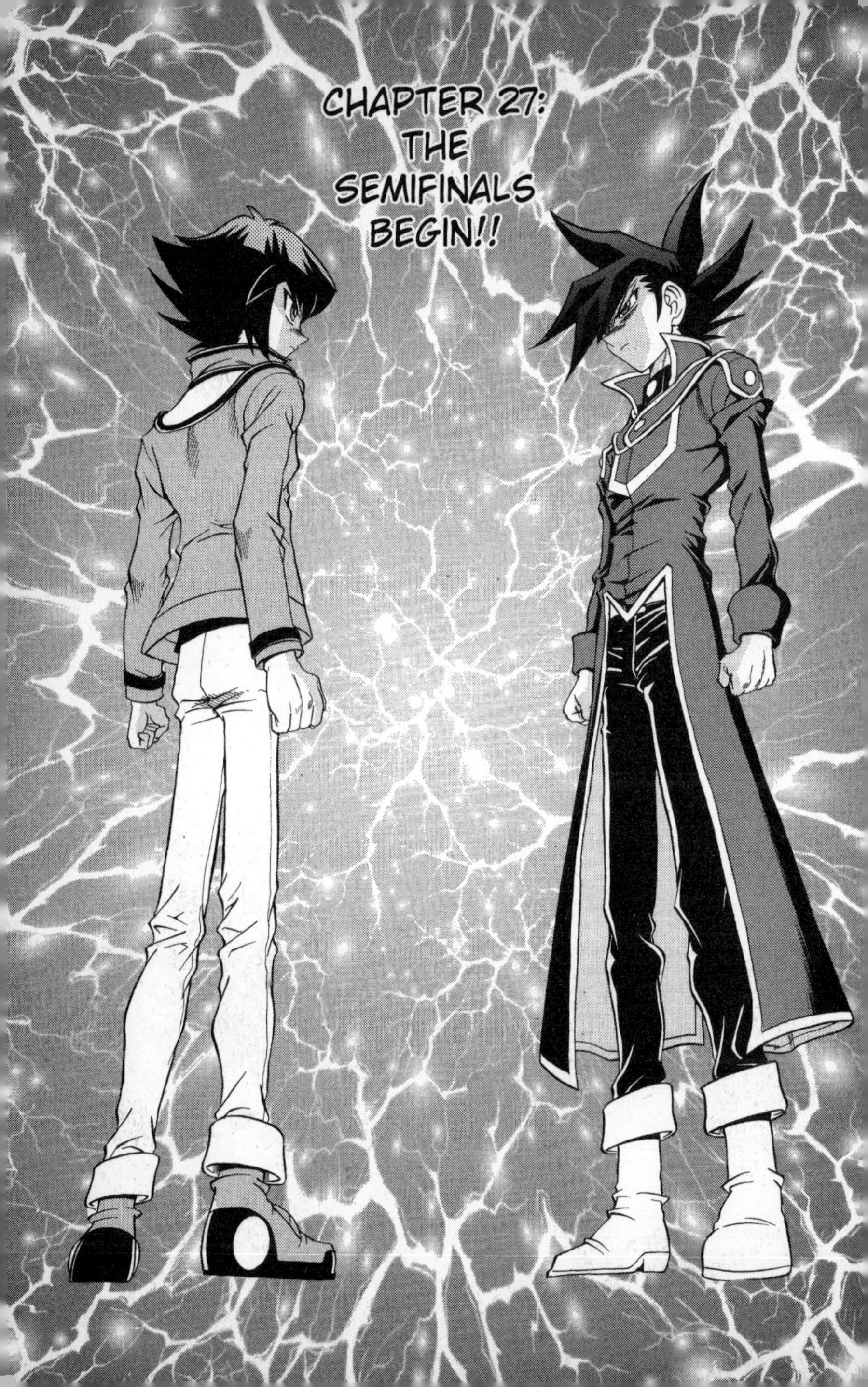
CHAPTER 27:
THE
SEMIFINALS
BEGIN!!

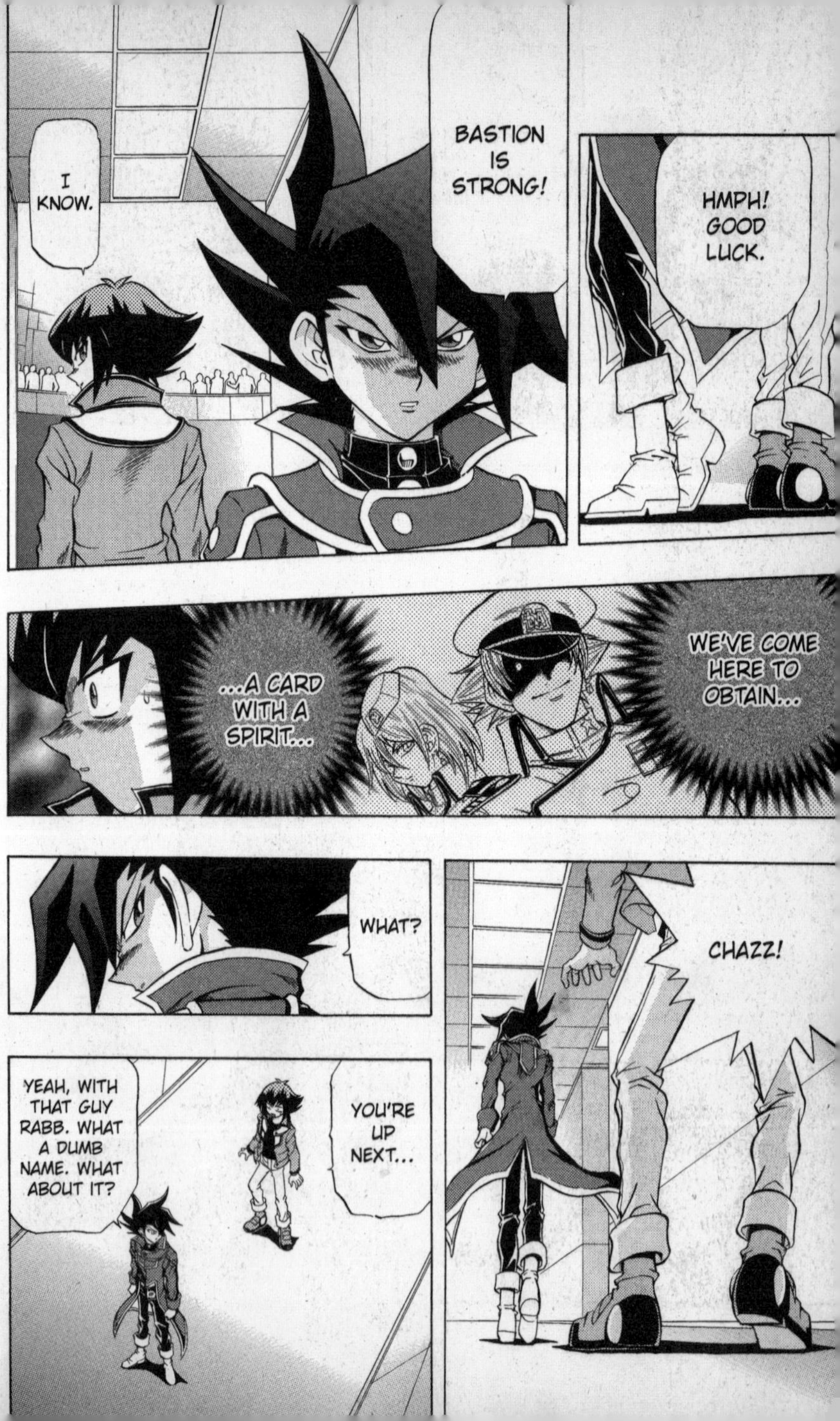
HMPH! GOOD LUCK.
BASTION IS STRONG!
I KNOW.
WE'VE COME HERE TO OBTAIN...
...A CARD WITH A SPIRIT...
CHAZZ!
WHAT?
YOU'RE UP NEXT...
YEAH, WITH THAT GUY RABB. WHAT A DUMB NAME. WHAT ABOUT IT?

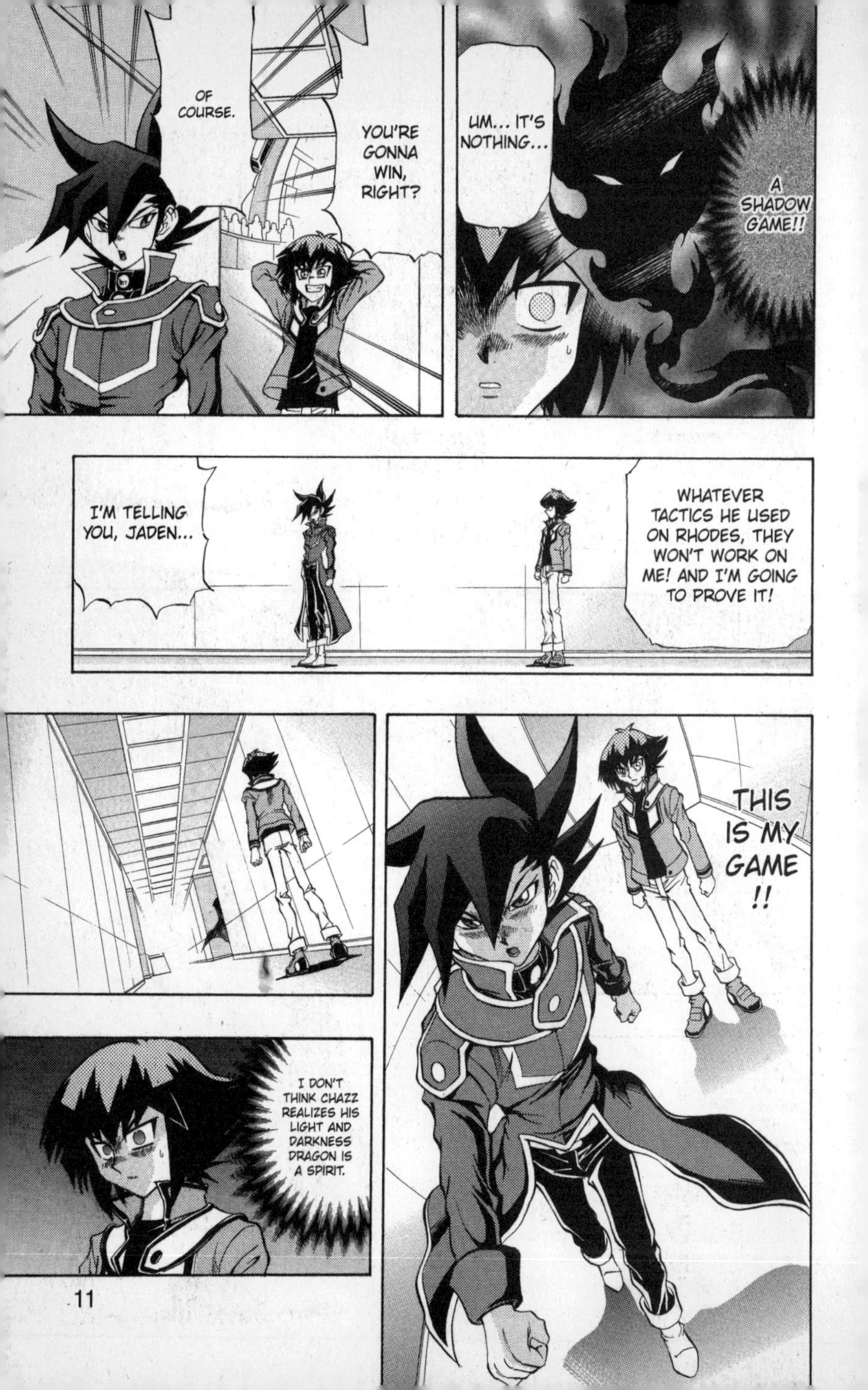
A SHADOW GAME!!
UM... IT'S NOTHING...
YOU'RE GONNA WIN, RIGHT?
OF COURSE.
WHATEVER TACTICS HE USED ON RHODES, THEY WON'T WORK ON ME! AND I'M GOING TO PROVE IT!
I'M TELLING YOU, JADEN...
THIS IS MY GAME!!
I DON'T THINK CHAZZ REALIZES HIS LIGHT AND DARKNESS DRAGON IS A SPIRIT.

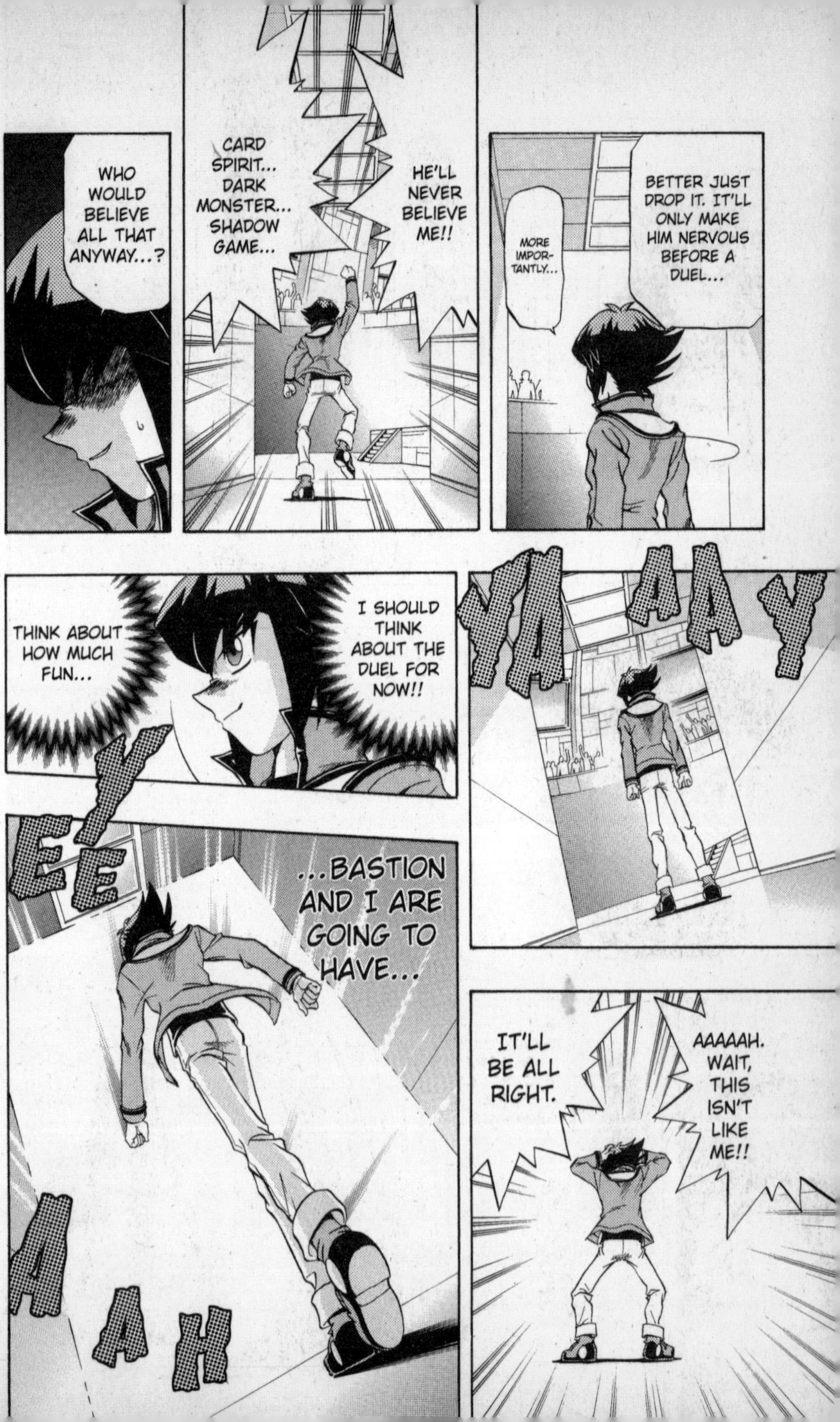
WHO WOULD BELIEVE ALL THAT ANYWAY...?
CARD SPIRIT... DARK MONSTER... SHADOW GAME...
HE'LL NEVER BELIEVE ME!!
BETTER JUST DROP IT. IT'LL ONLY MAKE HIM NERVOUS BEFORE A DUEL...
MORE IMPORTANTLY...
I SHOULD THINK ABOUT THE DUEL FOR NOW!!
THINK ABOUT HOW MUCH FUN...
YAAAY
...BASTION AND I ARE GOING TO HAVE...
YEE
AAH
IT'LL BE ALL RIGHT.
AAAAAH. WAIT, THIS ISN'T LIKE ME!!

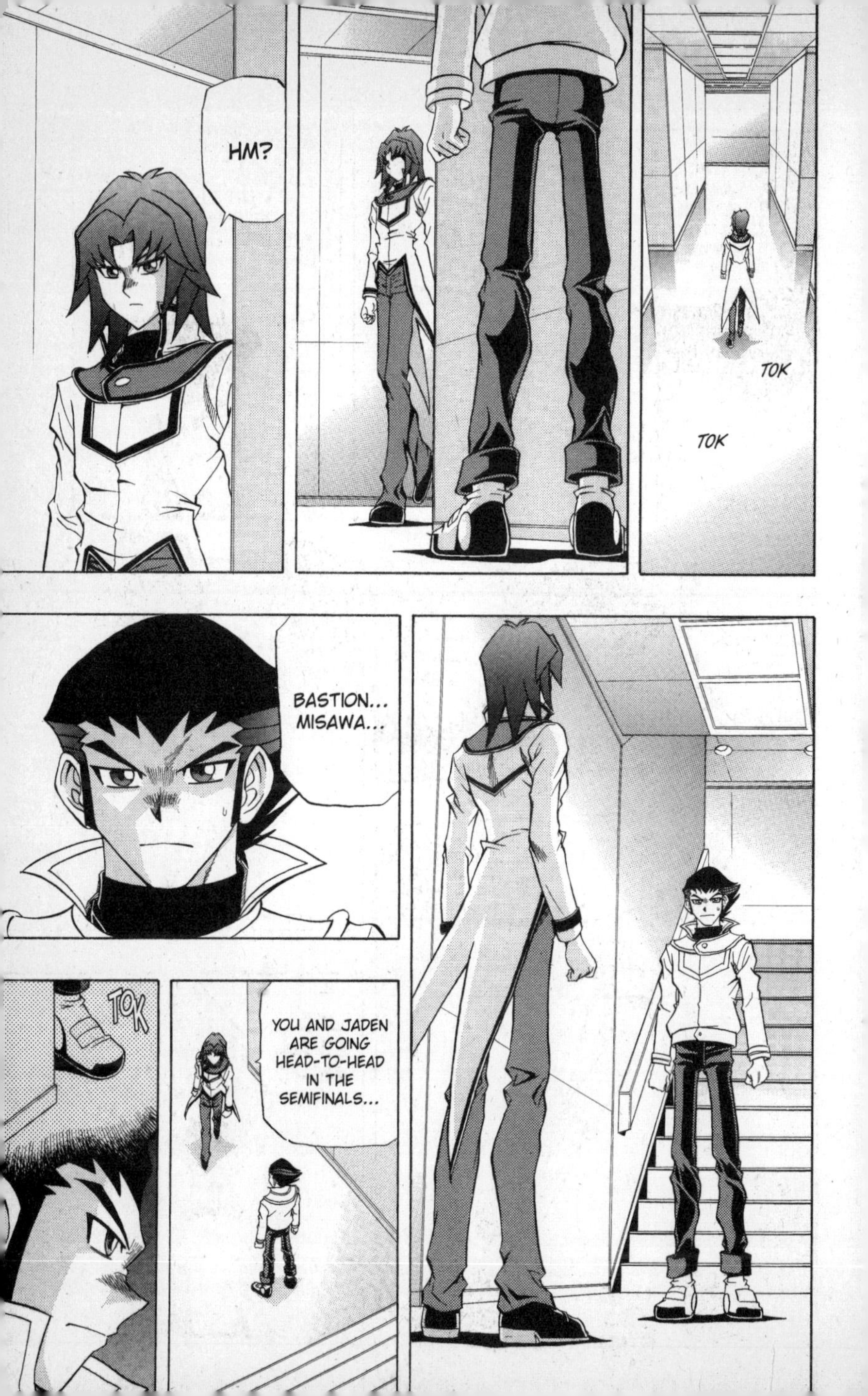
TOK
TOK
HM?
BASTION... MISAWA...
YOU AND JADEN ARE GOING HEAD-TO-HEAD IN THE SEMIFINALS...
TOK

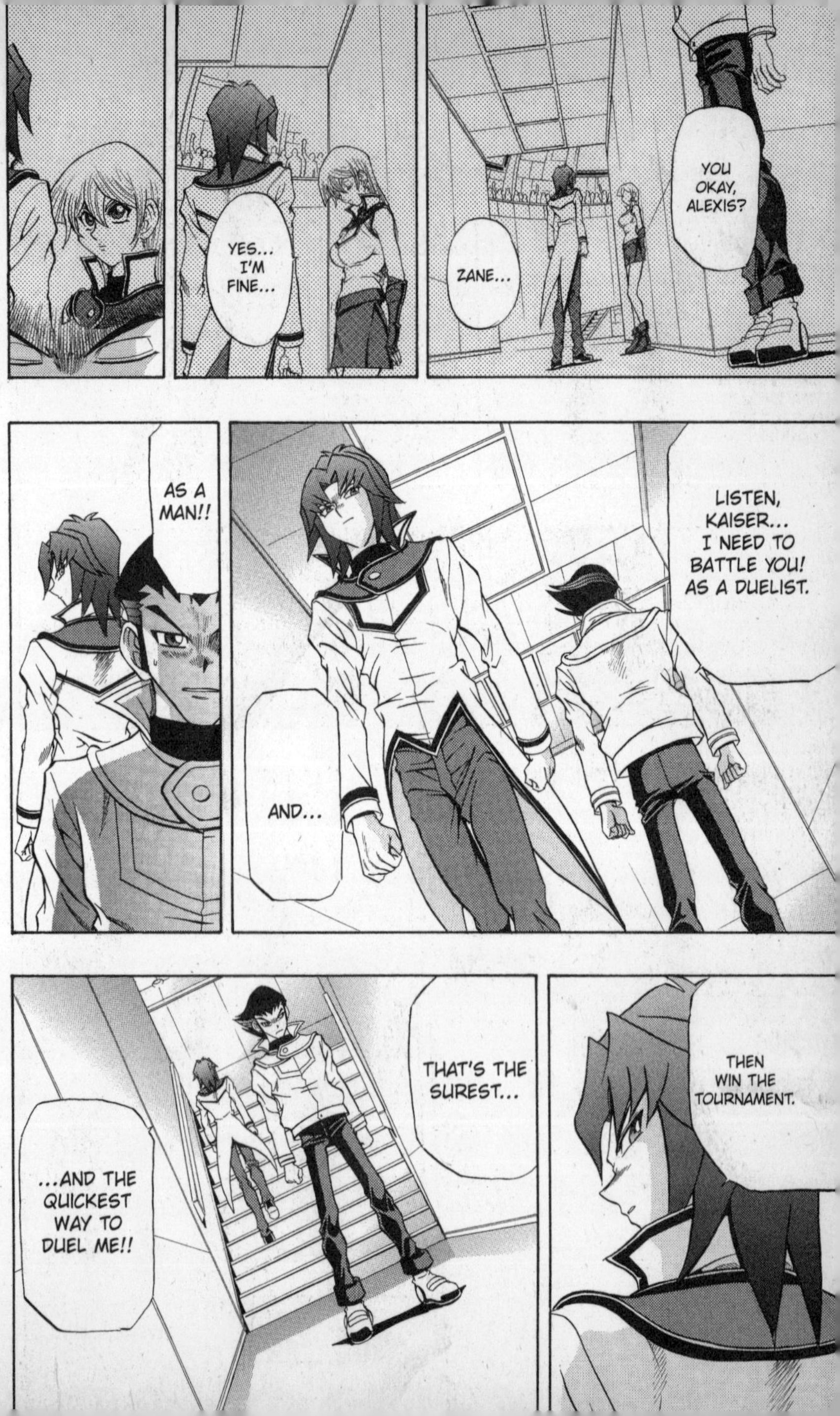
YOU OKAY, ALEXIS?
ZANE...
YES... I'M FINE...
LISTEN, KAISER... I NEED TO BATTLE YOU! AS A DUELIST.
AND...
AS A MAN!!
THEN WIN THE TOURNAMENT.
THAT'S THE SUREST...
...AND THE QUICKEST WAY TO DUEL ME!!

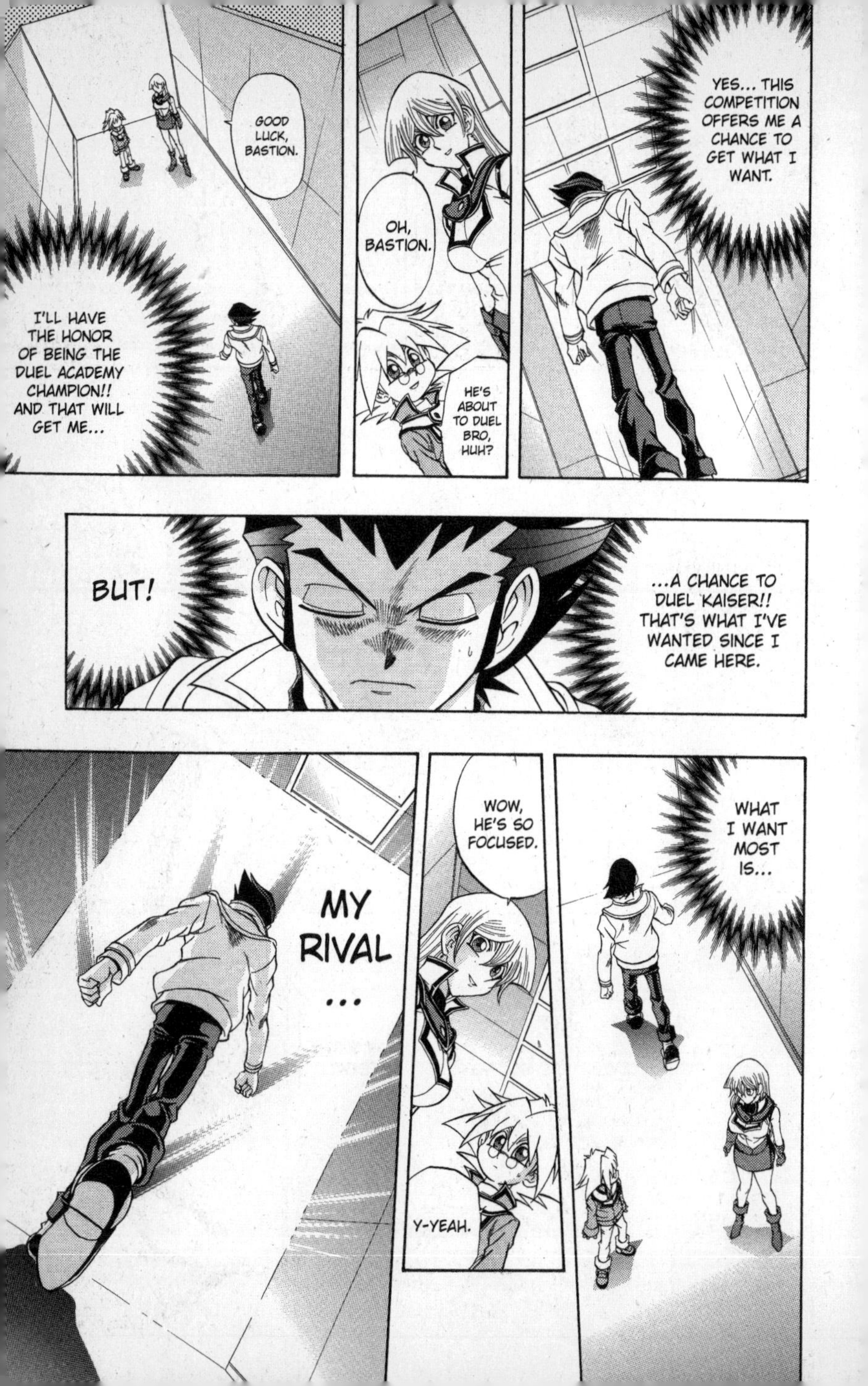
YES... THIS COMPETITION OFFERS ME A CHANCE TO GET WHAT I WANT.
OH, BASTION.
HE'S ABOUT TO DUEL BRO, HUH?
GOOD LUCK, BASTION.
I'LL HAVE THE HONOR OF BEING THE DUEL ACADEMY CHAMPION!! AND THAT WILL GET ME...
...A CHANCE TO DUEL KAISER!! THAT'S WHAT I'VE WANTED SINCE I CAME HERE.
BUT!
WHAT I WANT MOST IS...
WOW, HE'S SO FOCUSED.
Y-YEAH.
MY RIVAL ...

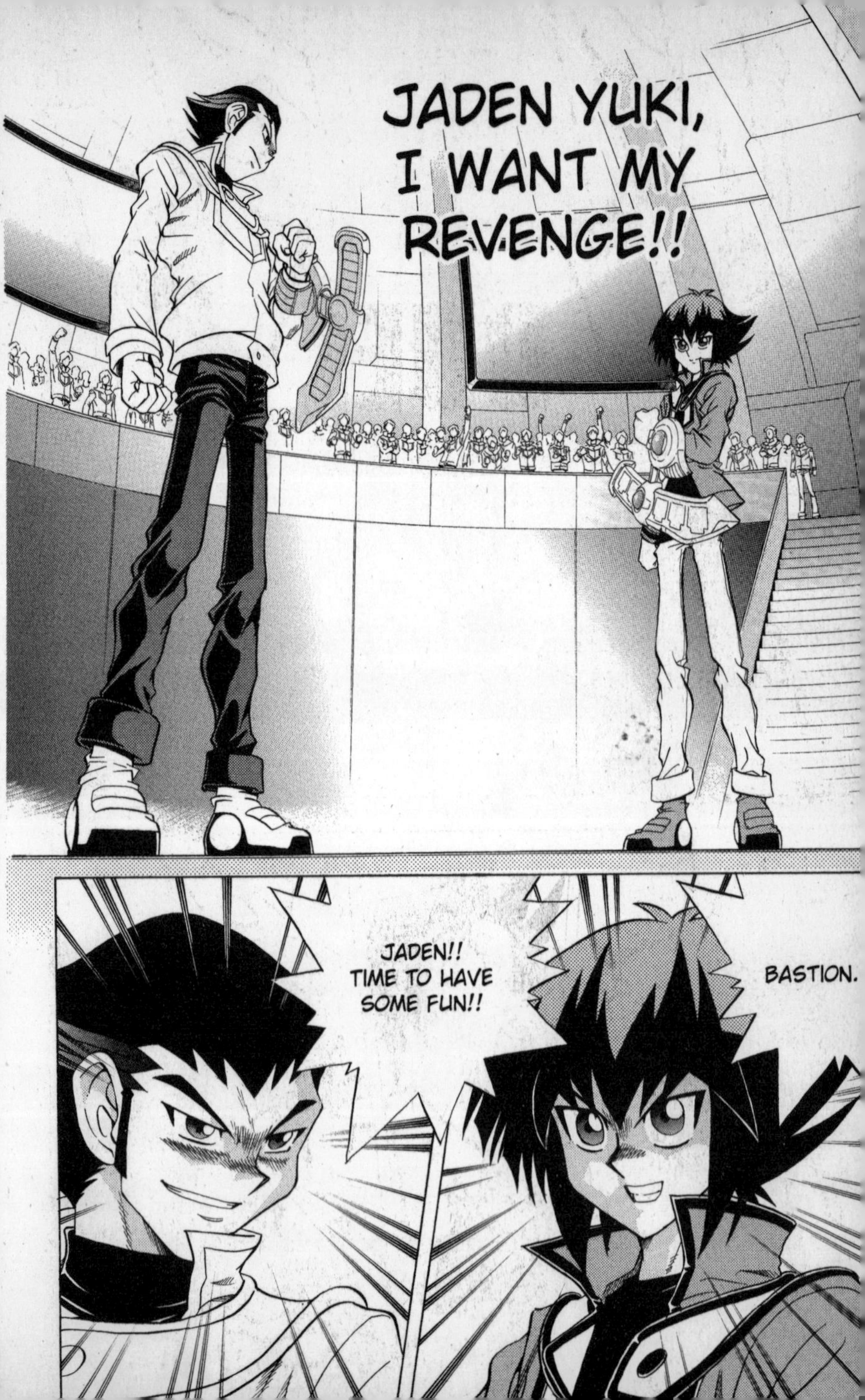
JADEN YUKI, I WANT MY REVENGE!!
BASTION.
JADEN!! TIME TO HAVE SOME FUN!!

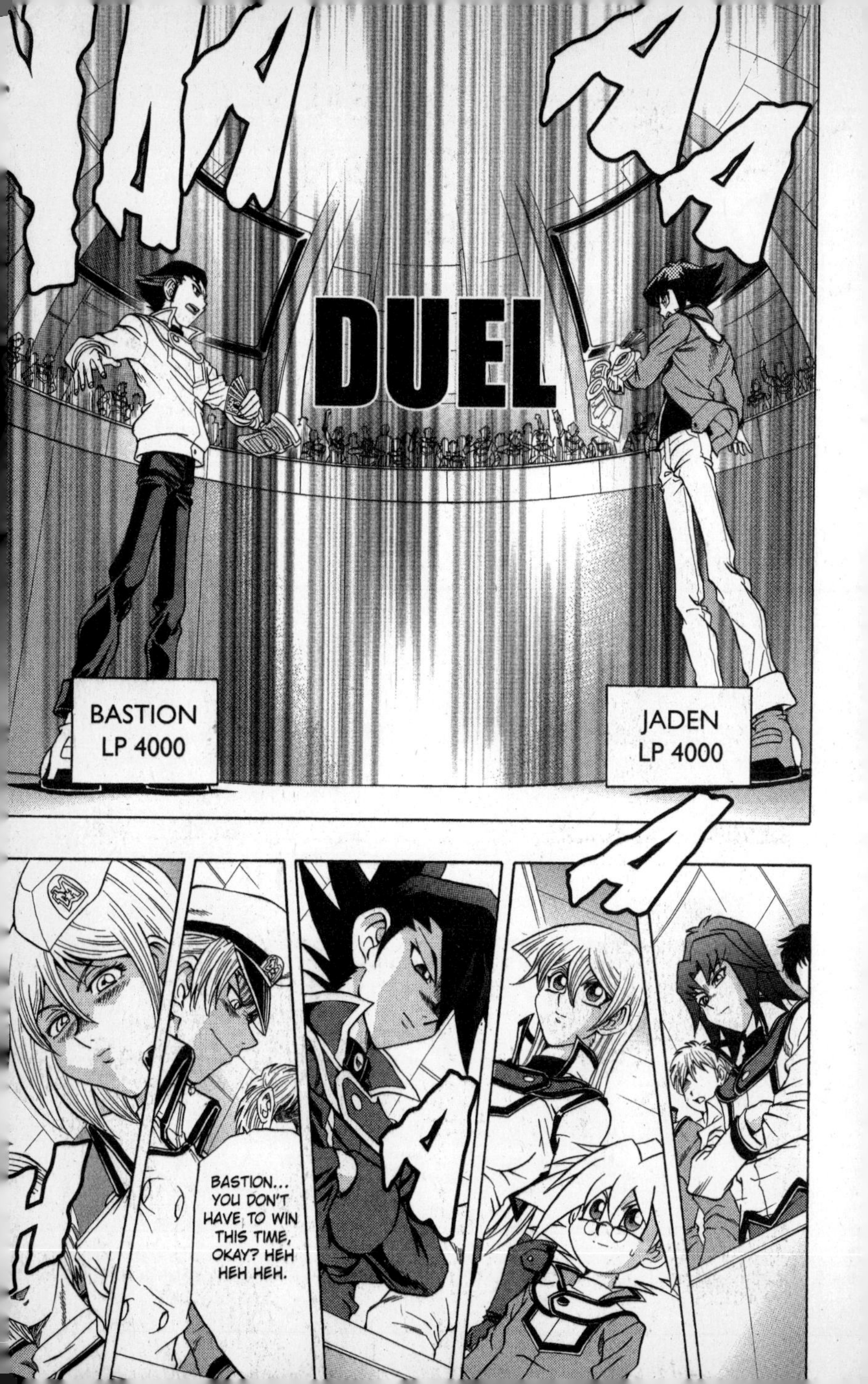
DUEL
JADEN LP 4000
BASTION LP 4000
BASTION... YOU DON'T HAVE TO WIN THIS TIME, OKAY? HEH HEH HEH.

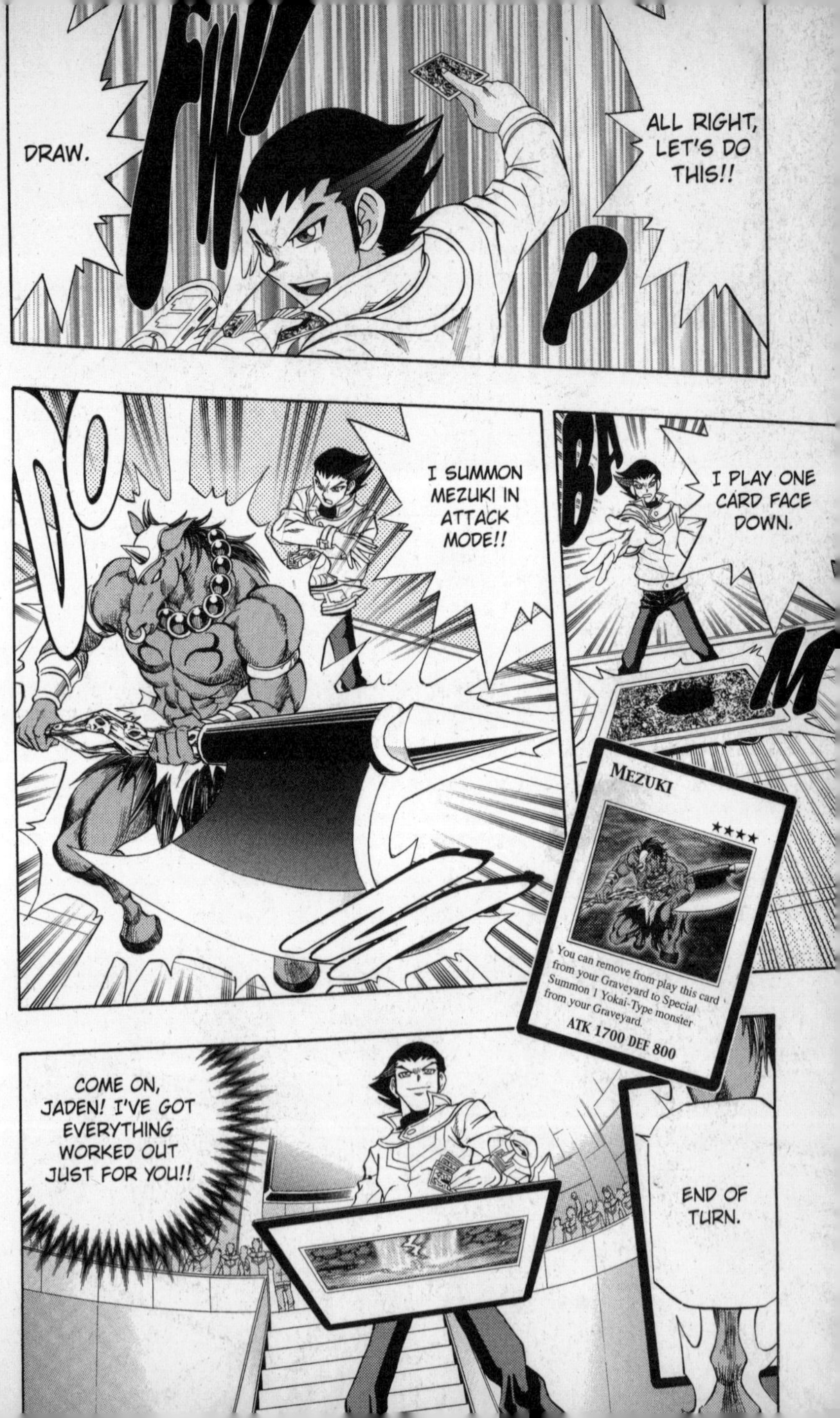
ALL RIGHT, LET'S DO THIS!!
DRAW.
FW
P
BA
I PLAY ONE CARD FACE DOWN.
DO
I SUMMON MEZUKI IN ATTACK MODE!!
MEZUKI
You can remove from play this card from your Graveyard to Special Summon 1 Yokai-Type monster from your Graveyard.
ATK 1700 DEF 800
END OF TURN.
COME ON, JADEN! I'VE GOT EVERYTHING WORKED OUT JUST FOR YOU!!

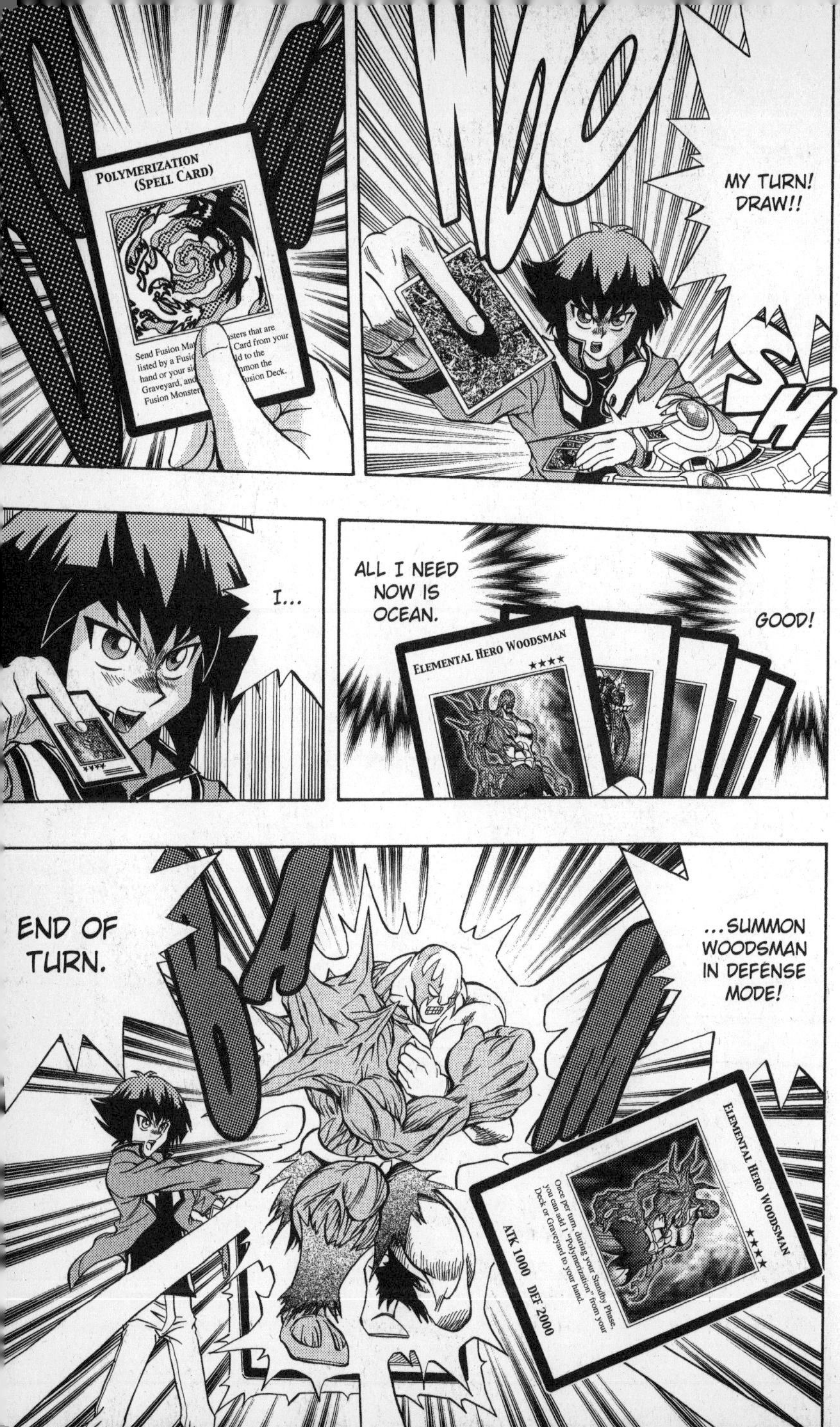
MY TURN! DRAW!!
SH
POLYMERIZATION (SPELL CARD)
GOOD!
ALL I NEED NOW IS OCEAN.
ELEMENTAL HERO WOODSMAN
I...
...SUMMON WOODSMAN IN DEFENSE MODE!
ELEMENTAL HERO WOODSMAN
Once per turn, during your Standby Phase, you can add 1 "Polymerization" from your Deck or Graveyard to your hand.
ATK 1000 DEF 2000
END OF TURN.

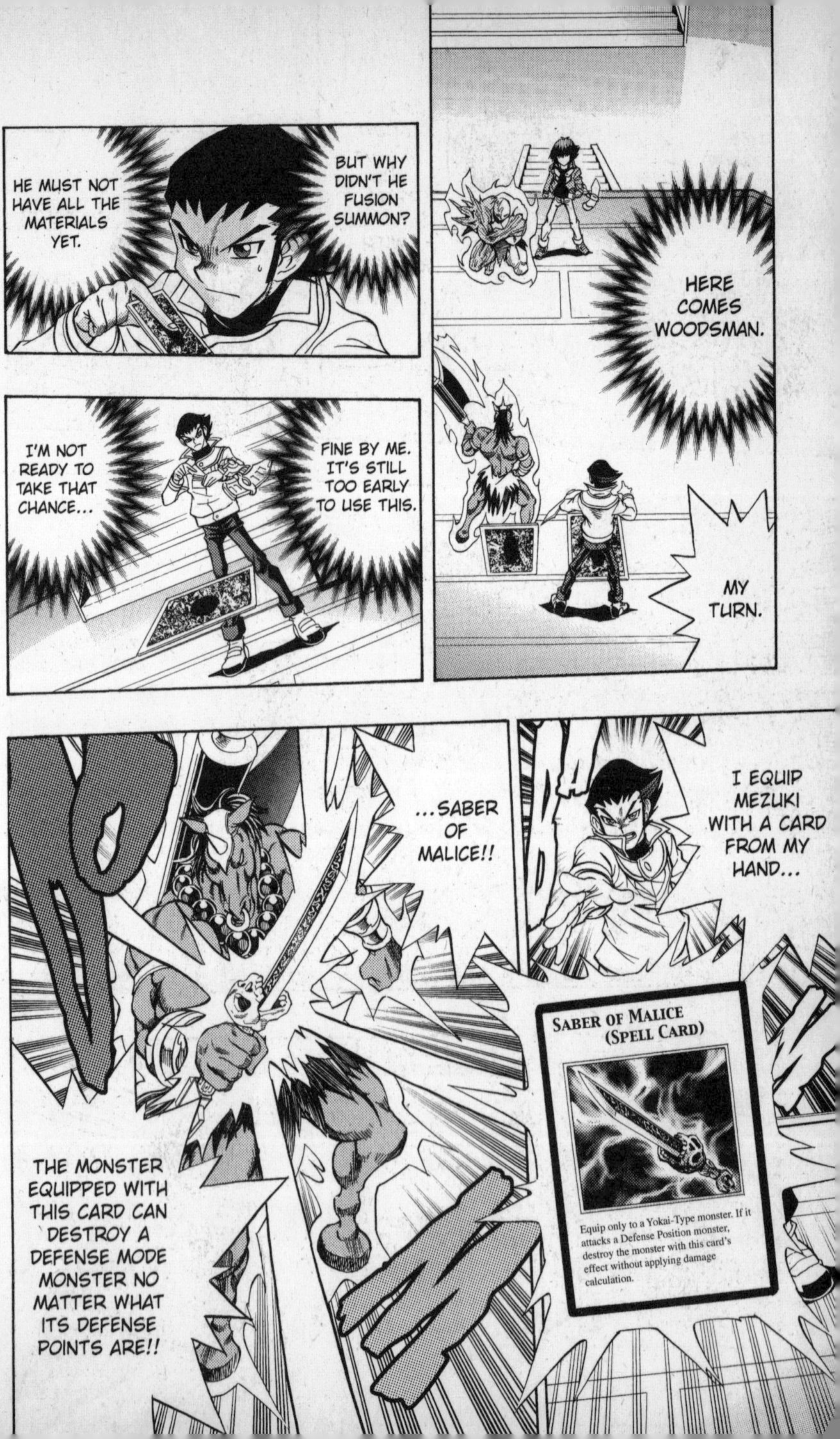

HERE COMES WOODSMAN.
MY TURN.
BUT WHY DIDN'T HE FUSION SUMMON?
HE MUST NOT HAVE ALL THE MATERIALS YET.
FINE BY ME. IT'S STILL TOO EARLY TO USE THIS.
I'M NOT READY TO TAKE THAT CHANCE...
I EQUIP MEZUKI WITH A CARD FROM MY HAND...
...SABER OF MALICE!!
SABER OF MALICE (SPELL CARD)
Equip only to a Yokai-Type monster. If it attacks a Defense Position monster, destroy the monster with this card's effect without applying damage calculation.
THE MONSTER EQUIPPED WITH THIS CARD CAN DESTROY A DEFENSE MODE MONSTER NO MATTER WHAT ITS DEFENSE POINTS ARE!!

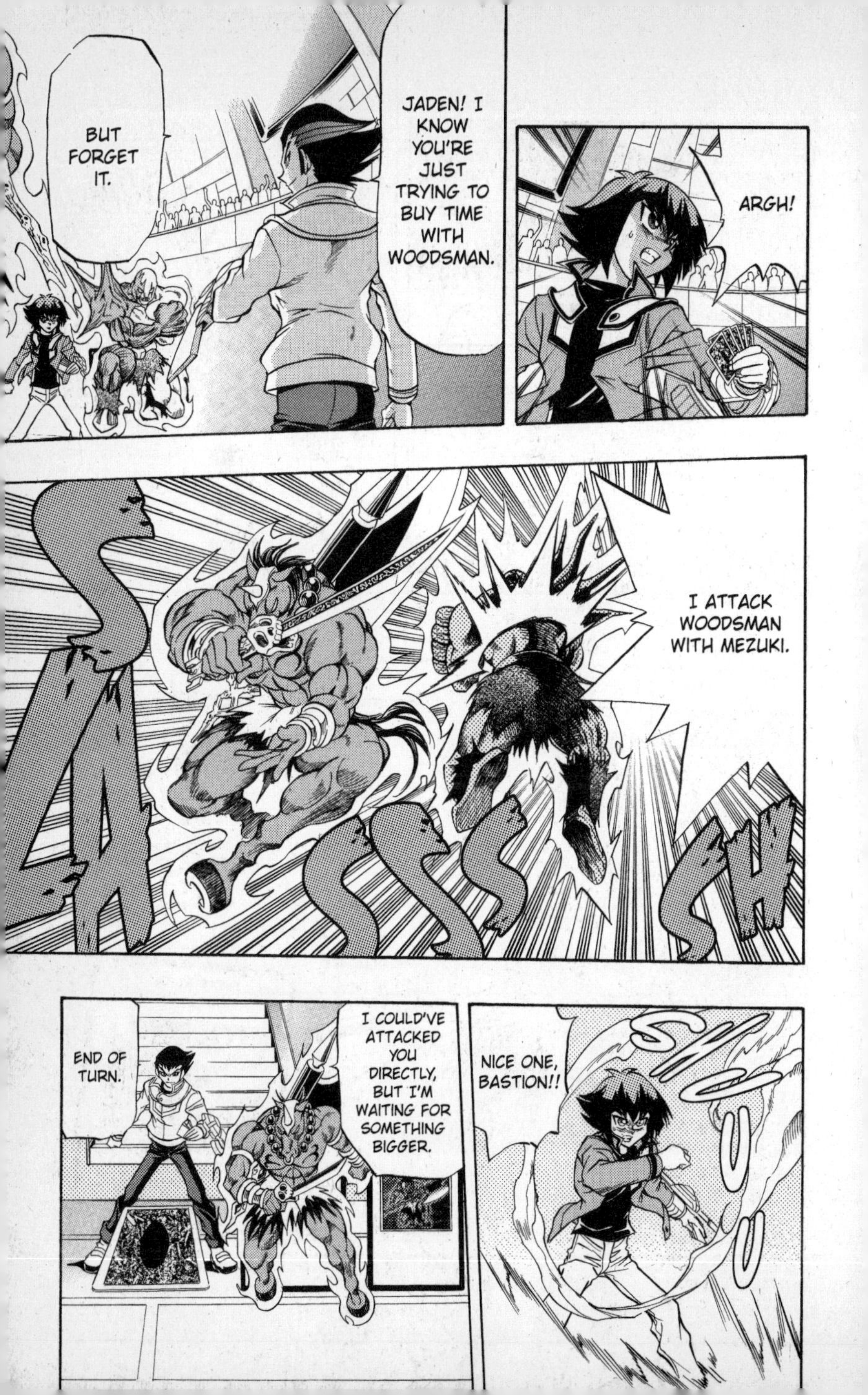
ARGH!
JADEN! I KNOW YOU'RE JUST TRYING TO BUY TIME WITH WOODSMAN.
BUT FORGET IT.
I ATTACK WOODSMAN WITH MEZUKI.
NICE ONE, BASTION!!
I COULD'VE ATTACKED YOU DIRECTLY, BUT I'M WAITING FOR SOMETHING BIGGER.
END OF TURN.

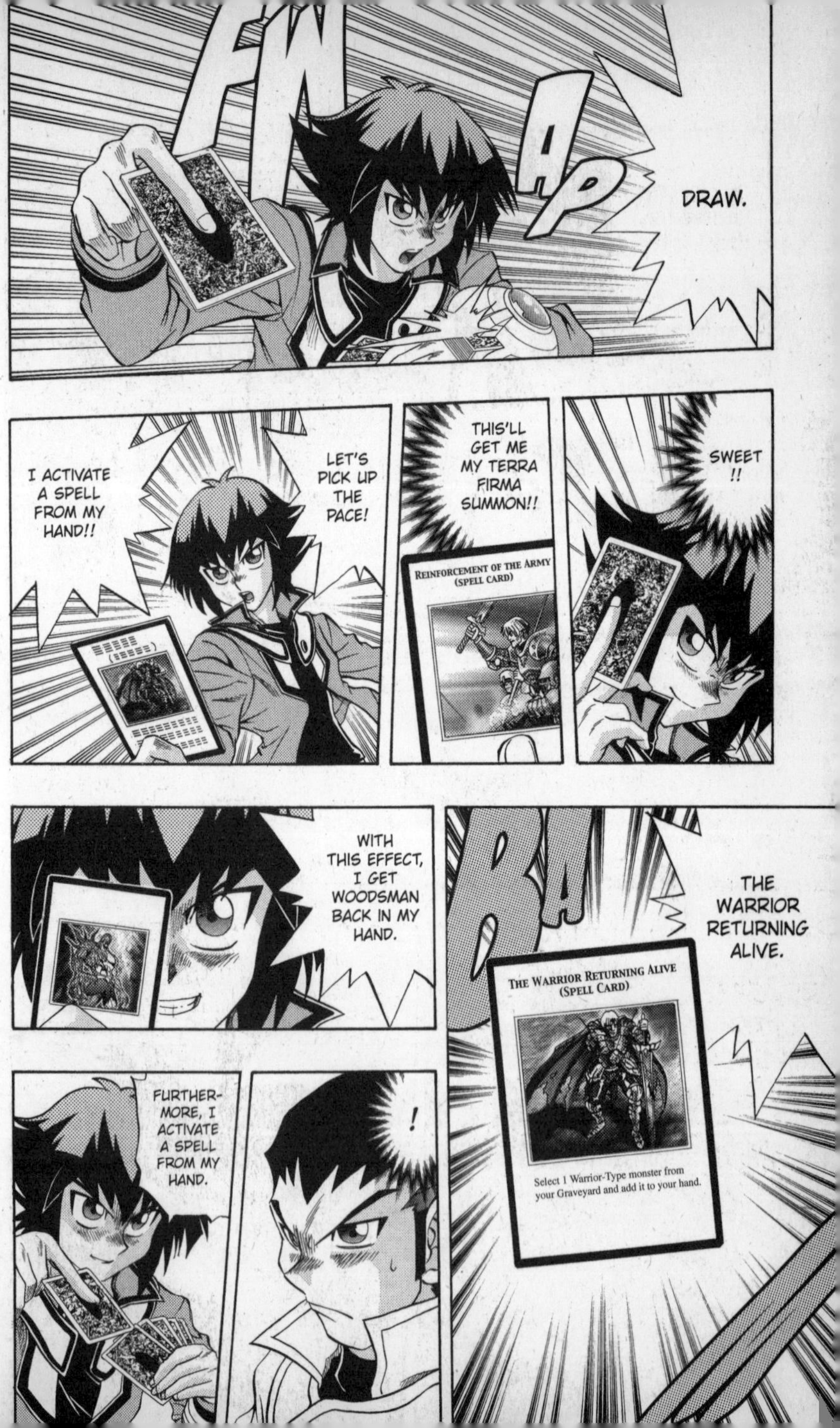
FWAP
DRAW.
SWEET!!
THIS'LL GET ME MY TERRA FIRMA SUMMON!!
REINFORCEMENT OF THE ARMY
(SPELL CARD)
LET'S PICK UP THE PACE!
I ACTIVATE A SPELL FROM MY HAND!!
BA
THE WARRIOR RETURNING ALIVE.
THE WARRIOR RETURNING ALIVE
(SPELL CARD)
Select 1 Warrior-Type monster from your Graveyard and add it to your hand.
WITH THIS EFFECT, I GET WOODSMAN BACK IN MY HAND.
!
FURTHER-MORE, I ACTIVATE A SPELL FROM MY HAND.

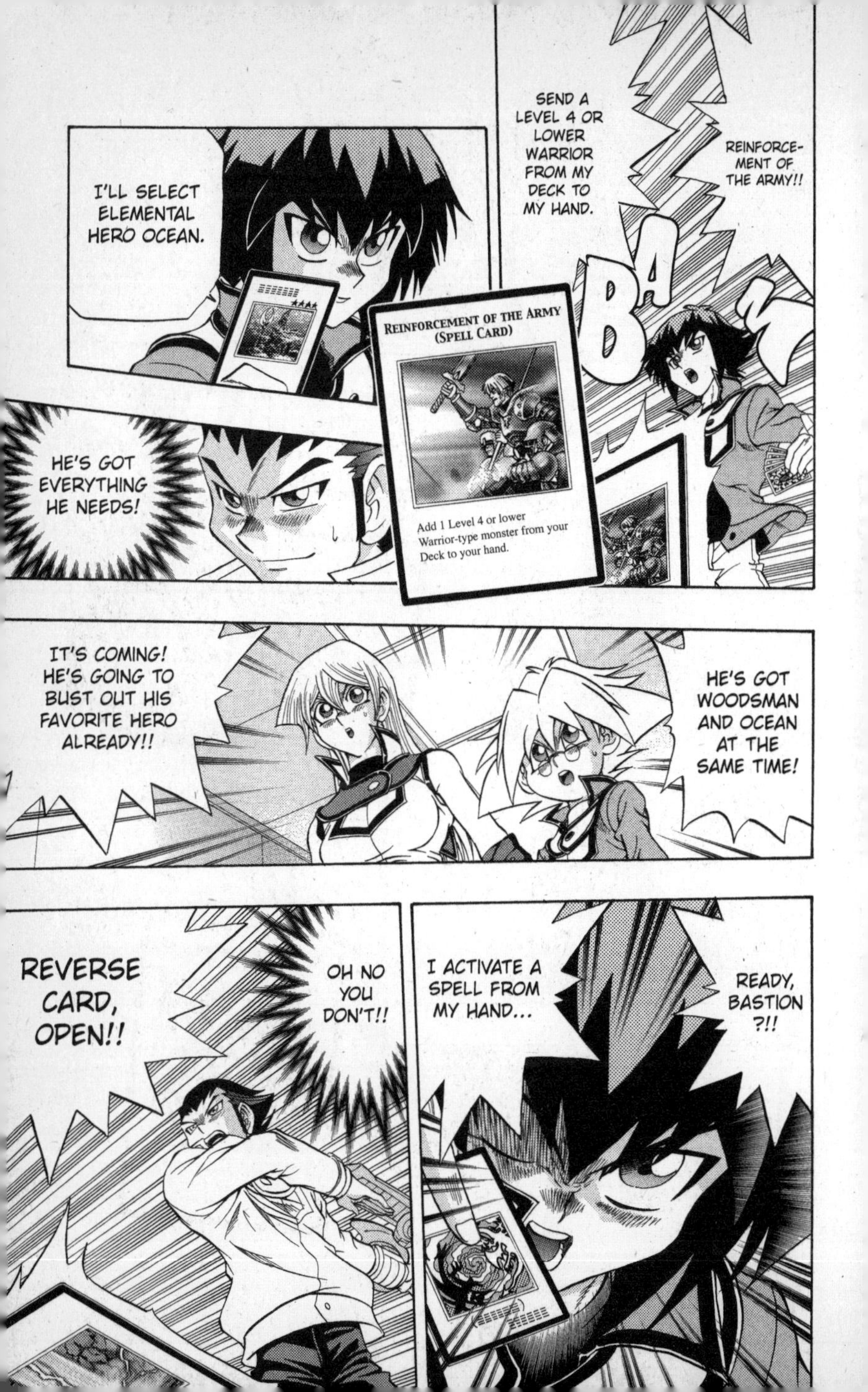
REINFORCEMENT OF THE ARMY!!
SEND A LEVEL 4 OR LOWER WARRIOR FROM MY DECK TO MY HAND.
BA
REINFORCEMENT OF THE ARMY (SPELL CARD)
Add 1 Level 4 or lower Warrior-type monster from your Deck to your hand.
I'LL SELECT ELEMENTAL HERO OCEAN.
HE'S GOT EVERYTHING HE NEEDS!
HE'S GOT WOODSMAN AND OCEAN AT THE SAME TIME!
IT'S COMING! HE'S GOING TO BUST OUT HIS FAVORITE HERO ALREADY!!
READY, BASTION ?!!
I ACTIVATE A SPELL FROM MY HAND...
OH NO YOU DON'T!!
REVERSE CARD, OPEN!!

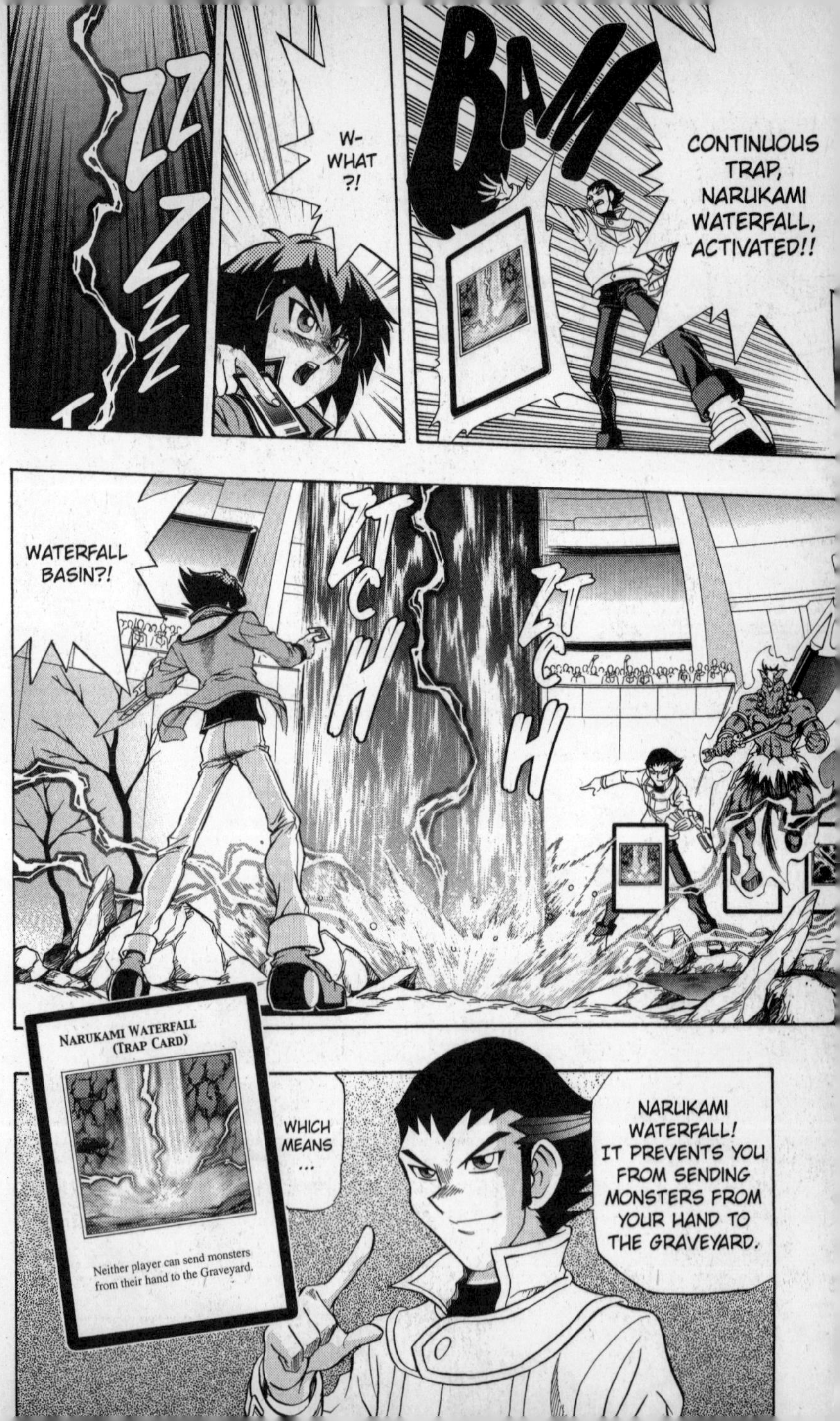
BAM
CONTINUOUS TRAP, NARUKAMI WATERFALL, ACTIVATED!!
W-WHAT?!
ZZZZZZT
ZZTCH
ZZTCH
WATERFALL BASIN?!
NARUKAMI WATERFALL! IT PREVENTS YOU FROM SENDING MONSTERS FROM YOUR HAND TO THE GRAVEYARD.
WHICH MEANS...
NARUKAMI WATERFALL (TRAP CARD)
Neither player can send monsters from their hand to the Graveyard.

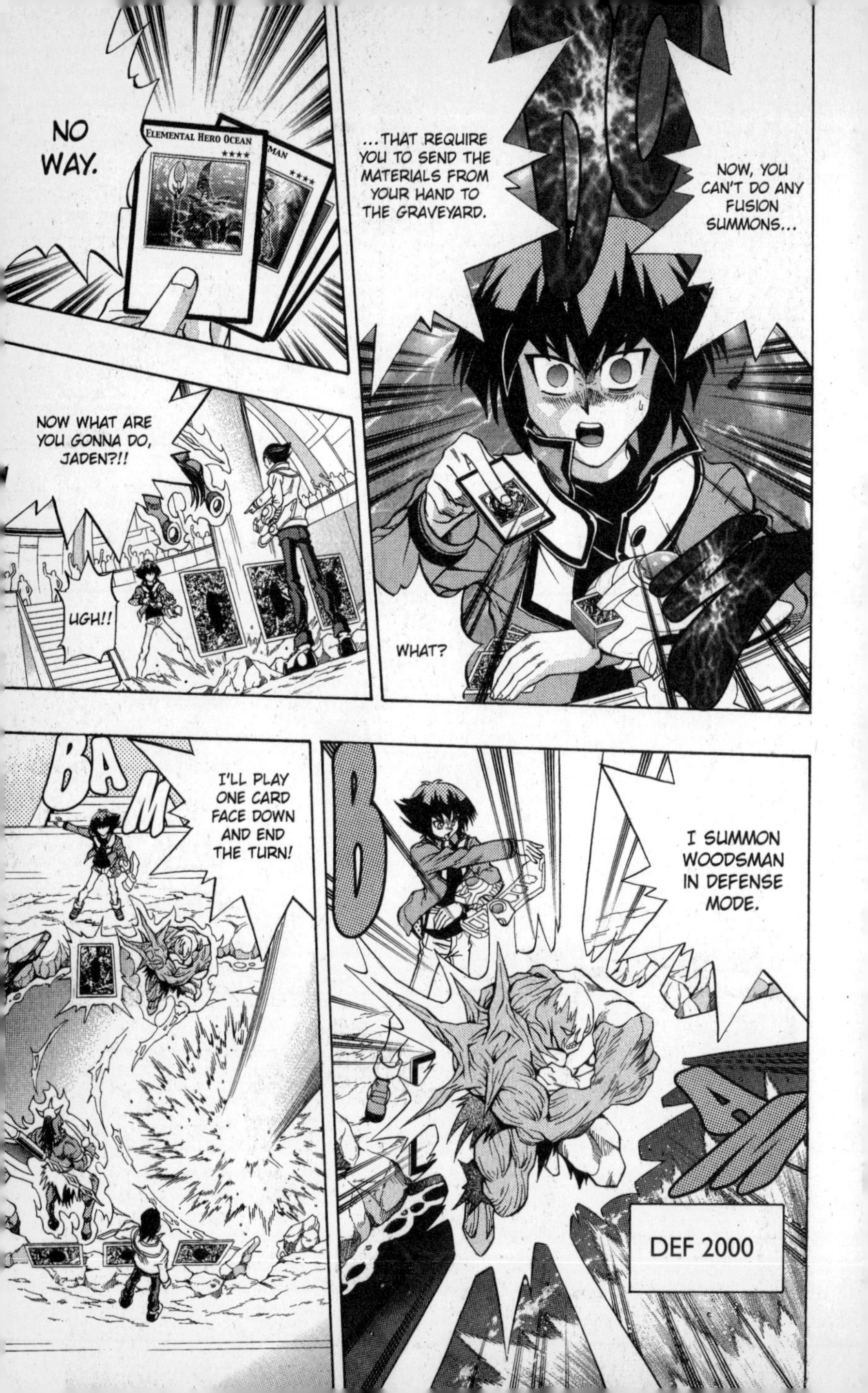
NOW, YOU CAN'T DO ANY FUSION SUMMONS...
...THAT REQUIRE YOU TO SEND THE MATERIALS FROM YOUR HAND TO THE GRAVEYARD.
WHAT?
NO WAY.
ELEMENTAL HERO OCEAN
NOW WHAT ARE YOU GONNA DO, JADEN?!!
UGH!!
I SUMMON WOODSMAN IN DEFENSE MODE.
DEF 2000
BAM
I'LL PLAY ONE CARD FACE DOWN AND END THE TURN!

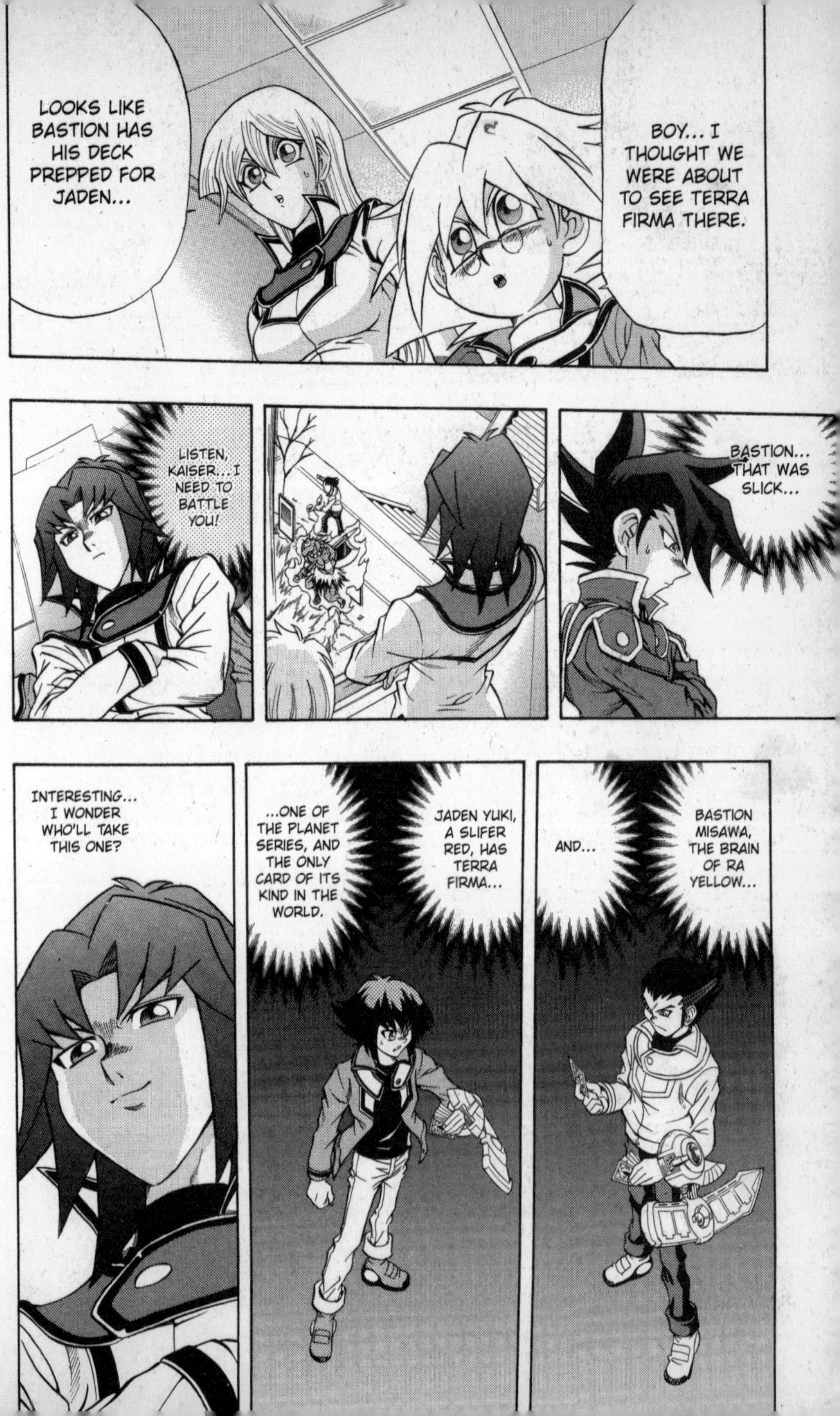
BOY... I THOUGHT WE WERE ABOUT TO SEE TERRA FIRMA THERE.
LOOKS LIKE BASTION HAS HIS DECK PREPPED FOR JADEN...
BASTION... THAT WAS SLICK...
LISTEN, KAISER... I NEED TO BATTLE YOU!
BASTION MISAWA, THE BRAIN OF RA YELLOW...
AND...
JADEN YUKI, A SLIFER RED, HAS TERRA FIRMA...
...ONE OF THE PLANET SERIES, AND THE ONLY CARD OF ITS KIND IN THE WORLD.
INTERESTING... I WONDER WHO'LL TAKE THIS ONE?

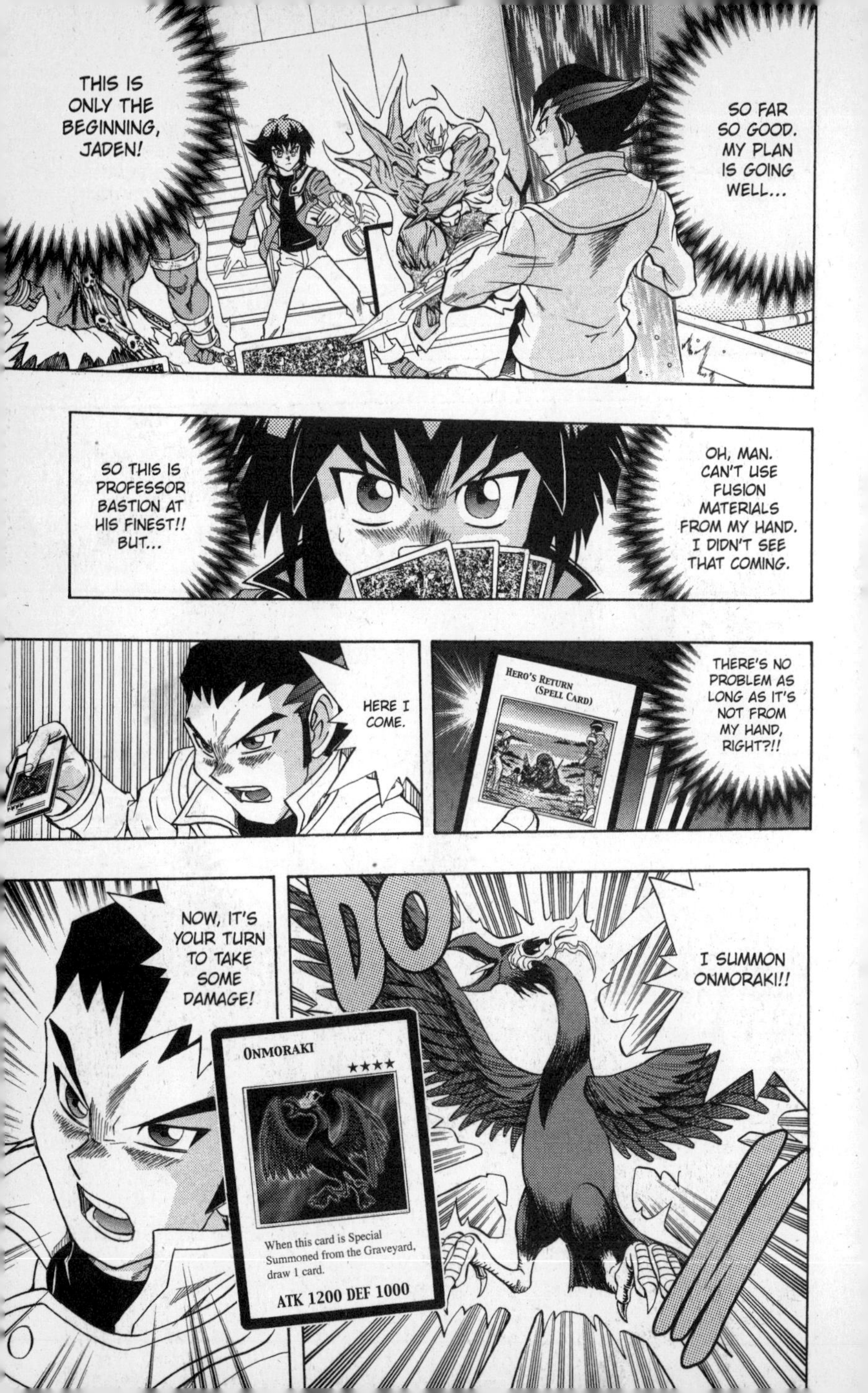
SO FAR SO GOOD. MY PLAN IS GOING WELL...
THIS IS ONLY THE BEGINNING, JADEN!
OH, MAN. CAN'T USE FUSION MATERIALS FROM MY HAND. I DIDN'T SEE THAT COMING.
SO THIS IS PROFESSOR BASTION AT HIS FINEST!! BUT...
THERE'S NO PROBLEM AS LONG AS IT'S NOT FROM MY HAND, RIGHT?!!
HERO'S RETURN (SPELL CARD)
HERE I COME.
I SUMMON ONMORAKI!!
DO
ONMORAKI
When this card is Special Summoned from the Graveyard, draw 1 card.
ATK 1200 DEF 1000
NOW, IT'S YOUR TURN TO TAKE SOME DAMAGE!

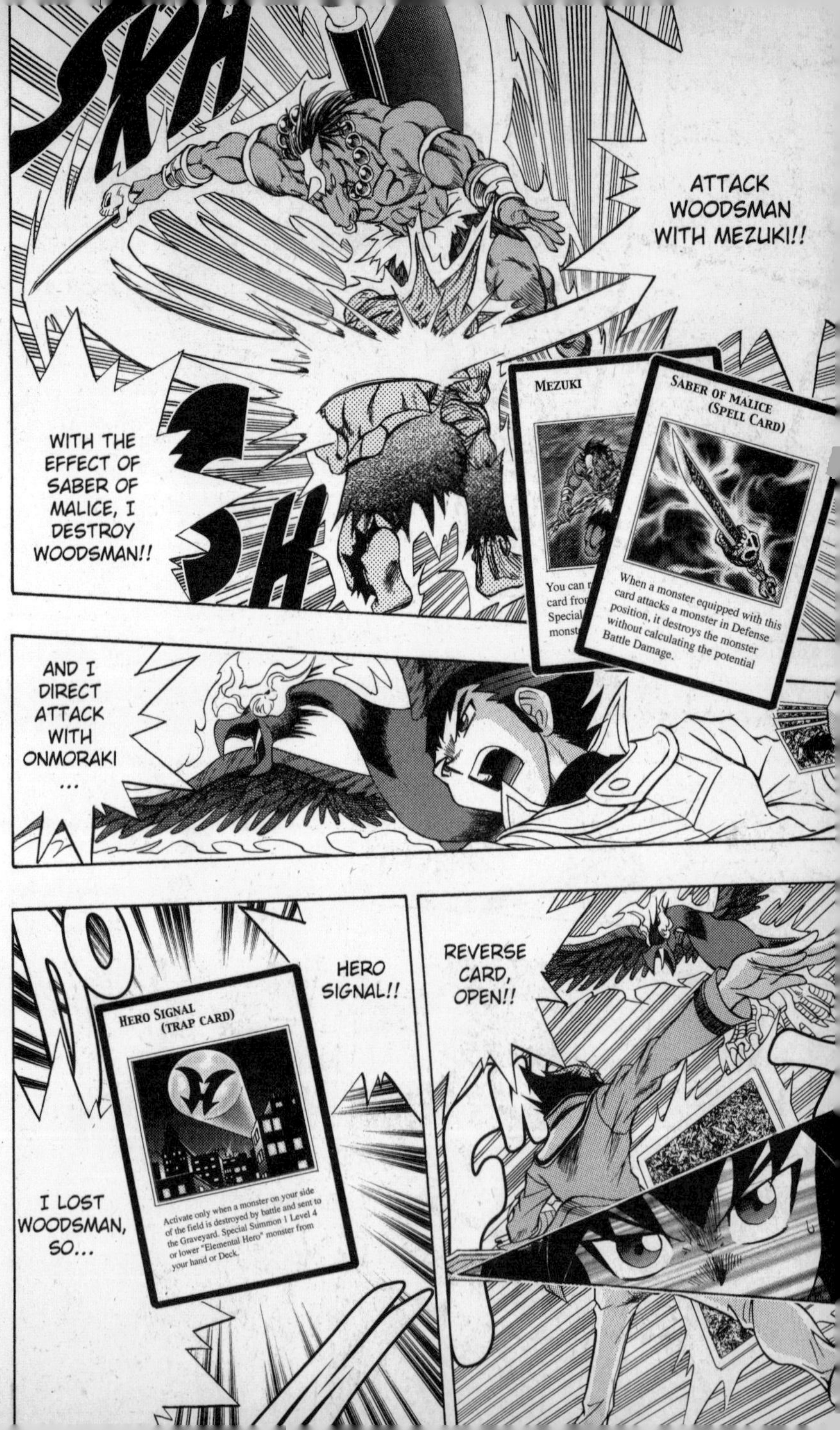
SKA
ATTACK WOODSMAN WITH MEZUKI!!
WITH THE EFFECT OF SABER OF MALICE, I DESTROY WOODSMAN!!
SH
MEZUKI
SABER OF MALICE (SPELL CARD)
When a monster equipped with this card attacks a monster in Defense position, it destroys the monster without calculating the potential Battle Damage.
AND I DIRECT ATTACK WITH ONMORAKI ...
REVERSE CARD, OPEN!!
HERO SIGNAL!!
HERO SIGNAL (TRAP CARD)
Activate only when a monster on your side of the field is destroyed by battle and sent to the Graveyard. Special Summon 1 Level 4 or lower "Elemental Hero" monster from your hand or Deck.
I LOST WOODSMAN, SO...

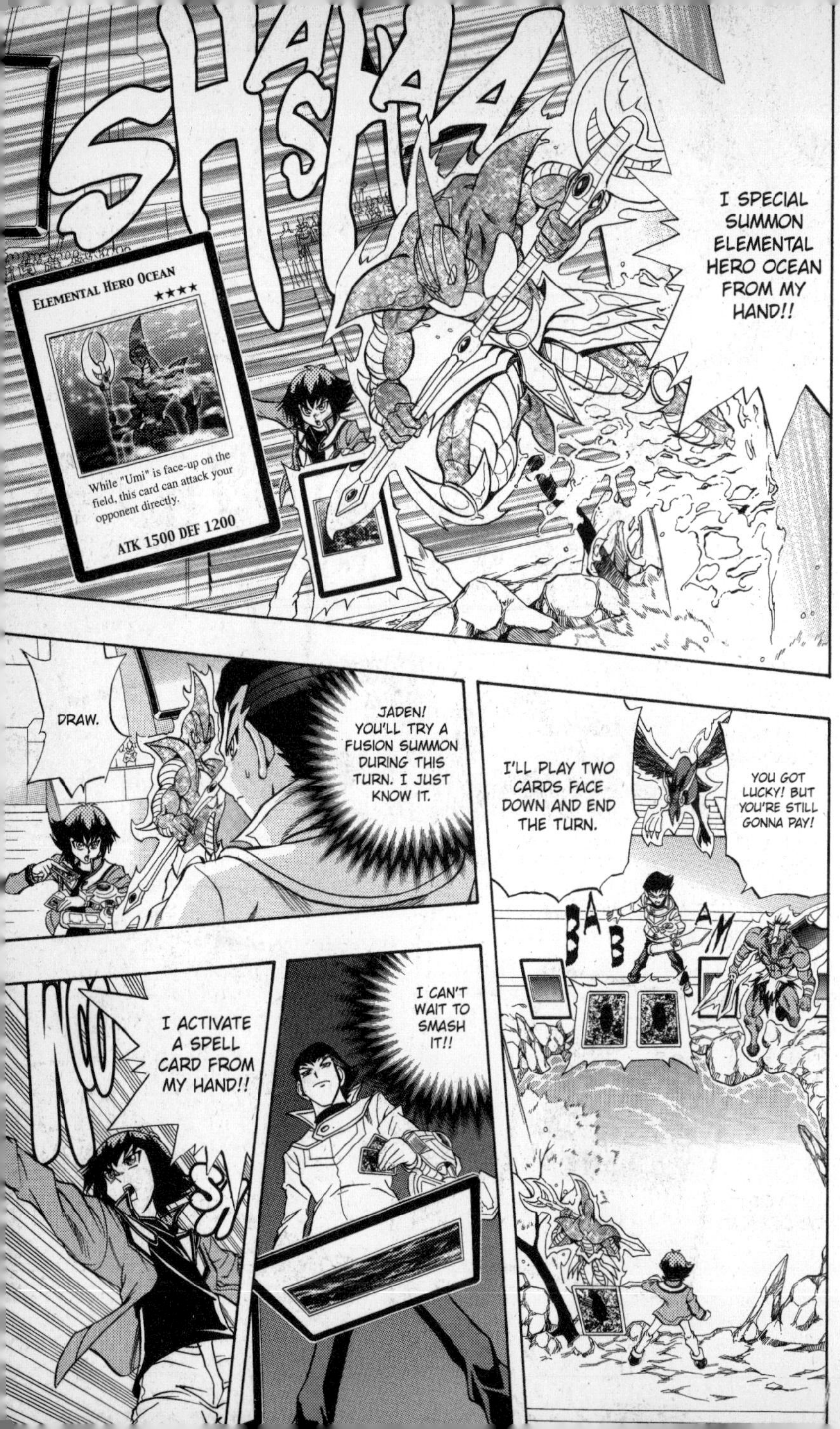
SHAAA
SHAA
ELEMENTAL HERO OCEAN ★★★★
While "Umi" is face-up on the field, this card can attack your opponent directly.
ATK 1500 DEF 1200
I SPECIAL SUMMON ELEMENTAL HERO OCEAN FROM MY HAND!!
YOU GOT LUCKY! BUT YOU'RE STILL GONNA PAY!
I'LL PLAY TWO CARDS FACE DOWN AND END THE TURN.
BABAAM
JADEN! YOU'LL TRY A FUSION SUMMON DURING THIS TURN. I JUST KNOW IT.
DRAW.
I CAN'T WAIT TO SMASH IT!!
I ACTIVATE A SPELL CARD FROM MY HAND!!

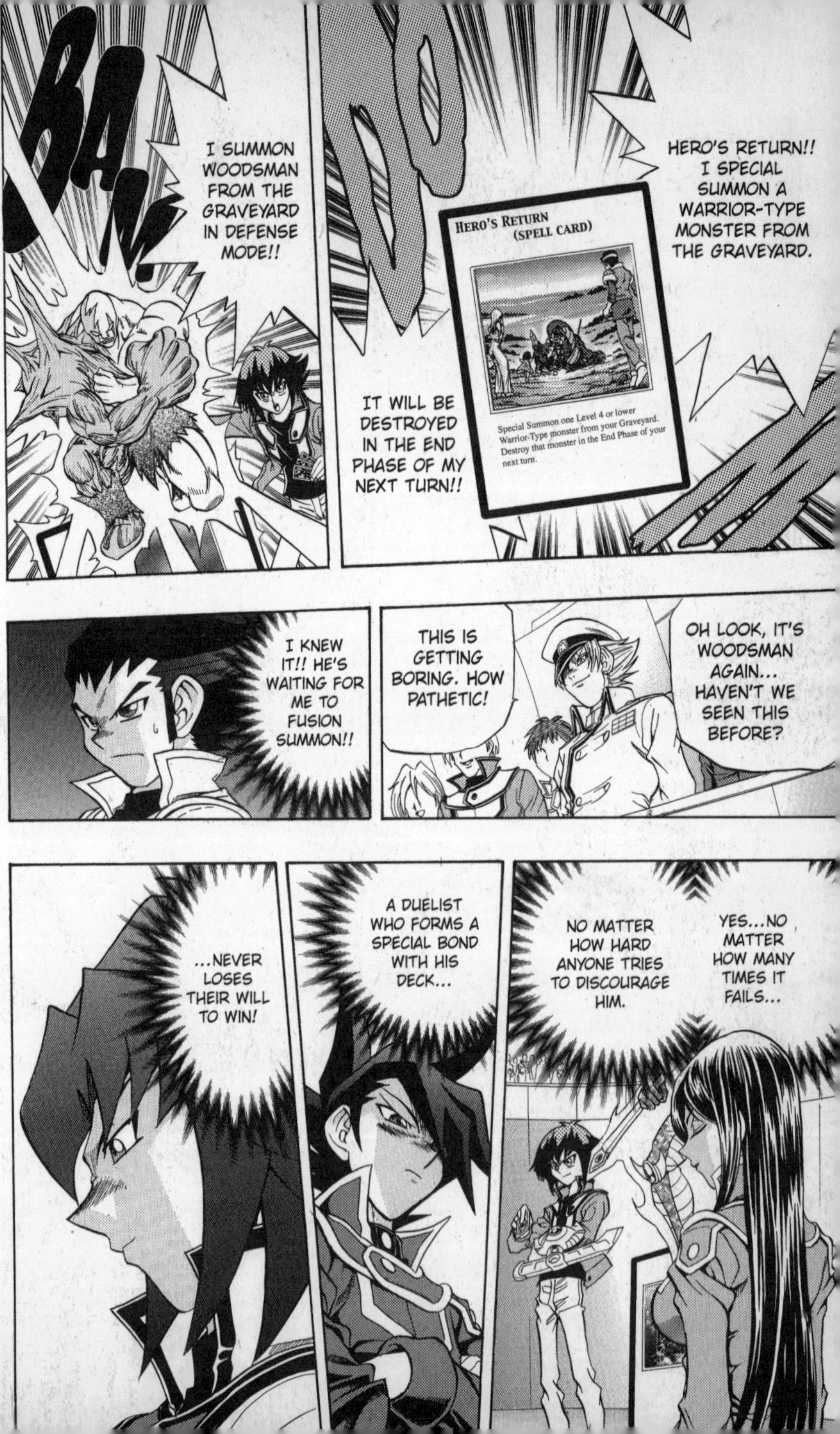
HERO'S RETURN!! I SPECIAL SUMMON A WARRIOR-TYPE MONSTER FROM THE GRAVEYARD.
HERO'S RETURN (SPELL CARD)
Special Summon one Level 4 or lower Warrior-Type monster from your Graveyard. Destroy that monster in the End Phase of your next turn.
IT WILL BE DESTROYED IN THE END PHASE OF MY NEXT TURN!!
BA
I SUMMON WOODSMAN FROM THE GRAVEYARD IN DEFENSE MODE!!
OH LOOK, IT'S WOODSMAN AGAIN... HAVEN'T WE SEEN THIS BEFORE?
THIS IS GETTING BORING. HOW PATHETIC!
I KNEW IT!! HE'S WAITING FOR ME TO FUSION SUMMON!!
YES...NO MATTER HOW MANY TIMES IT FAILS...
NO MATTER HOW HARD ANYONE TRIES TO DISCOURAGE HIM.
A DUELIST WHO FORMS A SPECIAL BOND WITH HIS DECK...
...NEVER LOSES THEIR WILL TO WIN!

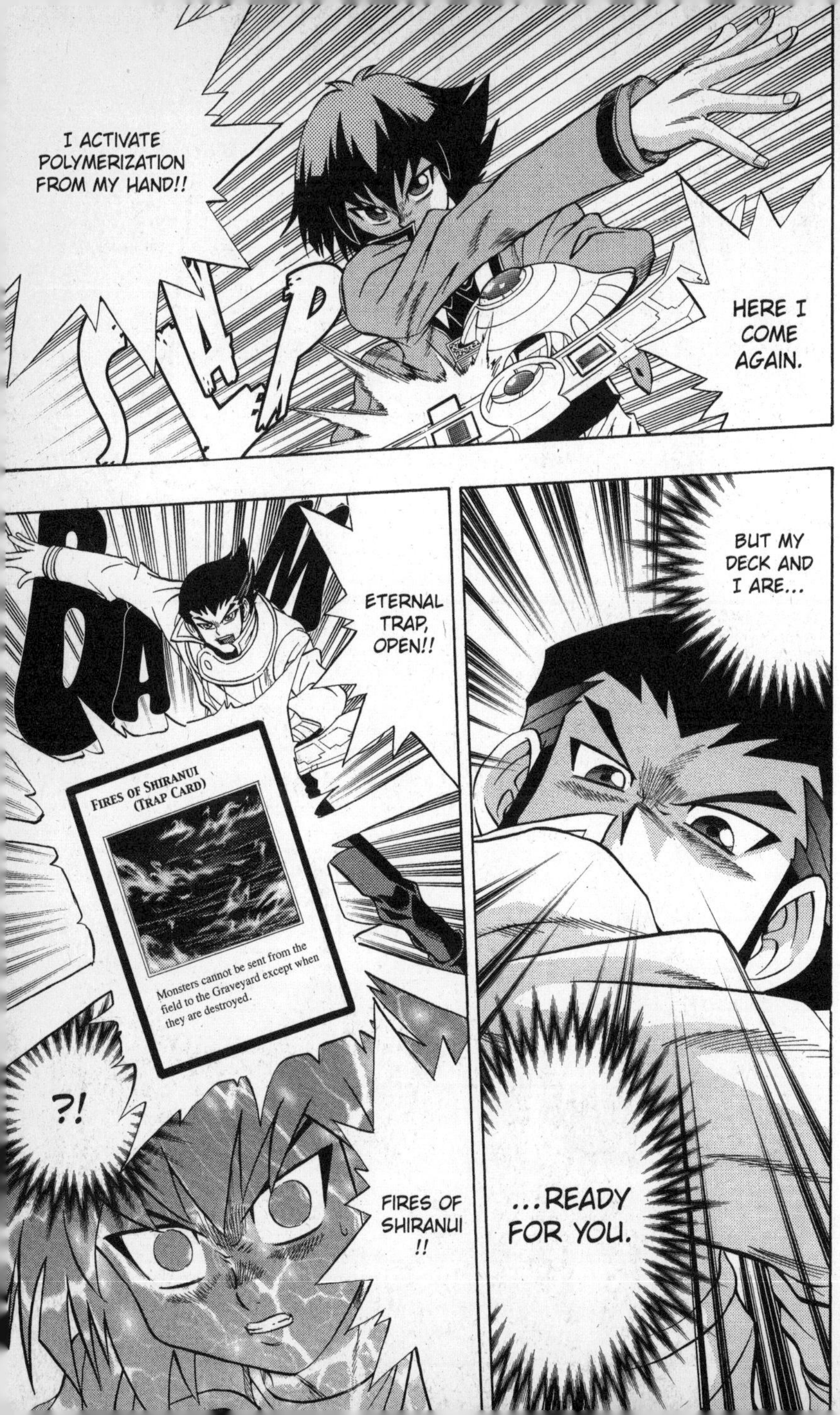
HERE I COME AGAIN.
I ACTIVATE POLYMERIZATION FROM MY HAND!!
BUT MY DECK AND I ARE...
...READY FOR YOU.
ETERNAL TRAP, OPEN!!
FIRES OF SHIRANUI (TRAP CARD)
Monsters cannot be sent from the field to the Graveyard except when they are destroyed.
?!
FIRES OF SHIRANUI !!

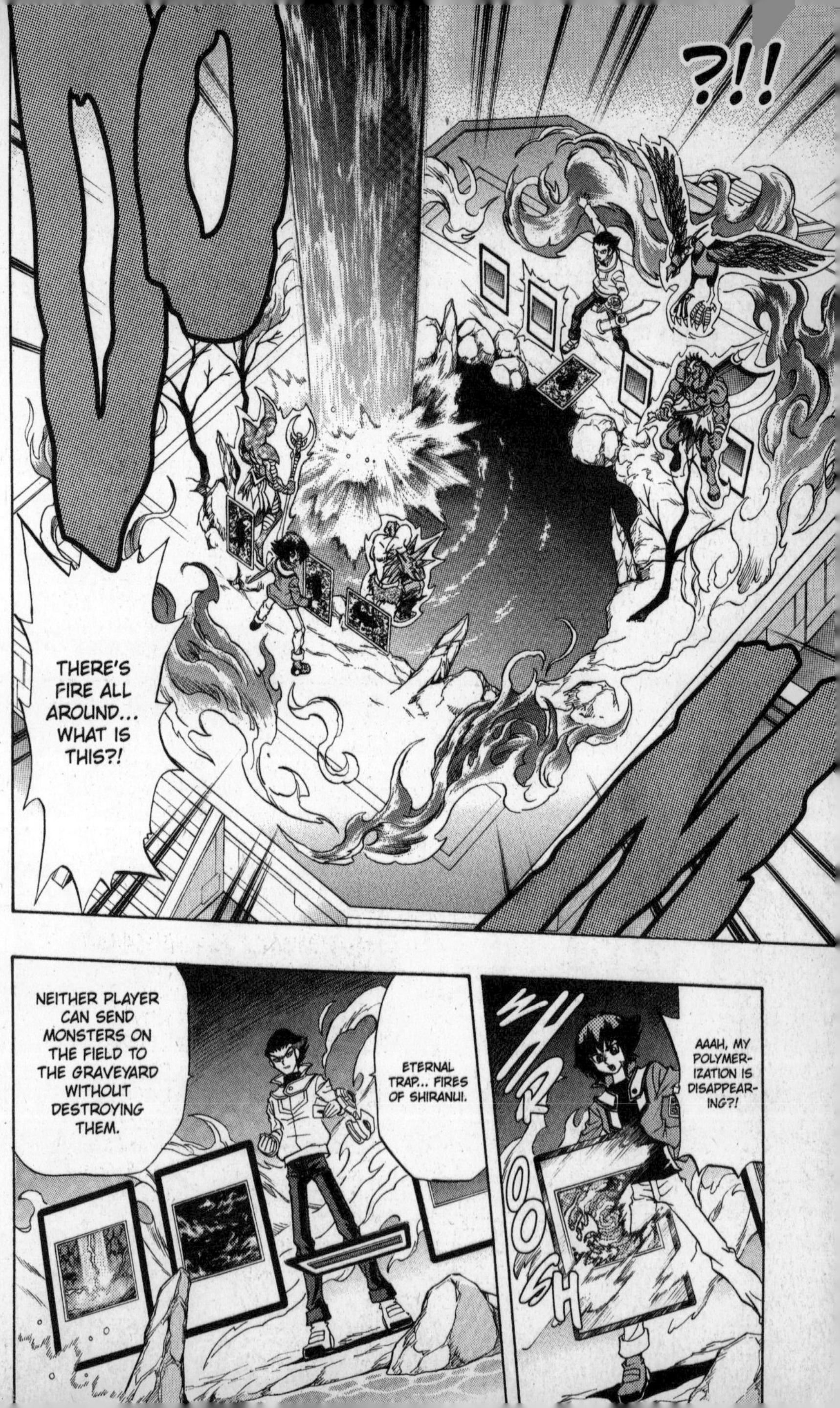
?!!
THERE'S FIRE ALL AROUND... WHAT IS THIS?!
WHOOOSH
AAAH, MY POLYMERIZATION IS DISAPPEARING?!
ETERNAL TRAP... FIRES OF SHIRANUI.
NEITHER PLAYER CAN SEND MONSTERS ON THE FIELD TO THE GRAVEYARD WITHOUT DESTROYING THEM.

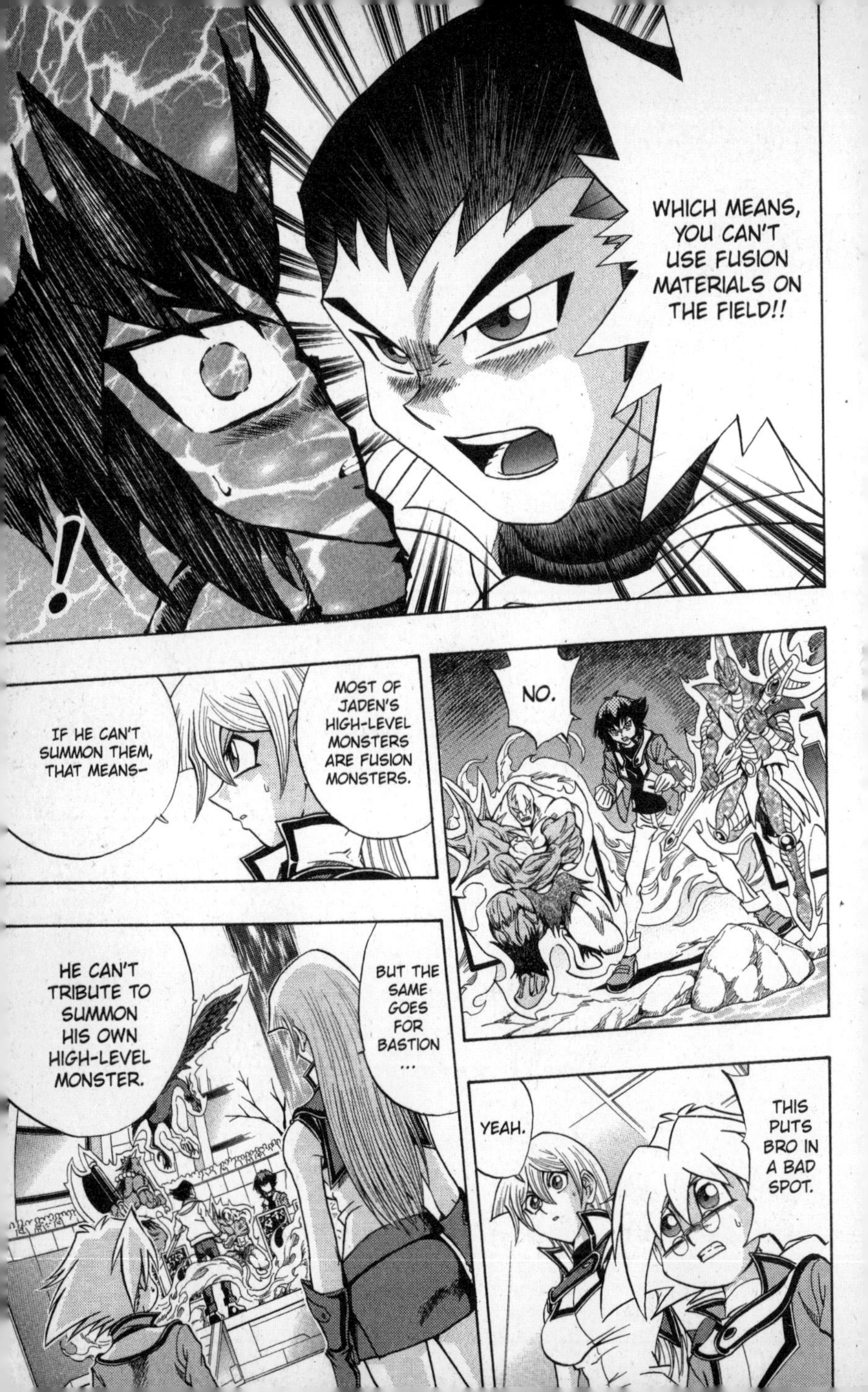
WHICH MEANS, YOU CAN'T USE FUSION MATERIALS ON THE FIELD!!
!
NO.
MOST OF JADEN'S HIGH-LEVEL MONSTERS ARE FUSION MONSTERS.
IF HE CAN'T SUMMON THEM, THAT MEANS—
BUT THE SAME GOES FOR BASTION ...
HE CAN'T TRIBUTE TO SUMMON HIS OWN HIGH-LEVEL MONSTER.
THIS PUTS BRO IN A BAD SPOT.
YEAH.

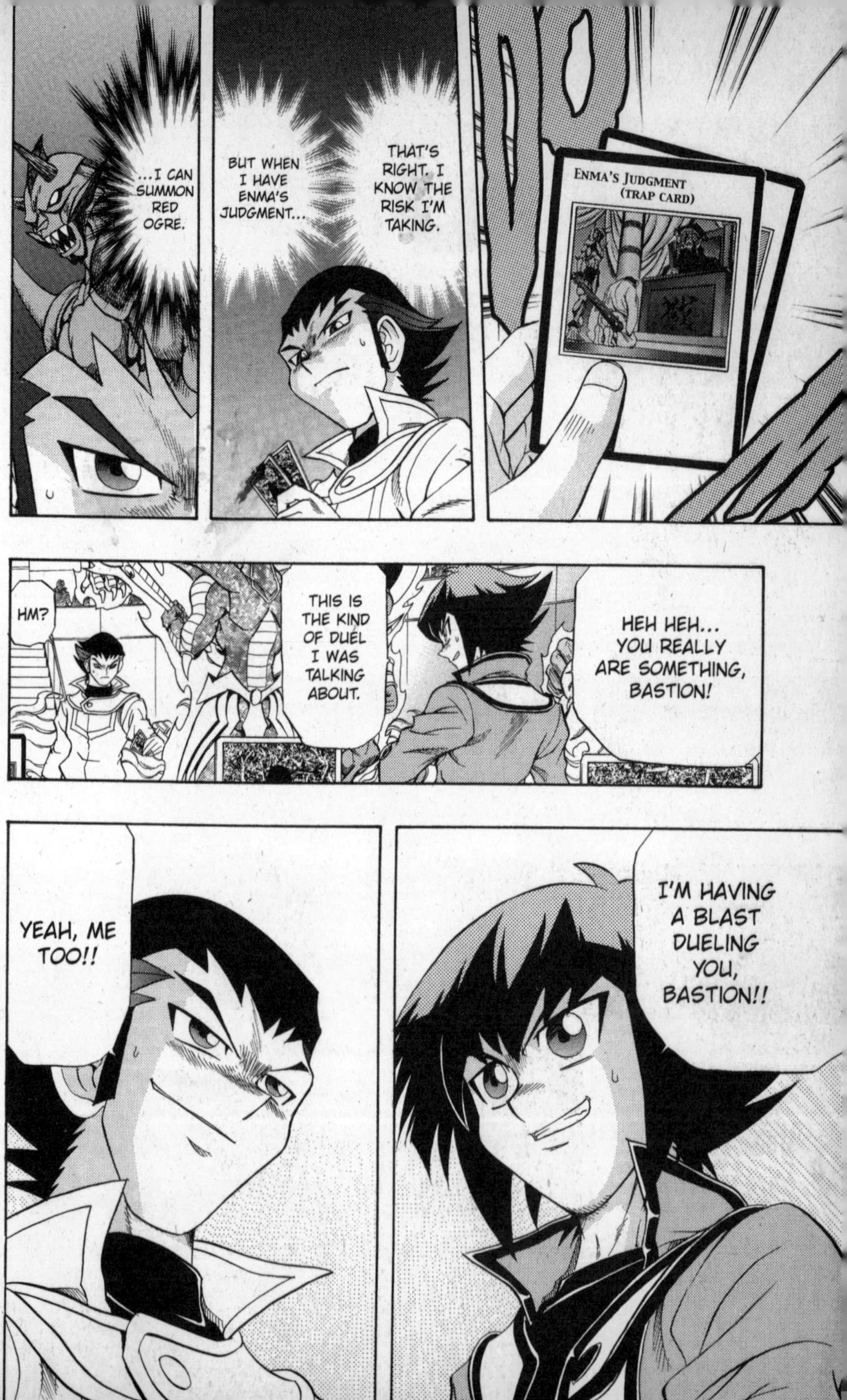
ENMA'S JUDGMENT
(TRAP CARD)
THAT'S RIGHT. I KNOW THE RISK I'M TAKING.
BUT WHEN I HAVE ENMA'S JUDGMENT...
...I CAN SUMMON RED OGRE.
HEH HEH... YOU REALLY ARE SOMETHING, BASTION!
THIS IS THE KIND OF DUEL I WAS TALKING ABOUT.
HM?
I'M HAVING A BLAST DUELING YOU, BASTION!!
YEAH, ME TOO!!

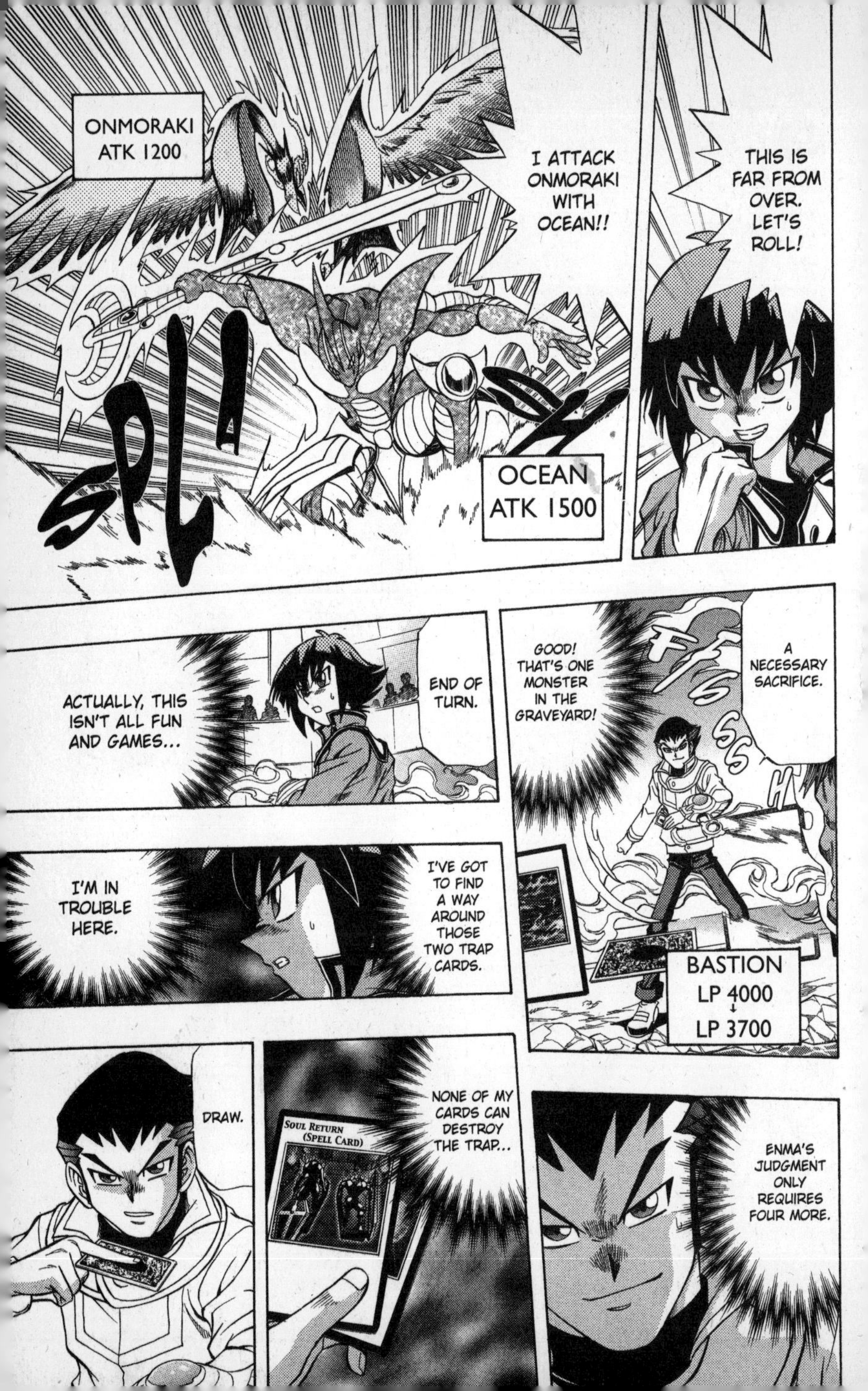
THIS IS FAR FROM OVER. LET'S ROLL!
I ATTACK ONMORAKI WITH OCEAN!!
ONMORAKI ATK 1200
OCEAN ATK 1500
SPLASH
A NECESSARY SACRIFICE.
GOOD! THAT'S ONE MONSTER IN THE GRAVEYARD!
FSSSH
BASTION LP 4000 → LP 3700
END OF TURN.
ACTUALLY, THIS ISN'T ALL FUN AND GAMES...
I'VE GOT TO FIND A WAY AROUND THOSE TWO TRAP CARDS.
I'M IN TROUBLE HERE.
ENMA'S JUDGMENT ONLY REQUIRES FOUR MORE.
NONE OF MY CARDS CAN DESTROY THE TRAP...
SOUL RETURN (SPELL CARD)
DRAW.

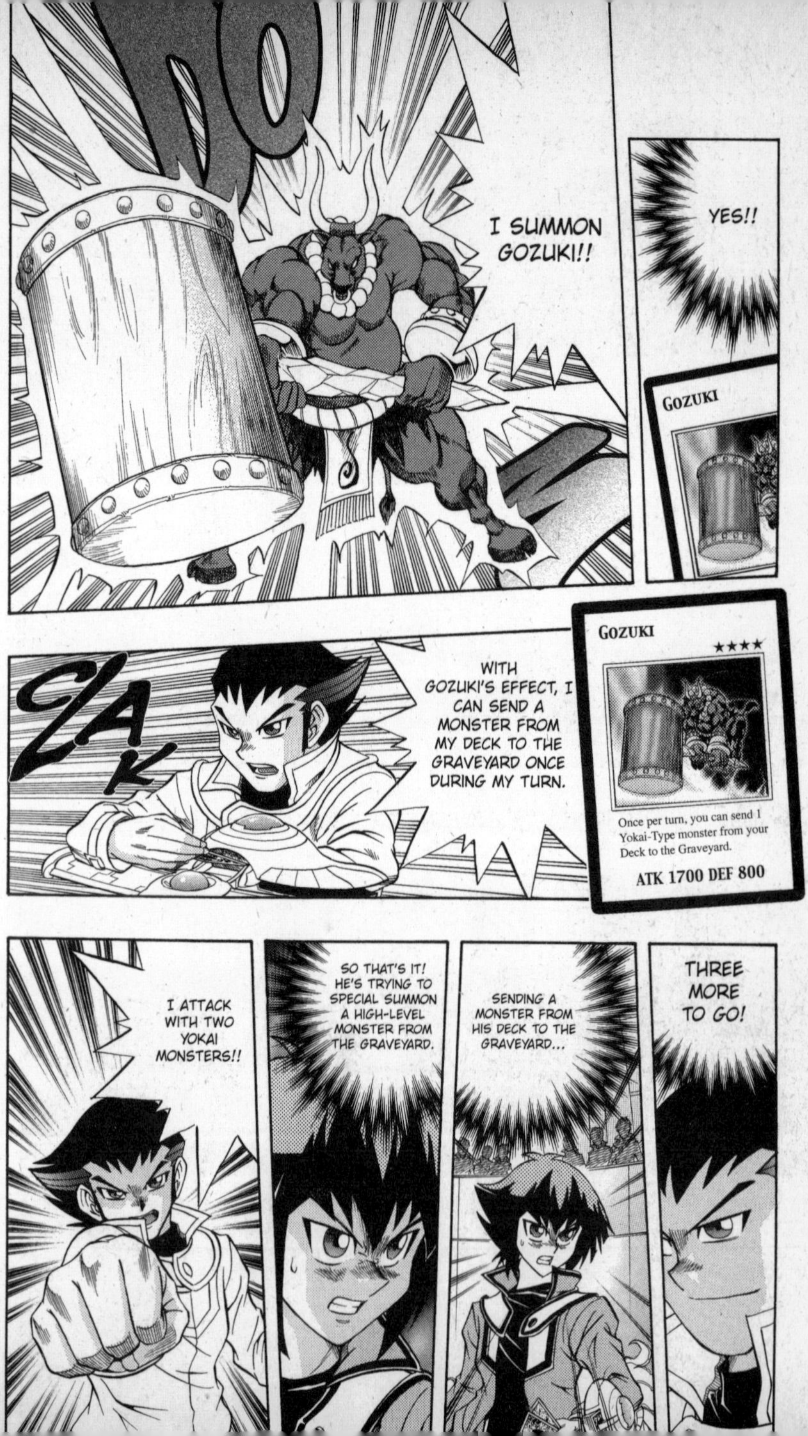

YES!!
GOZUKI
I SUMMON GOZUKI!!
GOZUKI
★★★★
Once per turn, you can send 1 Yokai-Type monster from your Deck to the Graveyard.
ATK 1700 DEF 800
WITH GOZUKI'S EFFECT, I CAN SEND A MONSTER FROM MY DECK TO THE GRAVEYARD ONCE DURING MY TURN.
CLAK
THREE MORE TO GO!
SENDING A MONSTER FROM HIS DECK TO THE GRAVEYARD...
SO THAT'S IT! HE'S TRYING TO SPECIAL SUMMON A HIGH-LEVEL MONSTER FROM THE GRAVEYARD.
I ATTACK WITH TWO YOKAI MONSTERS!!

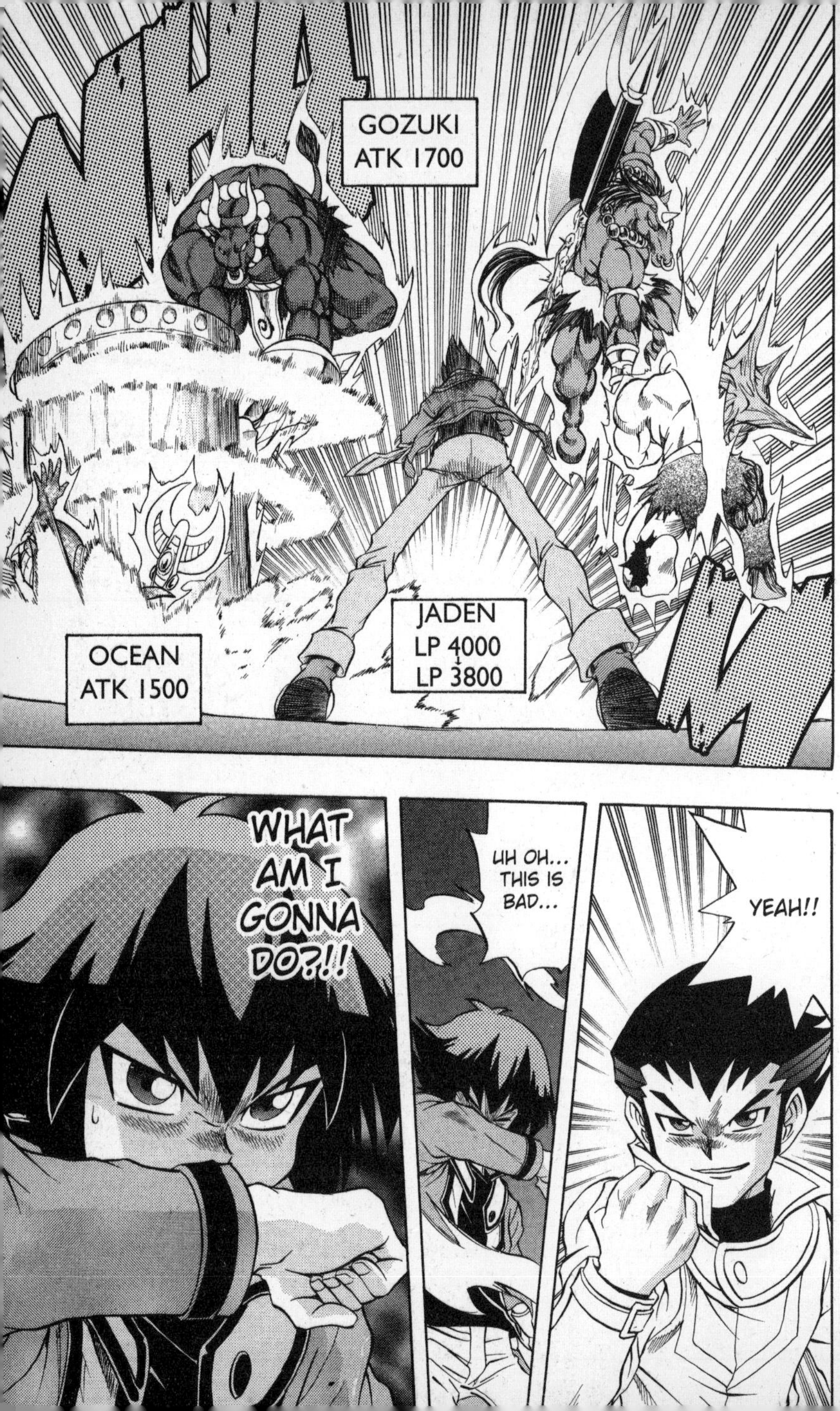
GOZUKI
ATK 1700
JADEN
LP 4000
LP 3800
OCEAN
ATK 1500
YEAH!!
UH OH... THIS IS BAD...
WHAT AM I GONNA DO?!!

In 2007
I WAS WORKING.
TAKAHASHI-SAN AND AKIRA WENT TO ISHIGAKI ISLAND ON VACATION IN EARLY JULY OF 2007.
?
RING-A-LING-LING
I WAS AT HOME WORKING ON MY STORYBOARD.
I GOT MAIL FROM TAKAHASHI-SAN.
I'm at the beach in Ishigaki. Akira went into the water with his mobile phone in his pocket! Can you believe that?
HUH ?!
HE'D JUST UPGRADED TO A NEW PHONE A MONTH AGO...
HE'S DEFINITELY MISSING A FEW CARDS FROM HIS DECK.
...
COME-UPPANCE!
GRIN...

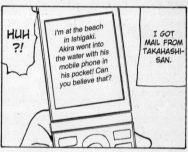

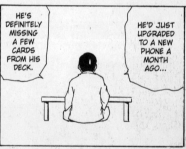

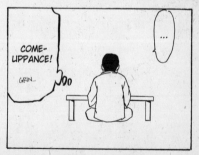

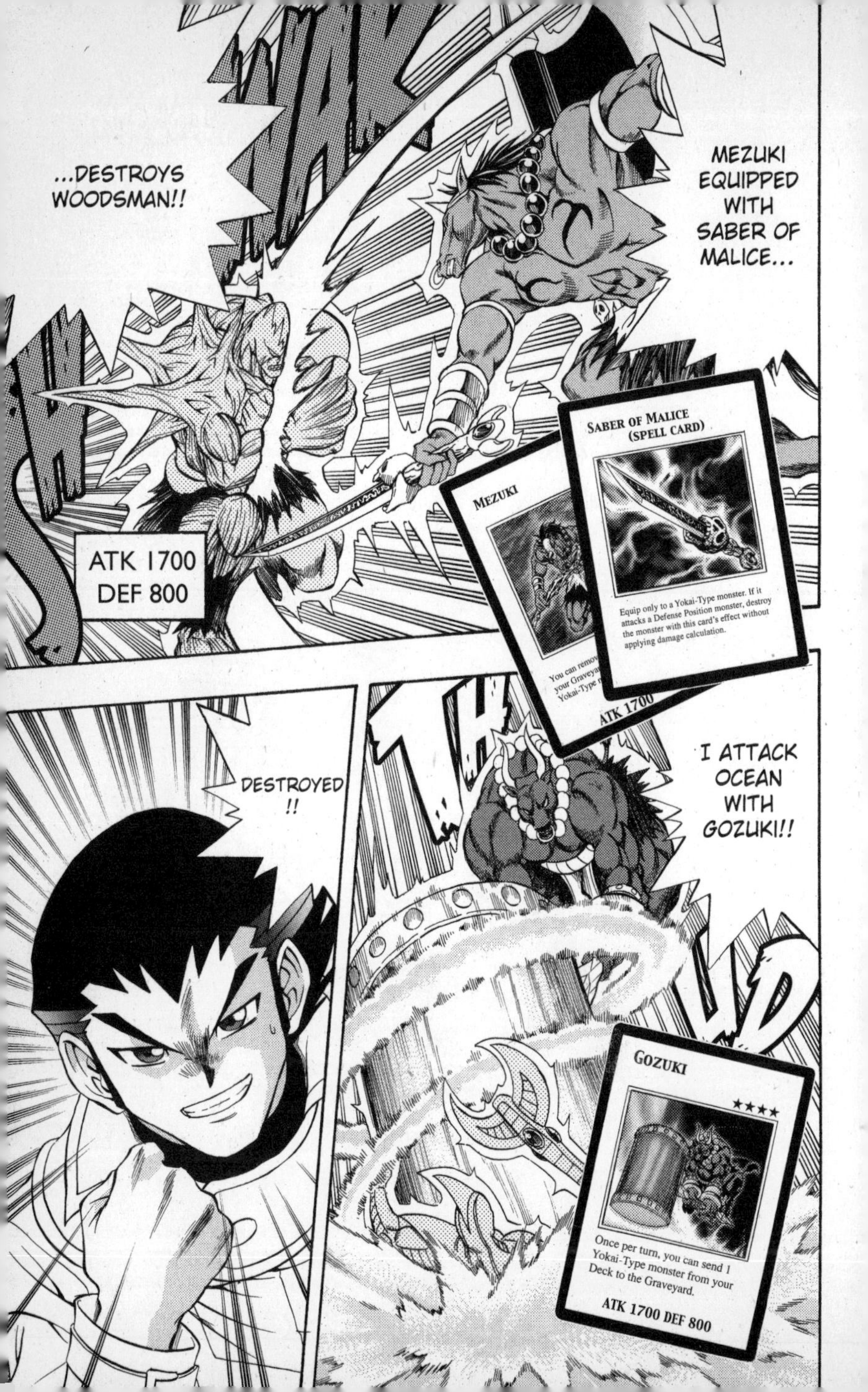
MEZUKI EQUIPPED WITH SABER OF MALICE...
...DESTROYS WOODSMAN!!
ATK 1700
DEF 800
MEZUKI
ATK 1700
SABER OF MALICE (SPELL CARD)
Equip only to a Yokai-Type monster. If it attacks a Defense Position monster, destroy the monster with this card's effect without applying damage calculation.
I ATTACK OCEAN WITH GOZUKI!!
GOZUKI
Once per turn, you can send 1 Yokai-Type monster from your Deck to the Graveyard.
ATK 1700 DEF 800
DESTROYED !!

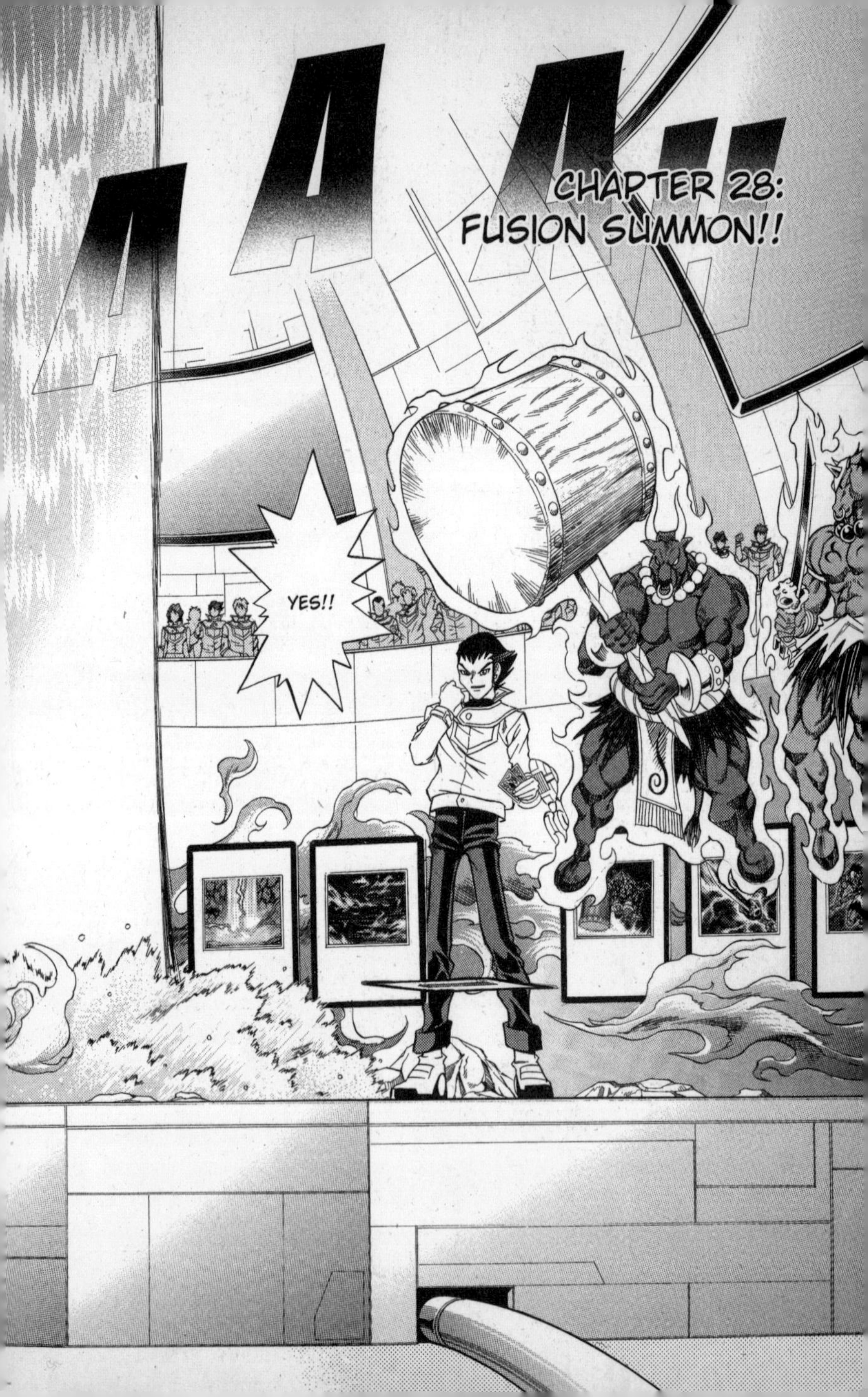
AAA!!
CHAPTER 28:
FUSION SUMMON!!
YES!!

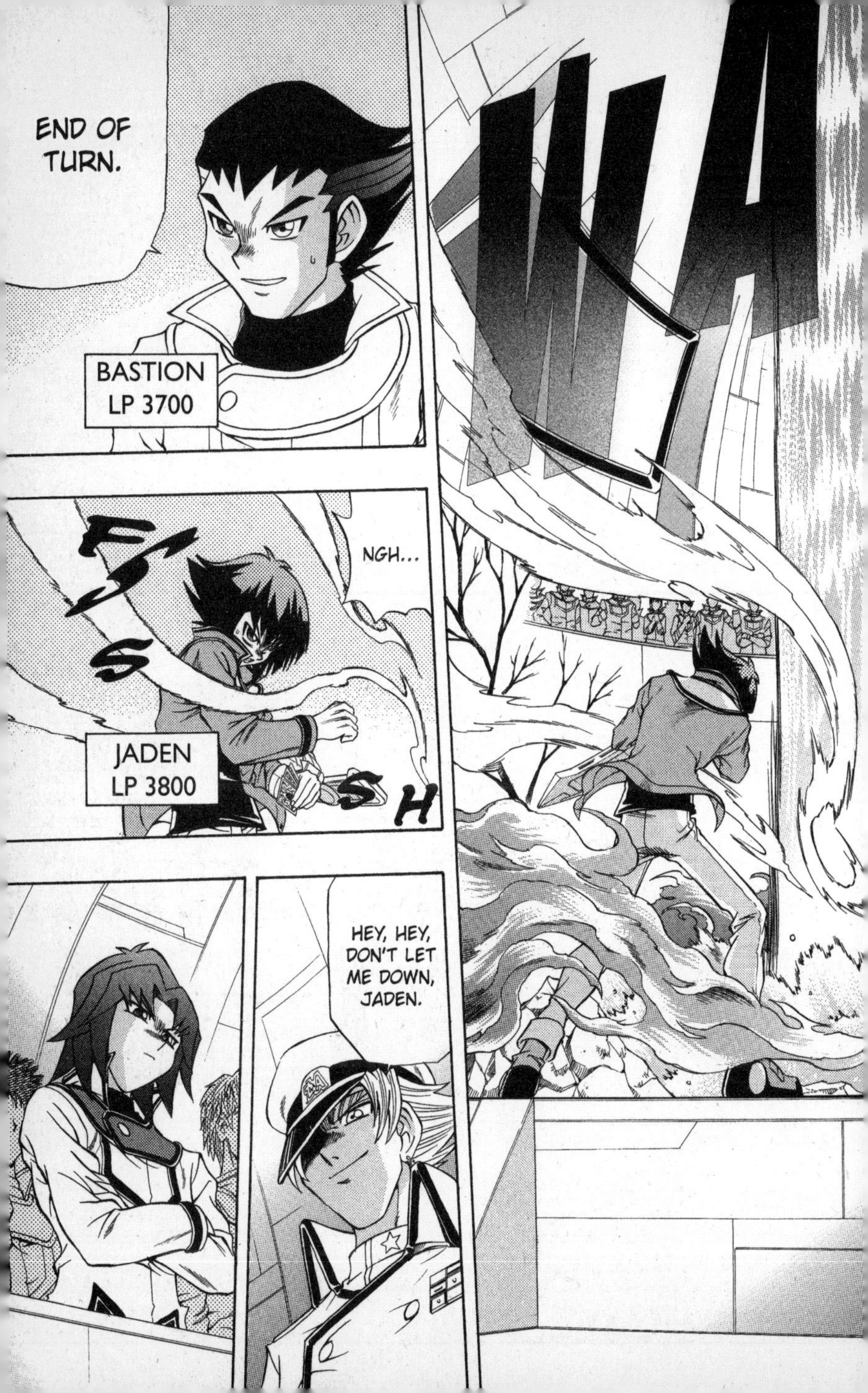
WA
END OF TURN.
BASTION
LP 3700
FSS
NGH...
SSH
JADEN
LP 3800
HEY, HEY, DON'T LET ME DOWN, JADEN.

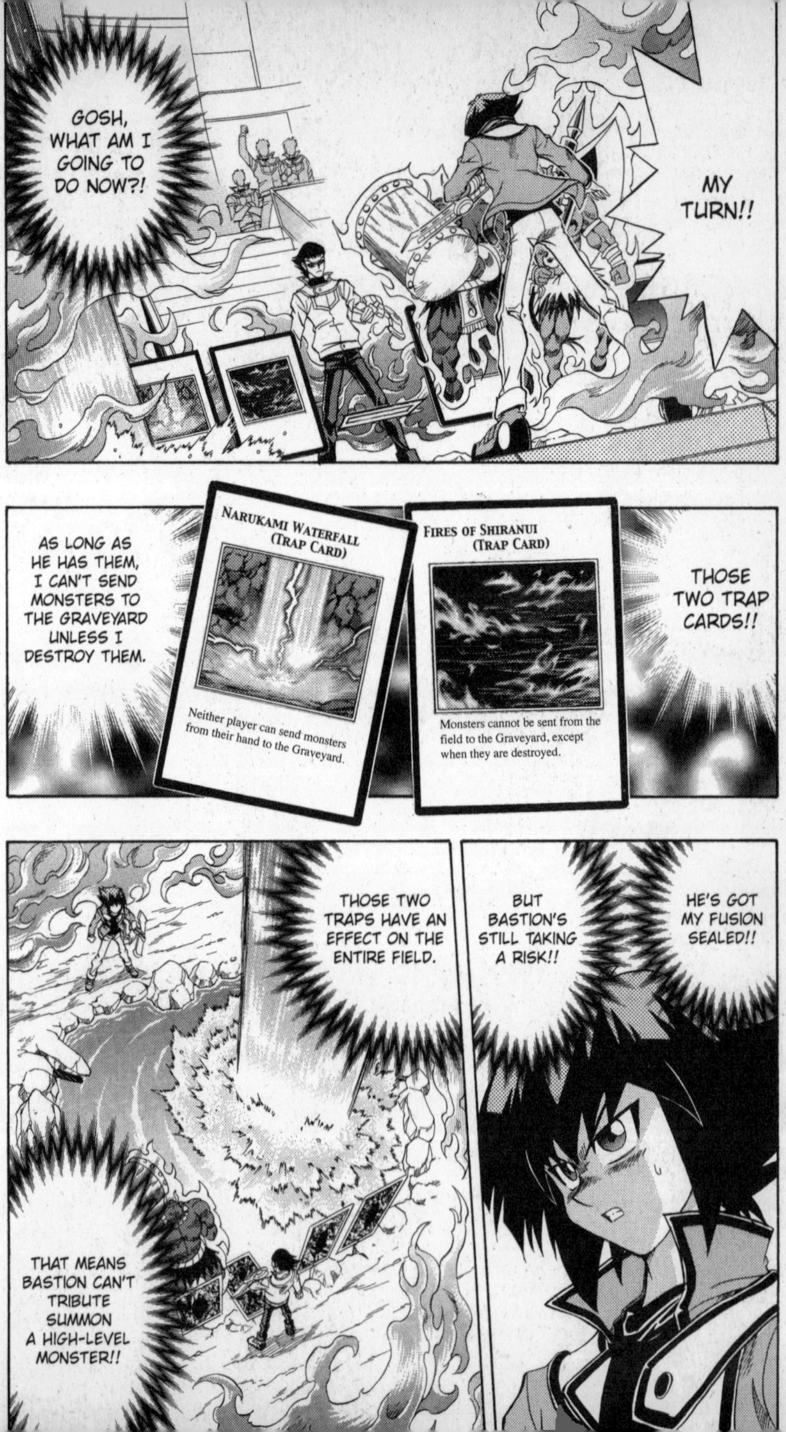
MY TURN!!
GOSH, WHAT AM I GOING TO DO NOW?!
THOSE TWO TRAP CARDS!!
FIRES OF SHIRANUI (TRAP CARD)
Monsters cannot be sent from the field to the Graveyard, except when they are destroyed.
NARUKAMI WATERFALL (TRAP CARD)
Neither player can send monsters from their hand to the Graveyard.
AS LONG AS HE HAS THEM, I CAN'T SEND MONSTERS TO THE GRAVEYARD UNLESS I DESTROY THEM.
HE'S GOT MY FUSION SEALED!!
BUT BASTION'S STILL TAKING A RISK!!
THOSE TWO TRAPS HAVE AN EFFECT ON THE ENTIRE FIELD.
THAT MEANS BASTION CAN'T TRIBUTE SUMMON A HIGH-LEVEL MONSTER!!

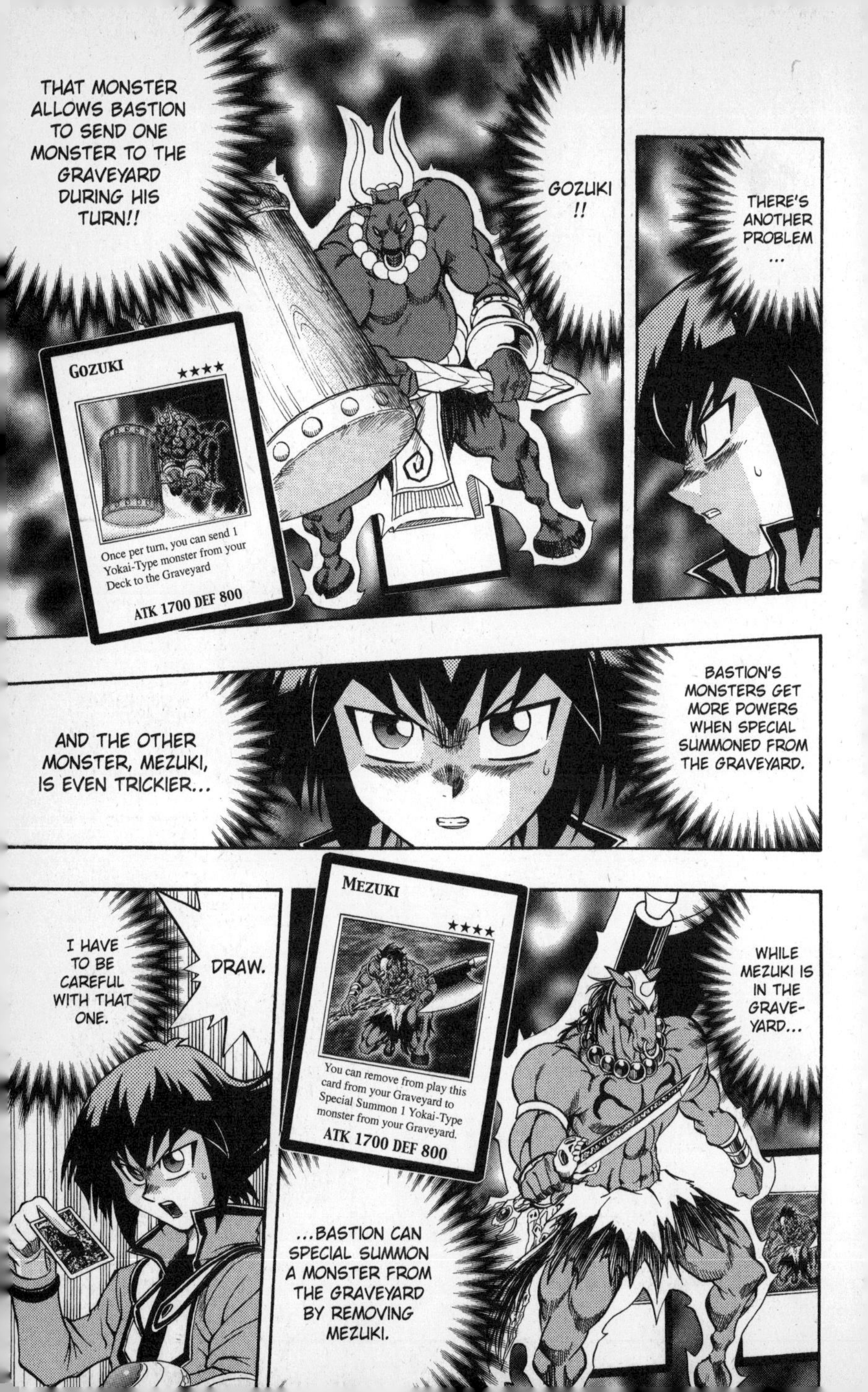
THERE'S ANOTHER PROBLEM ...
GOZUKI !!
THAT MONSTER ALLOWS BASTION TO SEND ONE MONSTER TO THE GRAVEYARD DURING HIS TURN!!
GOZUKI ★★★★
Once per turn, you can send 1 Yokai-Type monster from your Deck to the Graveyard
ATK 1700 DEF 800
BASTION'S MONSTERS GET MORE POWERS WHEN SPECIAL SUMMONED FROM THE GRAVEYARD.
AND THE OTHER MONSTER, MEZUKI, IS EVEN TRICKIER...
WHILE MEZUKI IS IN THE GRAVE-YARD...
MEZUKI ★★★★
You can remove from play this card from your Graveyard to Special Summon 1 Yokai-Type monster from your Graveyard.
ATK 1700 DEF 800
...BASTION CAN SPECIAL SUMMON A MONSTER FROM THE GRAVEYARD BY REMOVING MEZUKI.
DRAW.
I HAVE TO BE CAREFUL WITH THAT ONE.

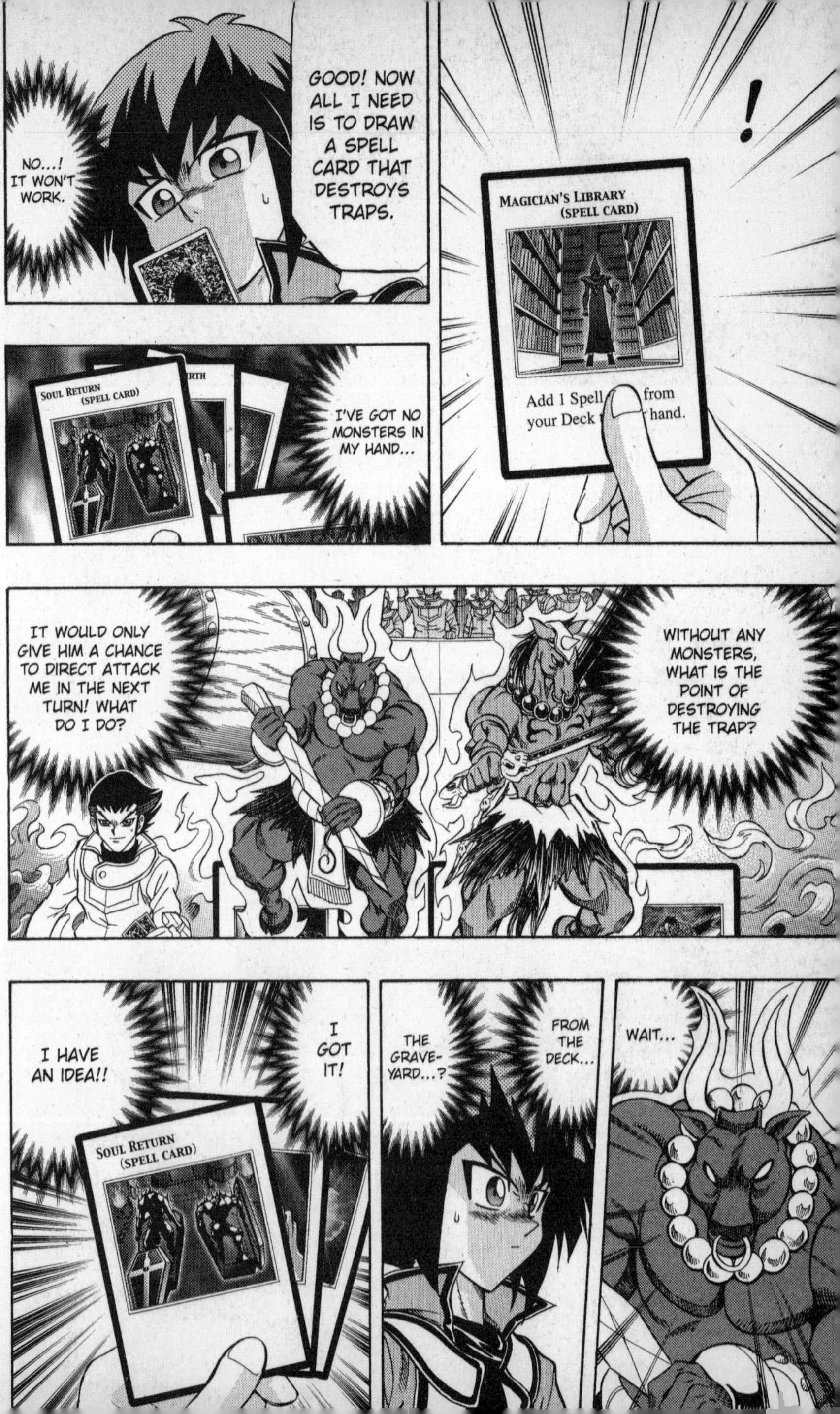
!
MAGICIAN'S LIBRARY (SPELL CARD)
Add 1 Spell
from
your Deck
hand.
GOOD! NOW ALL I NEED IS TO DRAW A SPELL CARD THAT DESTROYS TRAPS.
NO...! IT WON'T WORK.
I'VE GOT NO MONSTERS IN MY HAND...
SOUL RETURN (SPELL CARD)
WITHOUT ANY MONSTERS, WHAT IS THE POINT OF DESTROYING THE TRAP?
IT WOULD ONLY GIVE HIM A CHANCE TO DIRECT ATTACK ME IN THE NEXT TURN! WHAT DO I DO?
WAIT...
FROM THE DECK...
THE GRAVE-YARD...?
I GOT IT!
I HAVE AN IDEA!!
SOUL RETURN (SPELL CARD)

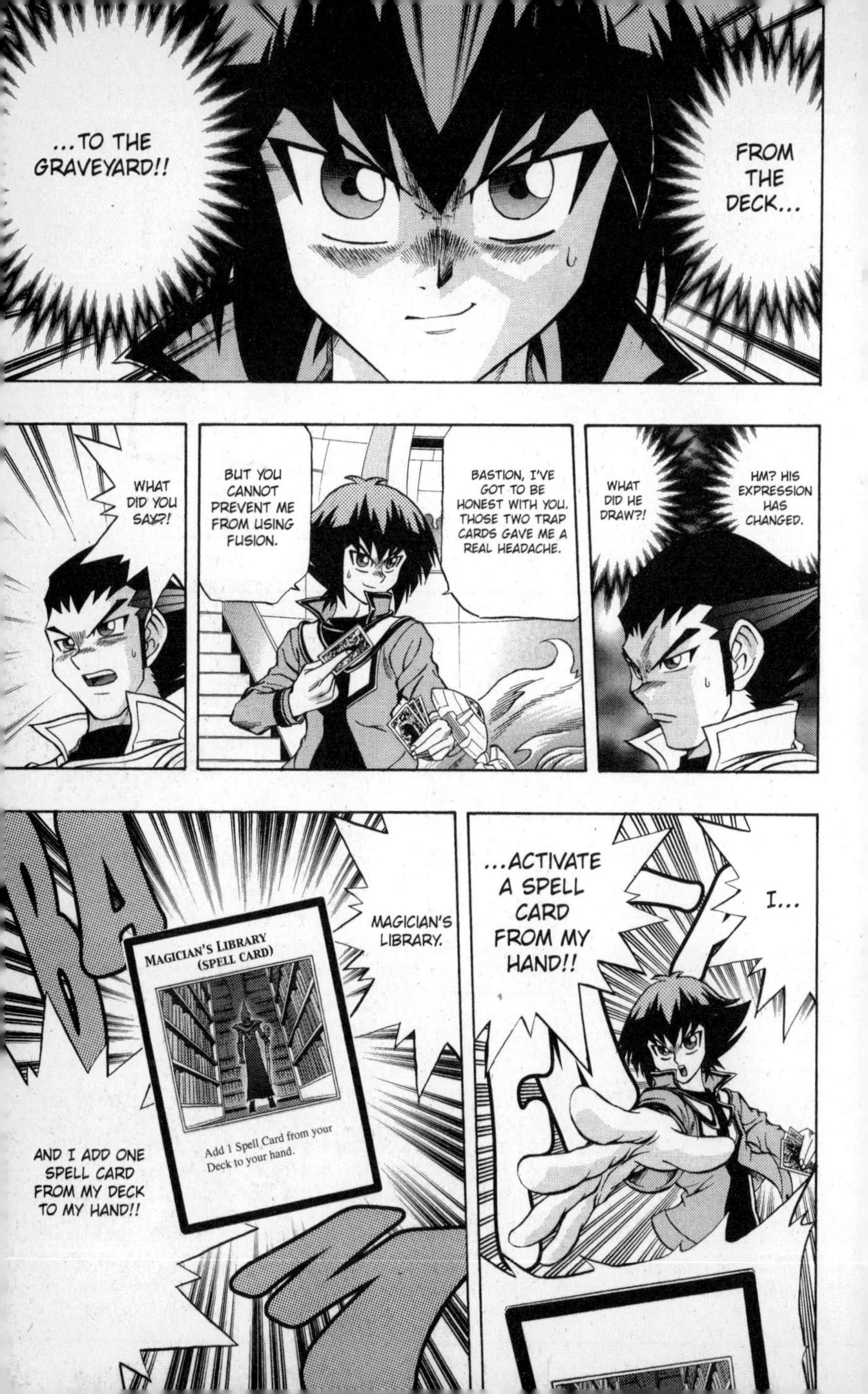
FROM THE DECK...
...TO THE GRAVEYARD!!
HM? HIS EXPRESSION HAS CHANGED.
WHAT DID HE DRAW?!
BASTION, I'VE GOT TO BE HONEST WITH YOU. THOSE TWO TRAP CARDS GAVE ME A REAL HEADACHE.
BUT YOU CANNOT PREVENT ME FROM USING FUSION.
WHAT DID YOU SAY?!
I...
...ACTIVATE A SPELL CARD FROM MY HAND!!
MAGICIAN'S LIBRARY.
MAGICIAN'S LIBRARY (SPELL CARD)
Add 1 Spell Card from your Deck to your hand.
AND I ADD ONE SPELL CARD FROM MY DECK TO MY HAND!!

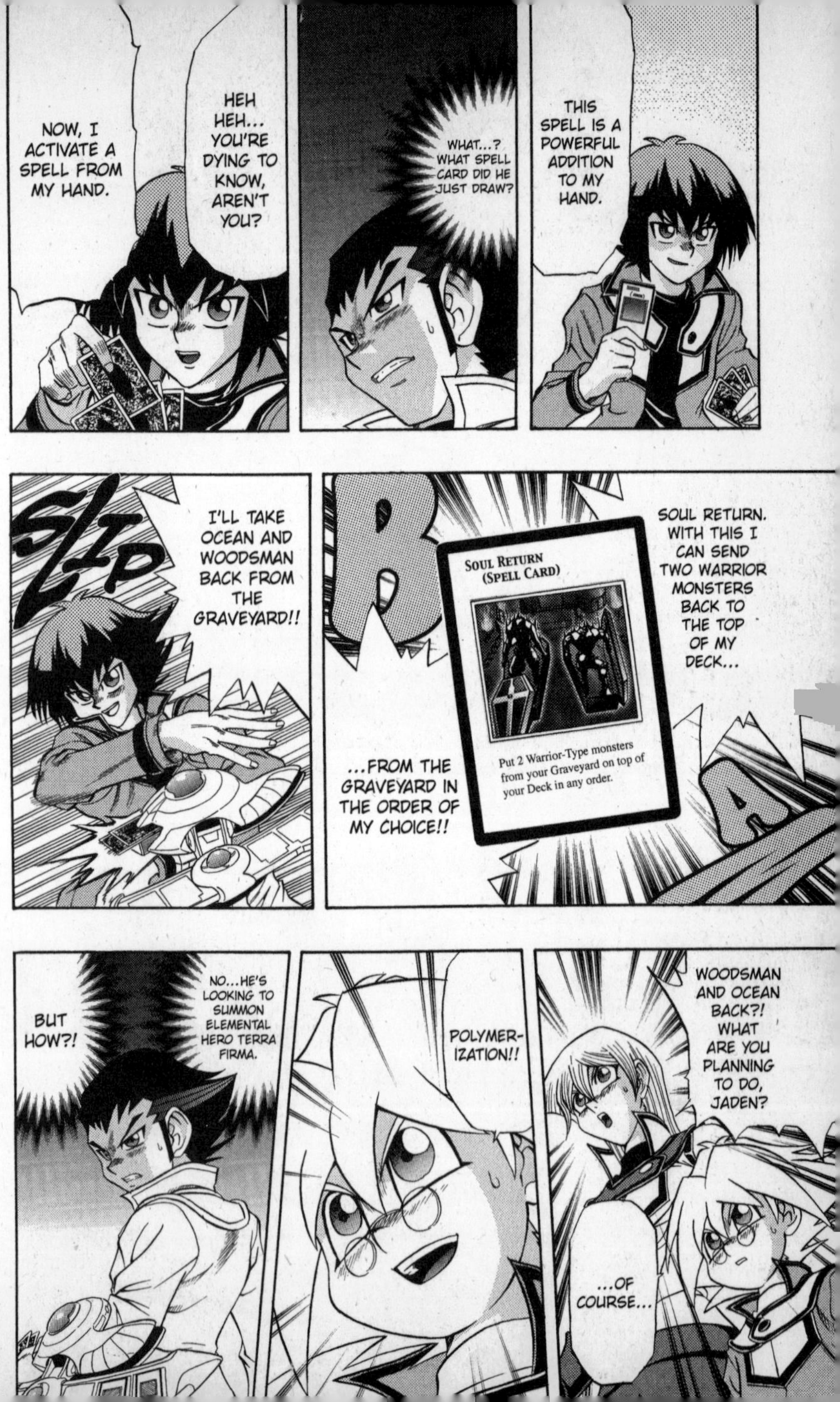
THIS SPELL IS A POWERFUL ADDITION TO MY HAND.
WHAT...? WHAT SPELL CARD DID HE JUST DRAW?
HEH HEH... YOU'RE DYING TO KNOW, AREN'T YOU?
NOW, I ACTIVATE A SPELL FROM MY HAND.
SOUL RETURN. WITH THIS I CAN SEND TWO WARRIOR MONSTERS BACK TO THE TOP OF MY DECK...
SOUL RETURN (SPELL CARD)
Put 2 Warrior-Type monsters from your Graveyard on top of your Deck in any order.
...FROM THE GRAVEYARD IN THE ORDER OF MY CHOICE!!
SLIP
I'LL TAKE OCEAN AND WOODSMAN BACK FROM THE GRAVEYARD!!
WOODSMAN AND OCEAN BACK?! WHAT ARE YOU PLANNING TO DO, JADEN?
...OF COURSE...
POLYMER-IZATION!!
NO...HE'S LOOKING TO SUMMON ELEMENTAL HERO TERRA FIRMA.
BUT HOW?!

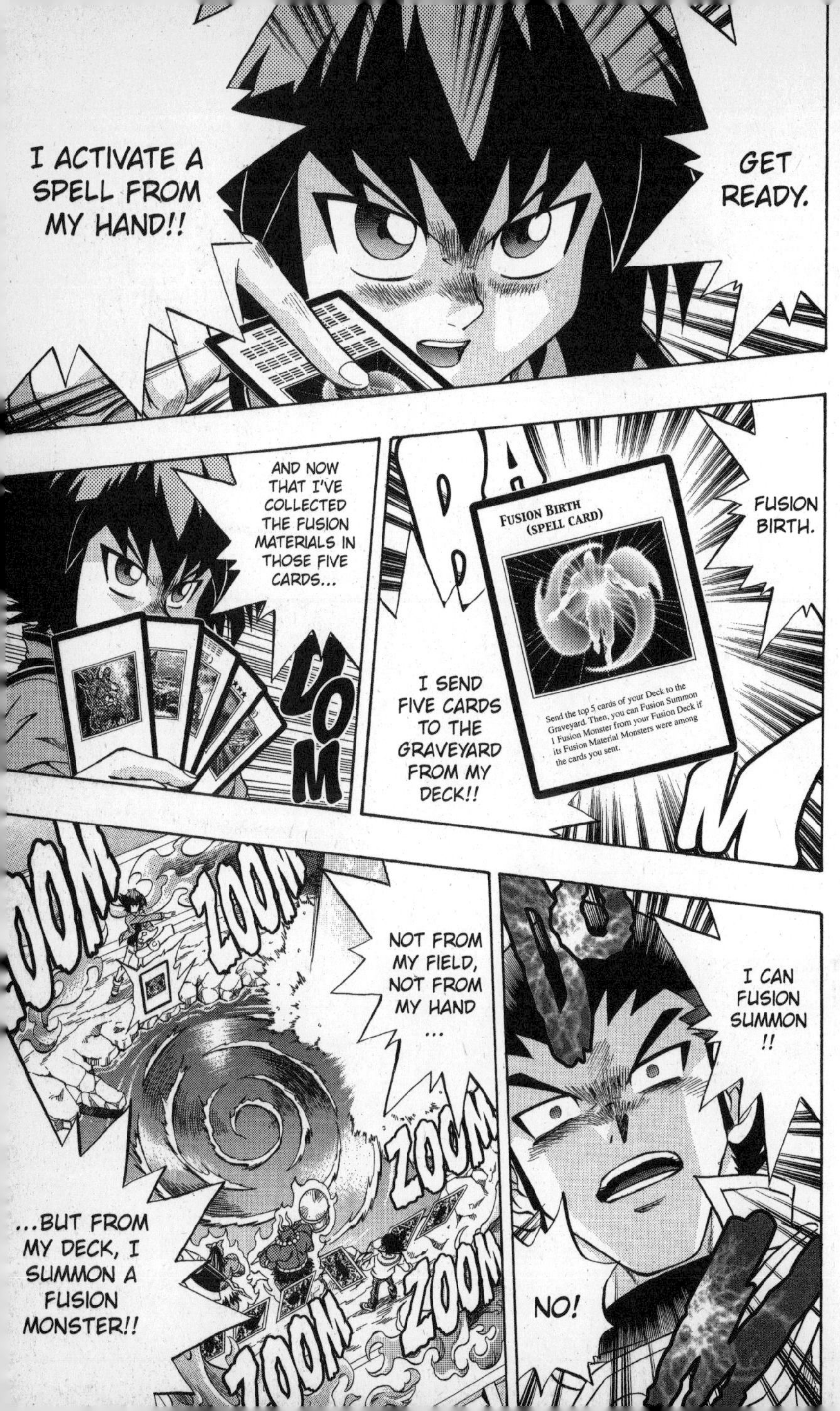
GET READY.
I ACTIVATE A SPELL FROM MY HAND!!
FUSION BIRTH.
FUSION BIRTH
(SPELL CARD)
Send the top 5 cards of your Deck to the Graveyard. Then, you can Fusion Summon 1 Fusion Monster from your Fusion Deck if its Fusion Material Monsters were among the cards you sent.
I SEND FIVE CARDS TO THE GRAVEYARD FROM MY DECK!!
AND NOW THAT I'VE COLLECTED THE FUSION MATERIALS IN THOSE FIVE CARDS...
DOM
I CAN FUSION SUMMON!!
NO!
ZOOM
NOT FROM MY FIELD, NOT FROM MY HAND ...
...BUT FROM MY DECK, I SUMMON A FUSION MONSTER!!
ZOOM
ZOOM
ZOOM

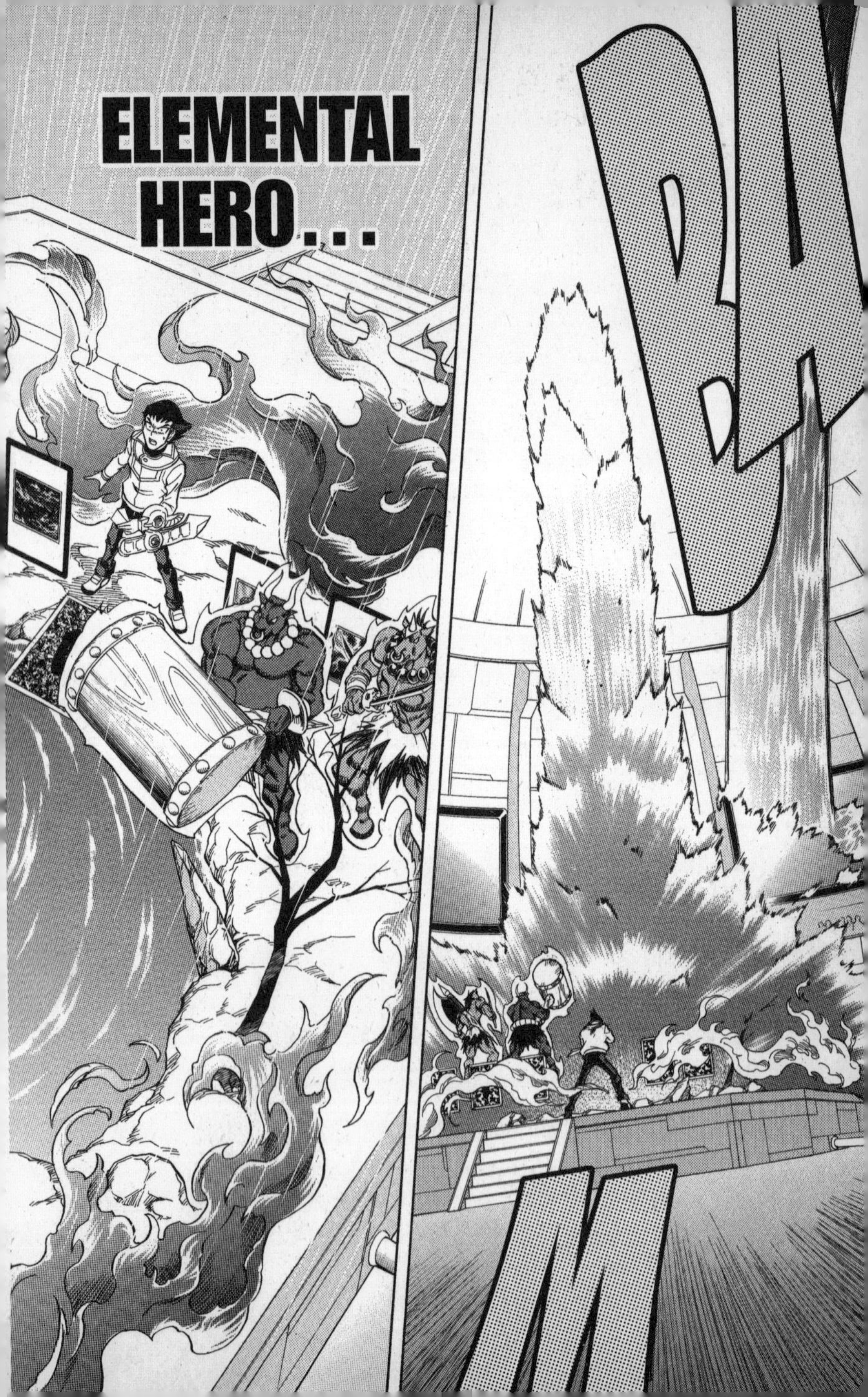
BAM
ELEMENTAL HERO...

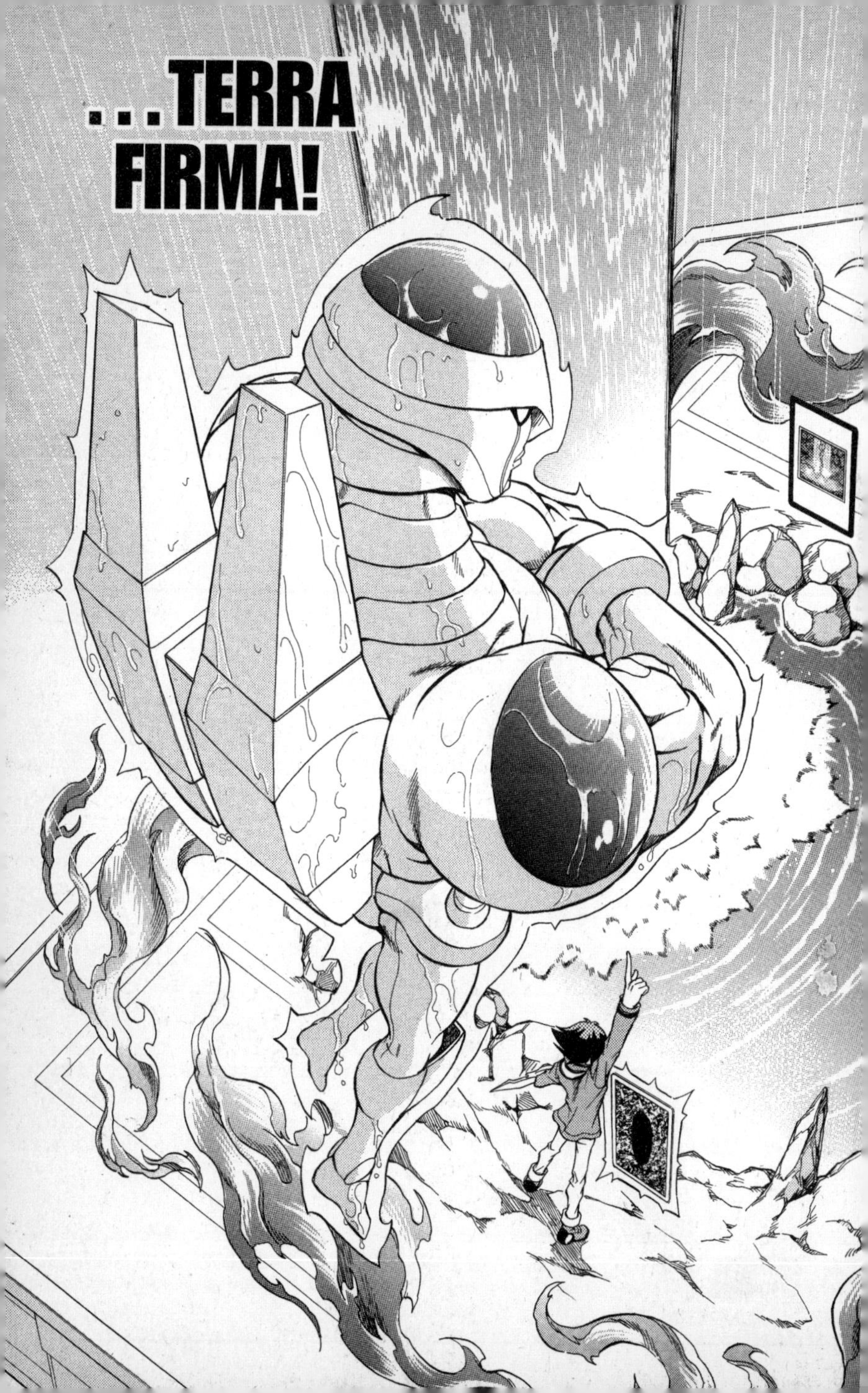
...TERRA FIRMA!

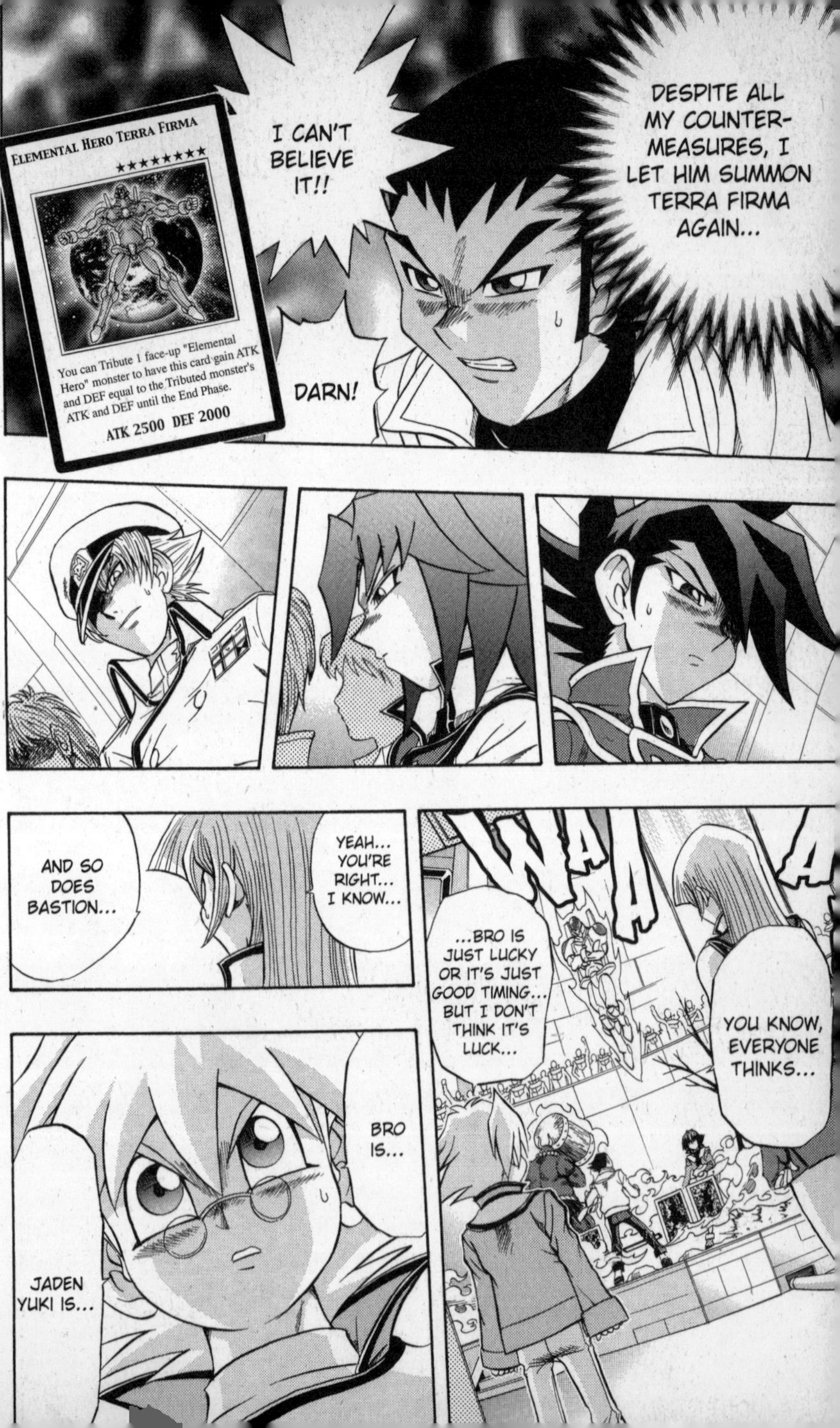
DESPITE ALL MY COUNTER-MEASURES, I LET HIM SUMMON TERRA FIRMA AGAIN...
I CAN'T BELIEVE IT!!
Elemental Hero Terra Firma
You can Tribute 1 face-up "Elemental Hero" monster to have this card gain ATK and DEF equal to the Tributed monster's ATK and DEF until the End Phase.
ATK 2500 DEF 2000
DARN!
YOU KNOW, EVERYONE THINKS...
...BRO IS JUST LUCKY OR IT'S JUST GOOD TIMING... BUT I DON'T THINK IT'S LUCK...
YEAH... YOU'RE RIGHT... I KNOW...
AND SO DOES BASTION...
BRO IS...
JADEN YUKI IS...

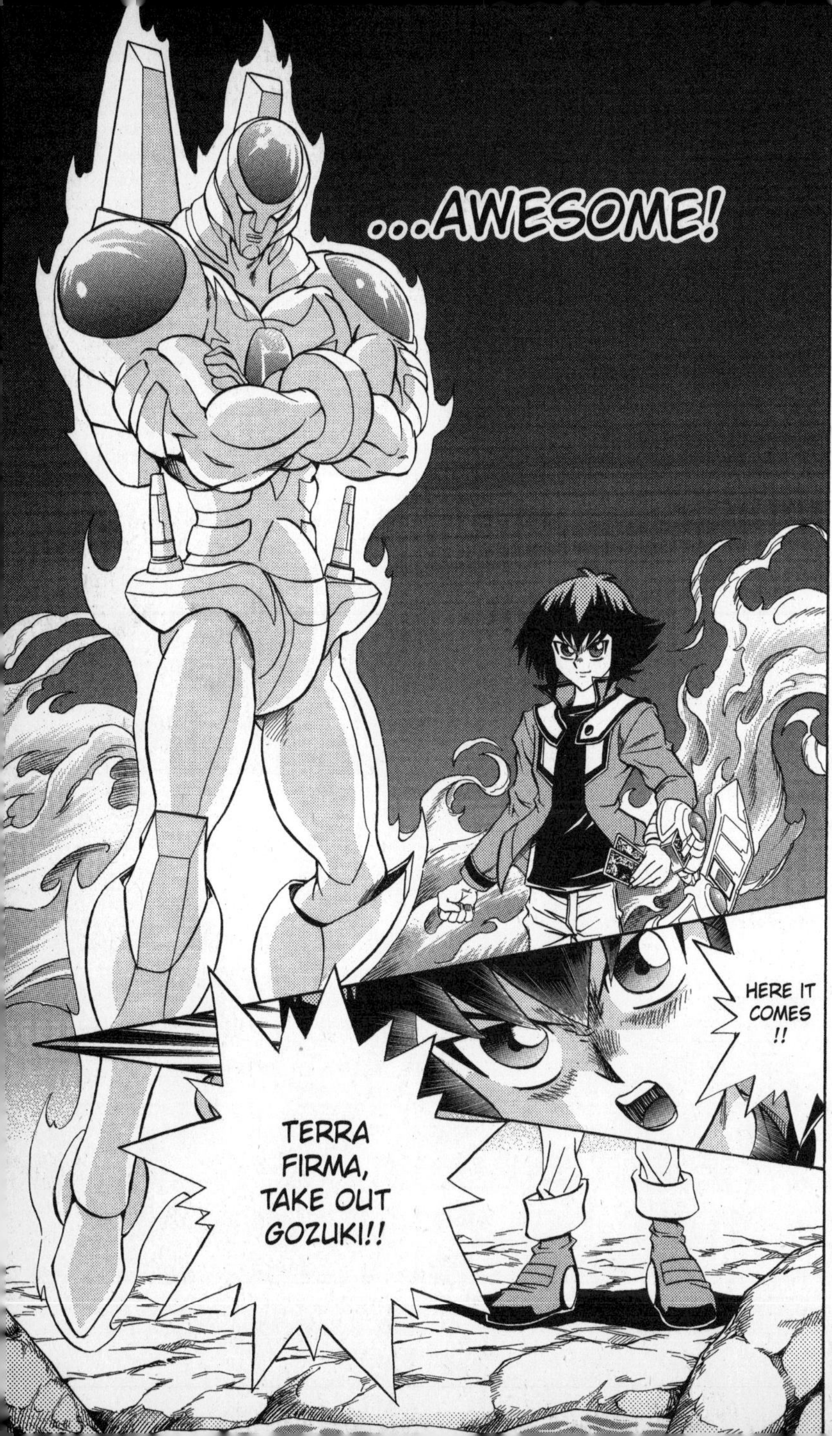
...AWESOME!
HERE IT COMES!!
TERRA FIRMA, TAKE OUT GOZUKI!!

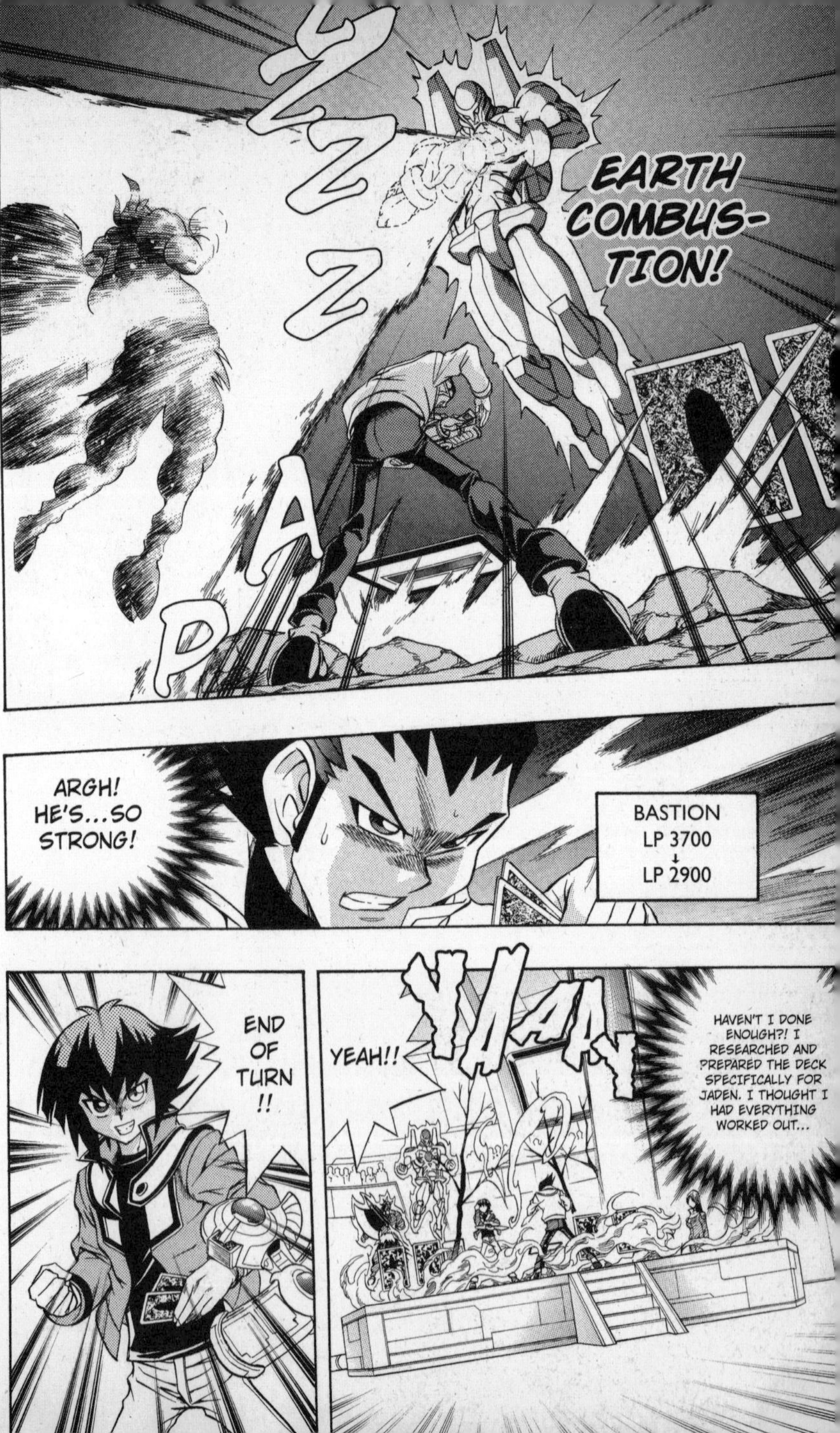
EARTH COMBUS-
TION!
ZZZAP
BASTION
LP 3700
↓
LP 2900
ARGH! HE'S...SO STRONG!
HAVEN'T I DONE ENOUGH?! I RESEARCHED AND PREPARED THE DECK SPECIFICALLY FOR JADEN. I THOUGHT I HAD EVERYTHING WORKED OUT...
YAAAY
YEAH!!
END OF TURN !!

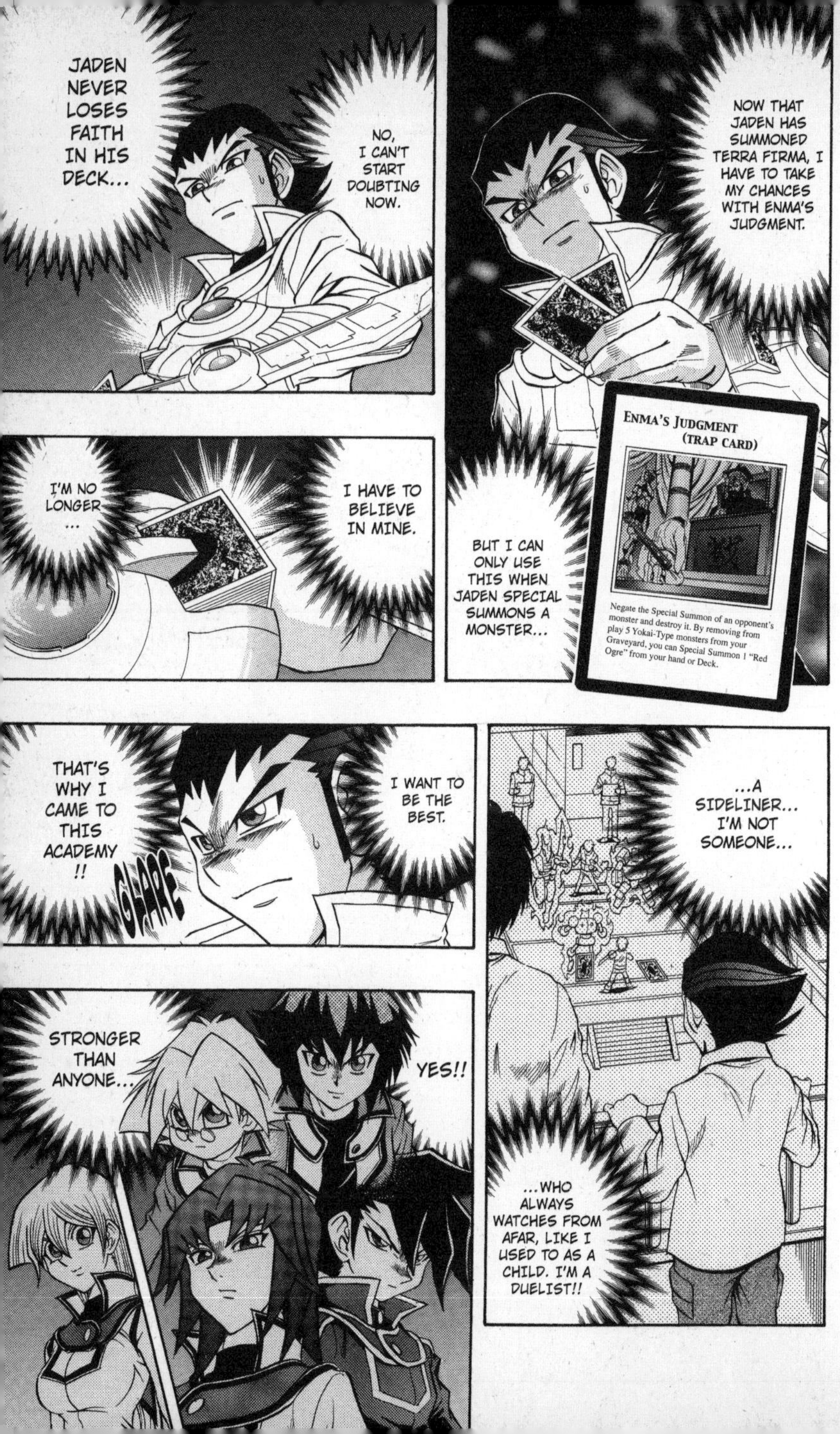
NOW THAT JADEN HAS SUMMONED TERRA FIRMA, I HAVE TO TAKE MY CHANCES WITH ENMA'S JUDGMENT.
NO, I CAN'T START DOUBTING NOW.
JADEN NEVER LOSES FAITH IN HIS DECK...
ENMA'S JUDGMENT (TRAP CARD)
Negate the Special Summon of an opponent's monster and destroy it. By removing from play 5 Yokai-Type monsters from your Graveyard, you can Special Summon 1 "Red Ogre" from your hand or Deck.
BUT I CAN ONLY USE THIS WHEN JADEN SPECIAL SUMMONS A MONSTER...
I HAVE TO BELIEVE IN MINE.
I'M NO LONGER ...
...A SIDELINER... I'M NOT SOMEONE...
...WHO ALWAYS WATCHES FROM AFAR, LIKE I USED TO AS A CHILD. I'M A DUELIST!!
I WANT TO BE THE BEST.
THAT'S WHY I CAME TO THIS ACADEMY !!
GLARE
YES!!
STRONGER THAN ANYONE...

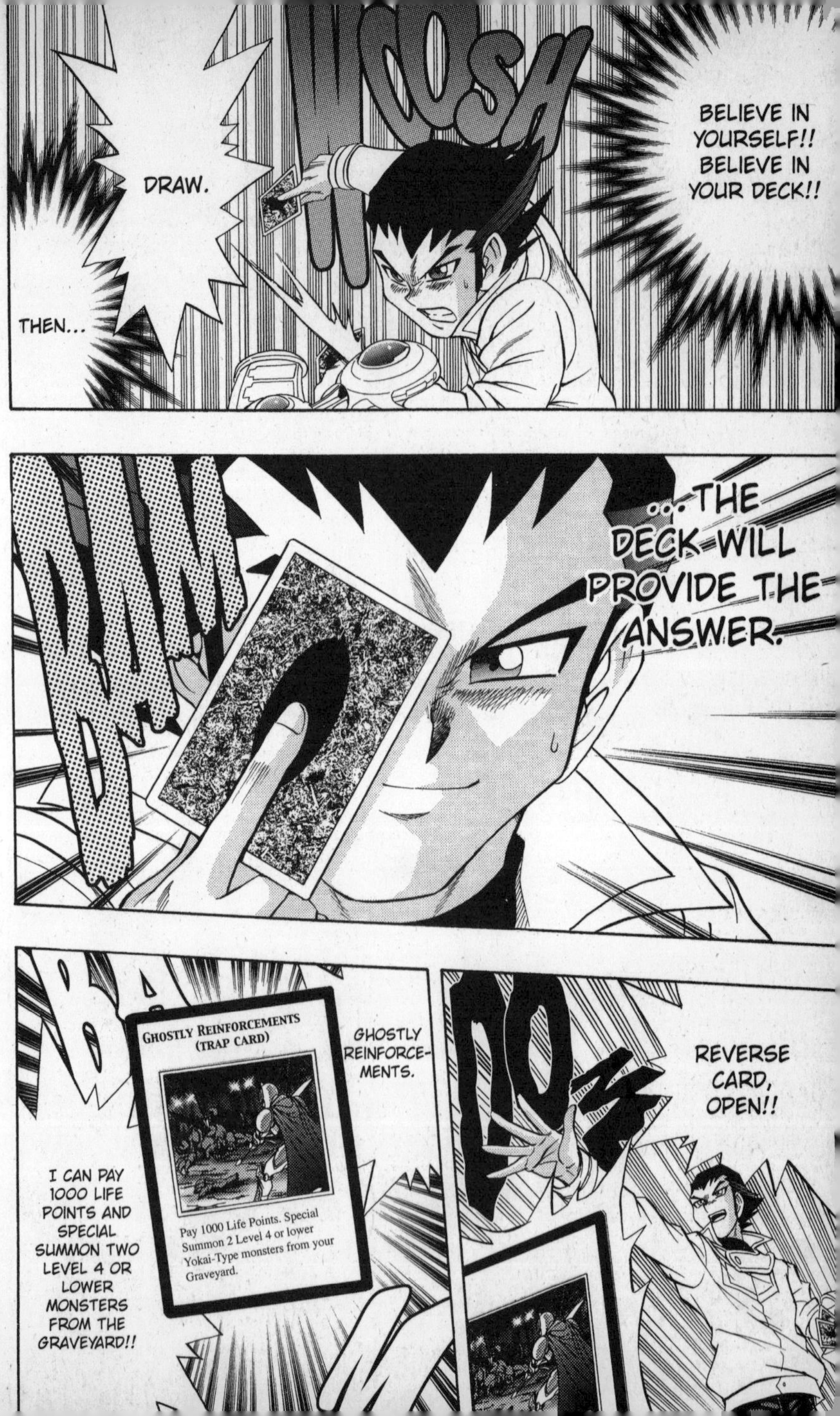
BELIEVE IN YOURSELF!! BELIEVE IN YOUR DECK!!
DRAW.
THEN...
...THE DECK WILL PROVIDE THE ANSWER.
REVERSE CARD, OPEN!!
GHOSTLY REINFORCEMENTS.
GHOSTLY REINFORCEMENTS
(TRAP CARD)
Pay 1000 Life Points. Special Summon 2 Level 4 or lower Yokai-Type monsters from your Graveyard.
I CAN PAY 1000 LIFE POINTS AND SPECIAL SUMMON TWO LEVEL 4 OR LOWER MONSTERS FROM THE GRAVEYARD!!

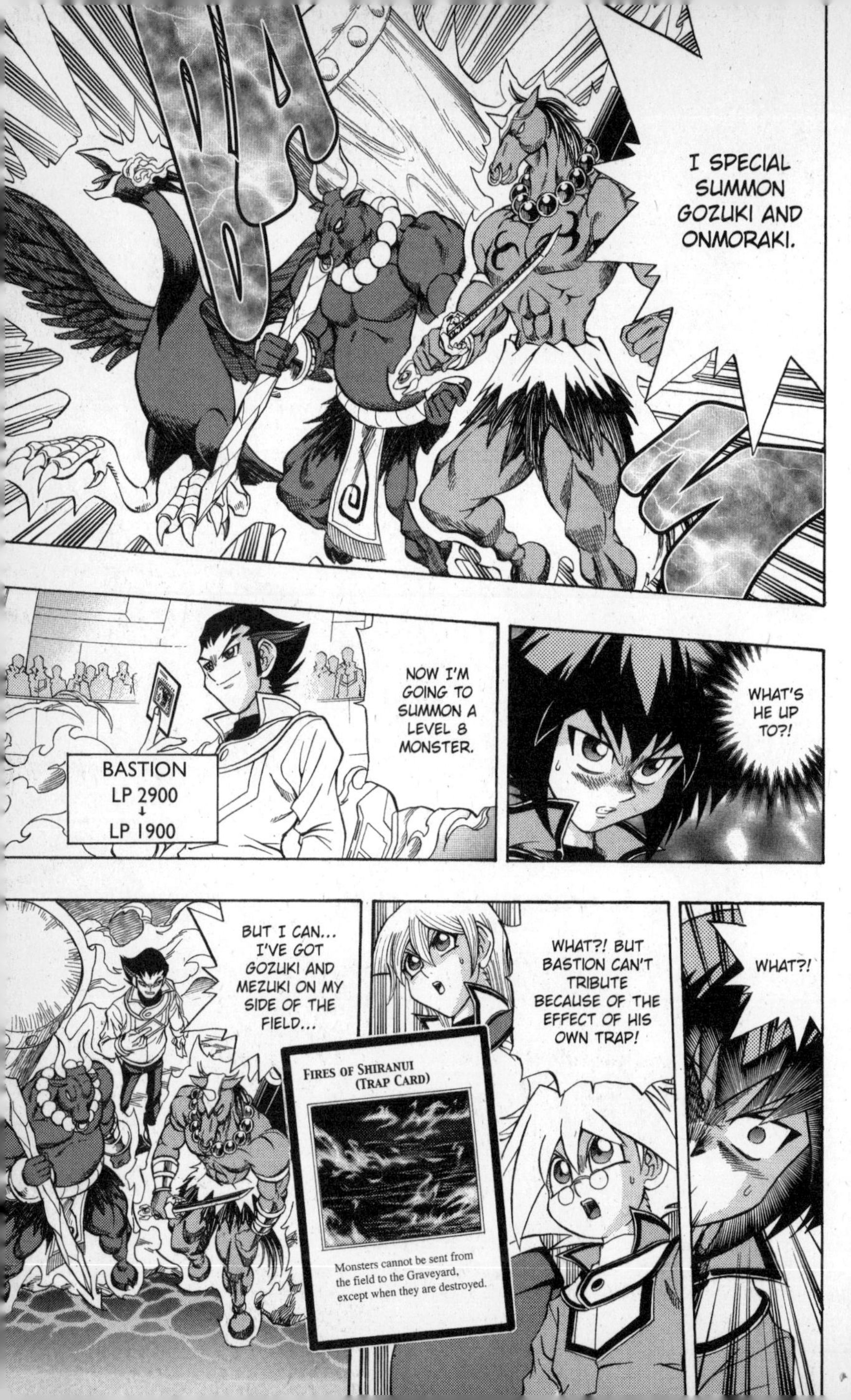
I SPECIAL SUMMON GOZUKI AND ONMORAKI.
WHAT'S HE UP TO?!
NOW I'M GOING TO SUMMON A LEVEL 8 MONSTER.
BASTION LP 2900 ↓ LP 1900
WHAT?!
WHAT?! BUT BASTION CAN'T TRIBUTE BECAUSE OF THE EFFECT OF HIS OWN TRAP!
FIRES OF SHIRANUI (TRAP CARD)
Monsters cannot be sent from the field to the Graveyard, except when they are destroyed.
BUT I CAN... I'VE GOT GOZUKI AND MEZUKI ON MY SIDE OF THE FIELD...

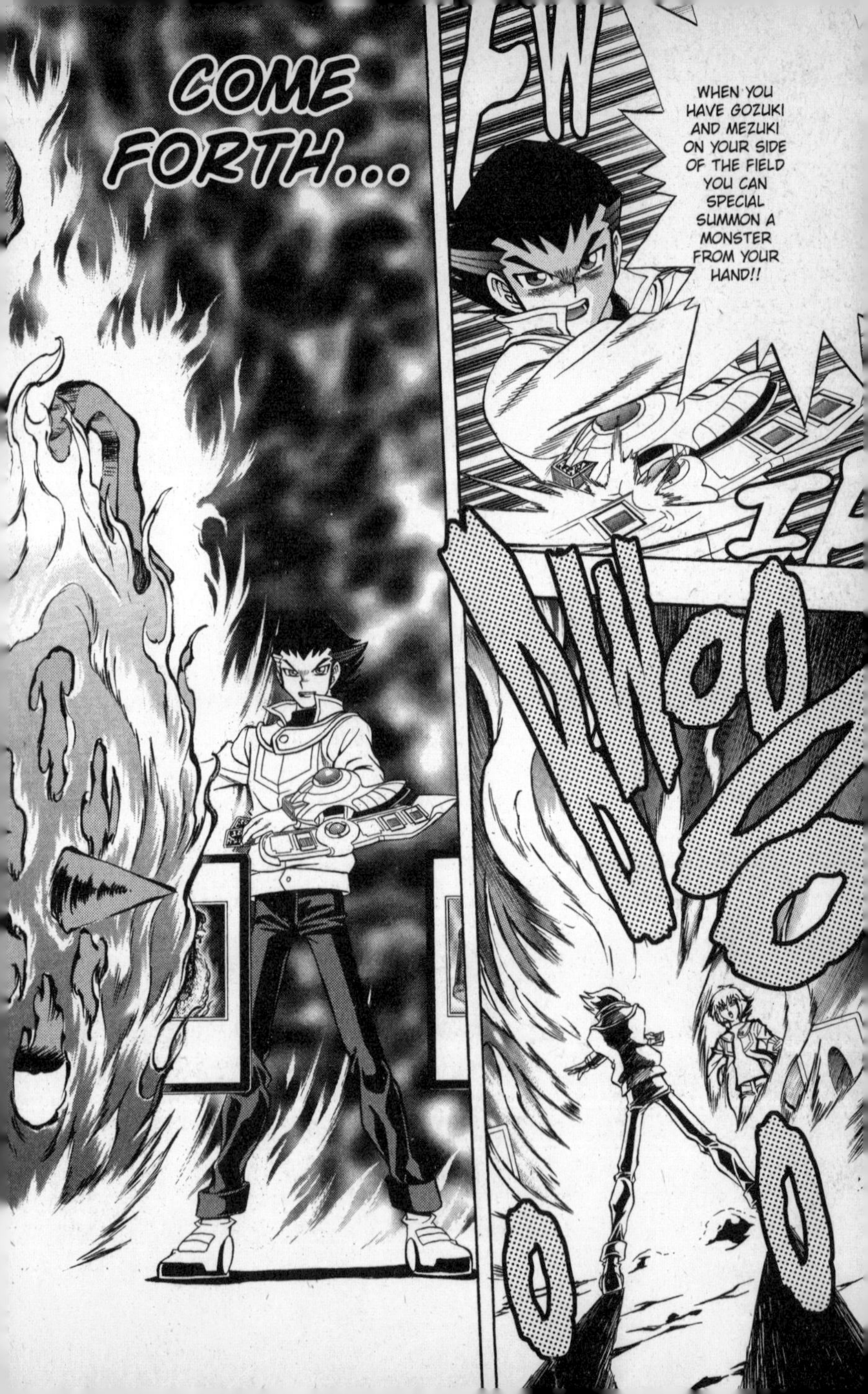
WHEN YOU HAVE GOZUKI AND MEZUKI ON YOUR SIDE OF THE FIELD YOU CAN SPECIAL SUMMON A MONSTER FROM YOUR HAND!!
COME FORTH...

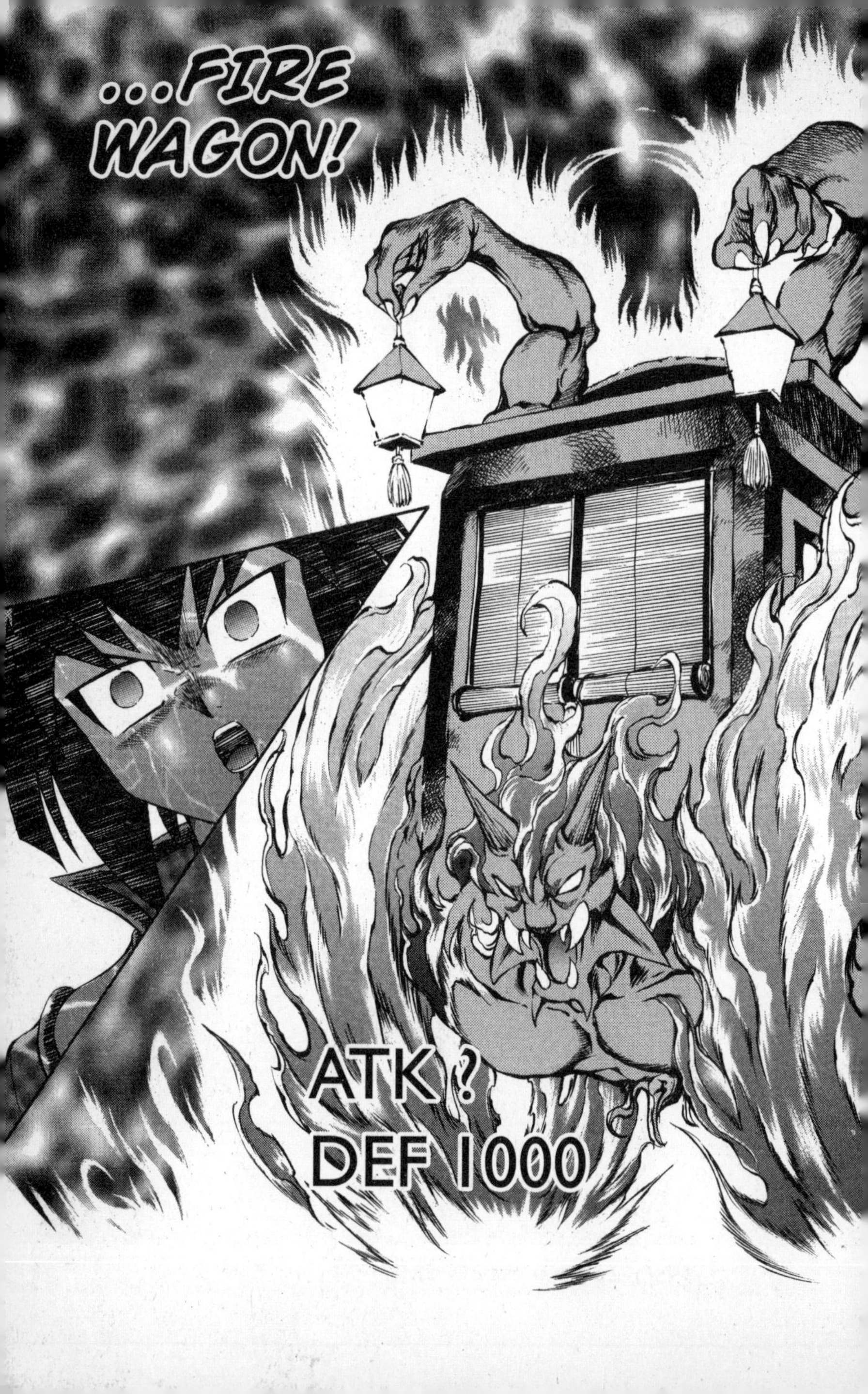
...FIRE WAGON!
ATK ?
DEF 1000

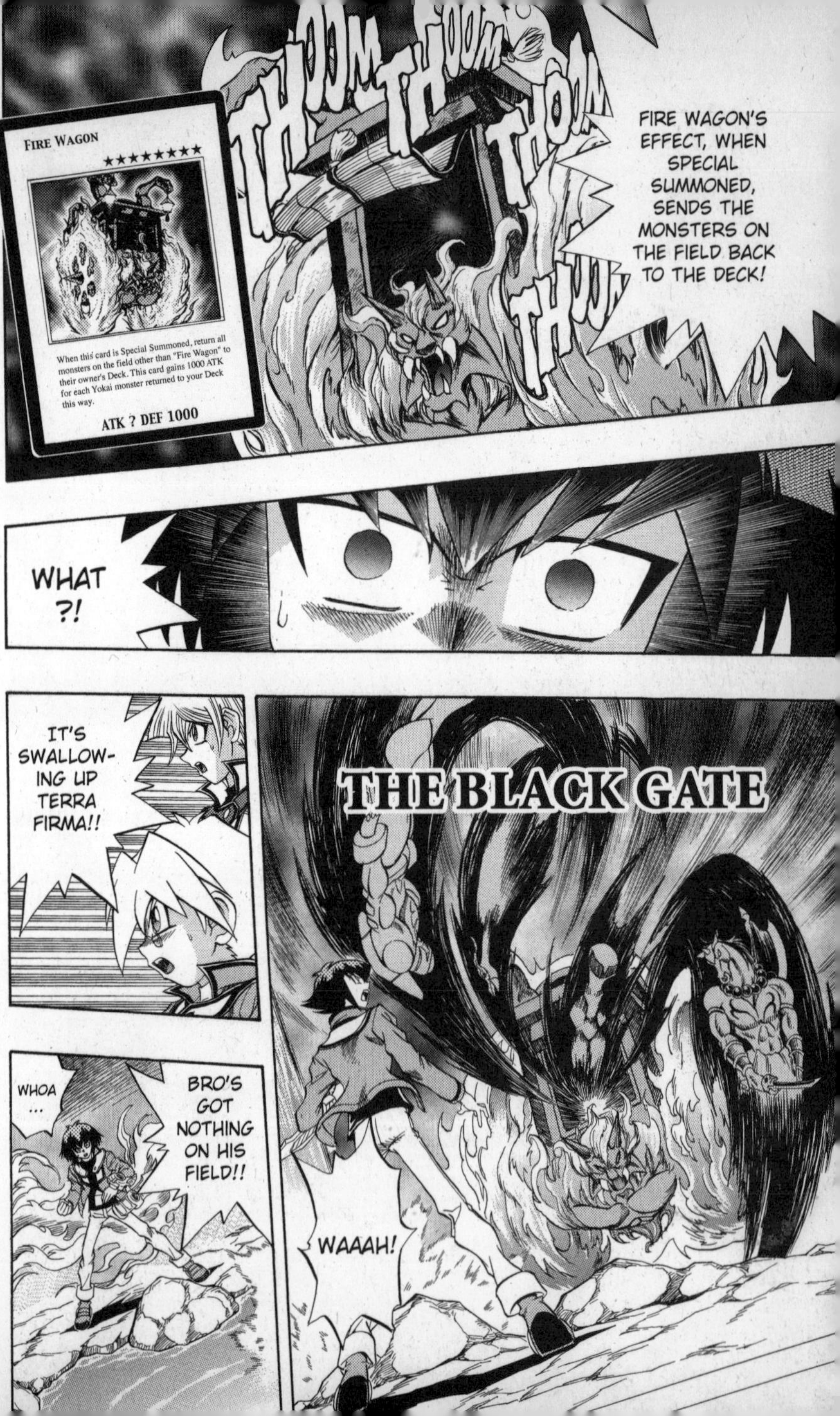
FIRE WAGON'S EFFECT, WHEN SPECIAL SUMMONED, SENDS THE MONSTERS ON THE FIELD BACK TO THE DECK!
THOOM
THOOM
THOOM
THOOM
THOOM
FIRE WAGON
When this card is Special Summoned, return all monsters on the field other than "Fire Wagon" to their owner's Deck. This card gains 1000 ATK for each Yokai monster returned to your Deck this way.
ATK ? DEF 1000
WHAT ?!
THE BLACK GATE
WAAAH!
IT'S SWALLOWING UP TERRA FIRMA!!
BRO'S GOT NOTHING ON HIS FIELD!!
WHOA ...

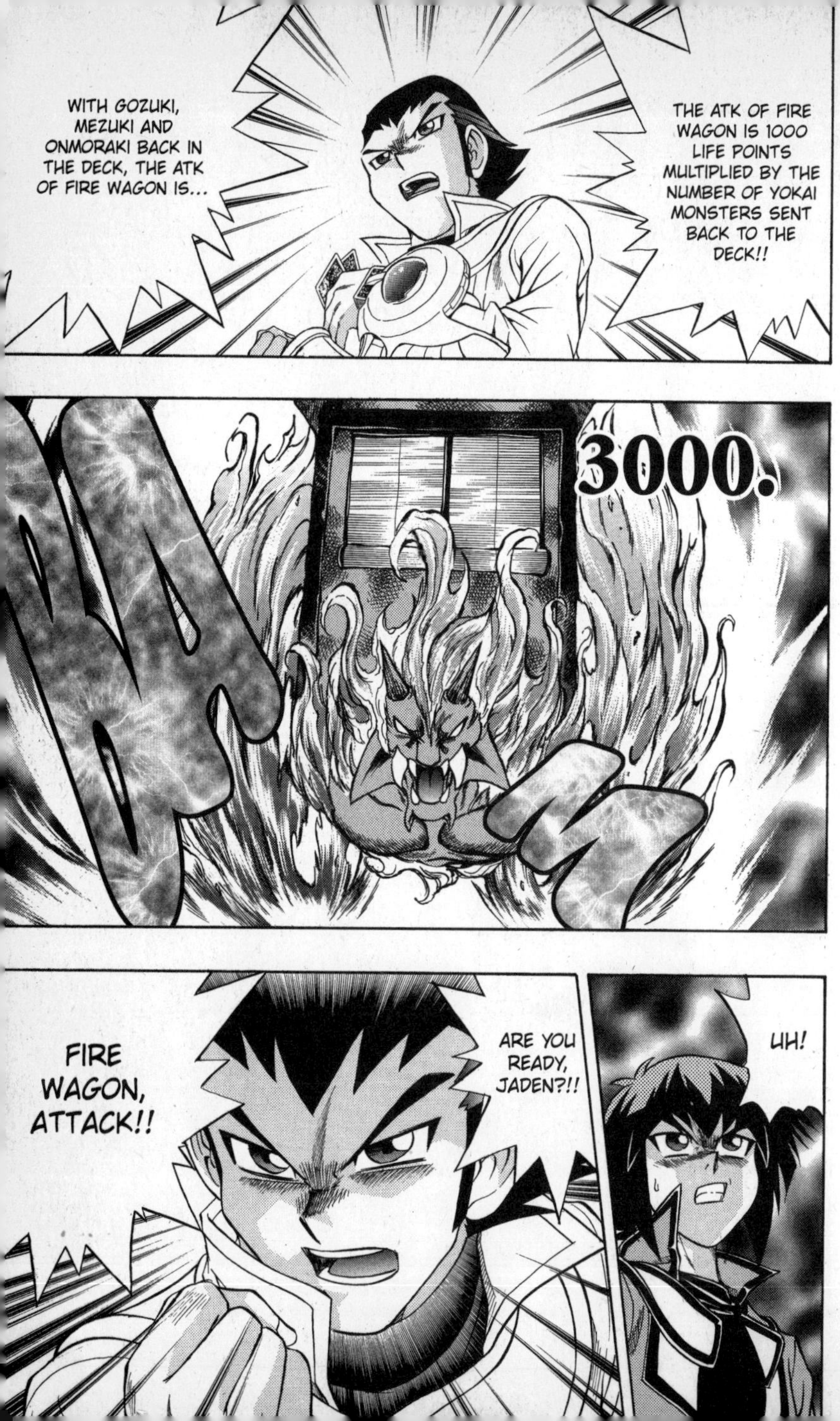
THE ATK OF FIRE WAGON IS 1000 LIFE POINTS MULTIPLIED BY THE NUMBER OF YOKAI MONSTERS SENT BACK TO THE DECK!!
WITH GOZUKI, MEZUKI AND ONMORAKI BACK IN THE DECK, THE ATK OF FIRE WAGON IS...
3000.
UH!
ARE YOU READY, JADEN?!!
FIRE WAGON, ATTACK!!

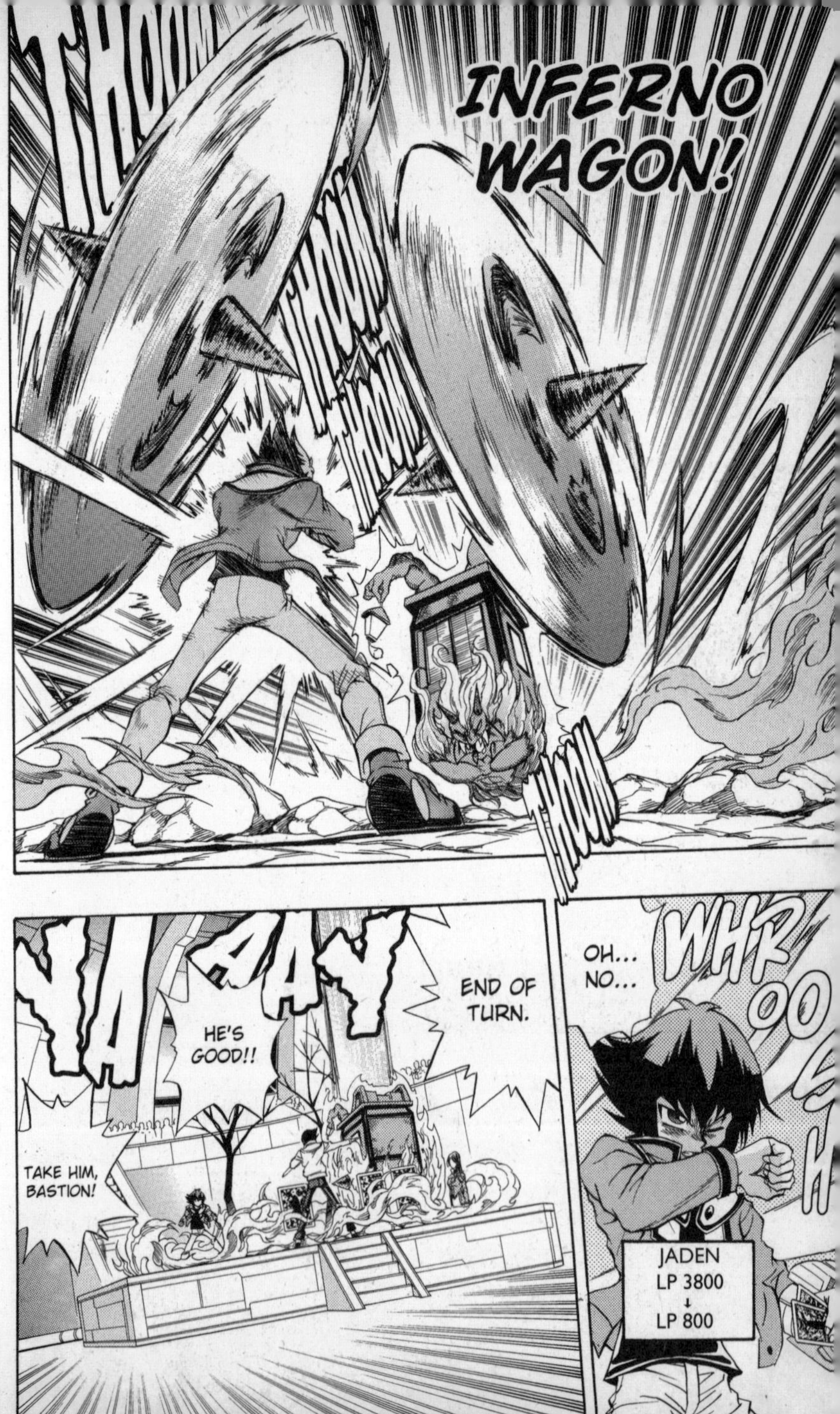
INFERNO WAGON!
THOOM
THOOM
THOOM
THOOM
OH... NO...
WHROOSH
JADEN LP 3800 ↓ LP 800
END OF TURN.
HE'S GOOD!!
YAAAY
TAKE HIM, BASTION!

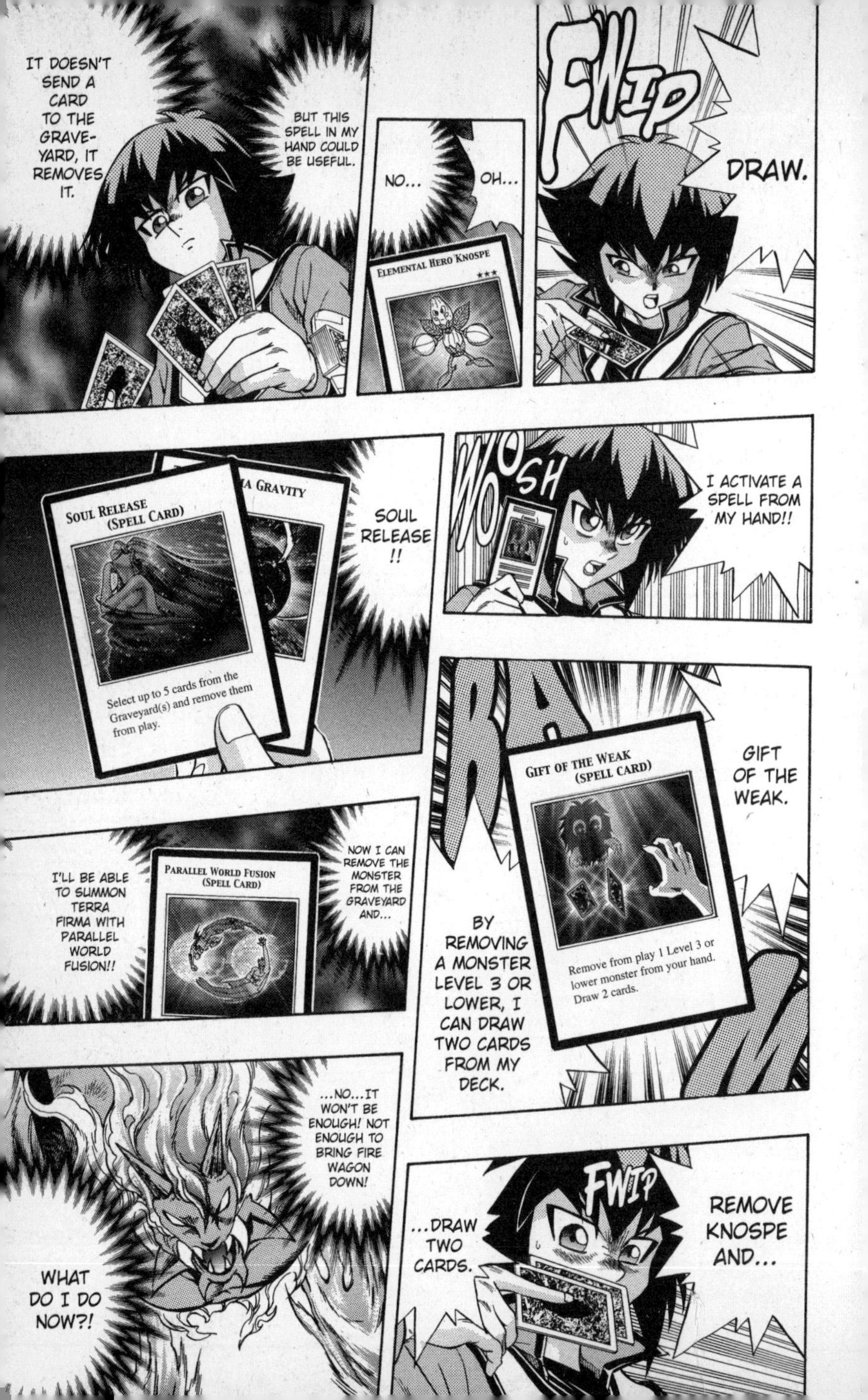
FWIP
DRAW.
OH...
NO...
ELEMENTAL HERO KNOSPE
BUT THIS SPELL IN MY HAND COULD BE USEFUL.
IT DOESN'T SEND A CARD TO THE GRAVEYARD, IT REMOVES IT.
WOOSH
I ACTIVATE A SPELL FROM MY HAND!!
SOUL RELEASE!!
SOUL RELEASE (SPELL CARD)
Select up to 5 cards from the Graveyard(s) and remove them from play.
GIFT OF THE WEAK.
GIFT OF THE WEAK (SPELL CARD)
Remove from play 1 Level 3 or lower monster from your hand. Draw 2 cards.
BY REMOVING A MONSTER LEVEL 3 OR LOWER, I CAN DRAW TWO CARDS FROM MY DECK.
NOW I CAN REMOVE THE MONSTER FROM THE GRAVEYARD AND...
PARALLEL WORLD FUSION (SPELL CARD)
I'LL BE ABLE TO SUMMON TERRA FIRMA WITH PARALLEL WORLD FUSION!!
REMOVE KNOSPE AND...
FWIP
...DRAW TWO CARDS.
...NO...IT WON'T BE ENOUGH! NOT ENOUGH TO BRING FIRE WAGON DOWN!
WHAT DO I DO NOW?!

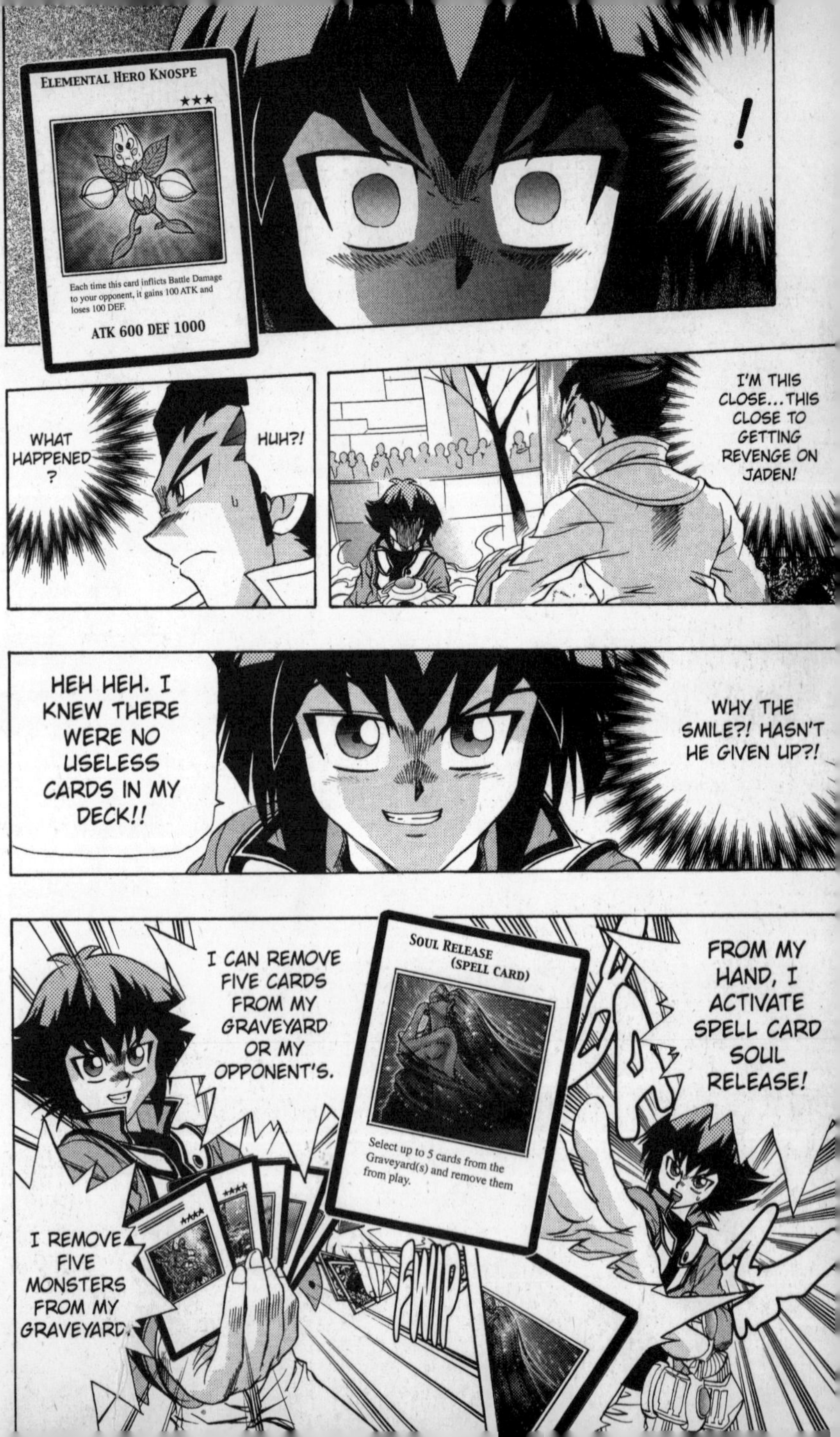
!
ELEMENTAL HERO KNOSPE
★★★
Each time this card inflicts Battle Damage to your opponent, it gains 100 ATK and loses 100 DEF.
ATK 600 DEF 1000
I'M THIS CLOSE...THIS CLOSE TO GETTING REVENGE ON JADEN!
HUH?!
WHAT HAPPENED?
WHY THE SMILE?! HASN'T HE GIVEN UP?!
HEH HEH. I KNEW THERE WERE NO USELESS CARDS IN MY DECK!!
FROM MY HAND, I ACTIVATE SPELL CARD SOUL RELEASE!
SOUL RELEASE (SPELL CARD)
Select up to 5 cards from the Graveyard(s) and remove them from play.
I CAN REMOVE FIVE CARDS FROM MY GRAVEYARD OR MY OPPONENT'S.
SWIP
I REMOVE FIVE MONSTERS FROM MY GRAVEYARD.

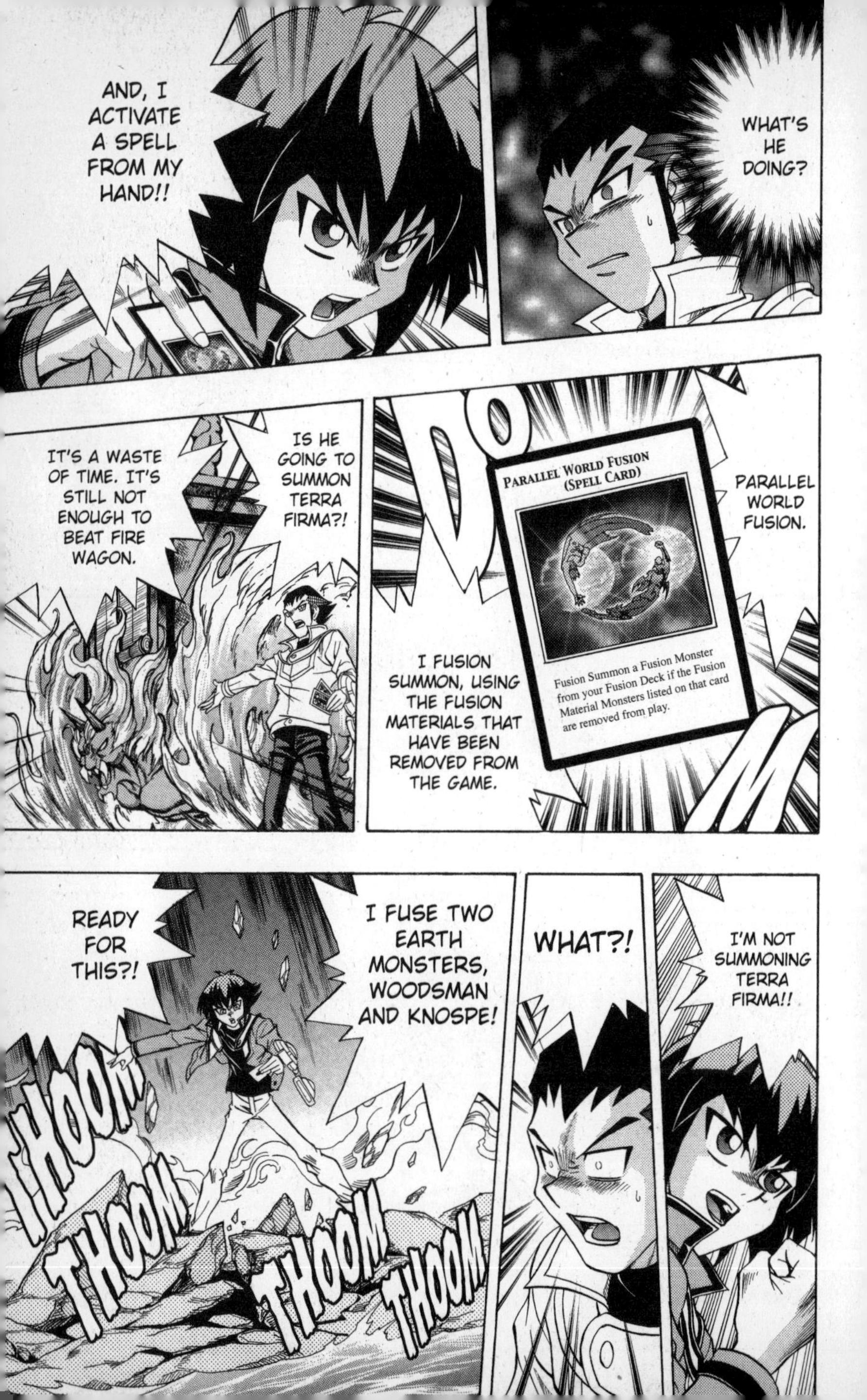
WHAT'S HE DOING?
AND, I ACTIVATE A SPELL FROM MY HAND!!
PARALLEL WORLD FUSION.
PARALLEL WORLD FUSION
(SPELL CARD)
Fusion Summon a Fusion Monster from your Fusion Deck if the Fusion Material Monsters listed on that card are removed from play.
I FUSION SUMMON, USING THE FUSION MATERIALS THAT HAVE BEEN REMOVED FROM THE GAME.
IS HE GOING TO SUMMON TERRA FIRMA?!
IT'S A WASTE OF TIME. IT'S STILL NOT ENOUGH TO BEAT FIRE WAGON.
I'M NOT SUMMONING TERRA FIRMA!!
WHAT?!
I FUSE TWO EARTH MONSTERS, WOODSMAN AND KNOSPE!
READY FOR THIS?!
THOOM
THOOM
THOOM
THOOM

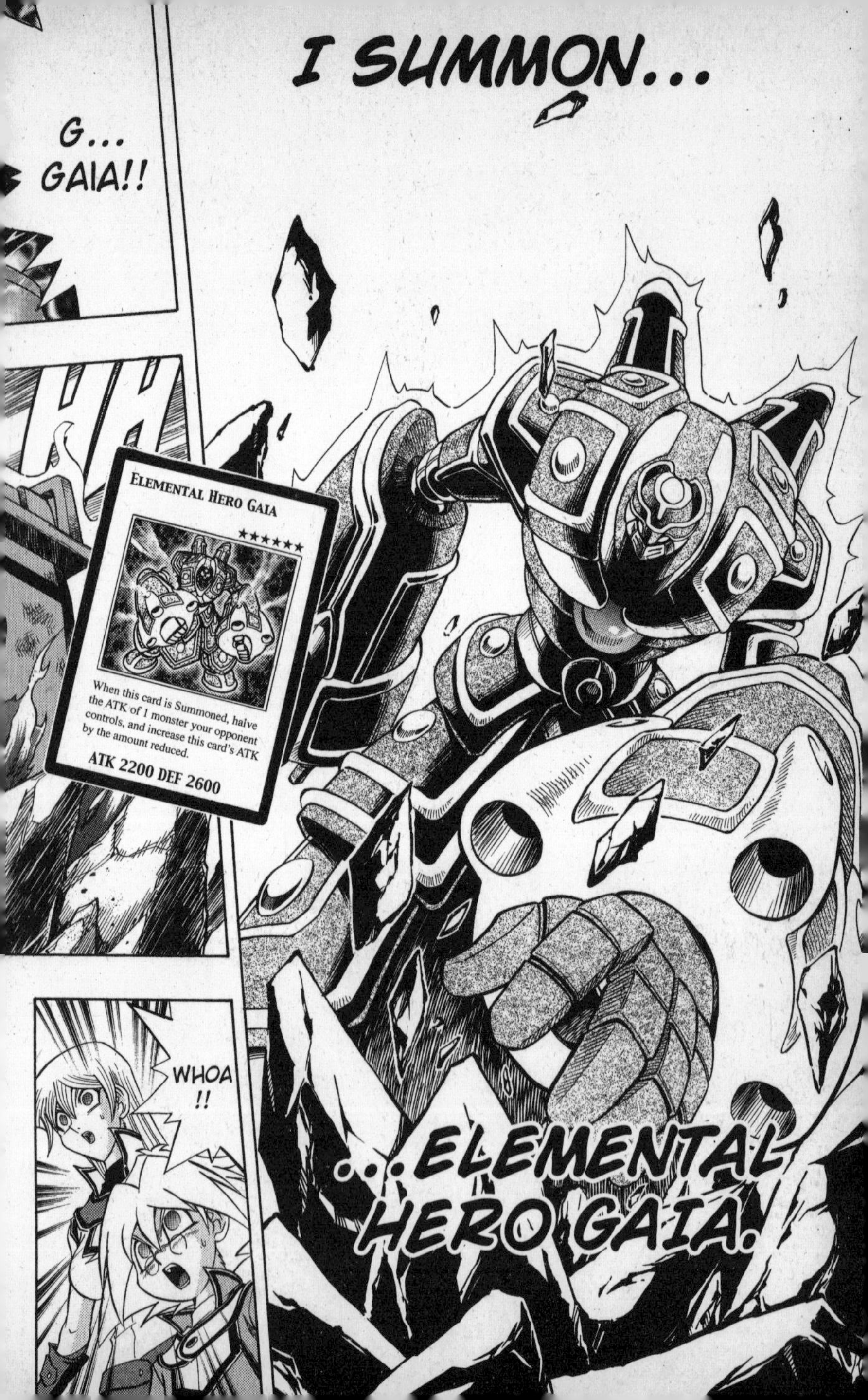
I SUMMON...
...ELEMENTAL HERO GAIA.
ELEMENTAL HERO GAIA
When this card is Summoned, halve the ATK of 1 monster your opponent controls, and increase this card's ATK by the amount reduced.
ATK 2200 DEF 2600
G... GAIA!!
WHOA !!

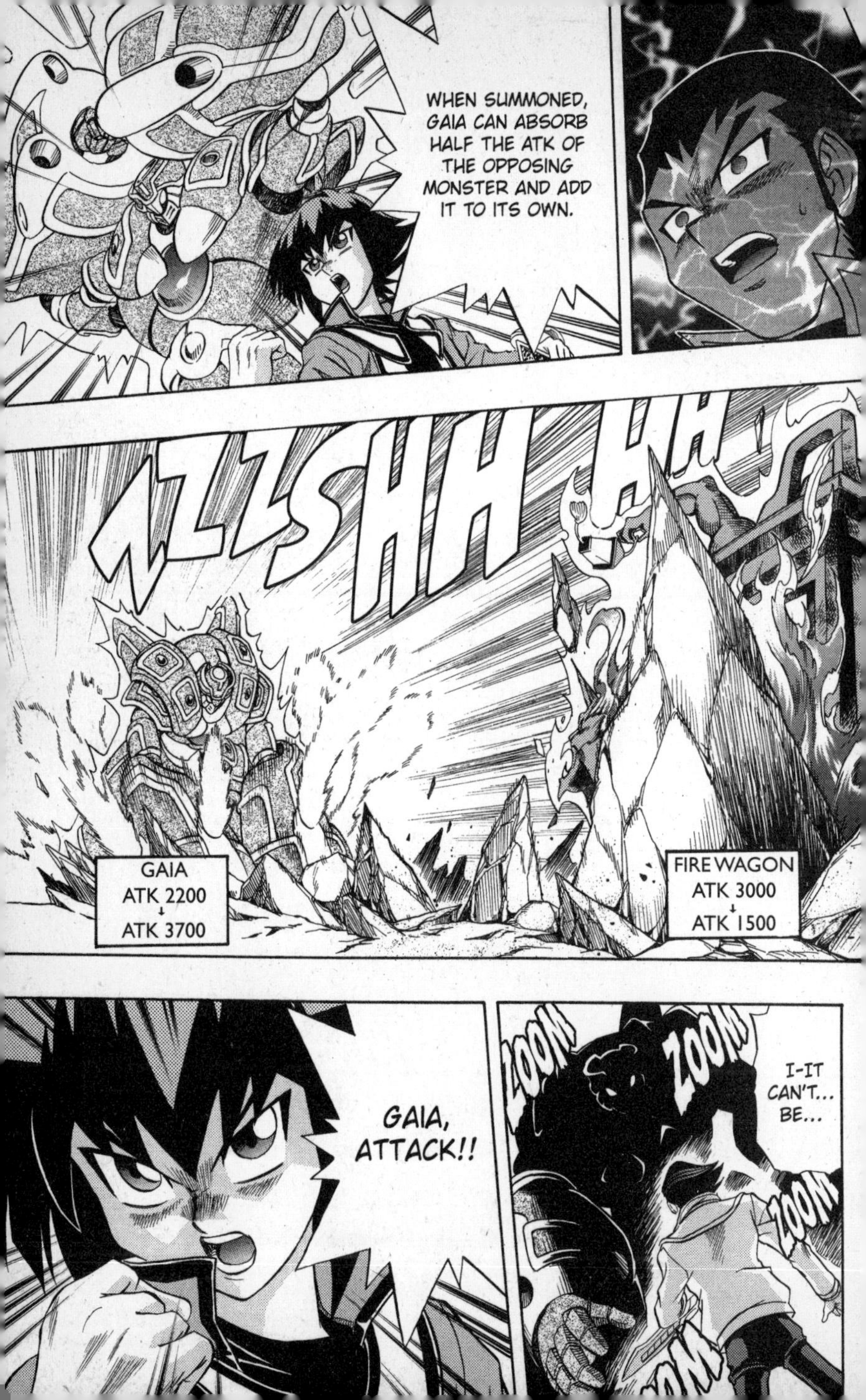
WHEN SUMMONED, GAIA CAN ABSORB HALF THE ATK OF THE OPPOSING MONSTER AND ADD IT TO ITS OWN.
FIRE WAGON
ATK 3000
ATK 1500
GAIA
ATK 2200
ATK 3700
ZOOM
ZOOM
I-IT CAN'T... BE...
ZOOM
GAIA, ATTACK!!

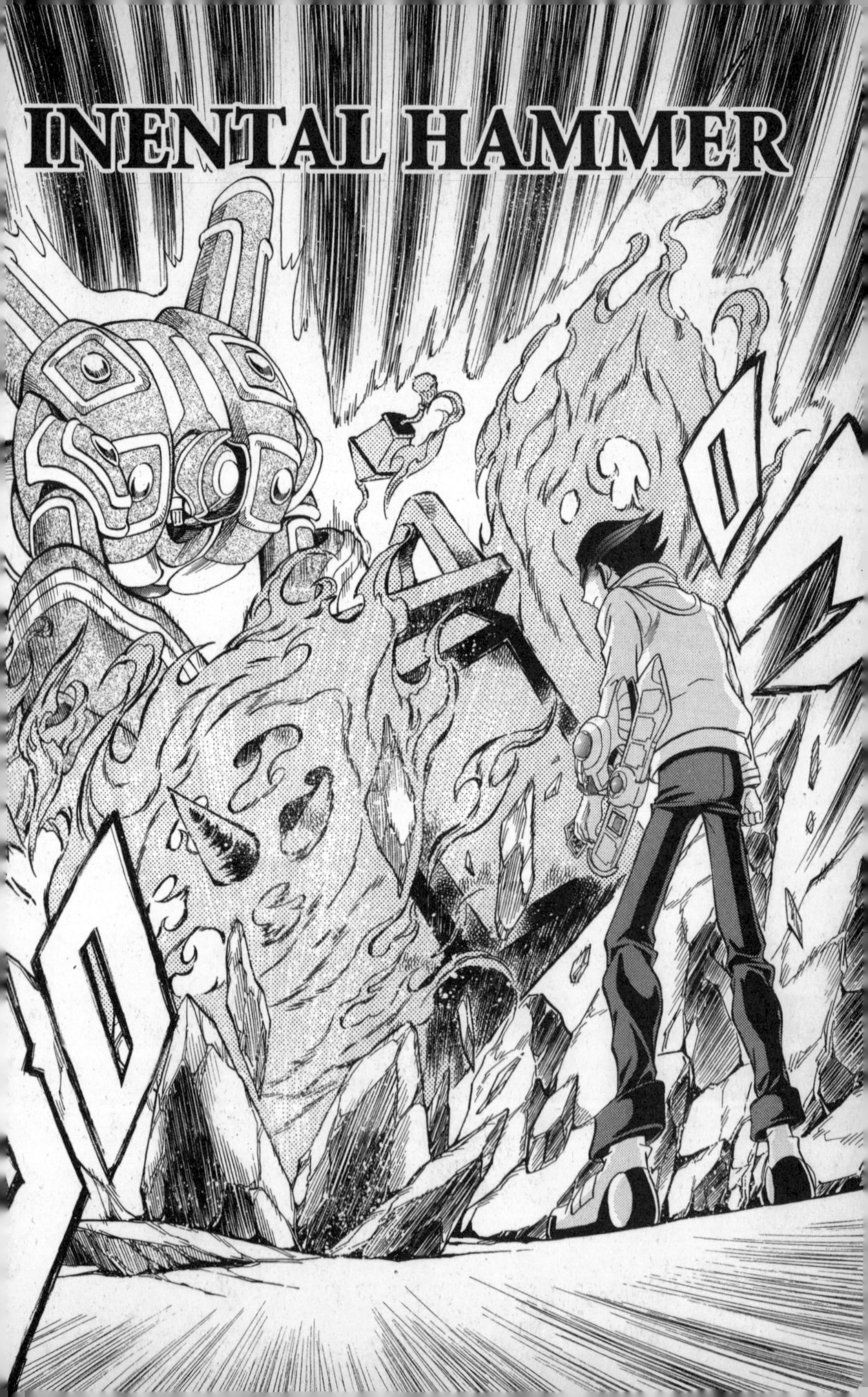
INENTAL HAMMER

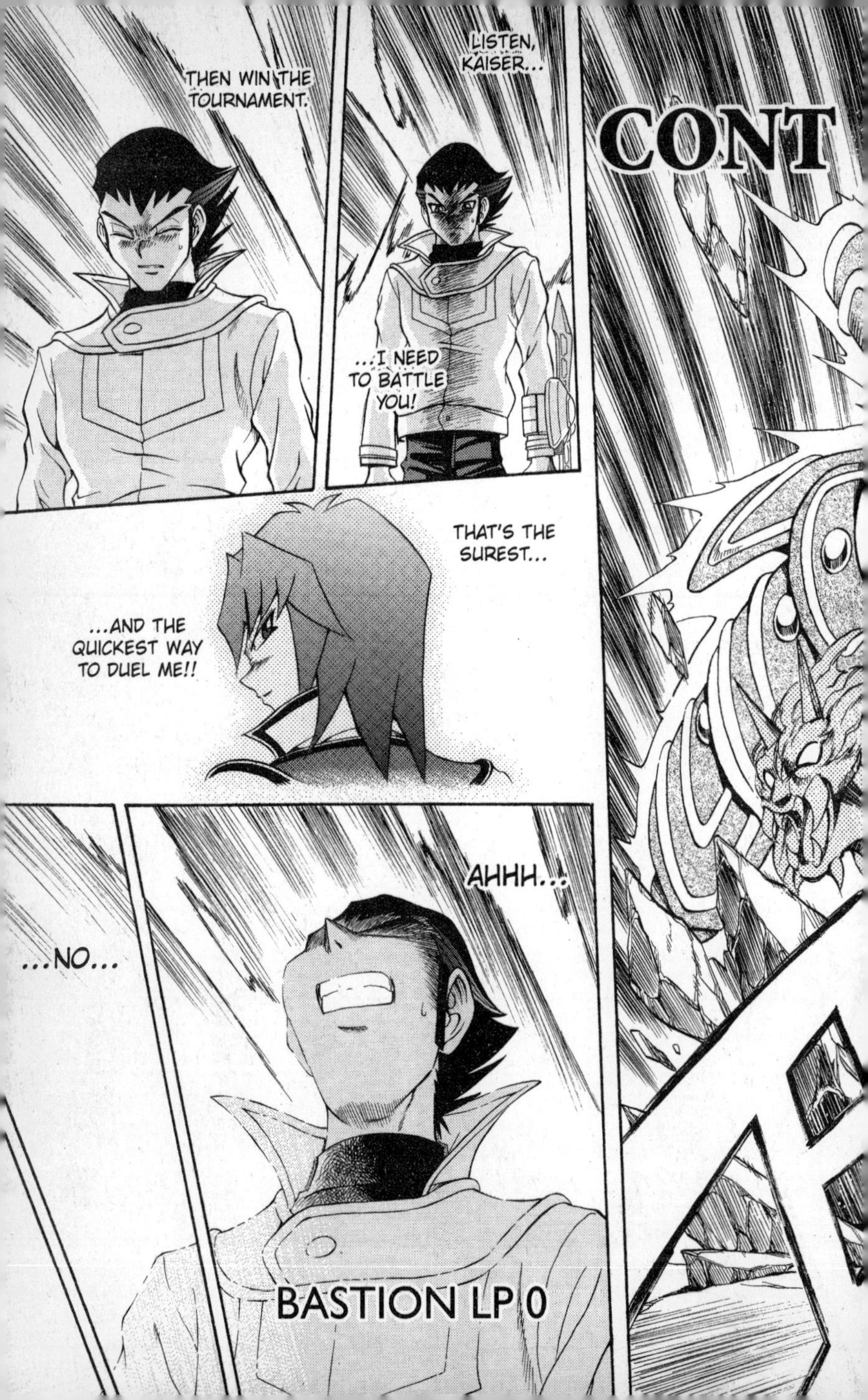
CONT
LISTEN, KAISER...
...I NEED TO BATTLE YOU!
THEN WIN THE TOURNAMENT.
THAT'S THE SUREST...
...AND THE QUICKEST WAY TO DUEL ME!!
AHHH...
...NO...
BASTION LP 0

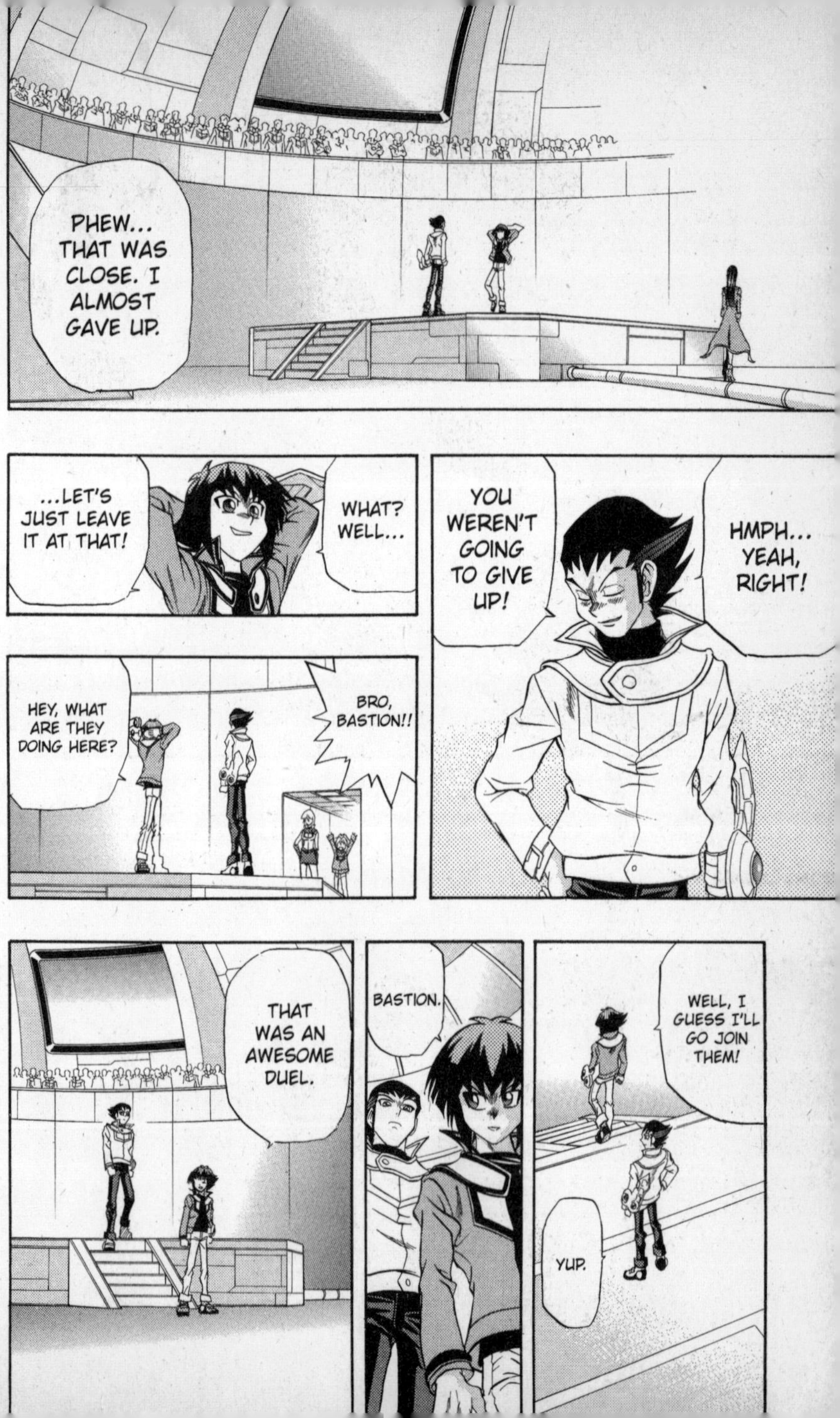
PHEW... THAT WAS CLOSE. I ALMOST GAVE UP.
HMPH... YEAH, RIGHT!
YOU WEREN'T GOING TO GIVE UP!
WHAT? WELL...
...LET'S JUST LEAVE IT AT THAT!
BRO, BASTION!!
HEY, WHAT ARE THEY DOING HERE?
WELL, I GUESS I'LL GO JOIN THEM!
YUP.
BASTION.
THAT WAS AN AWESOME DUEL.

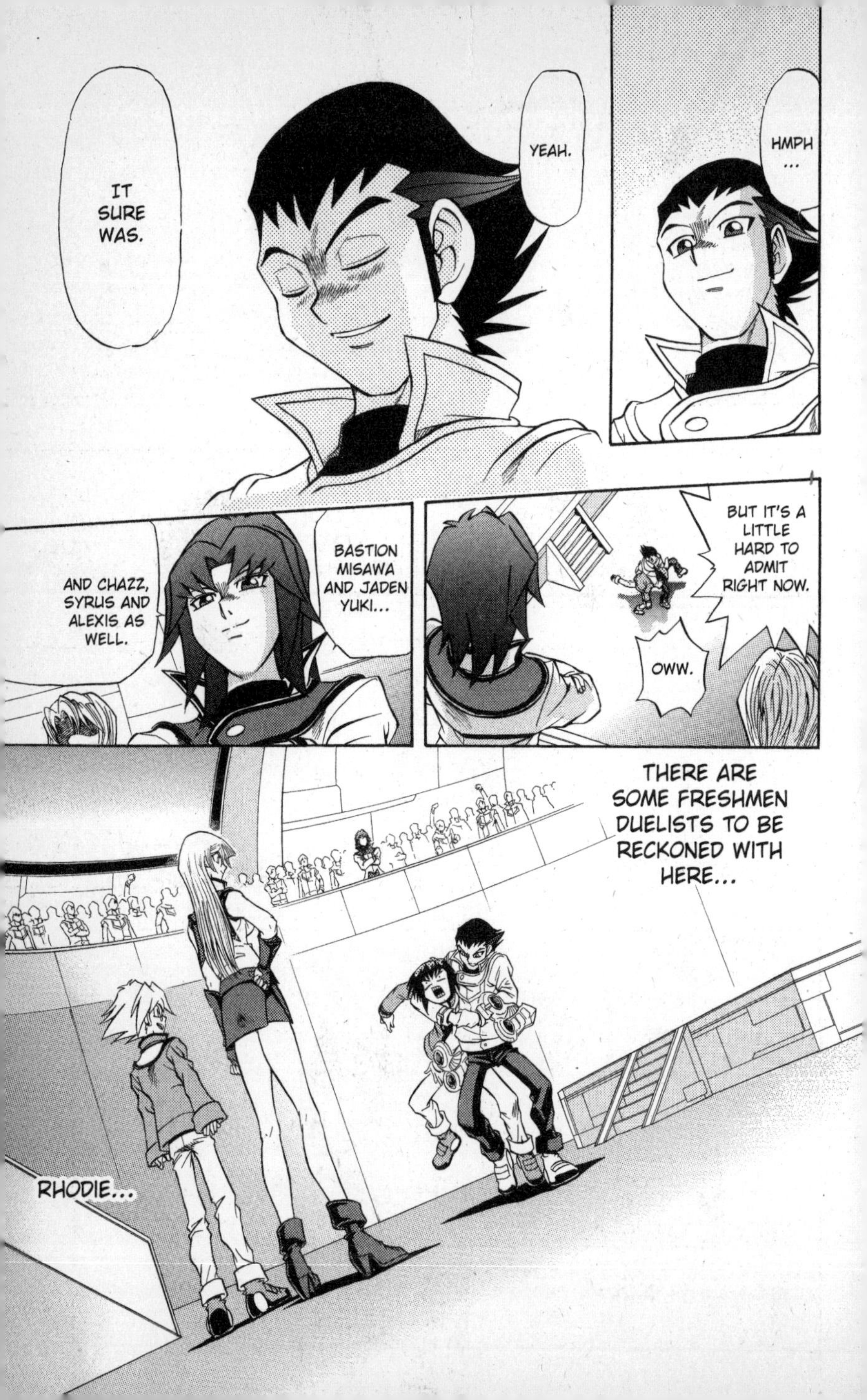
HMPH...
YEAH.
IT SURE WAS.
BUT IT'S A LITTLE HARD TO ADMIT RIGHT NOW.
OWW.
BASTION MISAWA AND JADEN YUKI...
AND CHAZZ, SYRUS AND ALEXIS AS WELL.
THERE ARE SOME FRESHMEN DUELISTS TO BE RECKONED WITH HERE...
RHODIE...

FROM ISHIGAKI ISLAND, 2008 PART 1

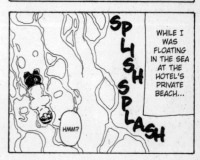

IN LATE JUNE OF 2008...
...ALL THE STUDIO DICE STAFF, AND SOME INVOLVED IN THE ANIME, WENT ON A TRIP TO ISHIGAKI ISLAND.
WHILE I WAS FLOATING IN THE SEA AT THE HOTEL'S PRIVATE BEACH...
SPLISH SPLASH
HMM?
SPLASH
SPLISH
TAKAHASHI-SAN WAS SWIMMING BUTTERFLY-STYLE.
SPLASH SPLASH
HE SWAM LONGER THAN ANY OF US...

I'D NEVER SEEN ANYONE DO THE BUTTERFLY, EXCEPT ON TV...

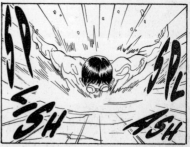

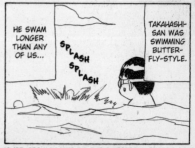

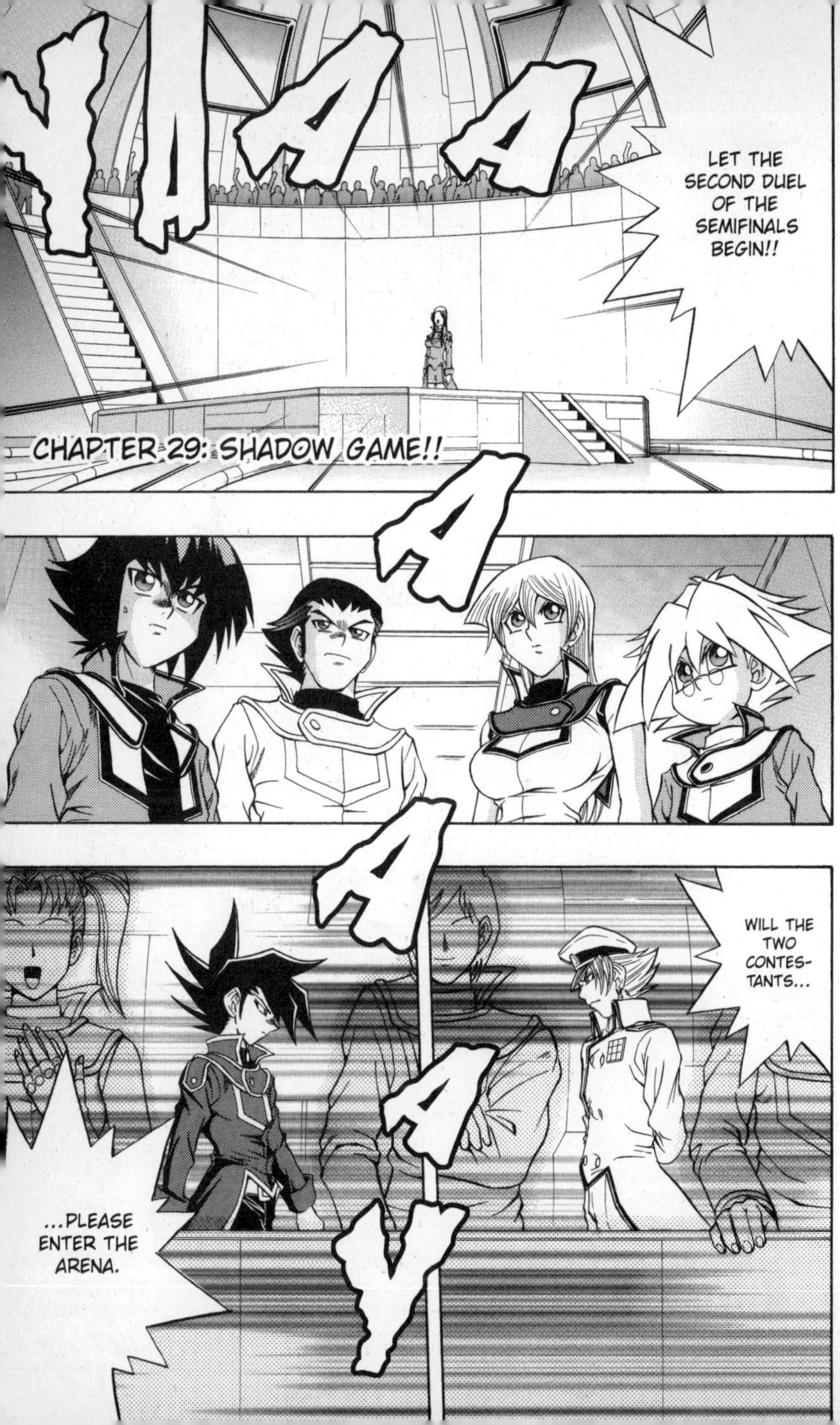
YAAAAAAY
LET THE SECOND DUEL OF THE SEMIFINALS BEGIN!!
CHAPTER 29: SHADOW GAME!!
WILL THE TWO CONTES-TANTS...
...PLEASE ENTER THE ARENA.

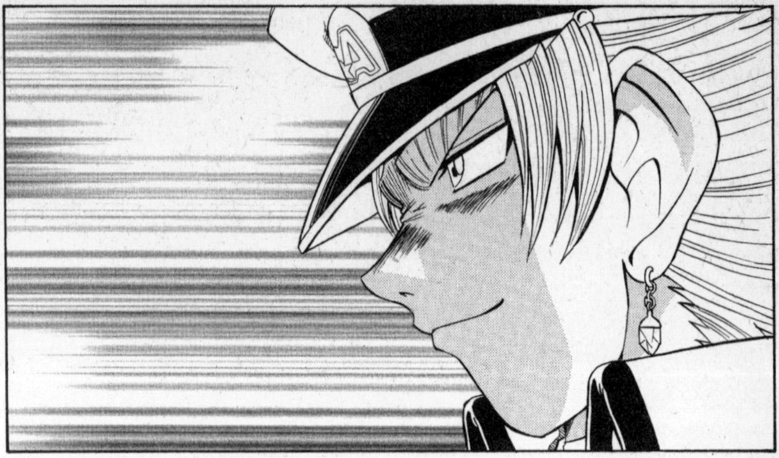

CHAPTER 29: SHADOW GAME!!

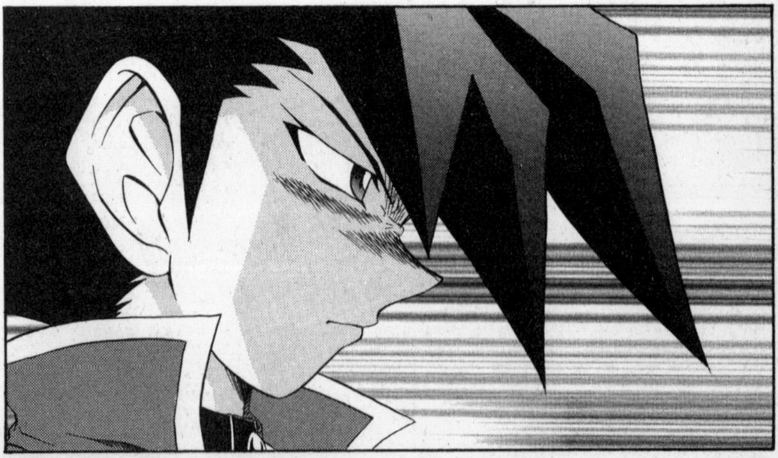

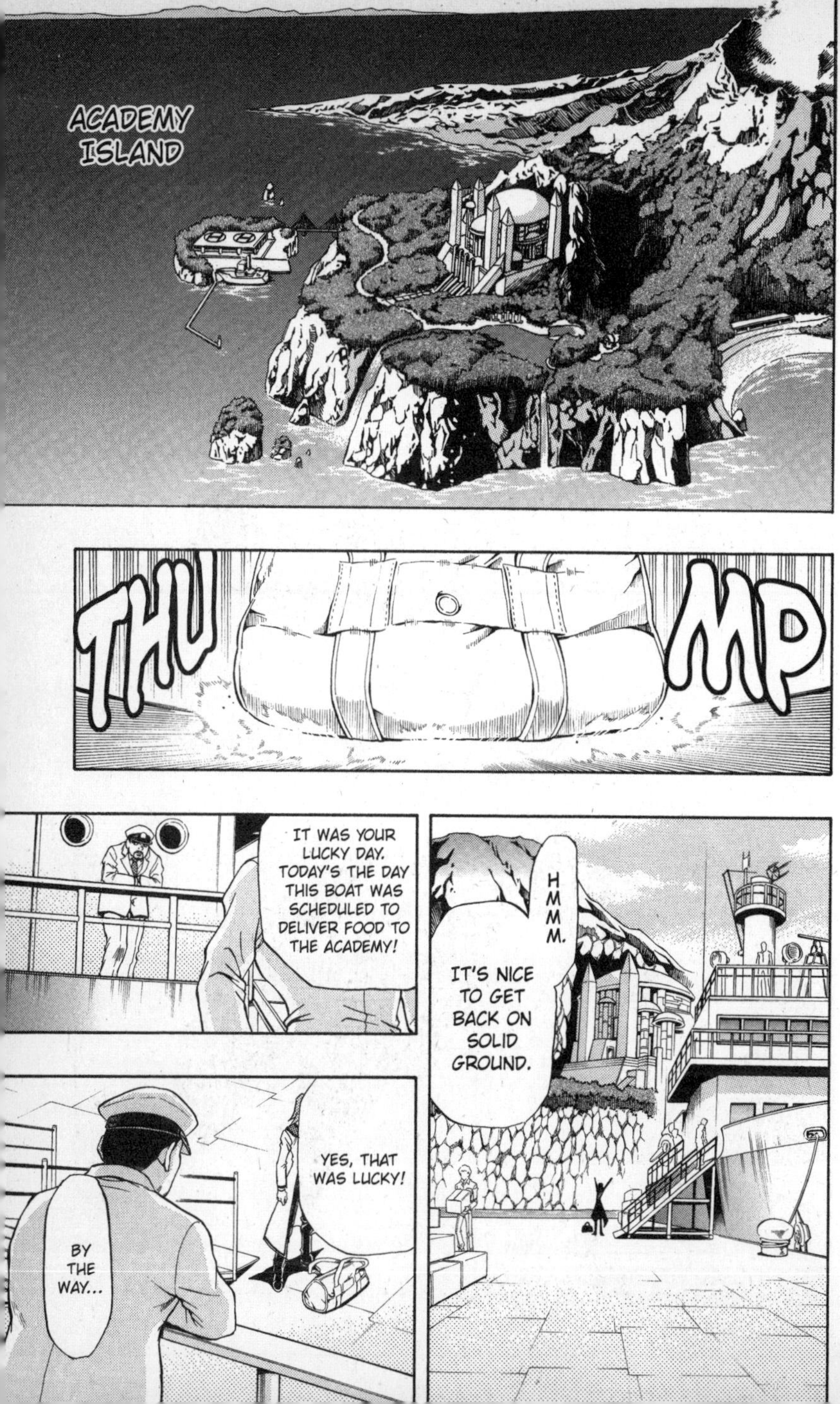
ACADEMY ISLAND
THUMP
HMMM.
IT'S NICE TO GET BACK ON SOLID GROUND.
IT WAS YOUR LUCKY DAY. TODAY'S THE DAY THIS BOAT WAS SCHEDULED TO DELIVER FOOD TO THE ACADEMY!
YES, THAT WAS LUCKY!
BY THE WAY...

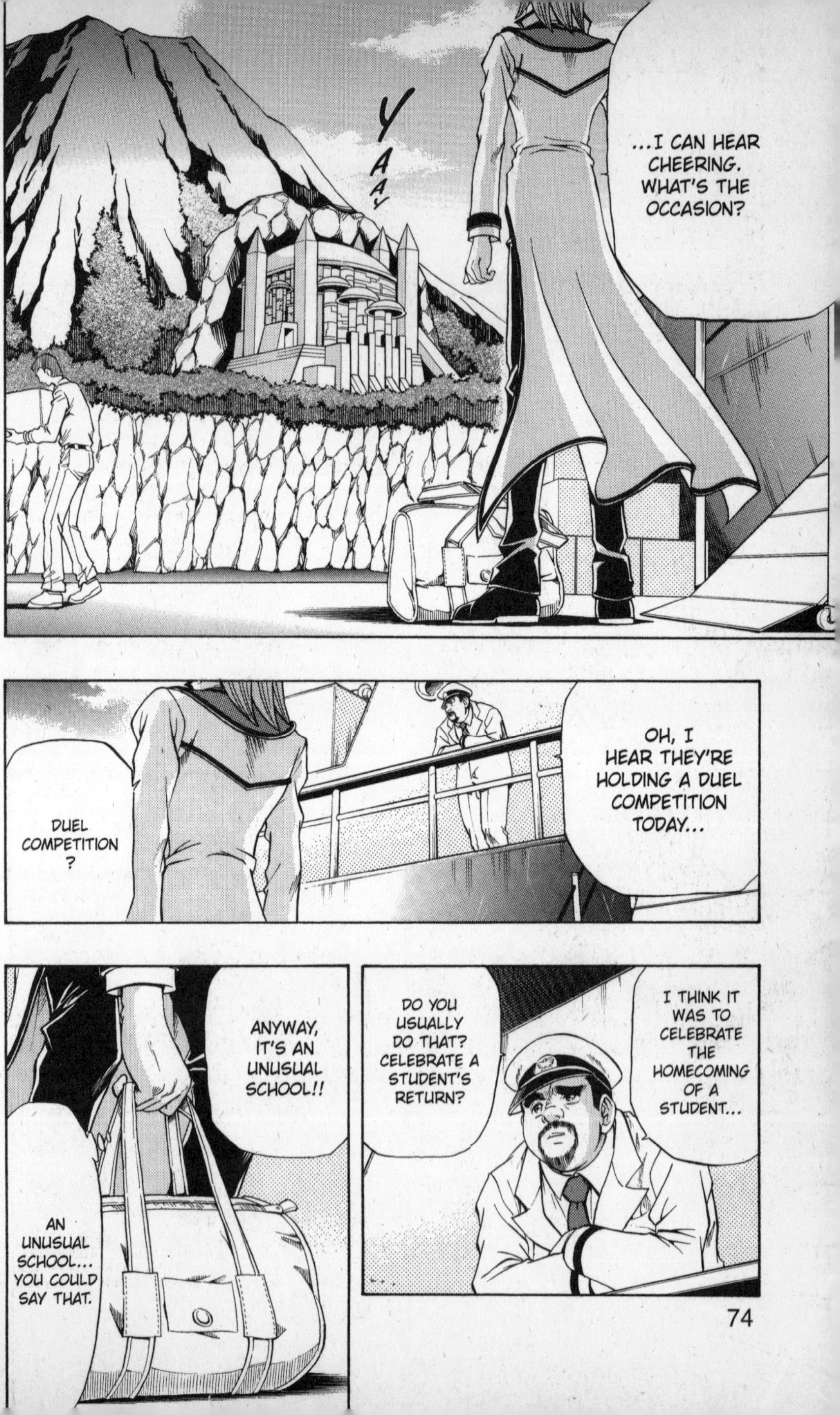
...I CAN HEAR CHEERING. WHAT'S THE OCCASION?
YAAY
OH, I HEAR THEY'RE HOLDING A DUEL COMPETITION TODAY...
DUEL COMPETITION ?
I THINK IT WAS TO CELEBRATE THE HOMECOMING OF A STUDENT...
DO YOU USUALLY DO THAT? CELEBRATE A STUDENT'S RETURN?
ANYWAY, IT'S AN UNUSUAL SCHOOL!!
AN UNUSUAL SCHOOL... YOU COULD SAY THAT.

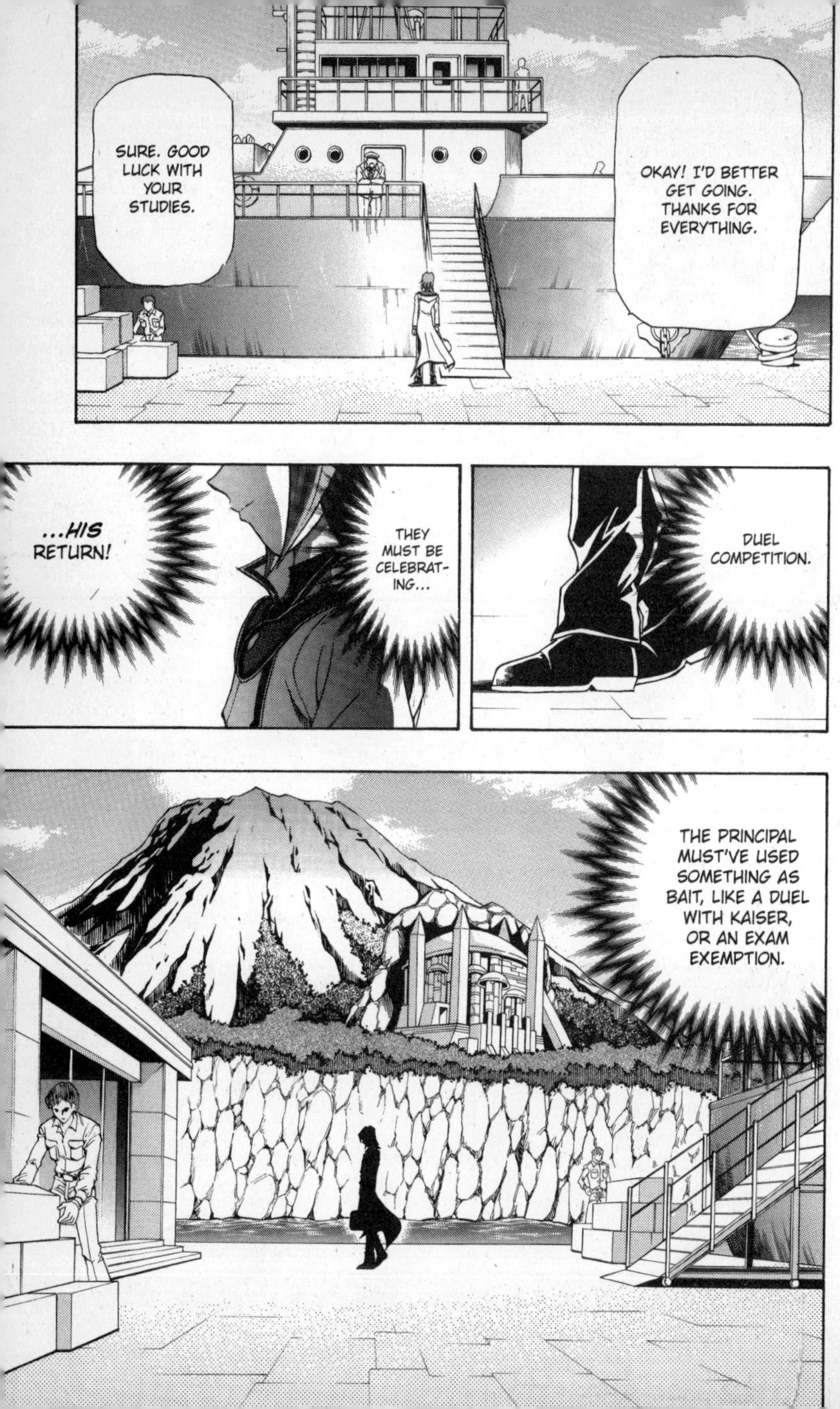
OKAY! I'D BETTER GET GOING. THANKS FOR EVERYTHING.
SURE. GOOD LUCK WITH YOUR STUDIES.
DUEL COMPETITION.
THEY MUST BE CELEBRAT-ING...
...HIS RETURN!
THE PRINCIPAL MUST'VE USED SOMETHING AS BAIT, LIKE A DUEL WITH KAISER, OR AN EXAM EXEMPTION.

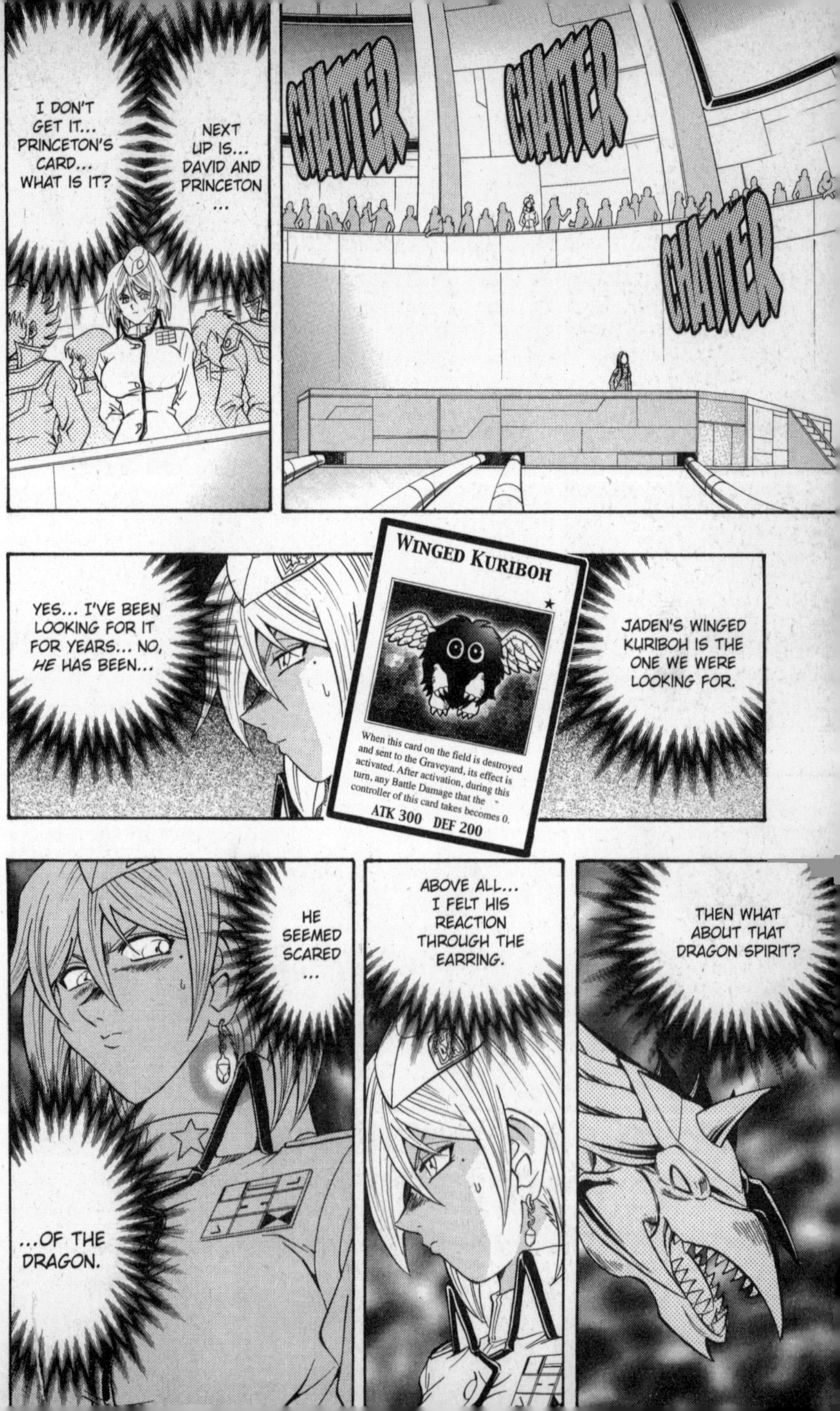
CHATTER
CHATTER
CHATTER
NEXT UP IS... DAVID AND PRINCETON...
I DON'T GET IT... PRINCETON'S CARD... WHAT IS IT?
JADEN'S WINGED KURIBOH IS THE ONE WE WERE LOOKING FOR.
WINGED KURIBOH
When this card on the field is destroyed and sent to the Graveyard, its effect is activated. After activation, during this turn, any Battle Damage that the controller of this card takes becomes 0.
ATK 300 DEF 200
YES... I'VE BEEN LOOKING FOR IT FOR YEARS... NO, *HE* HAS BEEN...
THEN WHAT ABOUT THAT DRAGON SPIRIT?
ABOVE ALL... I FELT HIS REACTION THROUGH THE EARRING.
HE SEEMED SCARED...
...OF THE DRAGON.

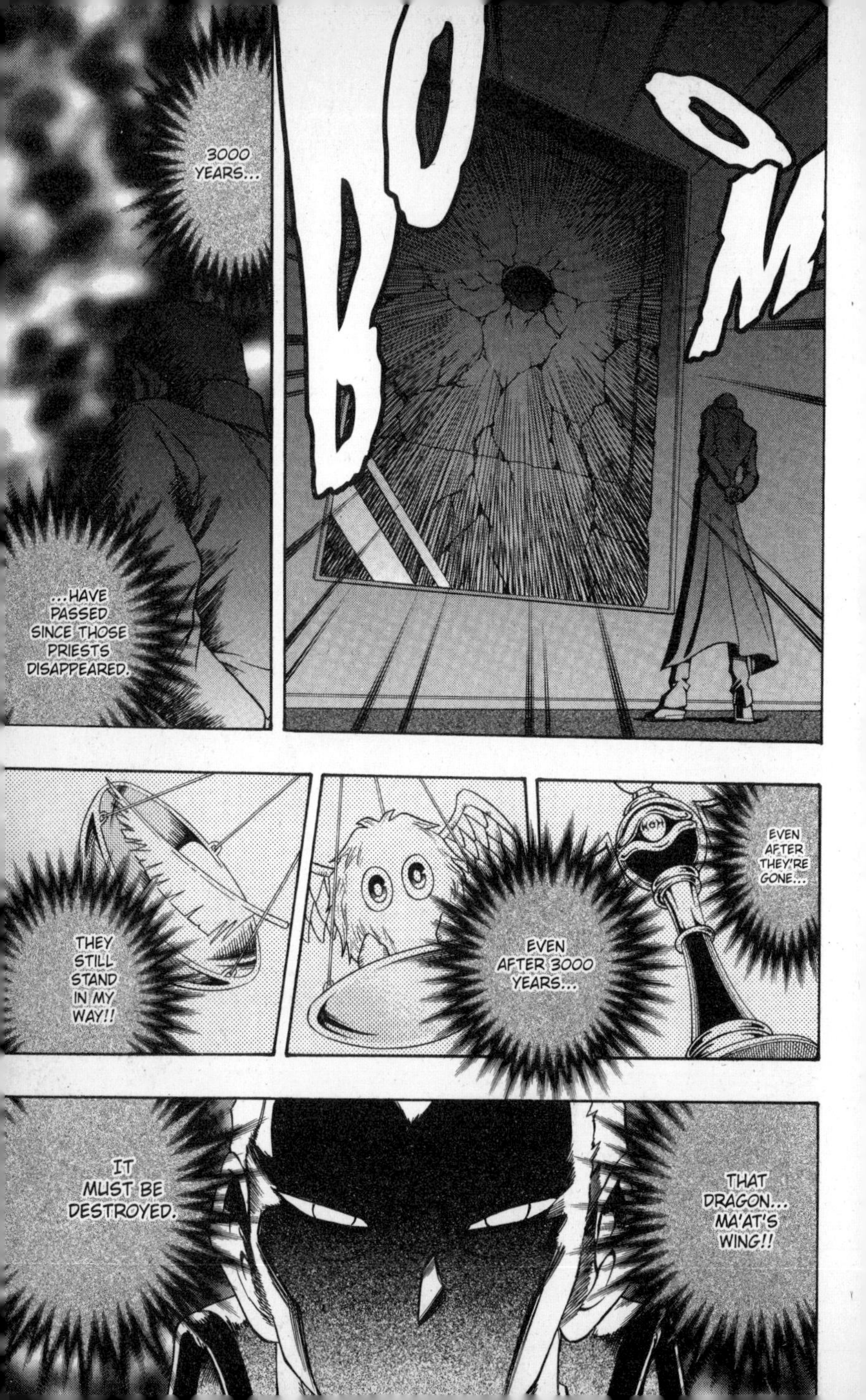
BOOM
3000 YEARS...
...HAVE PASSED SINCE THOSE PRIESTS DISAPPEARED.
EVEN AFTER THEY'RE GONE...
EVEN AFTER 3000 YEARS...
THEY STILL STAND IN MY WAY!!
THAT DRAGON... MA'AT'S WING!!
IT MUST BE DESTROYED.

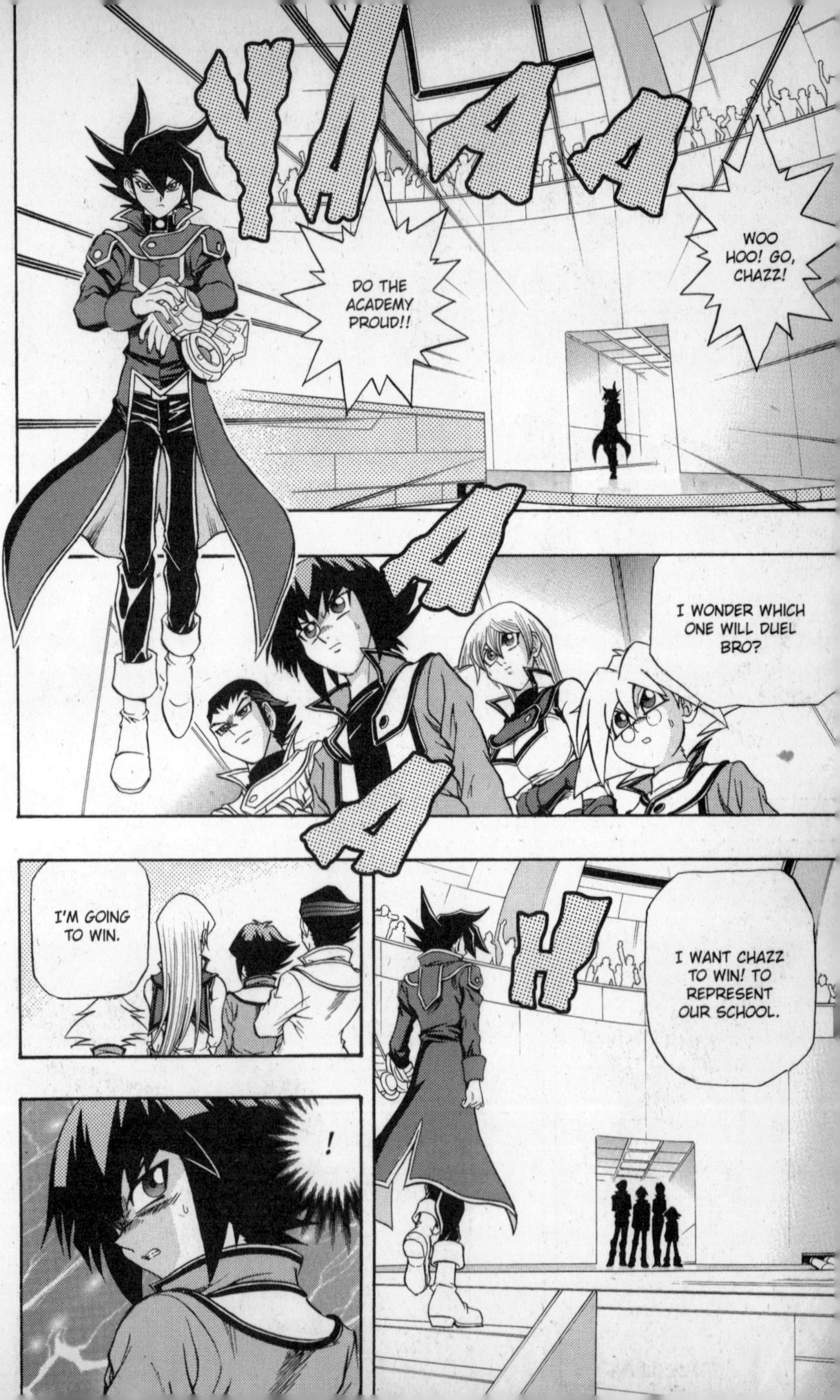
YAAAAAH
WOO HOO! GO, CHAZZ!
DO THE ACADEMY PROUD!!
I WONDER WHICH ONE WILL DUEL BRO?
I WANT CHAZZ TO WIN! TO REPRESENT OUR SCHOOL.
I'M GOING TO WIN.
!

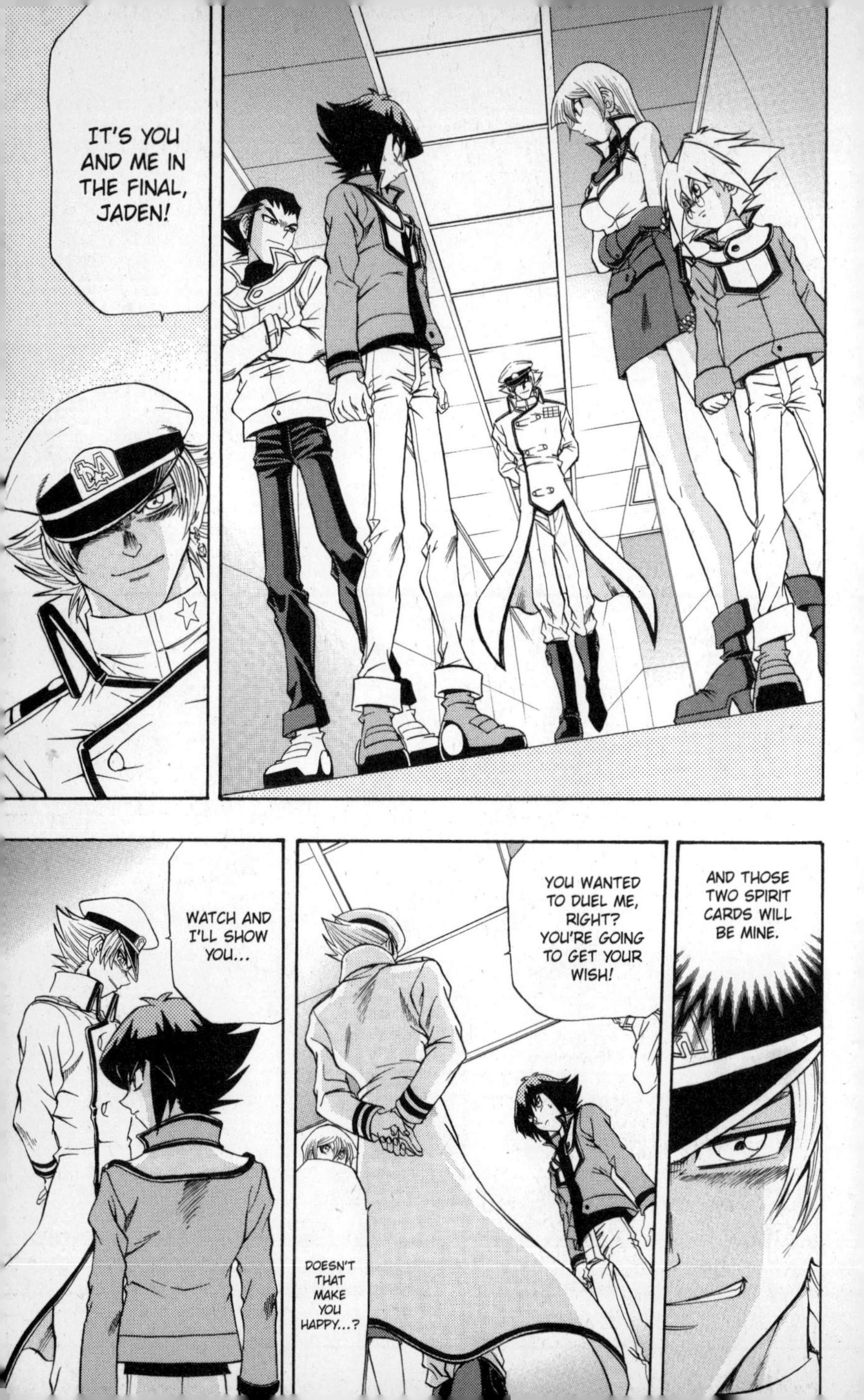
IT'S YOU AND ME IN THE FINAL, JADEN!
AND THOSE TWO SPIRIT CARDS WILL BE MINE.
YOU WANTED TO DUEL ME, RIGHT? YOU'RE GOING TO GET YOUR WISH!
DOESN'T THAT MAKE YOU HAPPY...?
WATCH AND I'LL SHOW YOU...

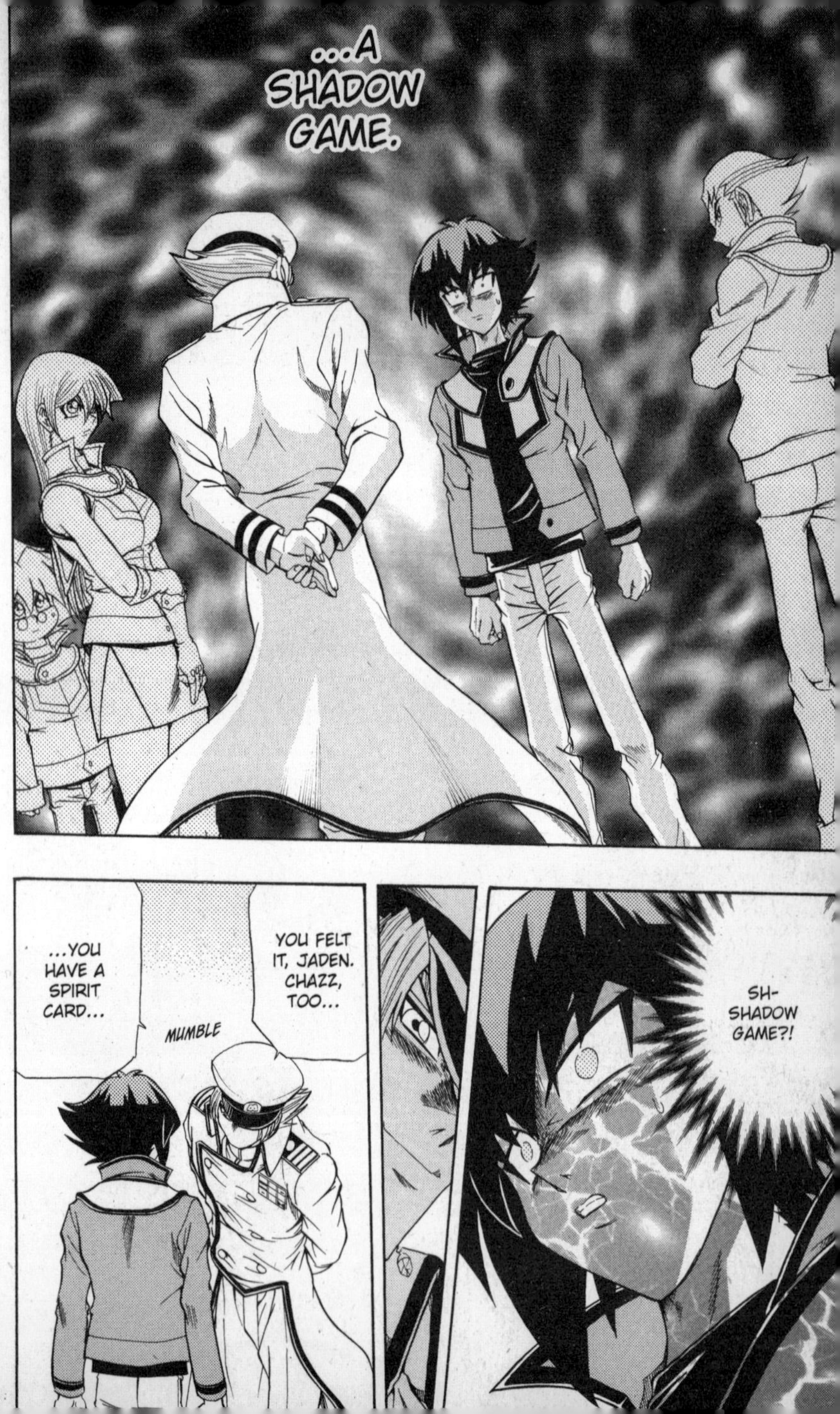
...A SHADOW GAME.
SH-SHADOW GAME?!
YOU FELT IT, JADEN. CHAZZ, TOO...
...YOU HAVE A SPIRIT CARD...
MUMBLE

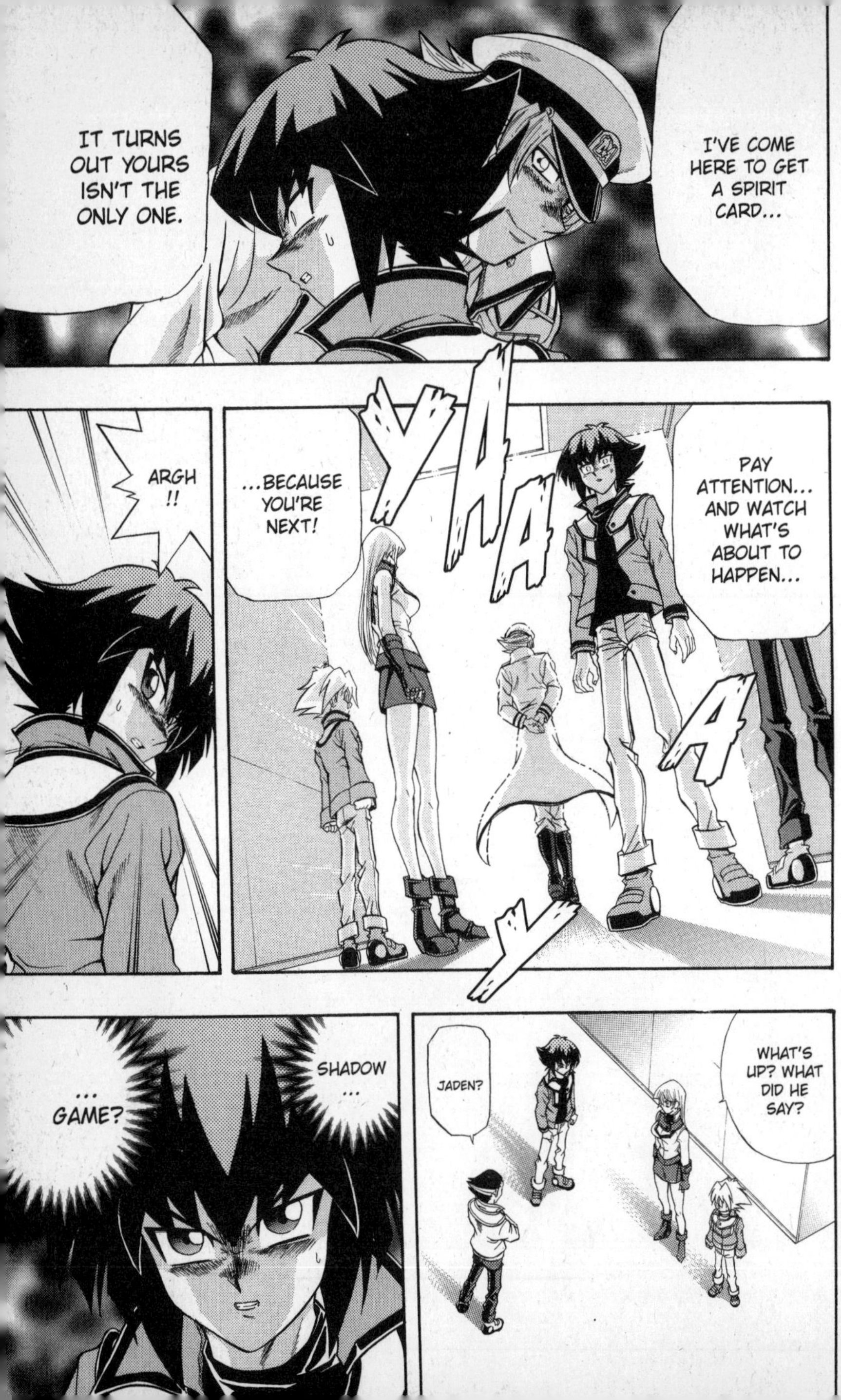
I'VE COME HERE TO GET A SPIRIT CARD...
IT TURNS OUT YOURS ISN'T THE ONLY ONE.
PAY ATTENTION... AND WATCH WHAT'S ABOUT TO HAPPEN...
...BECAUSE YOU'RE NEXT!
YAAAY
ARGH !!
WHAT'S UP? WHAT DID HE SAY?
JADEN?
SHADOW ...
... GAME?

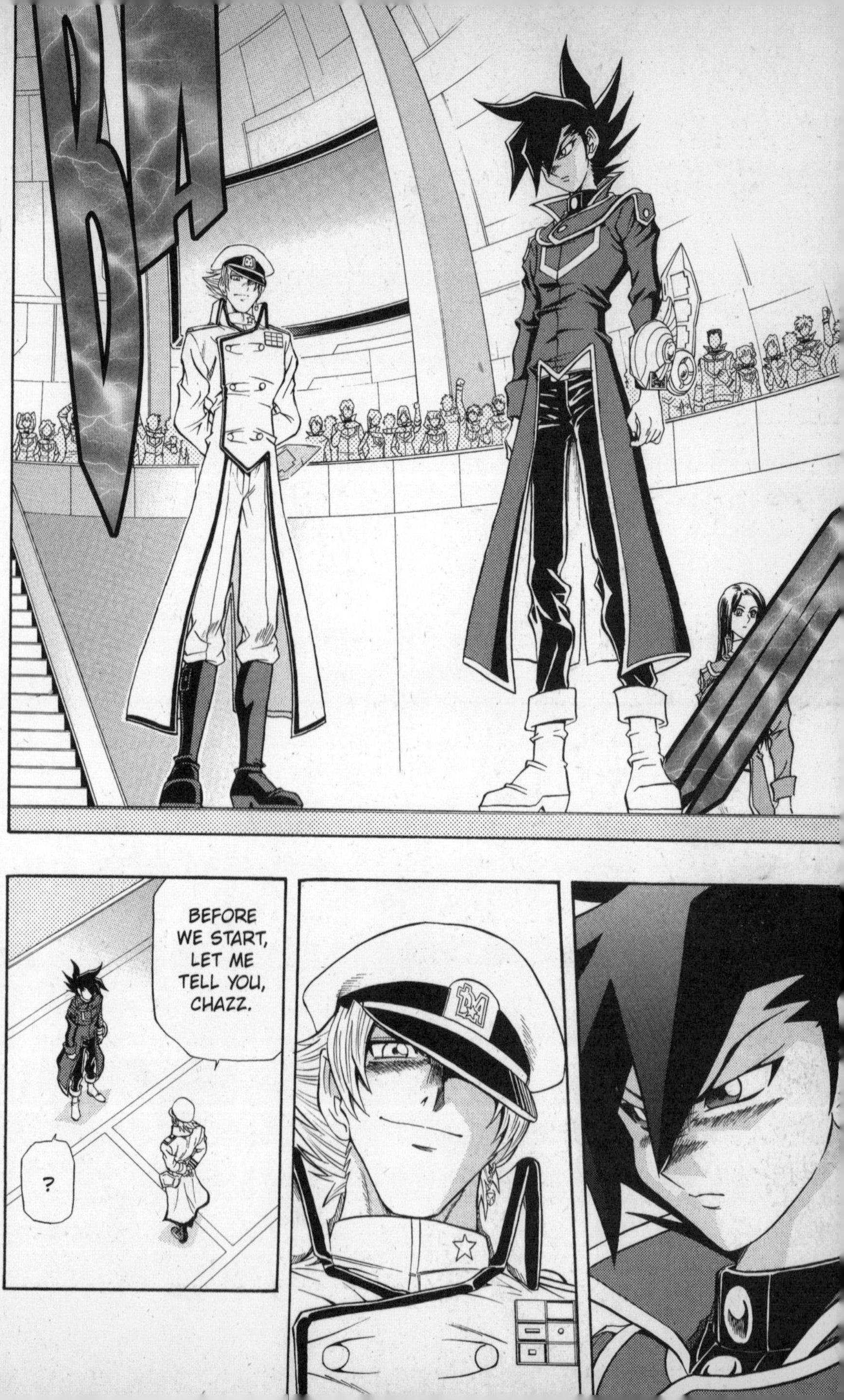
BEFORE WE START, LET ME TELL YOU, CHAZZ.
?

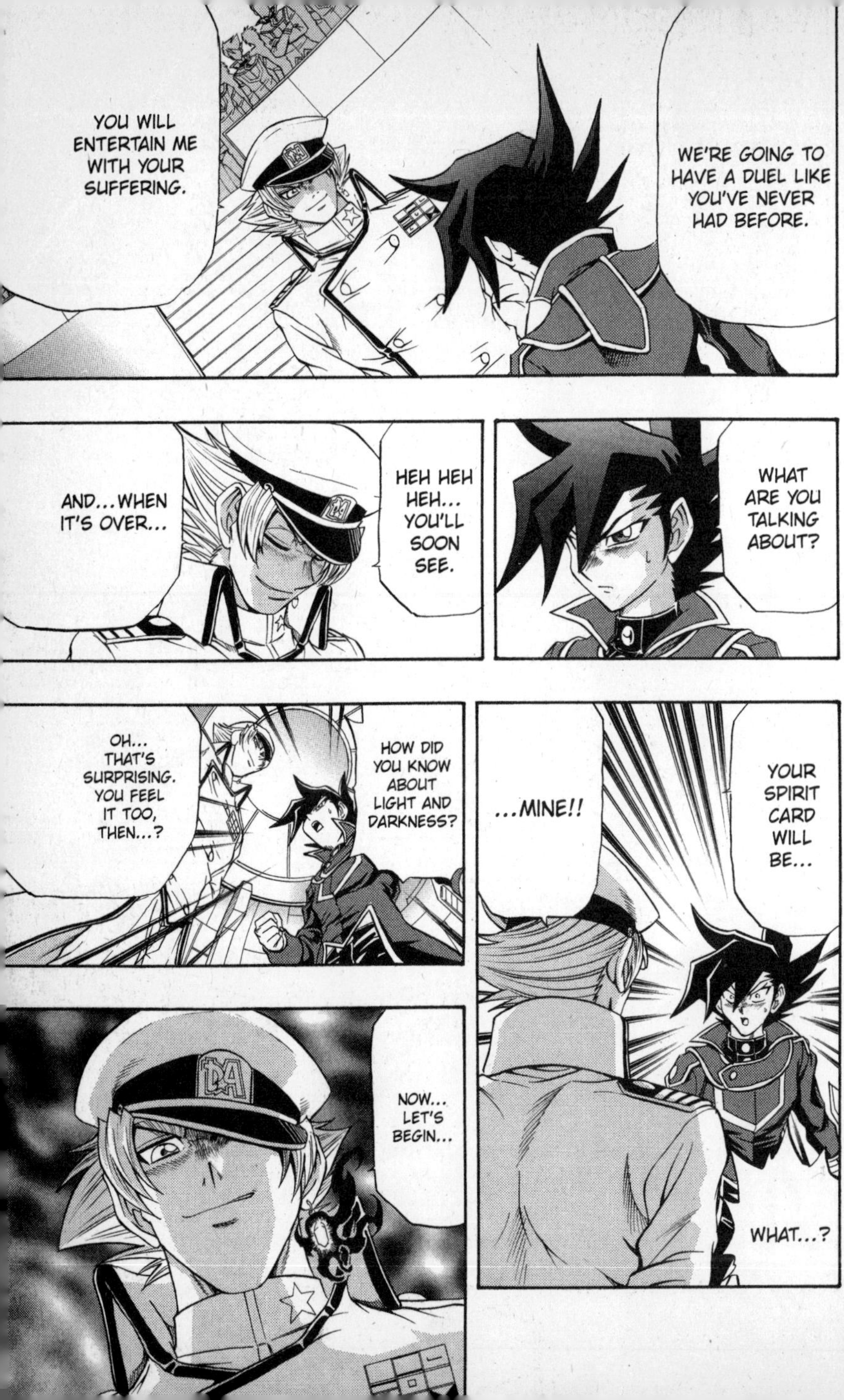
WE'RE GOING TO HAVE A DUEL LIKE YOU'VE NEVER HAD BEFORE.
YOU WILL ENTERTAIN ME WITH YOUR SUFFERING.
WHAT ARE YOU TALKING ABOUT?
HEH HEH HEH... YOU'LL SOON SEE.
AND...WHEN IT'S OVER...
YOUR SPIRIT CARD WILL BE...
...MINE!!
WHAT...?
HOW DID YOU KNOW ABOUT LIGHT AND DARKNESS?
OH... THAT'S SURPRISING. YOU FEEL IT TOO, THEN...?
NOW... LET'S BEGIN...

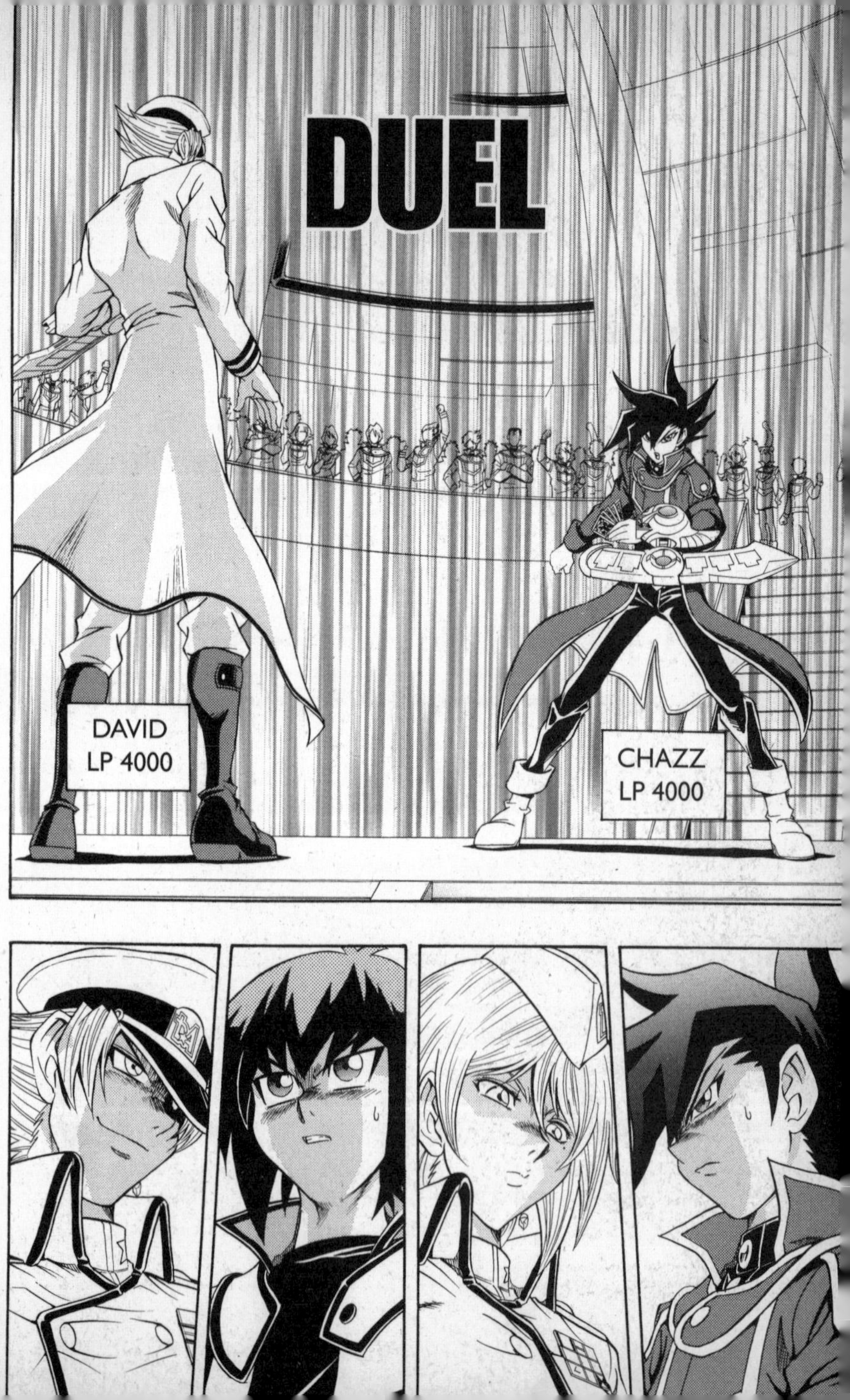
DUEL
CHAZZ
LP 4000
DAVID
LP 4000

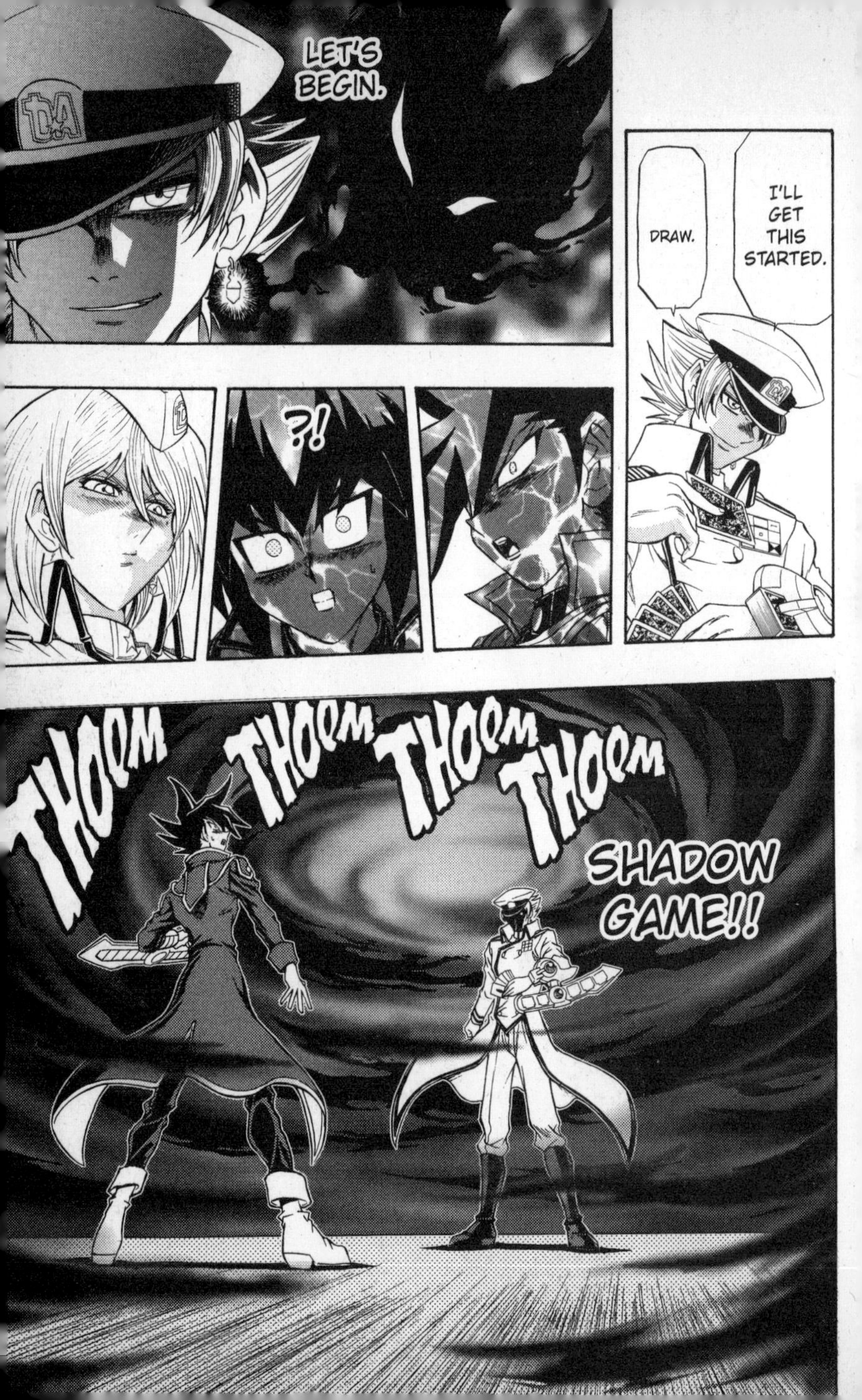
I'LL GET THIS STARTED.
DRAW.
LET'S BEGIN.
?!
THOOM
THOOM
THOOM
THOOM
SHADOW GAME!!

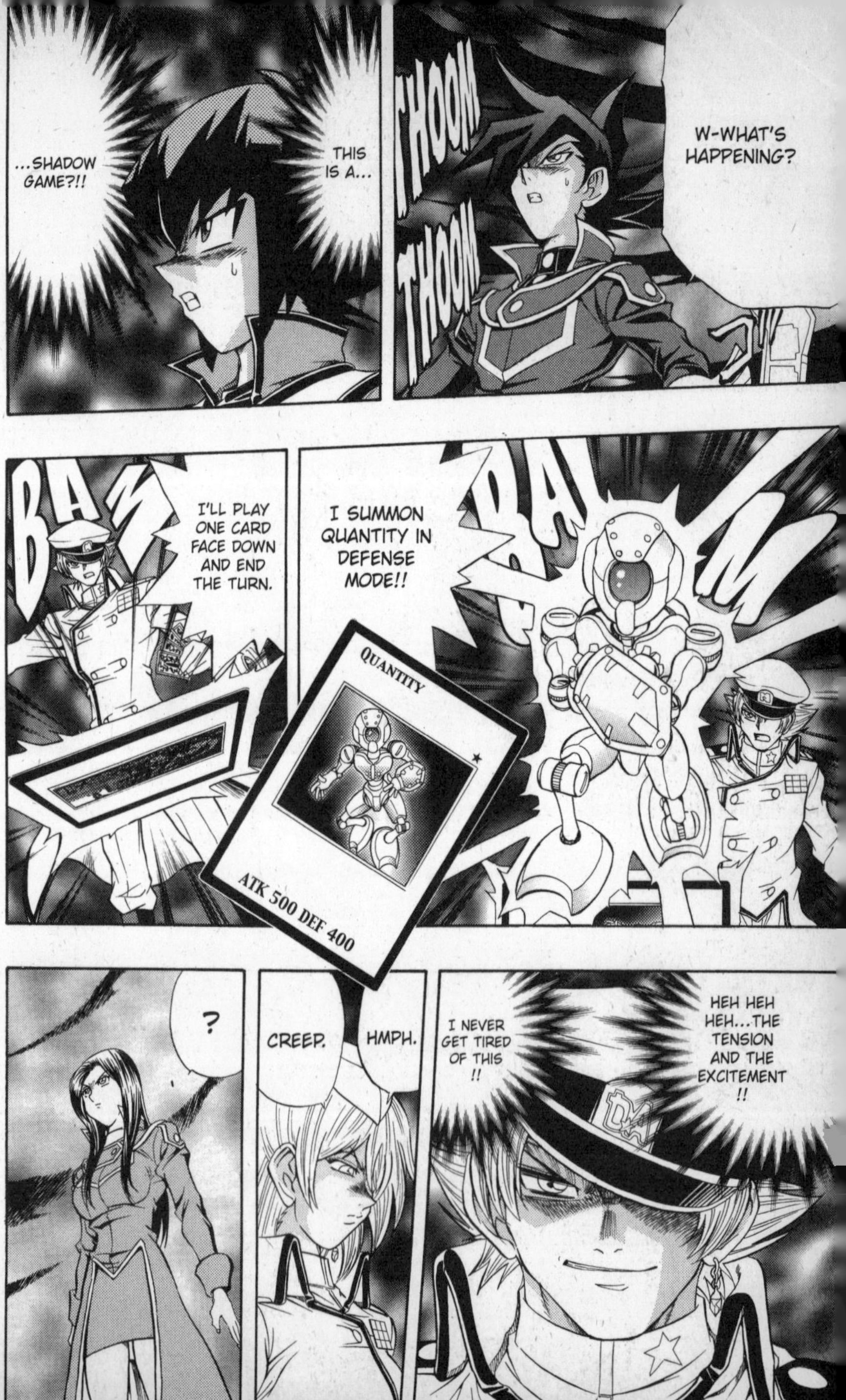
W-WHAT'S HAPPENING?
THOOM
THOOM
THIS IS A...
...SHADOW GAME?!!
BAM
I SUMMON QUANTITY IN DEFENSE MODE!!
QUANTITY
ATK 500 DEF 400
BAM
I'LL PLAY ONE CARD FACE DOWN AND END THE TURN.
HEH HEH HEH...THE TENSION AND THE EXCITEMENT !!
I NEVER GET TIRED OF THIS !!
HMPH.
CREEP.
?

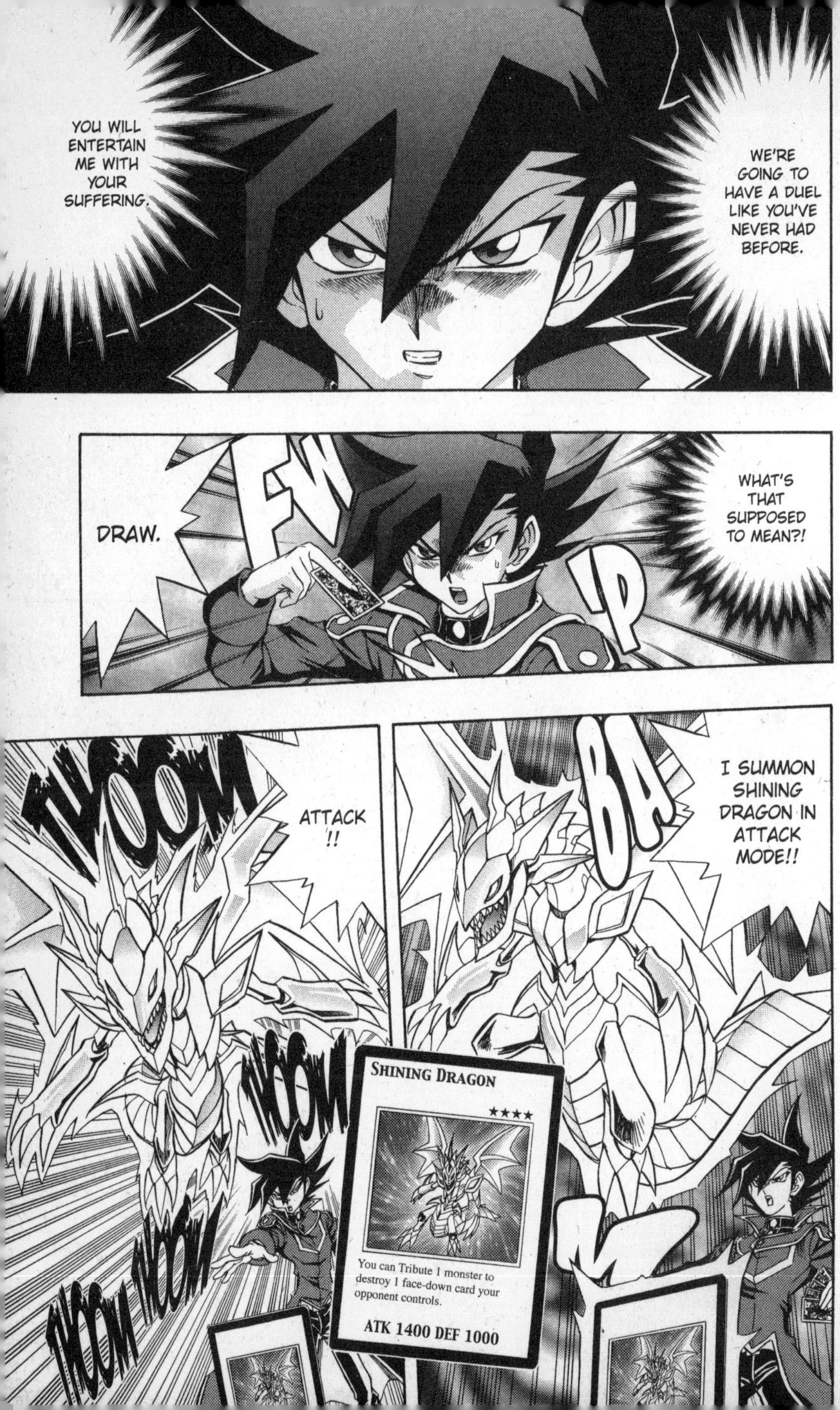
WE'RE GOING TO HAVE A DUEL LIKE YOU'VE NEVER HAD BEFORE.
YOU WILL ENTERTAIN ME WITH YOUR SUFFERING.
WHAT'S THAT SUPPOSED TO MEAN?!
'P
FW
DRAW.
I SUMMON SHINING DRAGON IN ATTACK MODE!!
BA
SHINING DRAGON
★★★★
You can Tribute 1 monster to destroy 1 face-down card your opponent controls.
ATK 1400 DEF 1000
ATTACK!!
THOOM
THOOM
THOOM THOOM

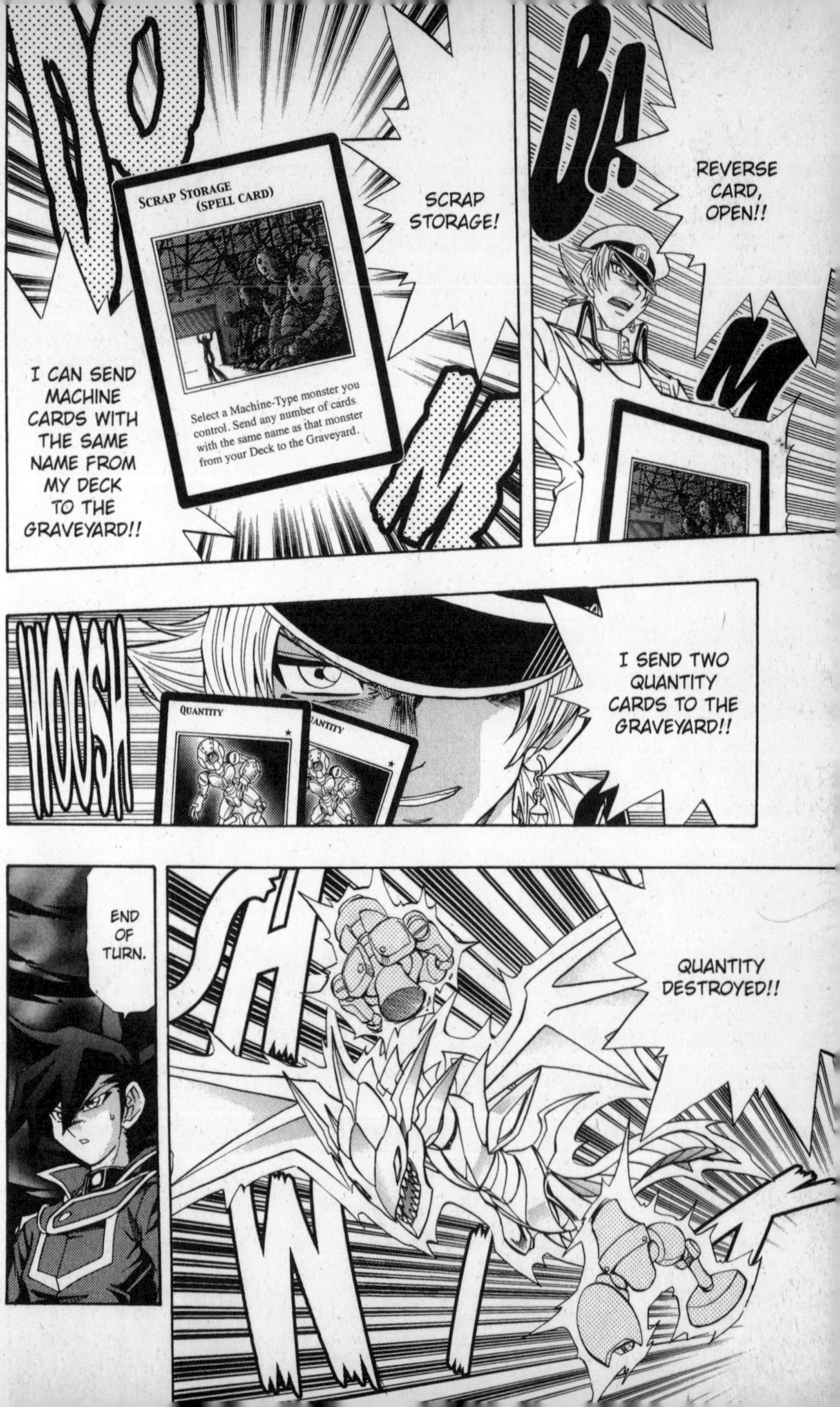
REVERSE CARD, OPEN!!
SCRAP STORAGE!
SCRAP STORAGE (SPELL CARD)
Select a Machine-Type monster you control. Send any number of cards with the same name as that monster from your Deck to the Graveyard.
I CAN SEND MACHINE CARDS WITH THE SAME NAME FROM MY DECK TO THE GRAVEYARD!!
I SEND TWO QUANTITY CARDS TO THE GRAVEYARD!!
QUANTITY
QUANTITY
WOOSH!
QUANTITY DESTROYED!!
END OF TURN.

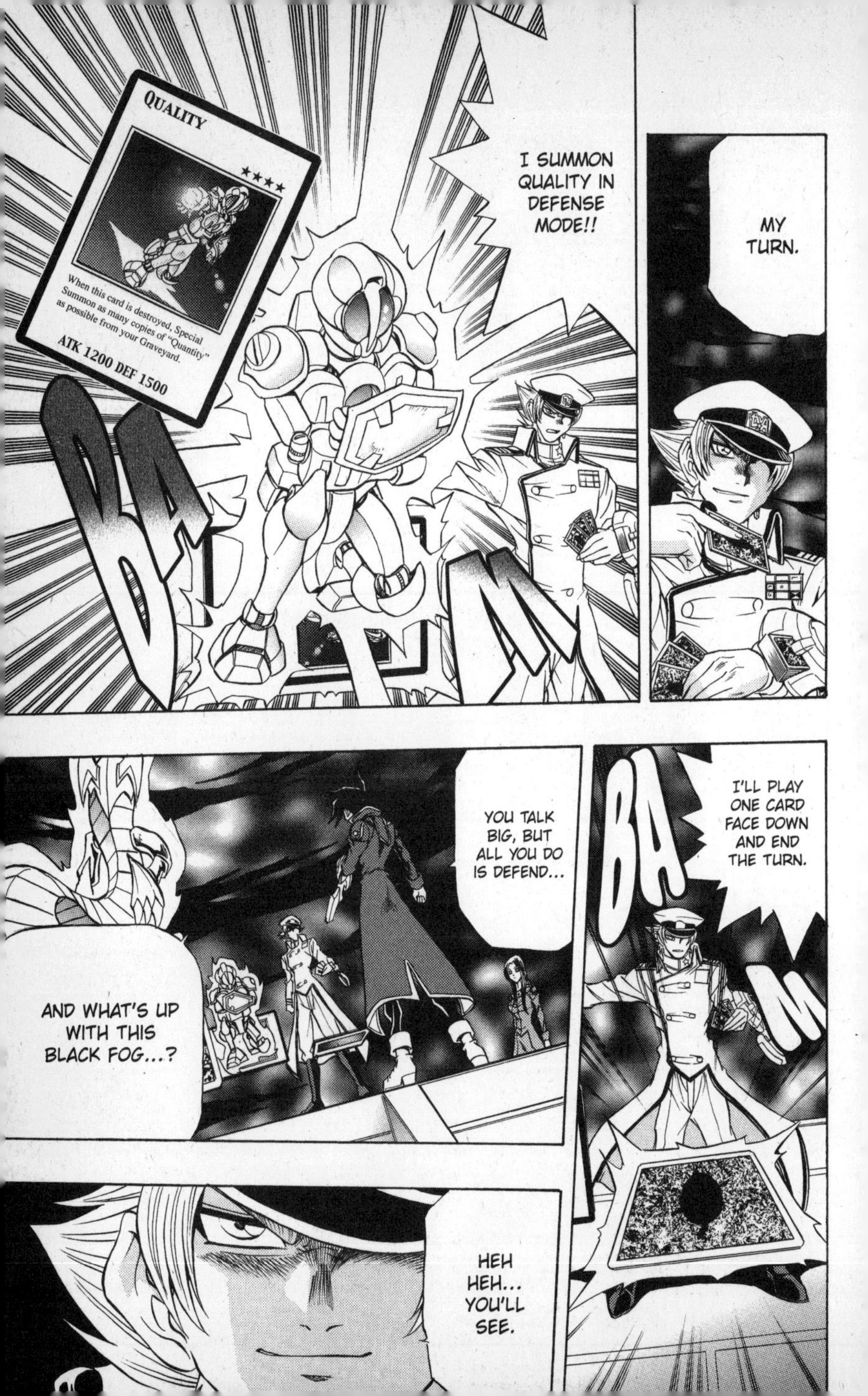
MY TURN.
QUALITY
When this card is destroyed, Special Summon as many copies of "Quantity" as possible from your Graveyard.
ATK 1200 DEF 1500
I SUMMON QUALITY IN DEFENSE MODE!!
BAM
BAM
I'LL PLAY ONE CARD FACE DOWN AND END THE TURN.
YOU TALK BIG, BUT ALL YOU DO IS DEFEND...
AND WHAT'S UP WITH THIS BLACK FOG...?
HEH HEH... YOU'LL SEE.

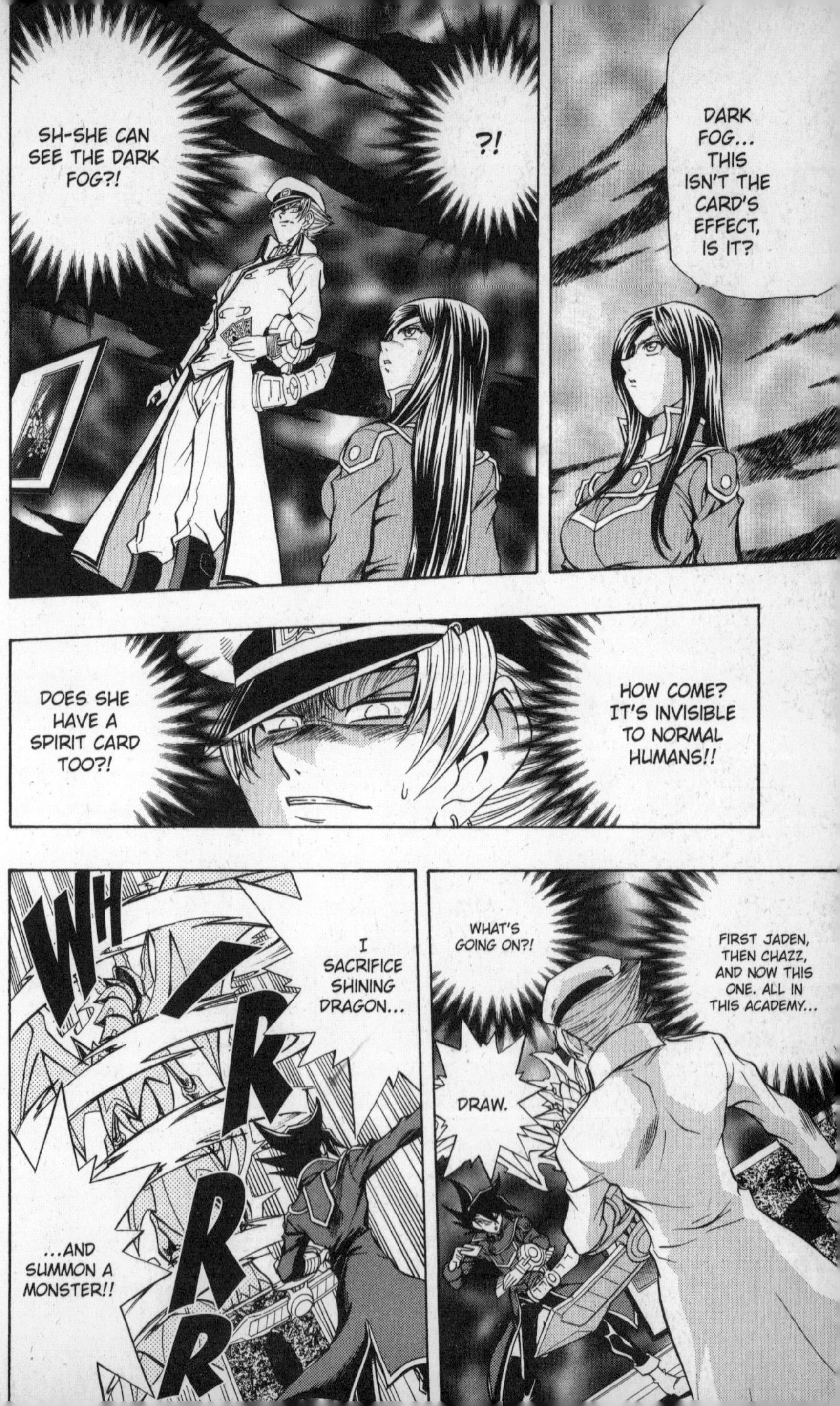
DARK FOG... THIS ISN'T THE CARD'S EFFECT, IS IT?
?!
SH-SHE CAN SEE THE DARK FOG?!
HOW COME? IT'S INVISIBLE TO NORMAL HUMANS!!
DOES SHE HAVE A SPIRIT CARD TOO?!
FIRST JADEN, THEN CHAZZ, AND NOW THIS ONE. ALL IN THIS ACADEMY...
WHAT'S GOING ON?!
DRAW.
I SACRIFICE SHINING DRAGON...
WHIRRR
...AND SUMMON A MONSTER!!

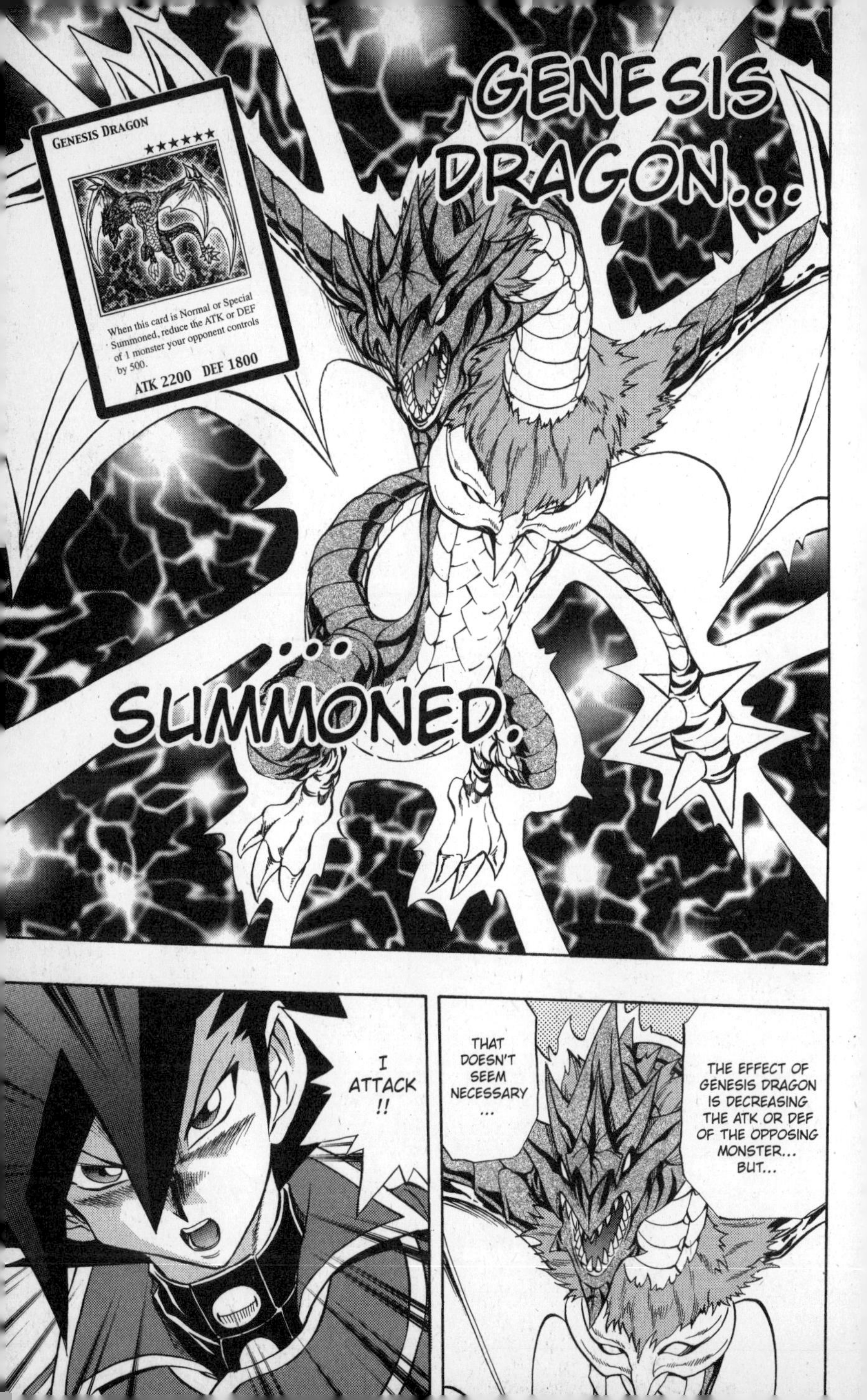
GENESIS DRAGON...
GENESIS DRAGON
When this card is Normal or Special Summoned, reduce the ATK or DEF of 1 monster your opponent controls by 500.
ATK 2200 DEF 1800
...SUMMONED.
THE EFFECT OF GENESIS DRAGON IS DECREASING THE ATK OR DEF OF THE OPPOSING MONSTER... BUT...
THAT DOESN'T SEEM NECESSARY...
I ATTACK!!

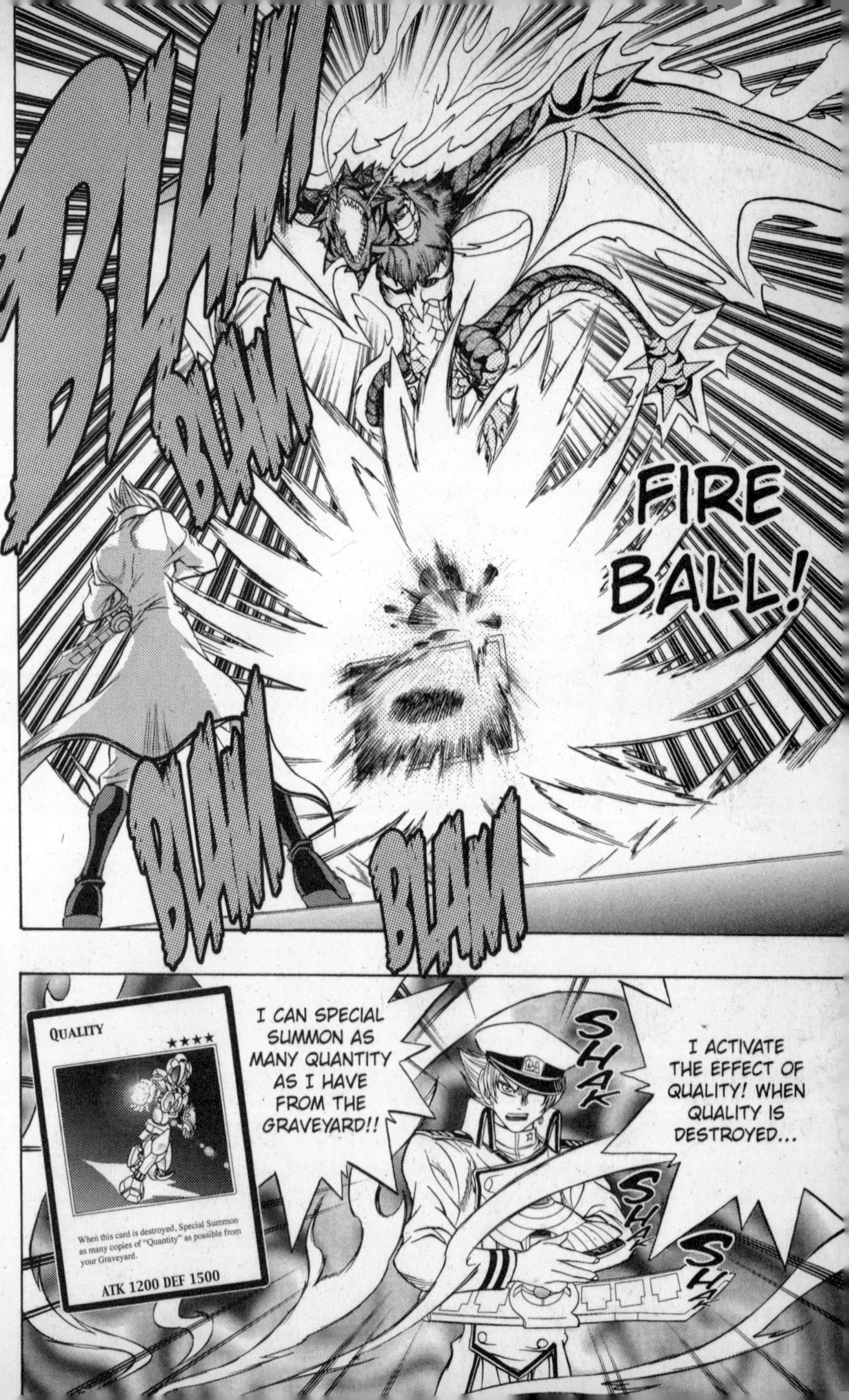
BLAM
BLAM
FIRE BALL!
BLAM
BLAM
I ACTIVATE THE EFFECT OF QUALITY! WHEN QUALITY IS DESTROYED...
SHAK
SHAK
SHAK
I CAN SPECIAL SUMMON AS MANY QUANTITY AS I HAVE FROM THE GRAVEYARD!!
QUALITY
★★★★
When this card is destroyed, Special Summon as many copies of "Quantity" as possible from your Graveyard.
ATK 1200 DEF 1500

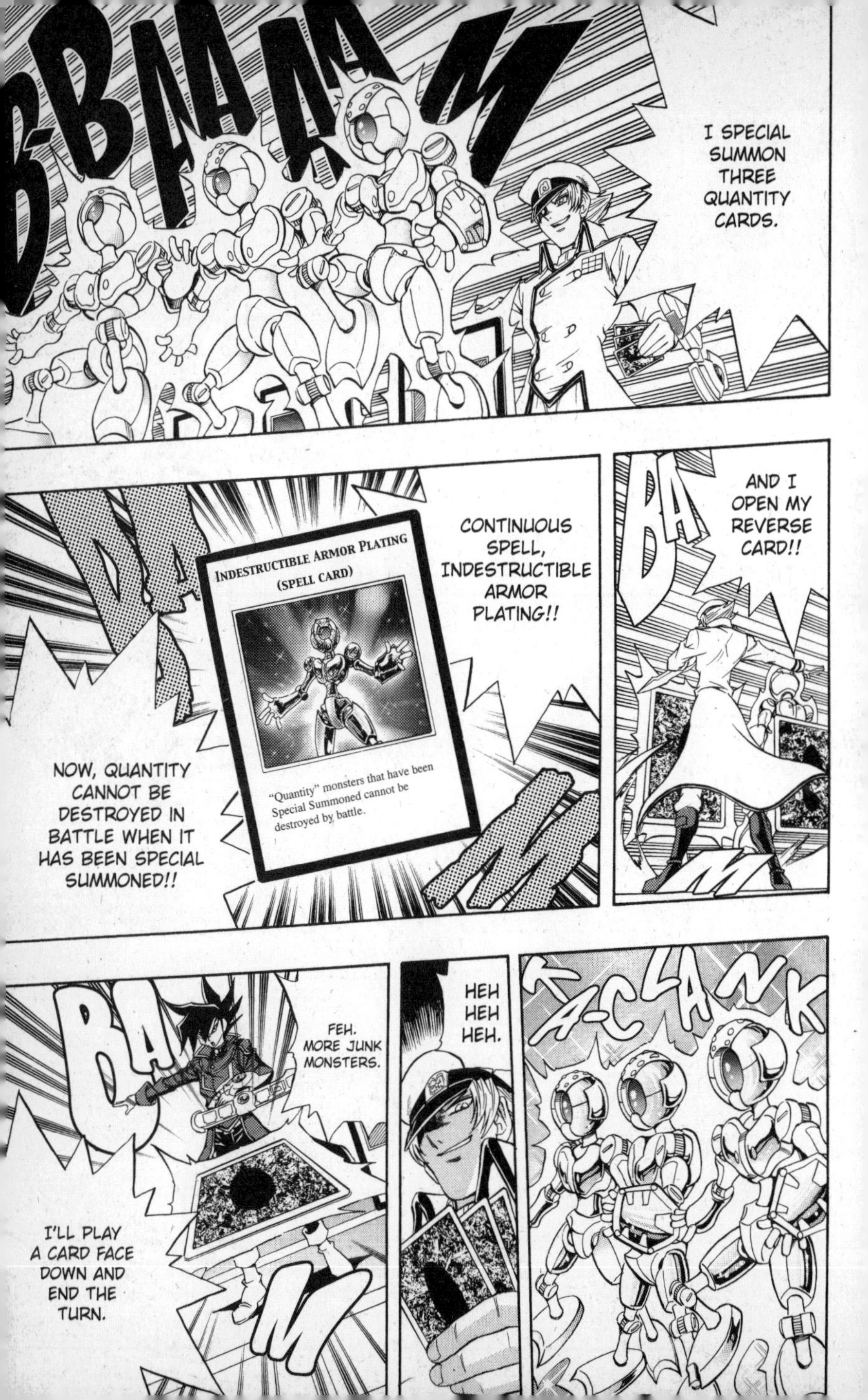
I SPECIAL SUMMON THREE QUANTITY CARDS.
AND I OPEN MY REVERSE CARD!!
CONTINUOUS SPELL, INDESTRUCTIBLE ARMOR PLATING!!
Indestructible Armor Plating
(Spell Card)
"Quantity" monsters that have been Special Summoned cannot be destroyed by battle.
NOW, QUANTITY CANNOT BE DESTROYED IN BATTLE WHEN IT HAS BEEN SPECIAL SUMMONED!!
KA-CLANK
HEH HEH HEH.
FEH. MORE JUNK MONSTERS.
I'LL PLAY A CARD FACE DOWN AND END THE TURN.

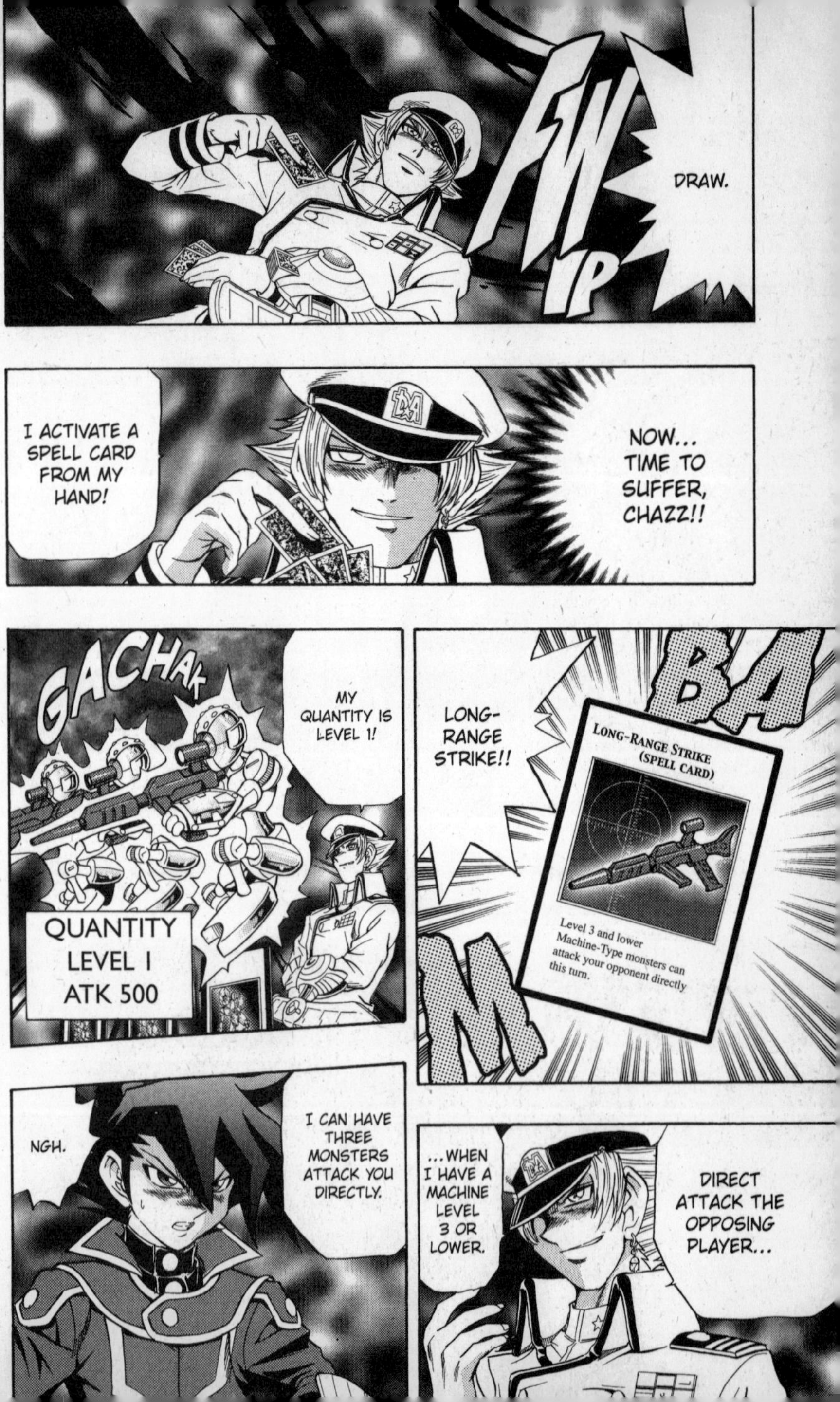
FWIP
DRAW.
NOW... TIME TO SUFFER, CHAZZ!!
I ACTIVATE A SPELL CARD FROM MY HAND!
BAM
LONG-RANGE STRIKE!!
LONG-RANGE STRIKE (SPELL CARD)
Level 3 and lower Machine-Type monsters can attack your opponent directly this turn.
MY QUANTITY IS LEVEL 1!
GACHAK
QUANTITY LEVEL 1 ATK 500
DIRECT ATTACK THE OPPOSING PLAYER...
...WHEN I HAVE A MACHINE LEVEL 3 OR LOWER.
I CAN HAVE THREE MONSTERS ATTACK YOU DIRECTLY.
NGH.

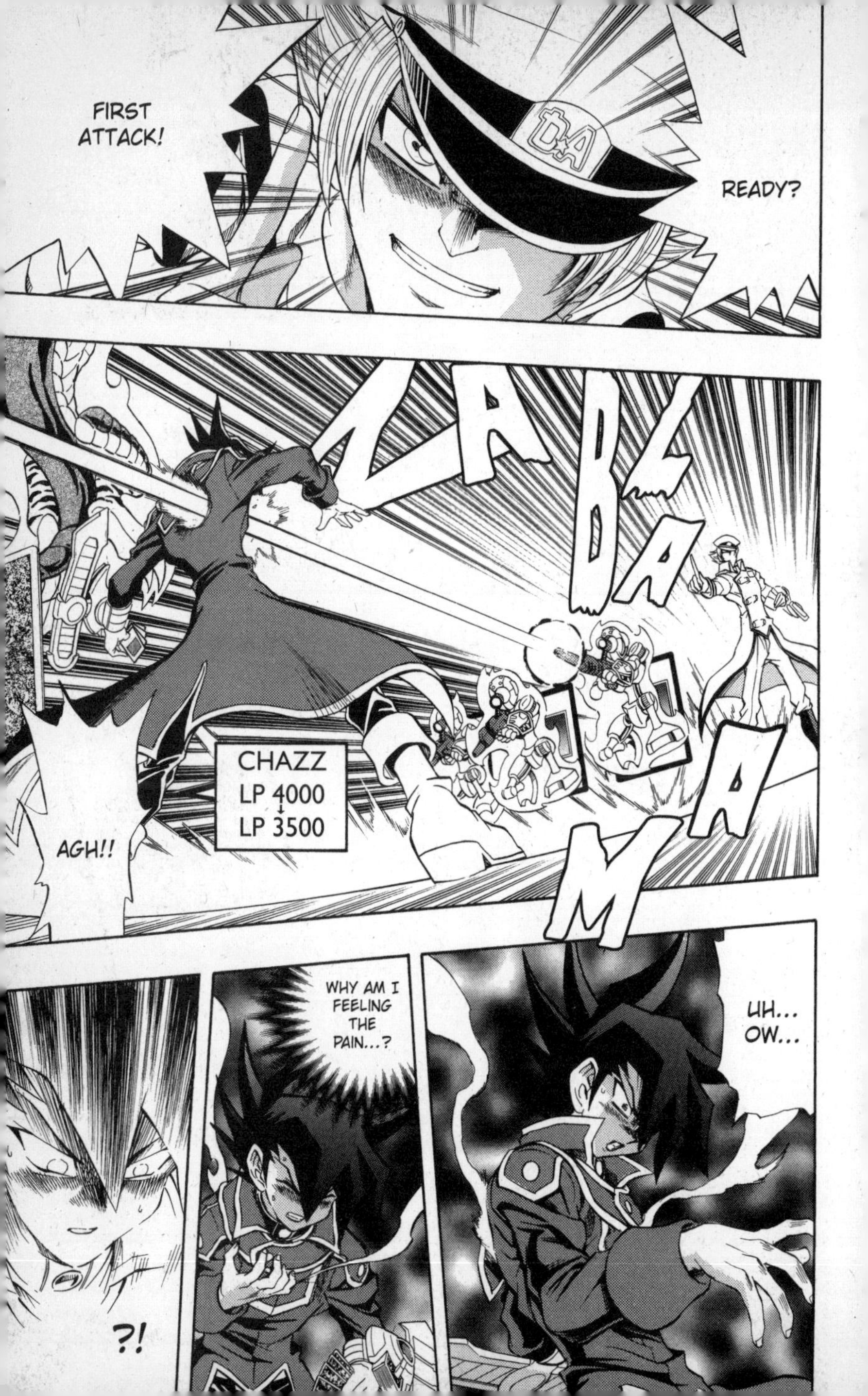
READY?
FIRST ATTACK!
CHAZZ
LP 4000
LP 3500
AGH!!
UH... OW...
WHY AM I FEELING THE PAIN...?
?!

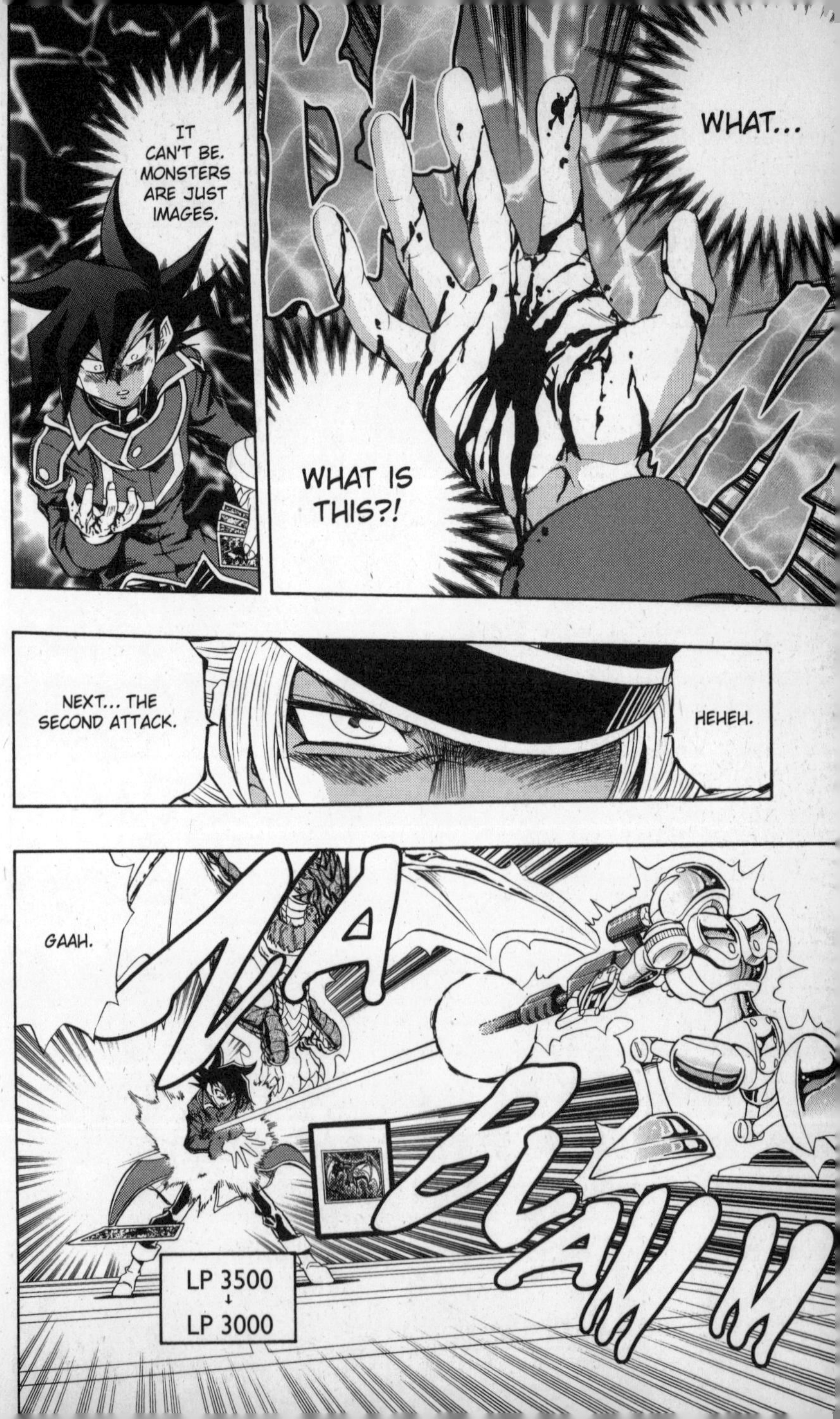
WHAT...
WHAT IS THIS?!
IT CAN'T BE. MONSTERS ARE JUST IMAGES.
HEHEH.
NEXT... THE SECOND ATTACK.
BLAM
LP 3500 ↓ LP 3000
GAAH.

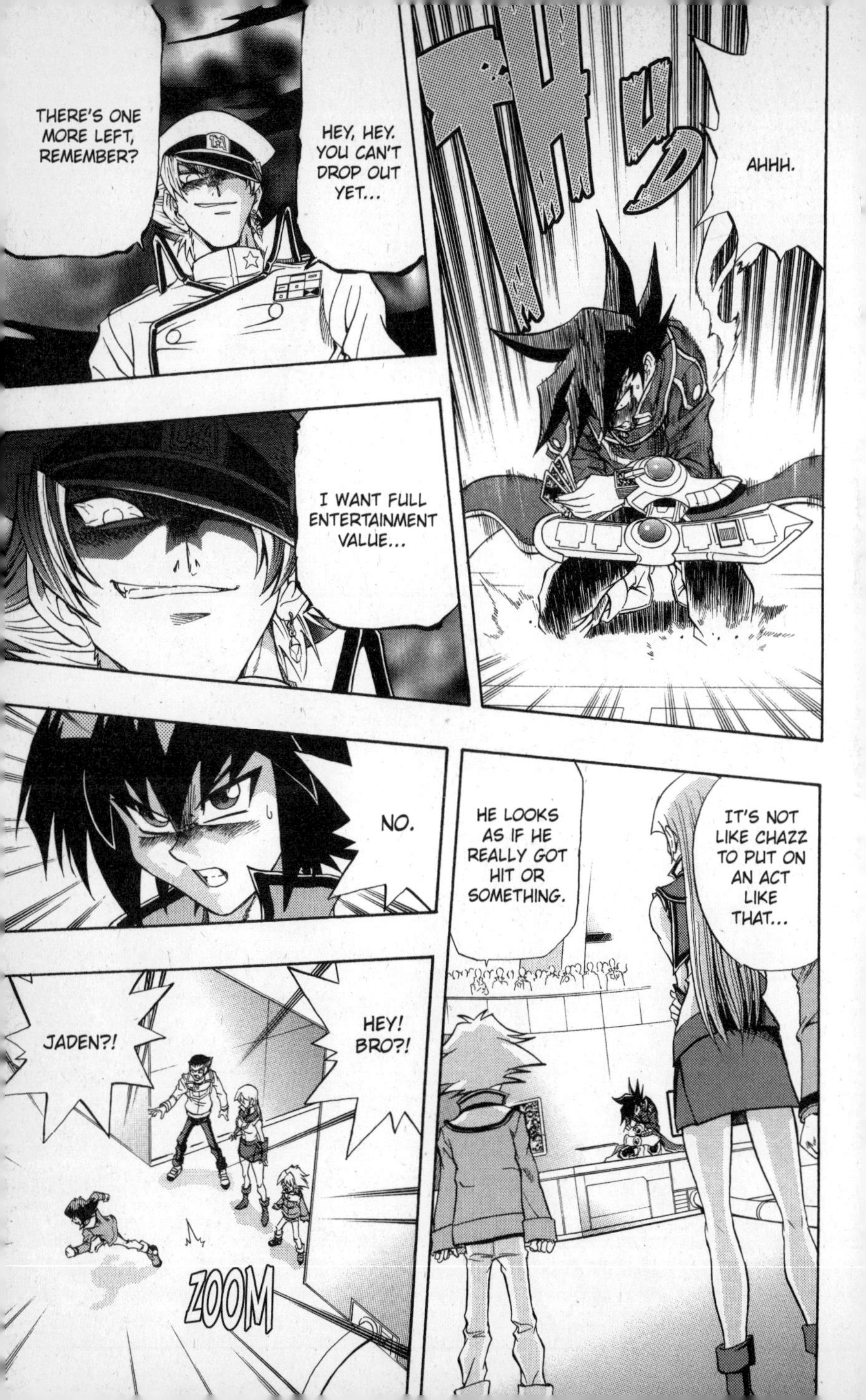
THUD
AHHH.
HEY, HEY. YOU CAN'T DROP OUT YET...
THERE'S ONE MORE LEFT, REMEMBER?
I WANT FULL ENTERTAINMENT VALUE...
IT'S NOT LIKE CHAZZ TO PUT ON AN ACT LIKE THAT...
HE LOOKS AS IF HE REALLY GOT HIT OR SOMETHING.
NO.
HEY! BRO?!
JADEN?!
ZOOM

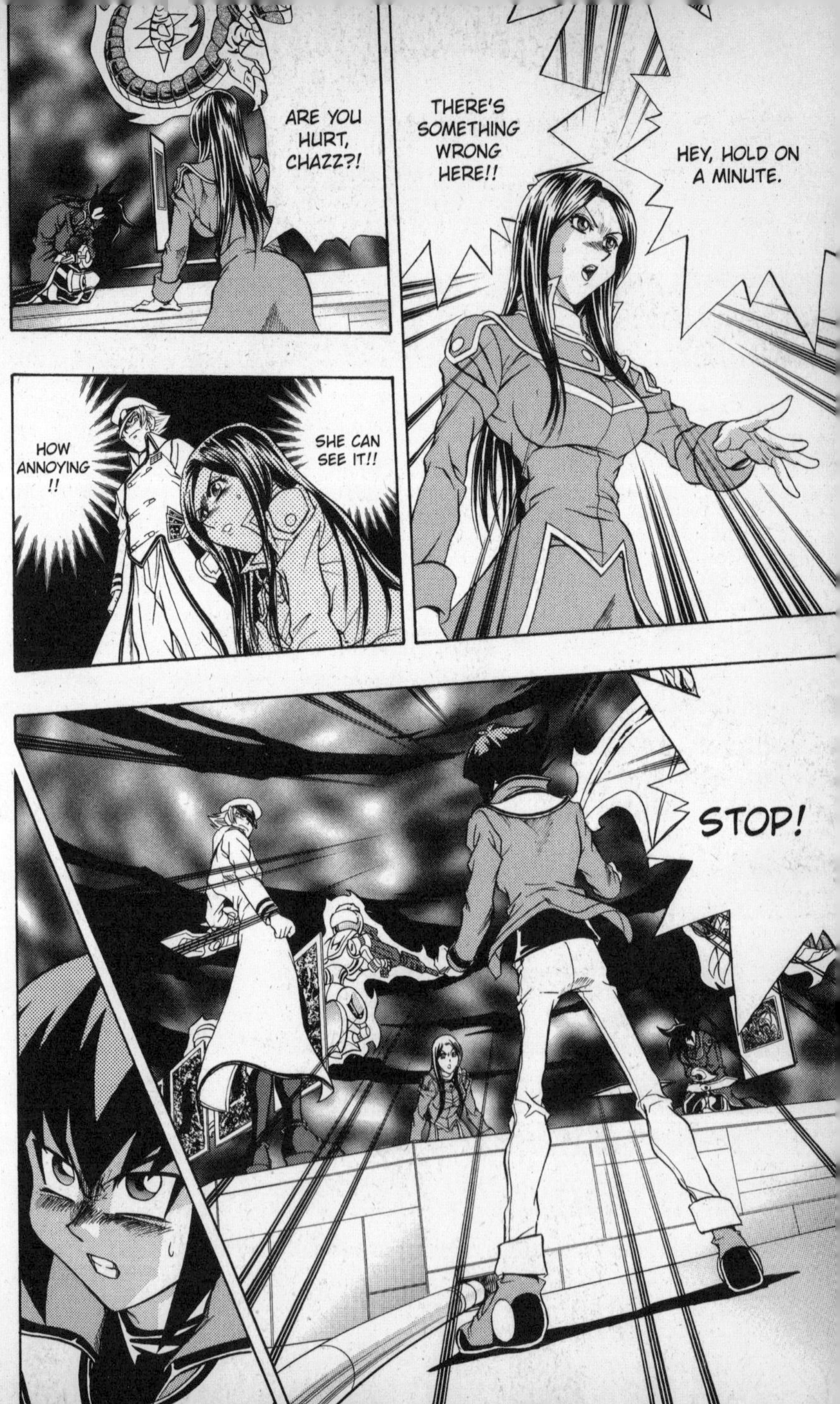
HEY, HOLD ON A MINUTE.
THERE'S SOMETHING WRONG HERE!!
ARE YOU HURT, CHAZZ?!
SHE CAN SEE IT!!
HOW ANNOYING!!
STOP!

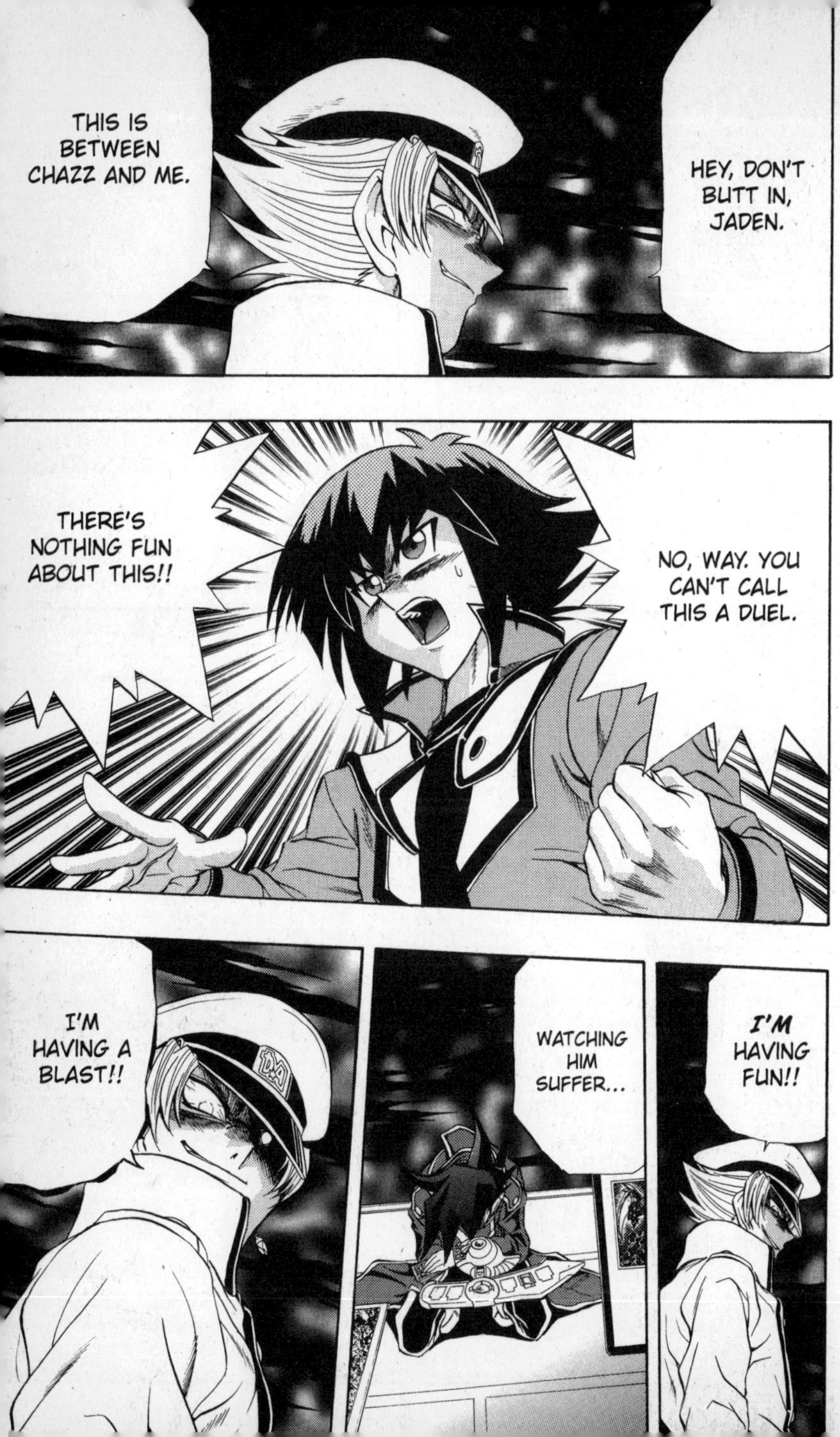
HEY, DON'T BUTT IN, JADEN.
THIS IS BETWEEN CHAZZ AND ME.
NO, WAY. YOU CAN'T CALL THIS A DUEL.
THERE'S NOTHING FUN ABOUT THIS!!
I'M HAVING FUN!!
WATCHING HIM SUFFER...
I'M HAVING A BLAST!!

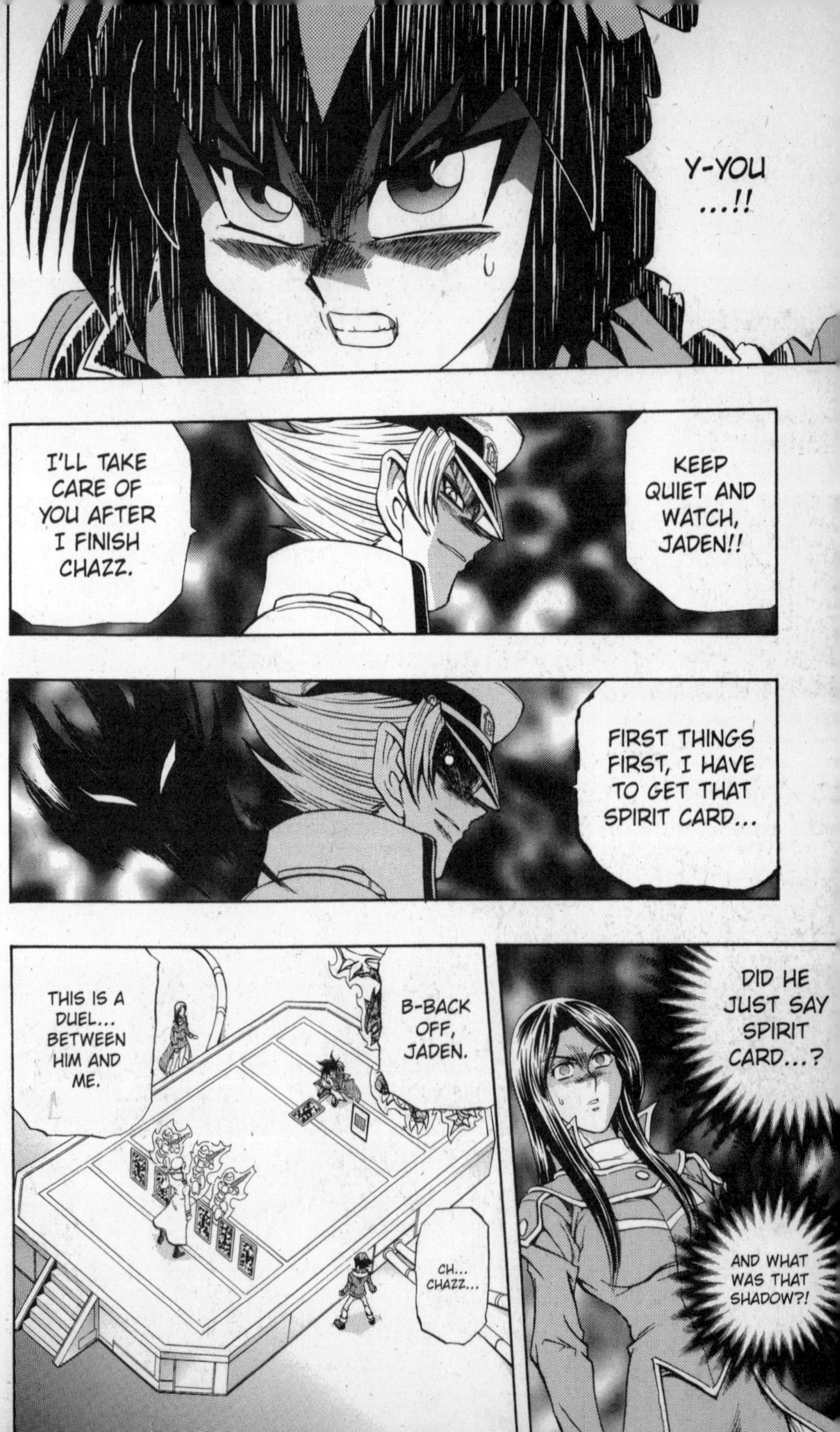
Y-YOU ...!!
KEEP QUIET AND WATCH, JADEN!!
I'LL TAKE CARE OF YOU AFTER I FINISH CHAZZ.
FIRST THINGS FIRST, I HAVE TO GET THAT SPIRIT CARD...
DID HE JUST SAY SPIRIT CARD...?
AND WHAT WAS THAT SHADOW?!
B-BACK OFF, JADEN.
THIS IS A DUEL... BETWEEN HIM AND ME.
CH... CHAZZ...

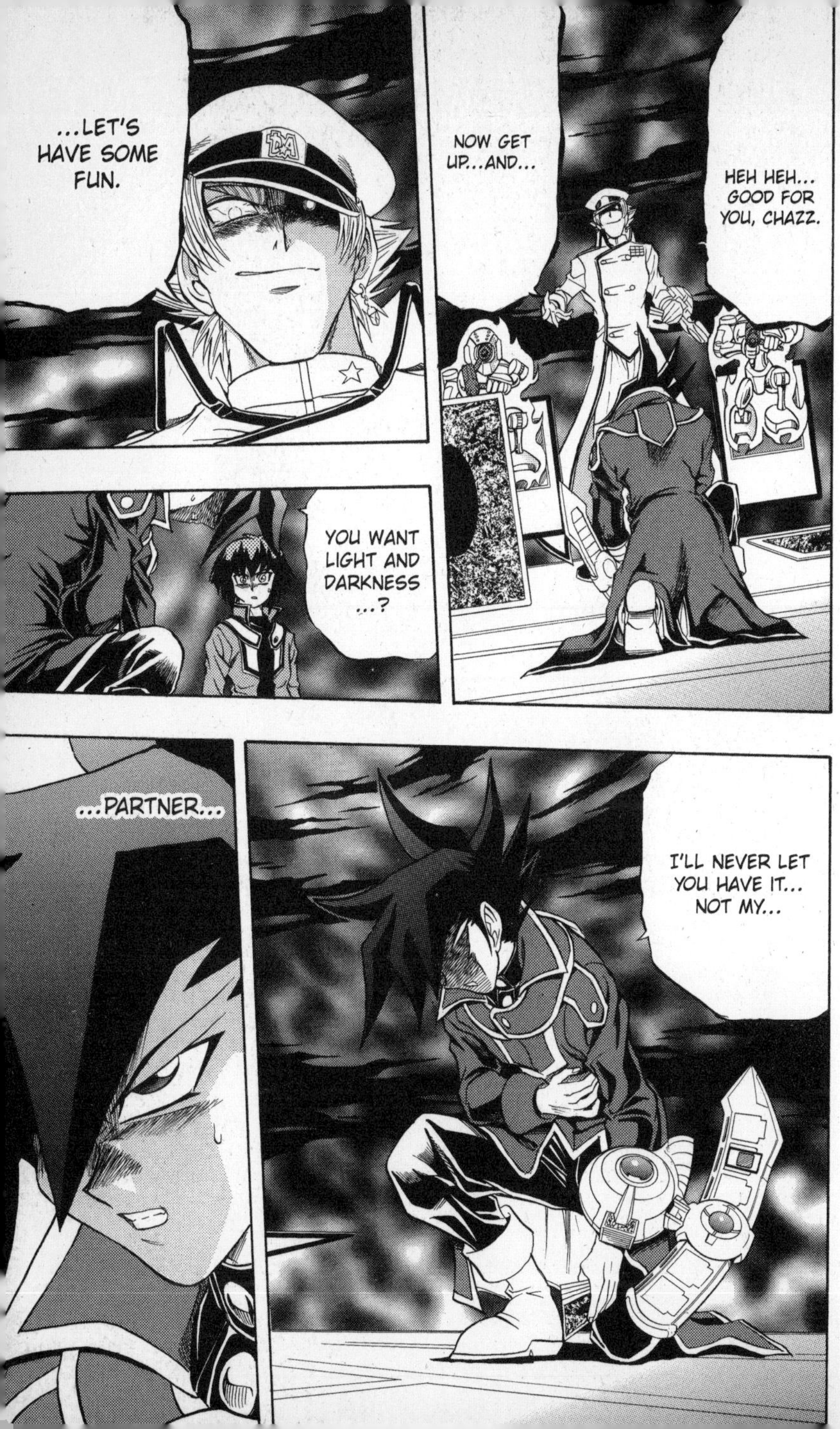
HEH HEH... GOOD FOR YOU, CHAZZ.
NOW GET UP...AND...
...LET'S HAVE SOME FUN.
YOU WANT LIGHT AND DARKNESS ...?
I'LL NEVER LET YOU HAVE IT... NOT MY...
...PARTNER...

FROM ISHIGAKI ISLAND, 2008 PART 2

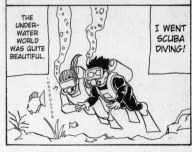

I WENT SCUBA DIVING!
THE UNDERWATER WORLD WAS QUITE BEAUTIFUL.
INSTRUCTOR
AFTER MY SCUBA DIVING EXPERIENCE, I DID MORE UNDERSEA OBSERVATION WITH A SNORKEL AND MASK.
FSHOO
BESIDES THOSE OF US WHO EXPERIENCED SCUBA DIVING FOR THE FIRST TIME...
TAKAHASHI-SAN, AKIRA AND THE DIRECTOR OF *YU-GI-OH 5D'S*, ONO-SAN...
...THE THREE WITH DIVING LICENSES...
...ENJOYED UNDERSEA STROLLING FOR NEARLY HALF AN HOUR.
HMMM. I WANT TO GET A LICENSE TOO...

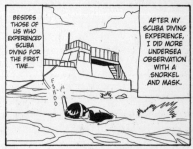

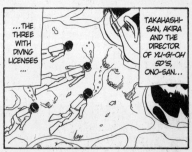

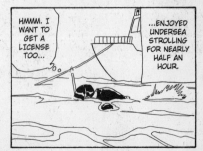

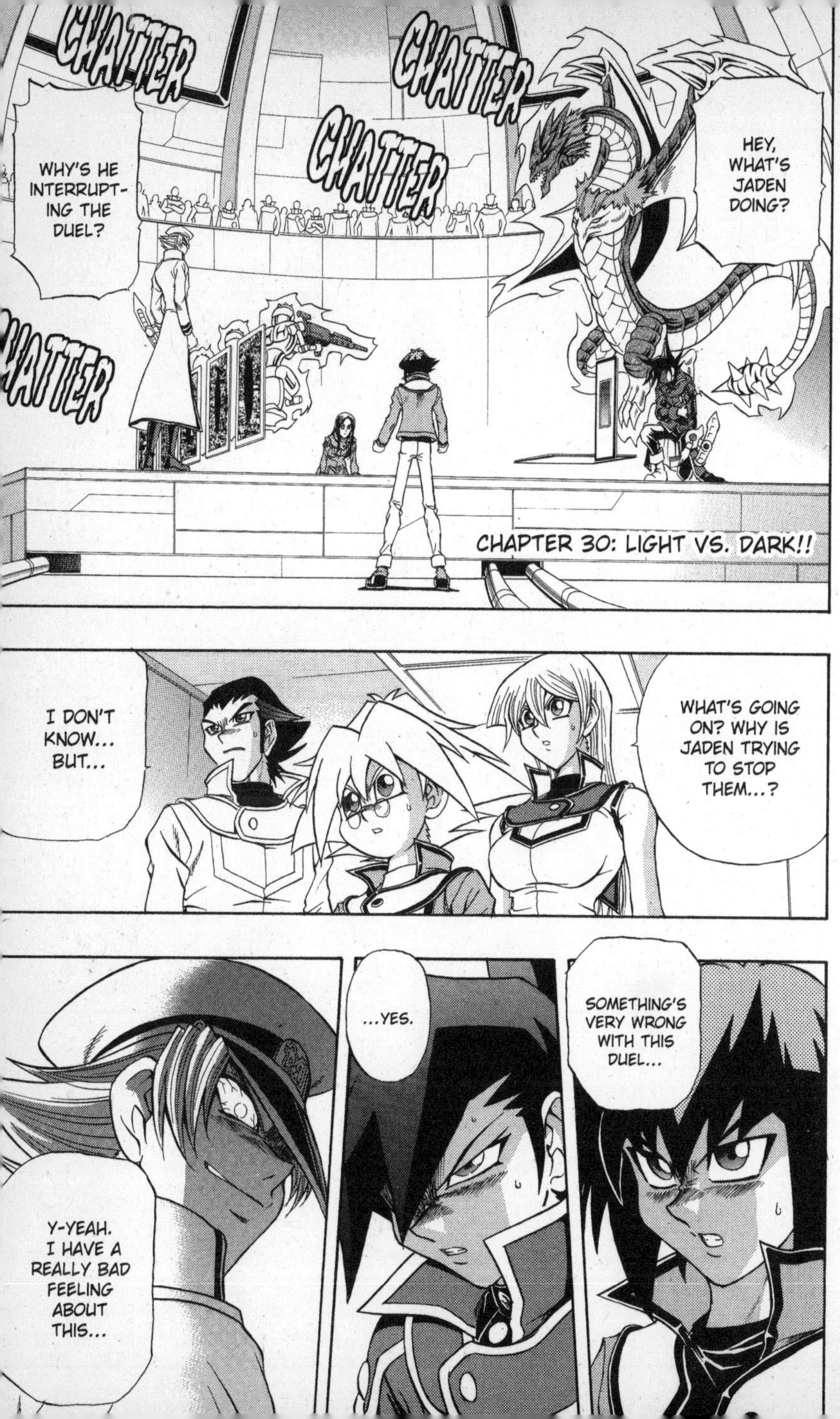
CHATTER
HEY, WHAT'S JADEN DOING?
CHATTER
CHATTER
WHY'S HE INTERRUPTING THE DUEL?
CHATTER
CHAPTER 30: LIGHT VS. DARK!!
WHAT'S GOING ON? WHY IS JADEN TRYING TO STOP THEM...?
I DON'T KNOW... BUT...
SOMETHING'S VERY WRONG WITH THIS DUEL...
...YES.
Y-YEAH. I HAVE A REALLY BAD FEELING ABOUT THIS...

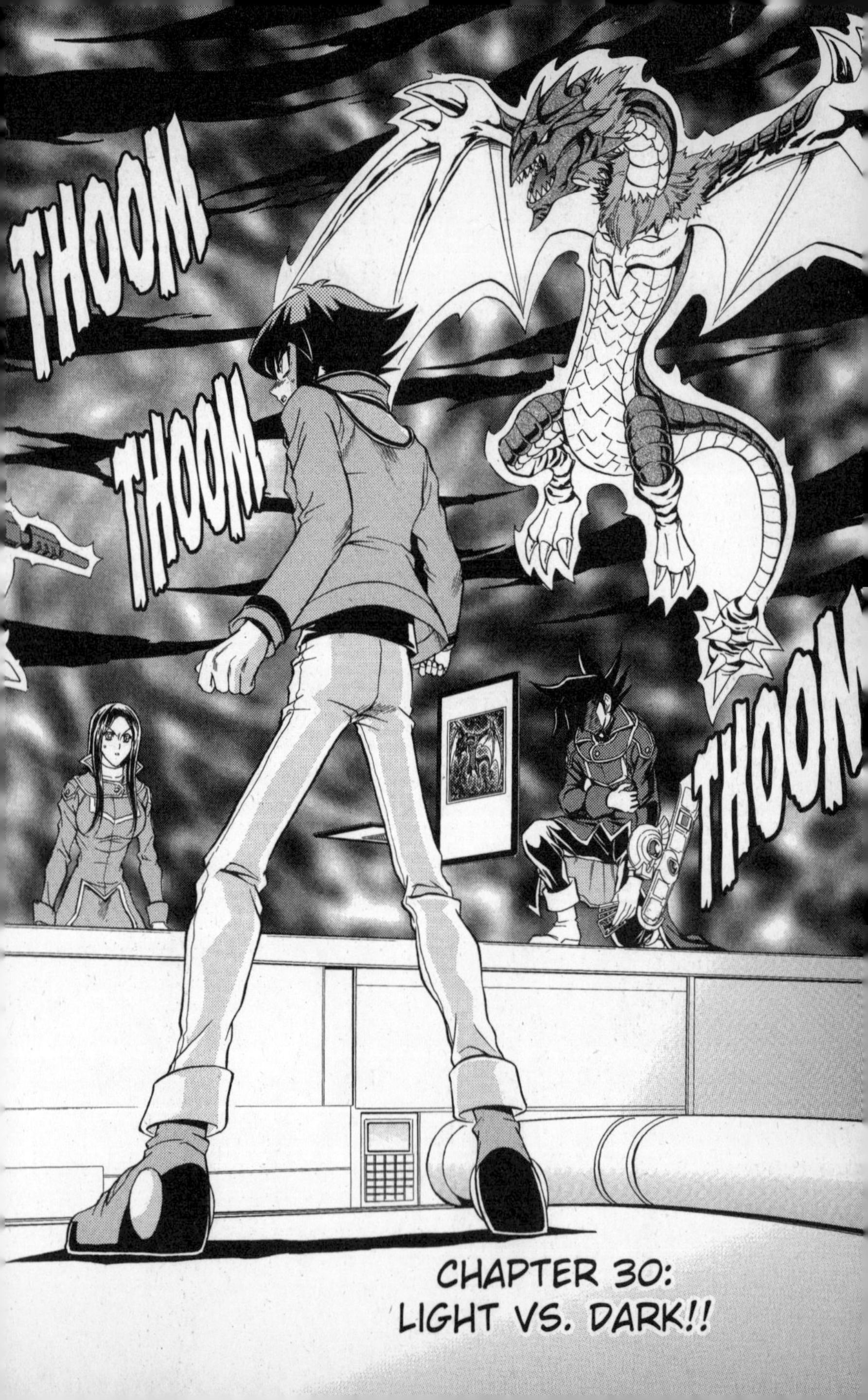
THOOM
THOOM
THOOM

CHAPTER 30: LIGHT VS. DARK!!

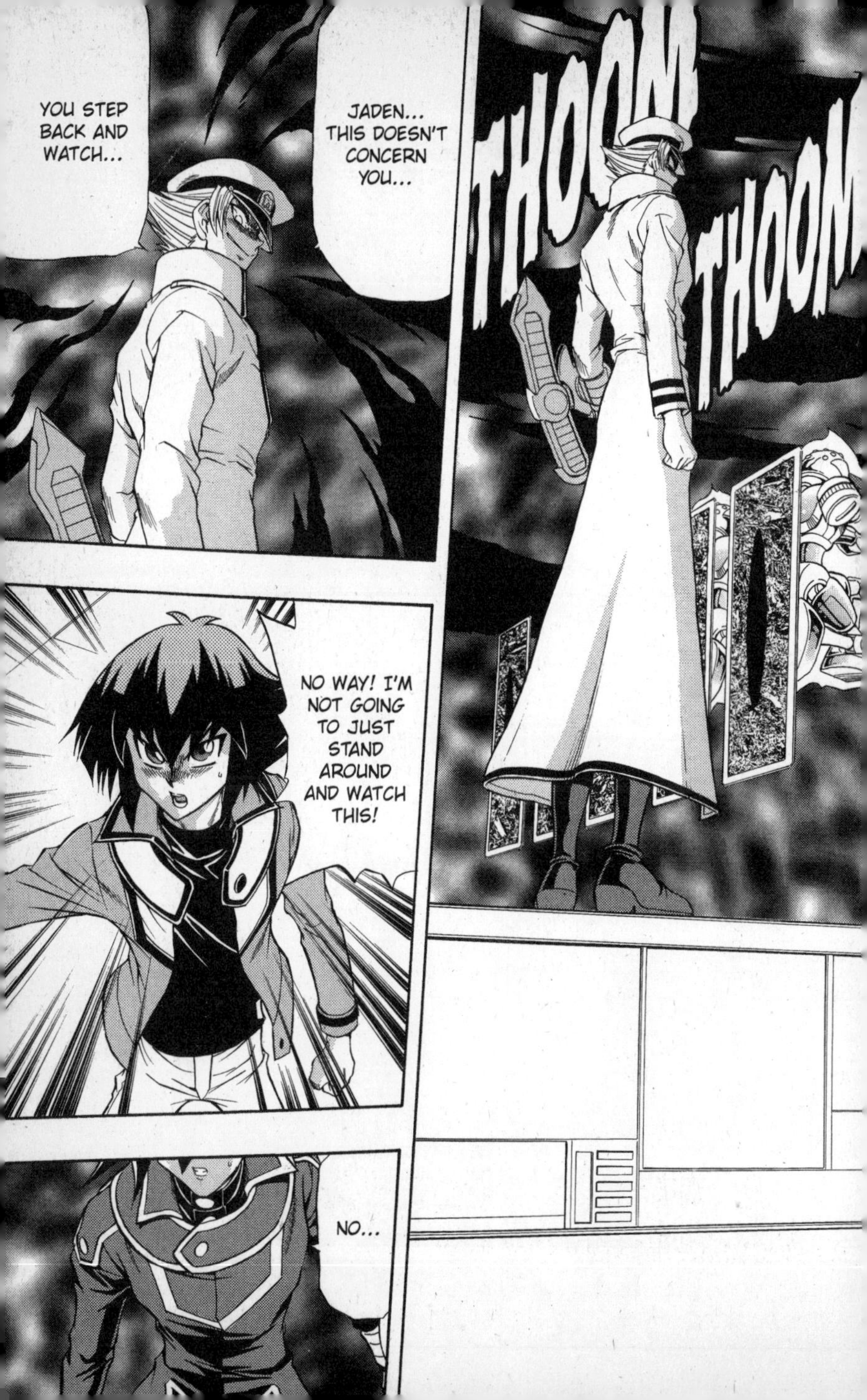
THOOM
THOOM
JADEN... THIS DOESN'T CONCERN YOU...
YOU STEP BACK AND WATCH...
NO WAY! I'M NOT GOING TO JUST STAND AROUND AND WATCH THIS!
NO...

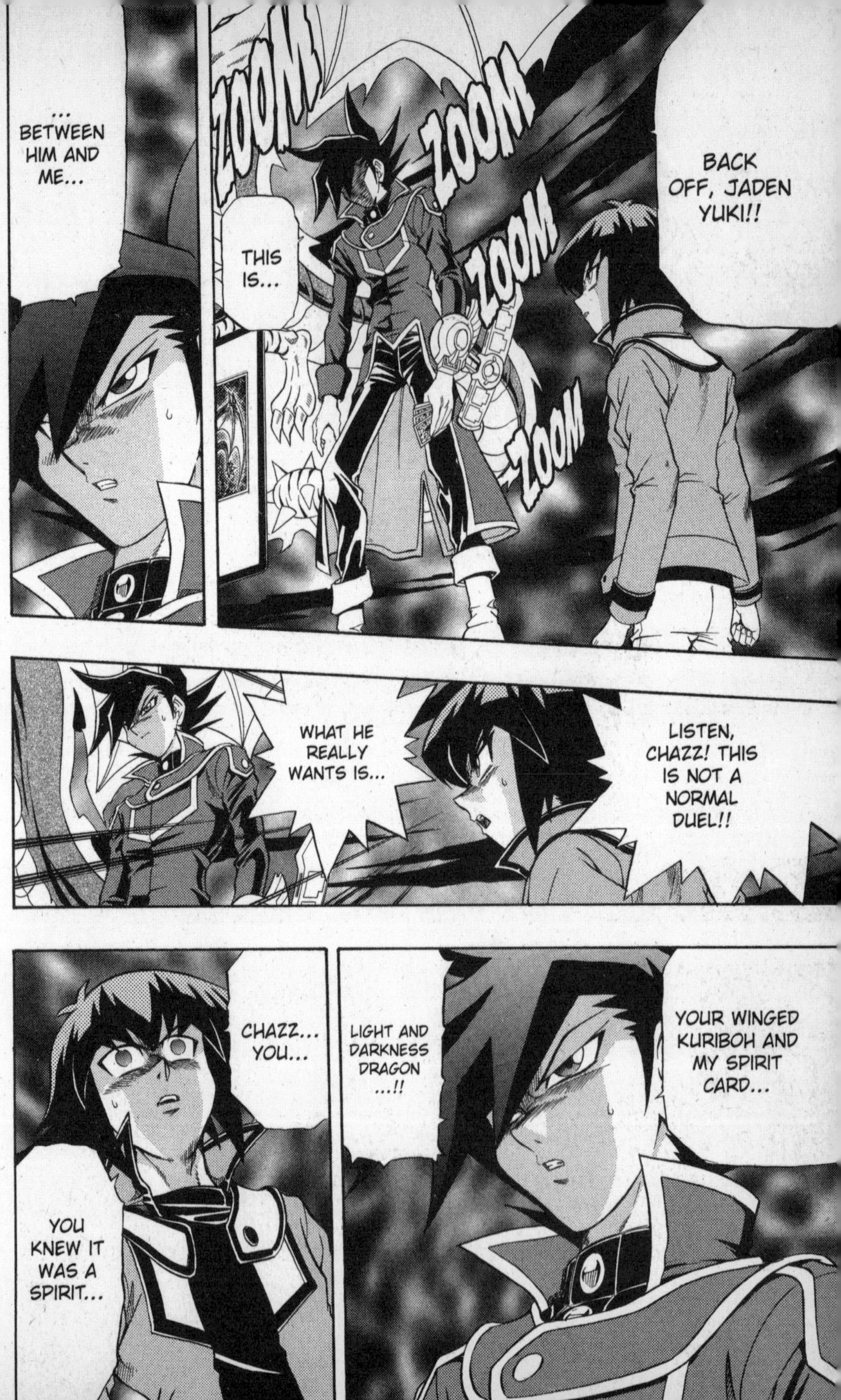
BACK OFF, JADEN YUKI!!
ZOOM
ZOOM
ZOOM
ZOOM
ZOOM
THIS IS...
... BETWEEN HIM AND ME...
LISTEN, CHAZZ! THIS IS NOT A NORMAL DUEL!!
WHAT HE REALLY WANTS IS...
YOUR WINGED KURIBOH AND MY SPIRIT CARD...
LIGHT AND DARKNESS DRAGON ...!!
CHAZZ... YOU...
YOU KNEW IT WAS A SPIRIT...

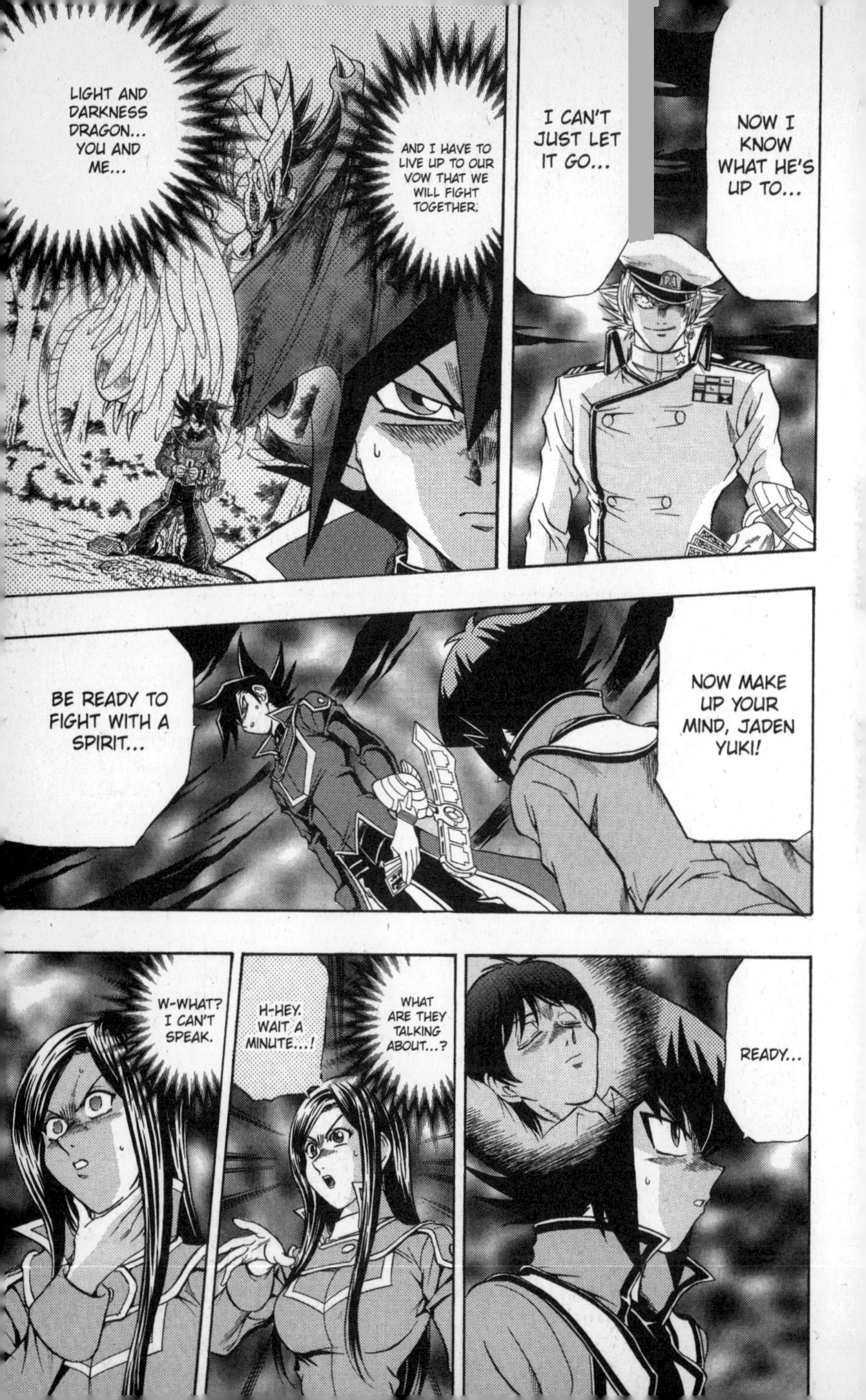

NOW I KNOW WHAT HE'S UP TO...
I CAN'T JUST LET IT GO...
LIGHT AND DARKNESS DRAGON... YOU AND ME...
AND I HAVE TO LIVE UP TO OUR VOW THAT WE WILL FIGHT TOGETHER.
NOW MAKE UP YOUR MIND, JADEN YUKI!
BE READY TO FIGHT WITH A SPIRIT...
READY...
WHAT ARE THEY TALKING ABOUT...?
H-HEY. WAIT A MINUTE...!
W-WHAT? I CAN'T SPEAK.

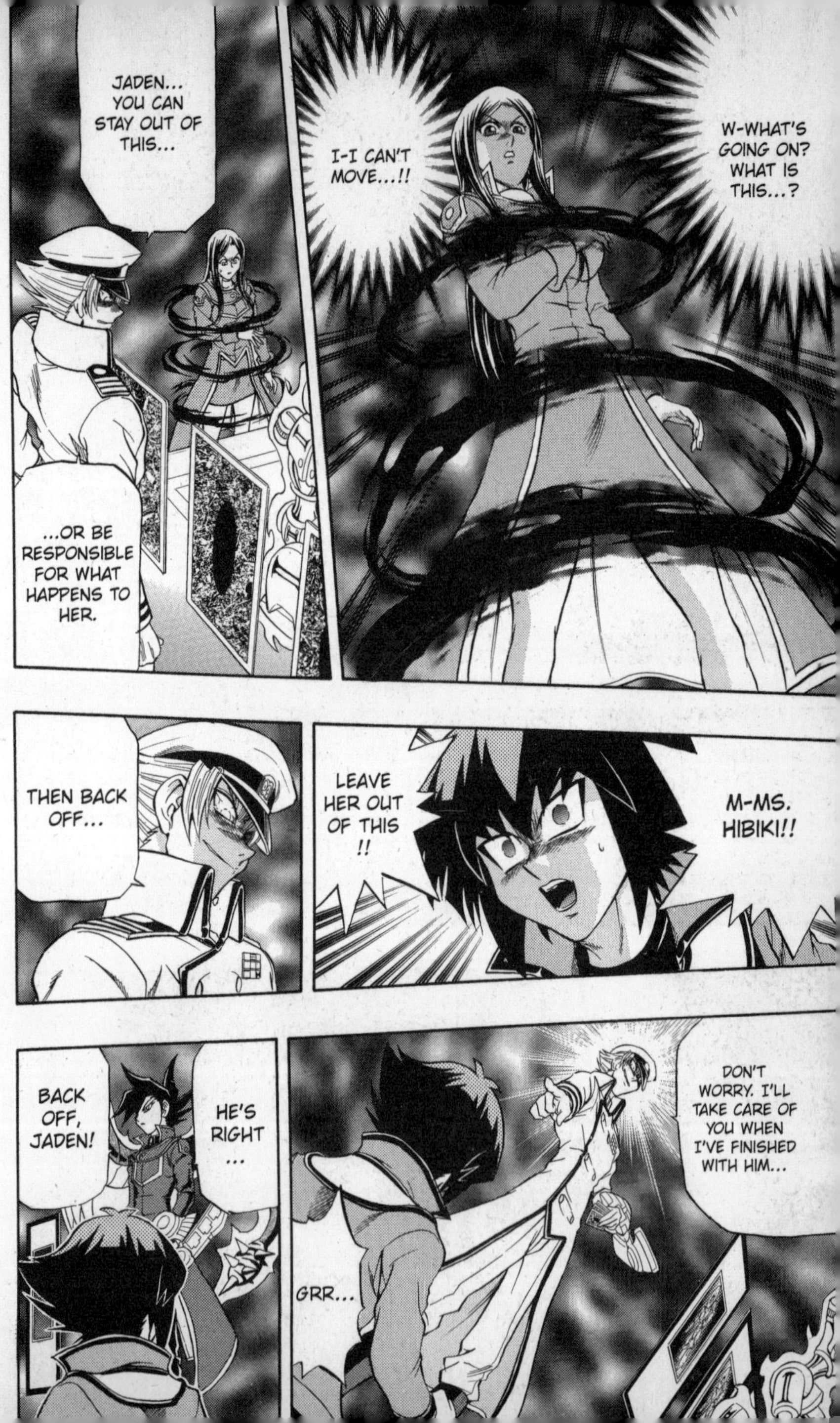
W-WHAT'S GOING ON? WHAT IS THIS...?
I-I CAN'T MOVE...!!
JADEN... YOU CAN STAY OUT OF THIS...
...OR BE RESPONSIBLE FOR WHAT HAPPENS TO HER.
M-MS. HIBIKI!!
LEAVE HER OUT OF THIS !!
THEN BACK OFF...
DON'T WORRY. I'LL TAKE CARE OF YOU WHEN I'VE FINISHED WITH HIM...
GRR...
HE'S RIGHT ...
BACK OFF, JADEN!

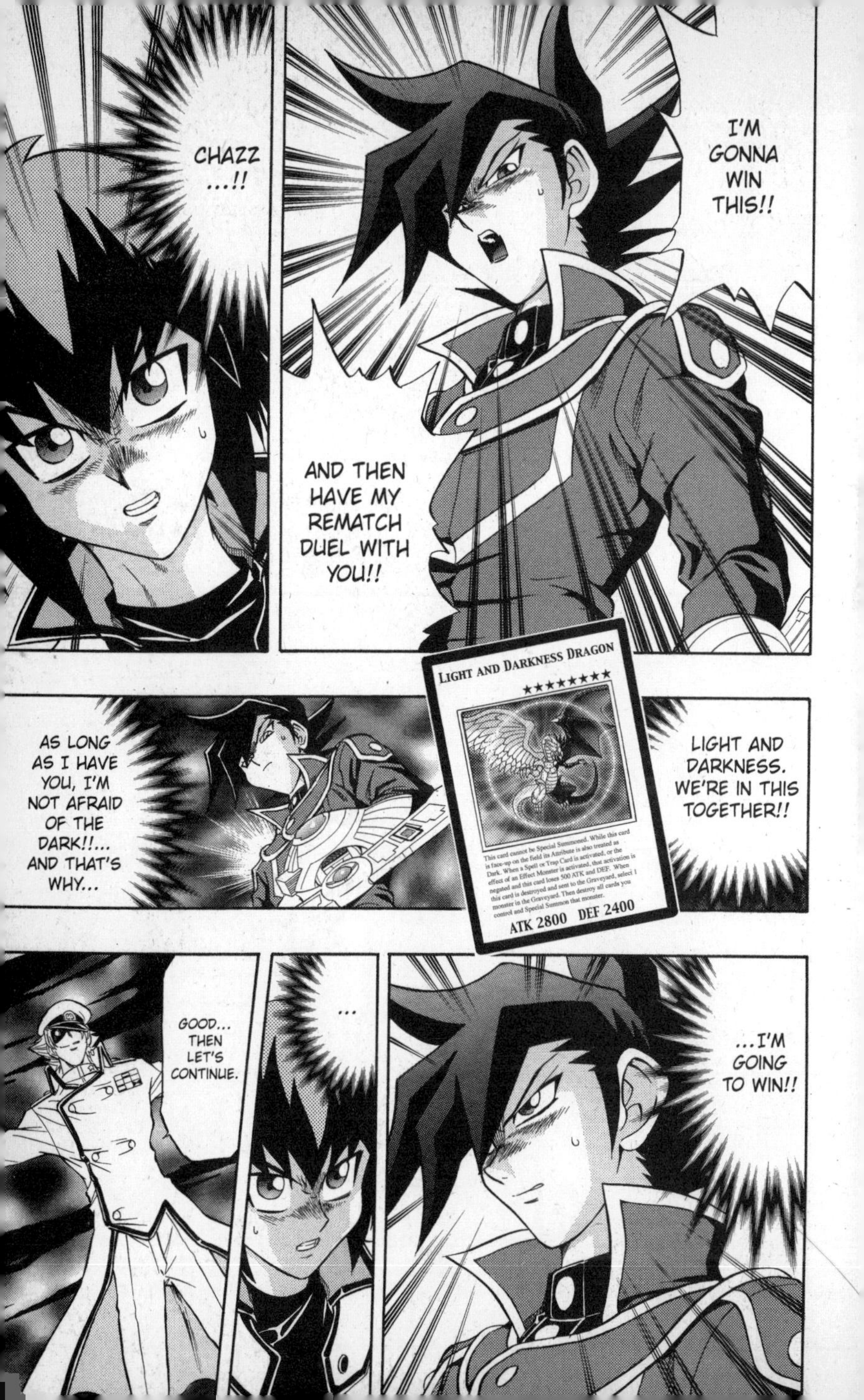
I'M GONNA WIN THIS!!
AND THEN HAVE MY REMATCH DUEL WITH YOU!!
CHAZZ ...!!
LIGHT AND DARKNESS. WE'RE IN THIS TOGETHER!!
LIGHT AND DARKNESS DRAGON
This card cannot be Special Summoned. While this card is face-up on the field its Attribute is also treated as Dark. When a Spell or Trap Card is activated, or the effect of an Effect Monster is activated, that activation is negated and this card loses 500 ATK and DEF. When this card is destroyed and sent to the Graveyard, select 1 monster in the Graveyard. Then destroy all cards you control and Special Summon that monster.
ATK 2800 DEF 2400
AS LONG AS I HAVE YOU, I'M NOT AFRAID OF THE DARK!!... AND THAT'S WHY...
...I'M GOING TO WIN!!
...
GOOD... THEN LET'S CONTINUE.

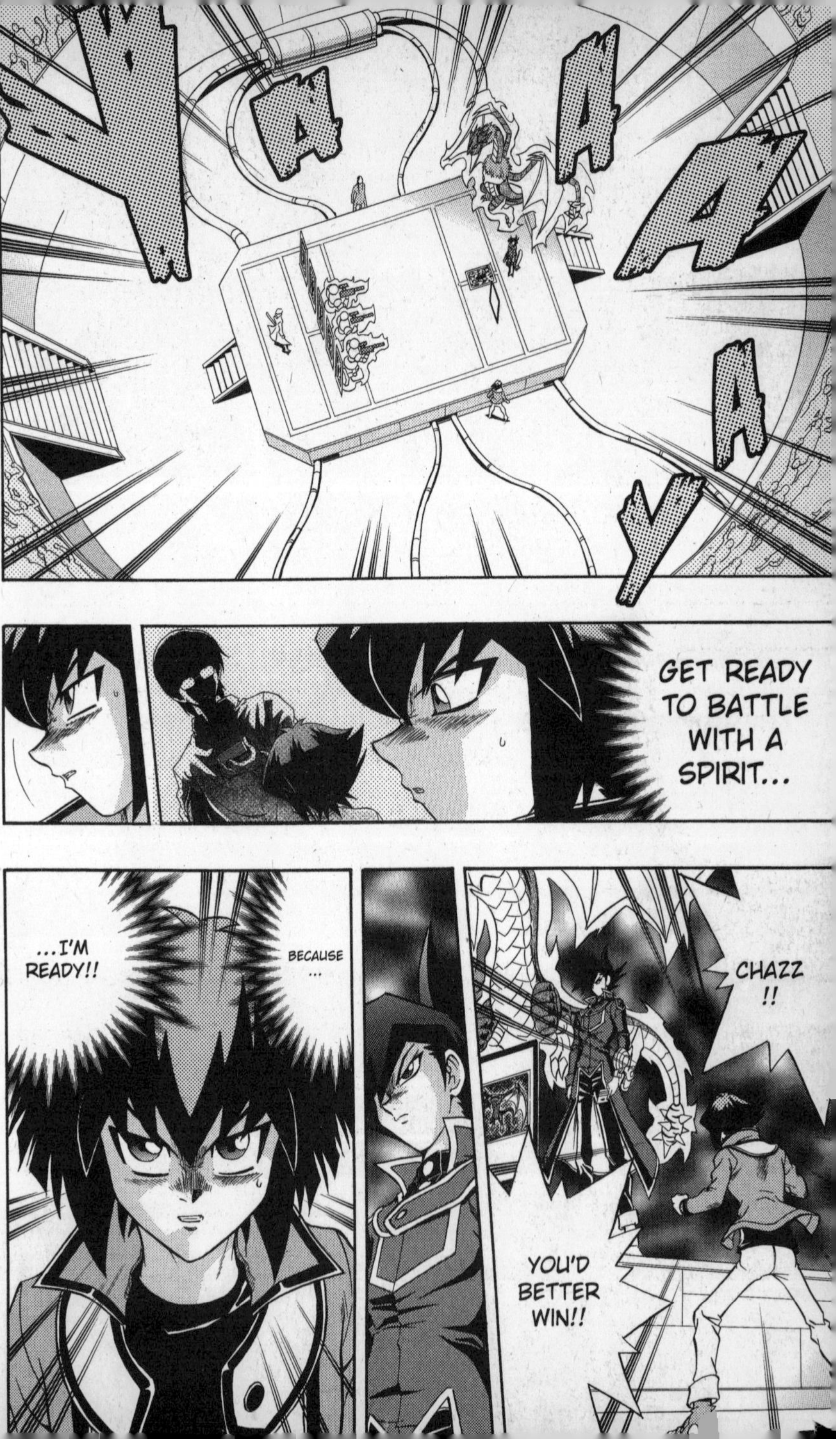
WAAAAY
GET READY TO BATTLE WITH A SPIRIT...
CHAZZ !!
YOU'D BETTER WIN!!
BECAUSE ...
...I'M READY!!

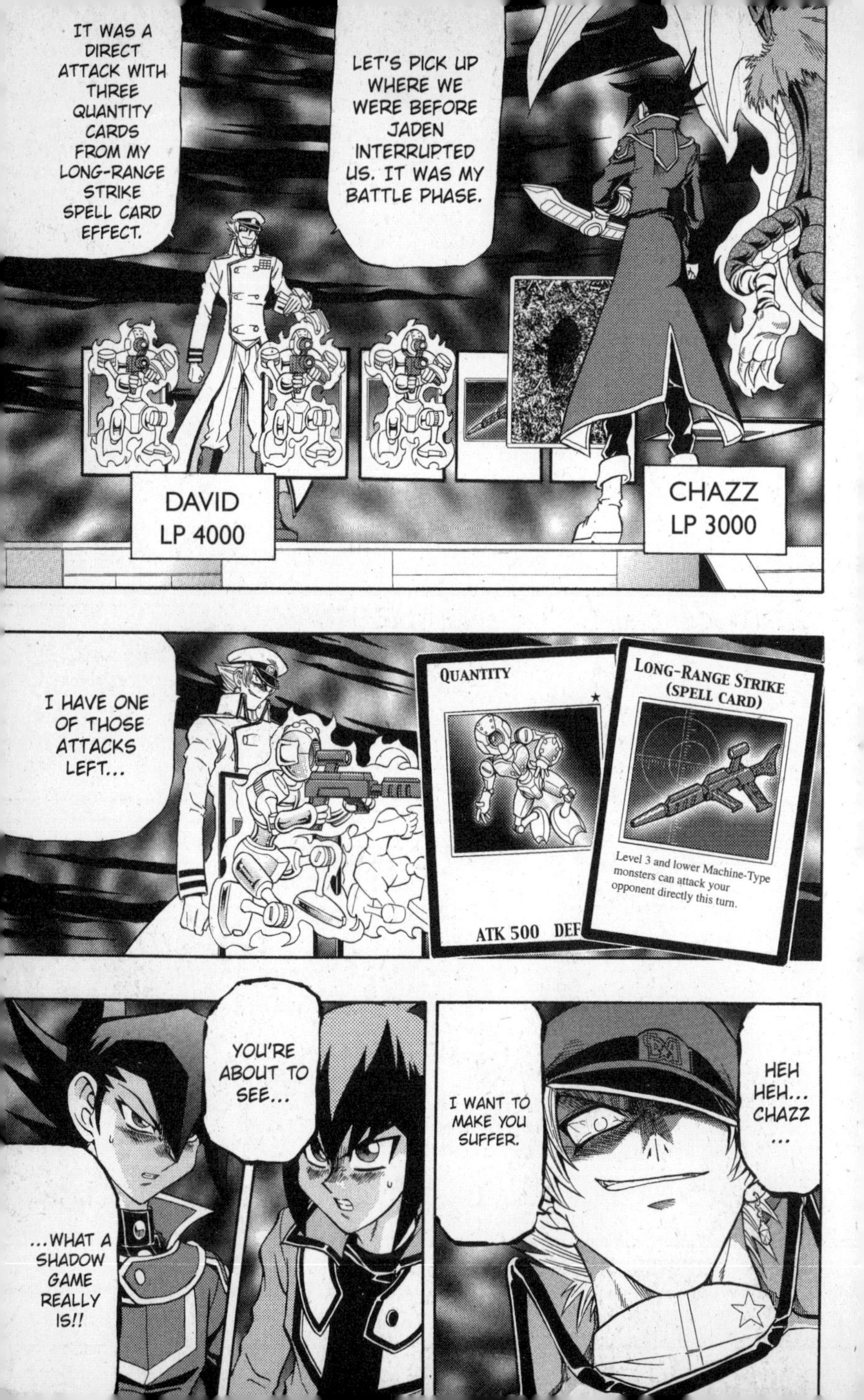
LET'S PICK UP WHERE WE WERE BEFORE JADEN INTERRUPTED US. IT WAS MY BATTLE PHASE.
IT WAS A DIRECT ATTACK WITH THREE QUANTITY CARDS FROM MY LONG-RANGE STRIKE SPELL CARD EFFECT.
CHAZZ
LP 3000
DAVID
LP 4000
LONG-RANGE STRIKE (SPELL CARD)
Level 3 and lower Machine-Type monsters can attack your opponent directly this turn.
QUANTITY
ATK 500 DEF
I HAVE ONE OF THOSE ATTACKS LEFT...
HEH HEH... CHAZZ...
I WANT TO MAKE YOU SUFFER.
YOU'RE ABOUT TO SEE...
...WHAT A SHADOW GAME REALLY IS!!

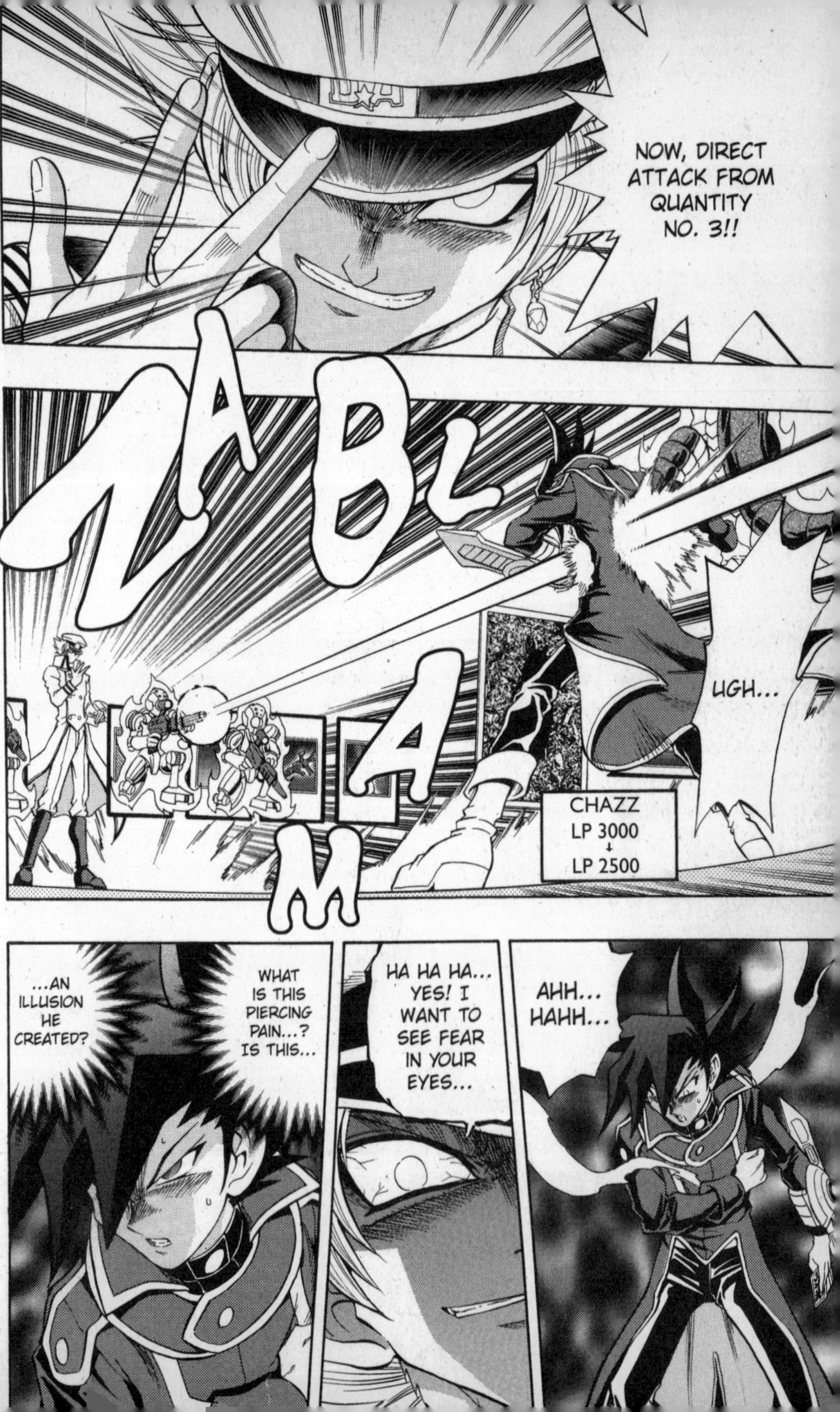
NOW, DIRECT ATTACK FROM QUANTITY NO. 3!!
ZABLAAM
UGH...
CHAZZ LP 3000 ↓ LP 2500
AHH... HAHH...
HA HA HA... YES! I WANT TO SEE FEAR IN YOUR EYES...
WHAT IS THIS PIERCING PAIN...? IS THIS...
...AN ILLUSION HE CREATED?

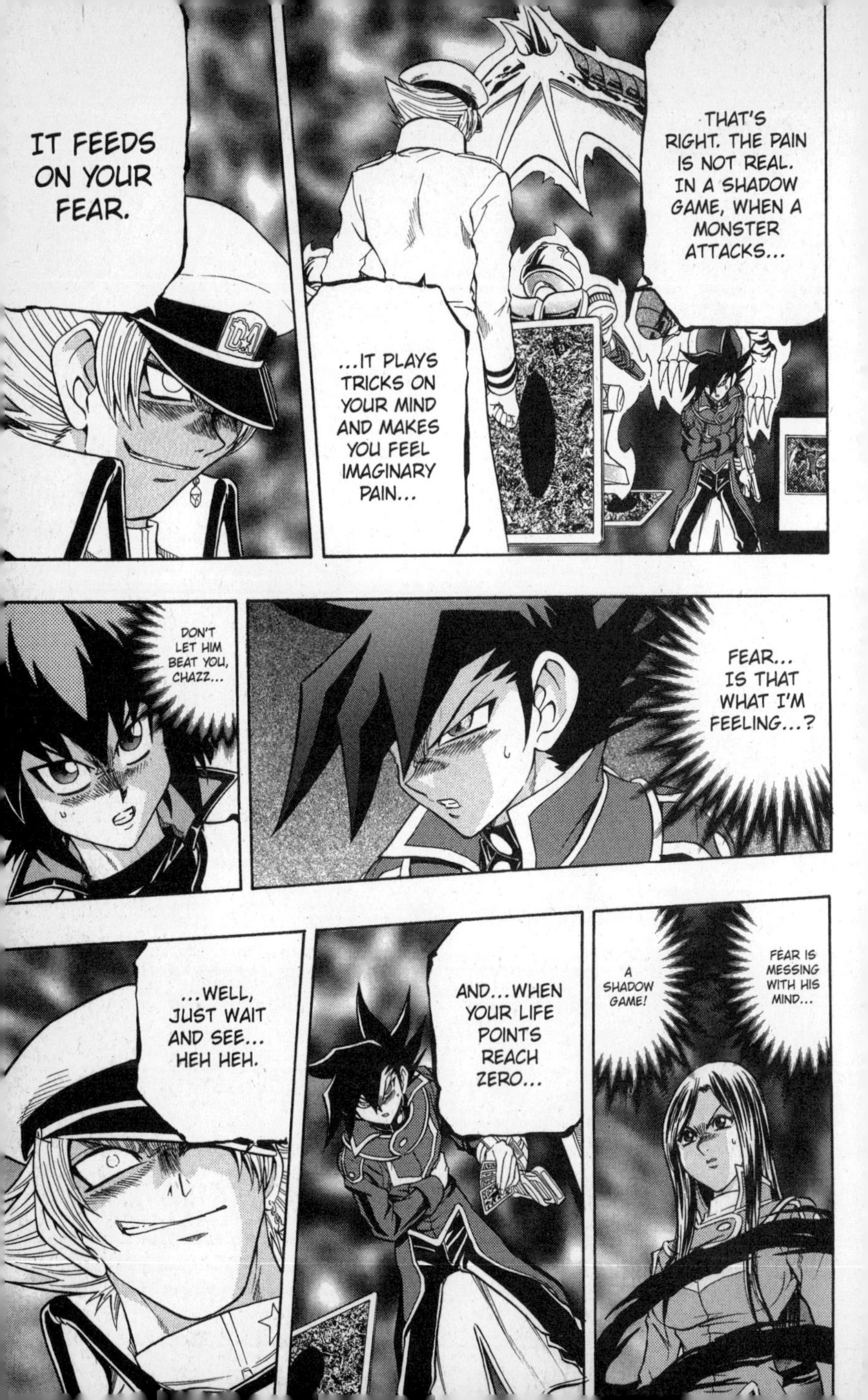
THAT'S RIGHT. THE PAIN IS NOT REAL. IN A SHADOW GAME, WHEN A MONSTER ATTACKS...
...IT PLAYS TRICKS ON YOUR MIND AND MAKES YOU FEEL IMAGINARY PAIN...
IT FEEDS ON YOUR FEAR.
FEAR... IS THAT WHAT I'M FEELING...?
DON'T LET HIM BEAT YOU, CHAZZ...
FEAR IS MESSING WITH HIS MIND...
A SHADOW GAME!
AND...WHEN YOUR LIFE POINTS REACH ZERO...
...WELL, JUST WAIT AND SEE... HEH HEH.

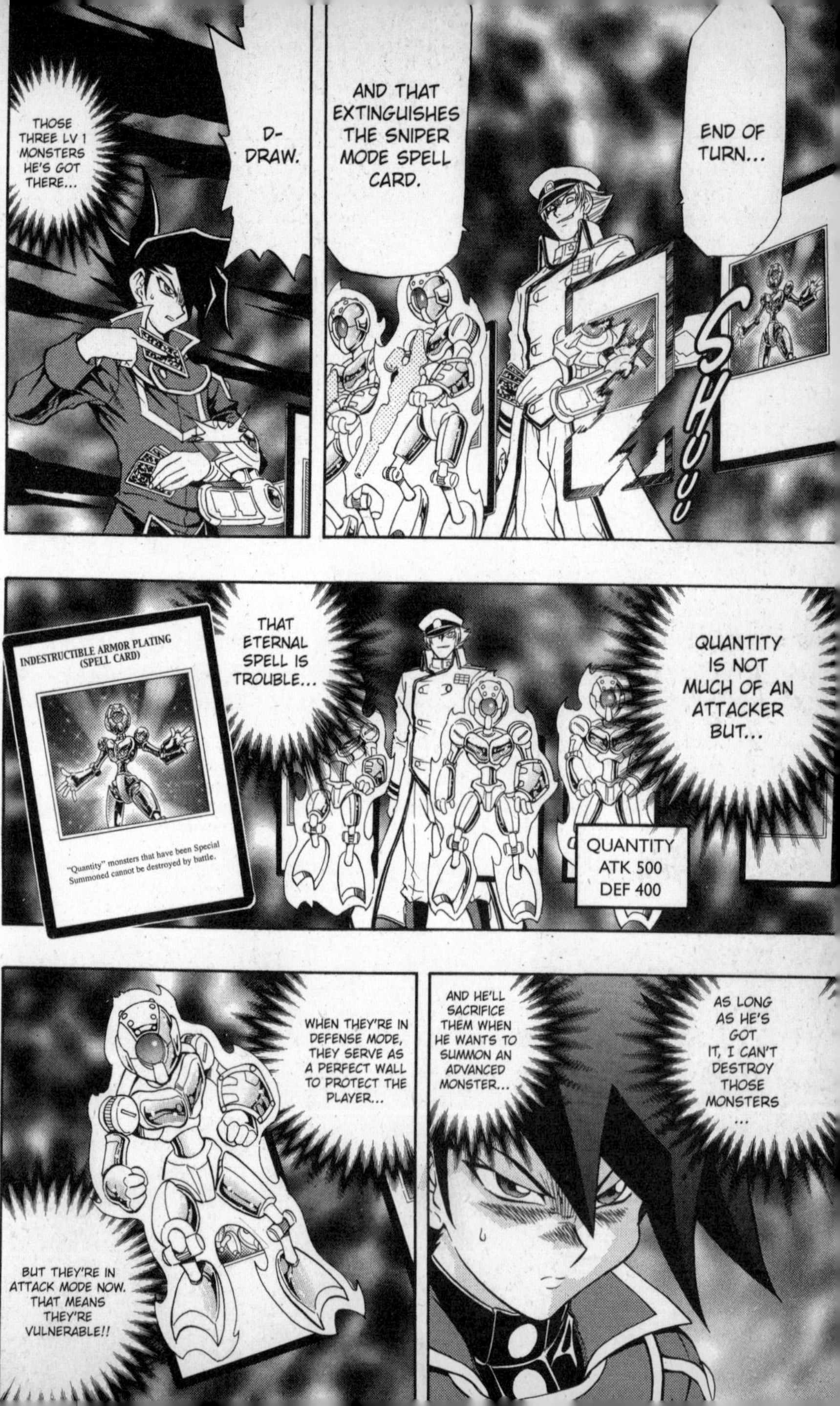
AND THAT EXTINGUISHES THE SNIPER MODE SPELL CARD.
END OF TURN...
SHUUU
D-DRAW.
THOSE THREE LV 1 MONSTERS HE'S GOT THERE...
QUANTITY IS NOT MUCH OF AN ATTACKER BUT...
QUANTITY
ATK 500
DEF 400
THAT ETERNAL SPELL IS TROUBLE...
INDESTRUCTIBLE ARMOR PLATING (SPELL CARD)
"Quantity" monsters that have been Special Summoned cannot be destroyed by battle.
AS LONG AS HE'S GOT IT, I CAN'T DESTROY THOSE MONSTERS...
AND HE'LL SACRIFICE THEM WHEN HE WANTS TO SUMMON AN ADVANCED MONSTER...
WHEN THEY'RE IN DEFENSE MODE, THEY SERVE AS A PERFECT WALL TO PROTECT THE PLAYER...
BUT THEY'RE IN ATTACK MODE NOW. THAT MEANS THEY'RE VULNERABLE!!

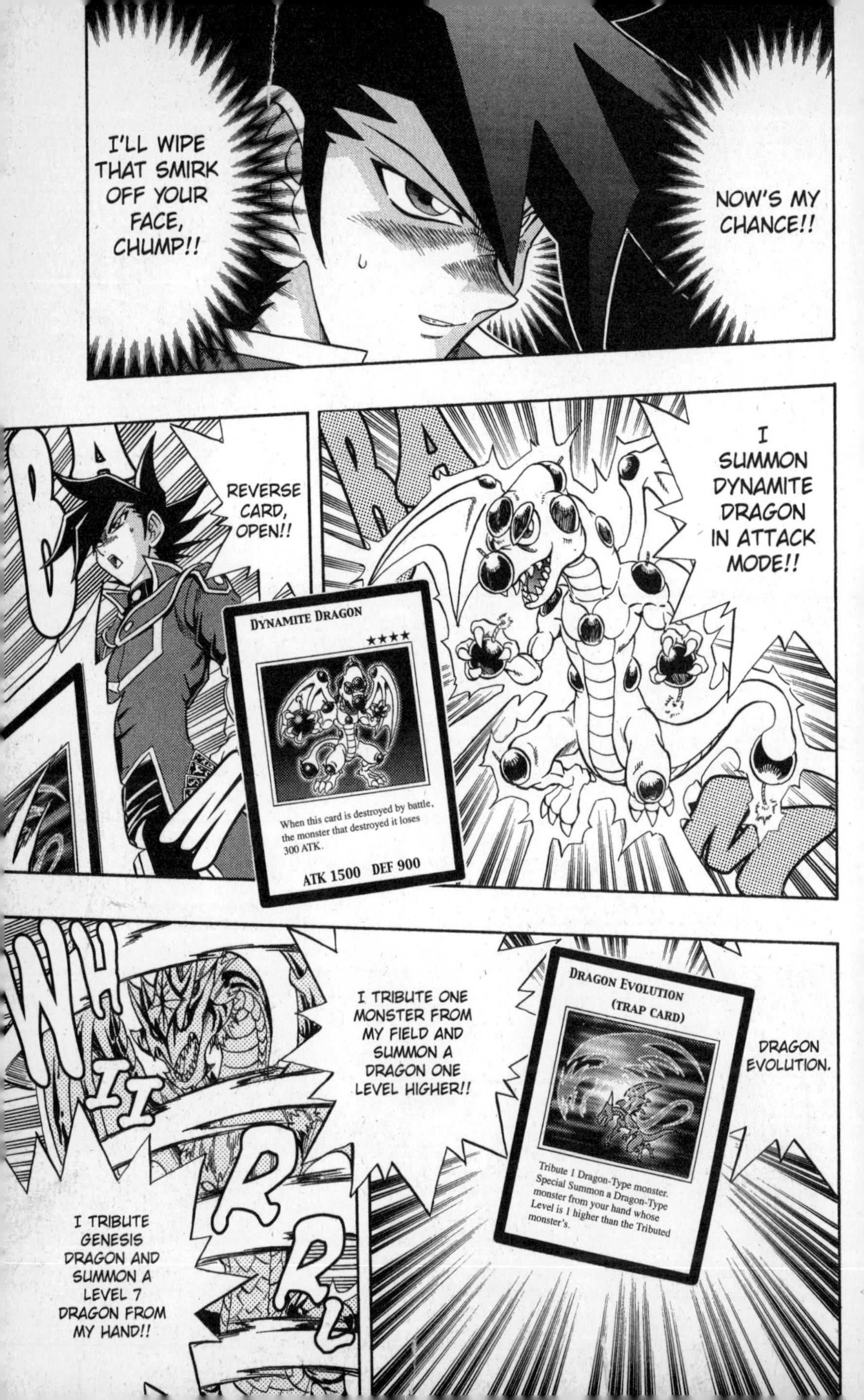
NOW'S MY CHANCE!!
I'LL WIPE THAT SMIRK OFF YOUR FACE, CHUMP!!
I SUMMON DYNAMITE DRAGON IN ATTACK MODE!!
DYNAMITE DRAGON
★★★★
When this card is destroyed by battle, the monster that destroyed it loses 300 ATK.
ATK 1500 DEF 900
REVERSE CARD, OPEN!!
DRAGON EVOLUTION.
DRAGON EVOLUTION
(TRAP CARD)
Tribute 1 Dragon-Type monster. Special Summon a Dragon-Type monster from your hand whose Level is 1 higher than the Tributed monster's.
I TRIBUTE ONE MONSTER FROM MY FIELD AND SUMMON A DRAGON ONE LEVEL HIGHER!!
I TRIBUTE GENESIS DRAGON AND SUMMON A LEVEL 7 DRAGON FROM MY HAND!!

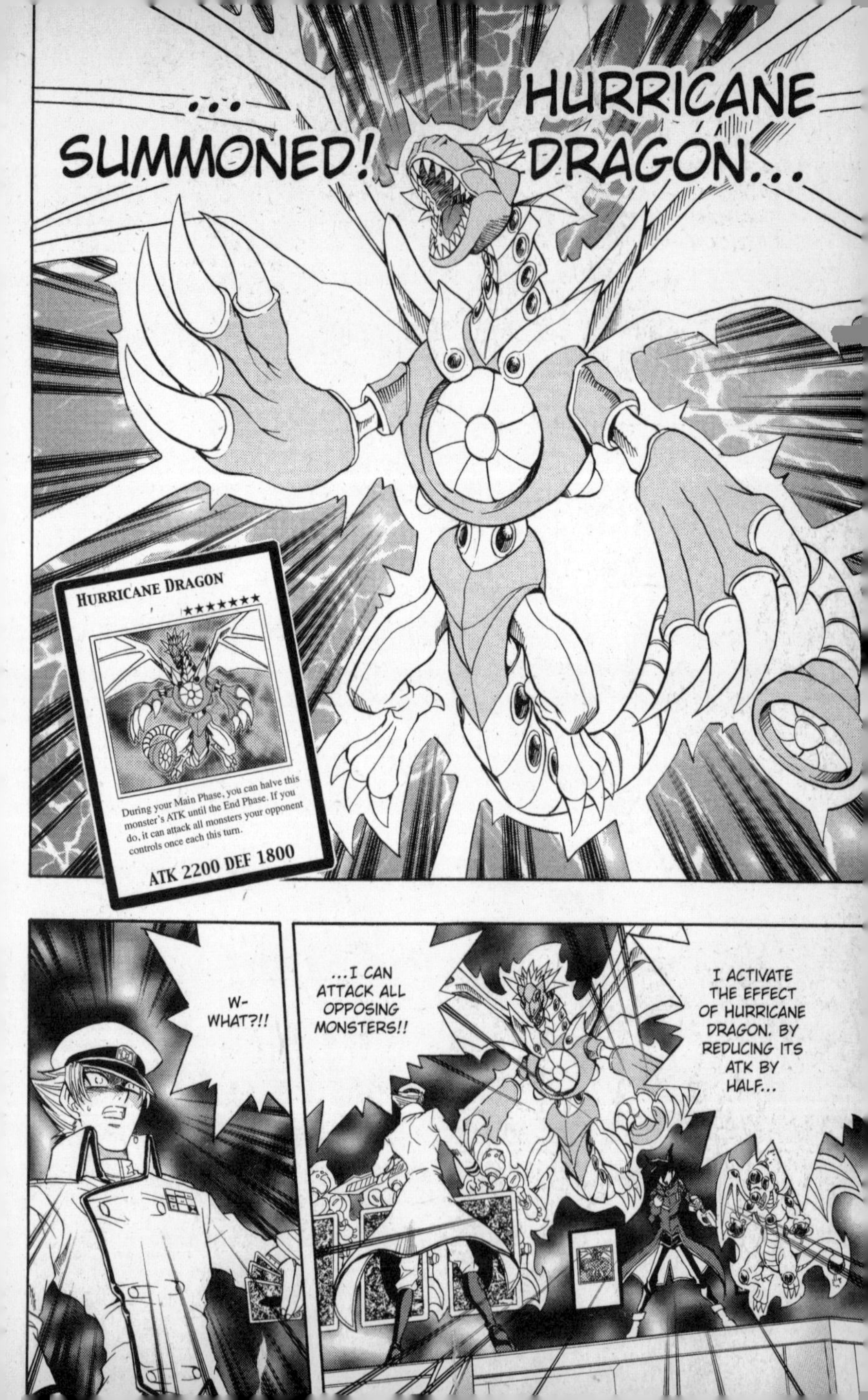
HURRICANE DRAGON...
...SUMMONED!
HURRICANE DRAGON
During your Main Phase, you can halve this monster's ATK until the End Phase. If you do, it can attack all monsters your opponent controls once each this turn.
ATK 2200 DEF 1800
I ACTIVATE THE EFFECT OF HURRICANE DRAGON. BY REDUCING ITS ATK BY HALF...
...I CAN ATTACK ALL OPPOSING MONSTERS!!
W-WHAT?!!

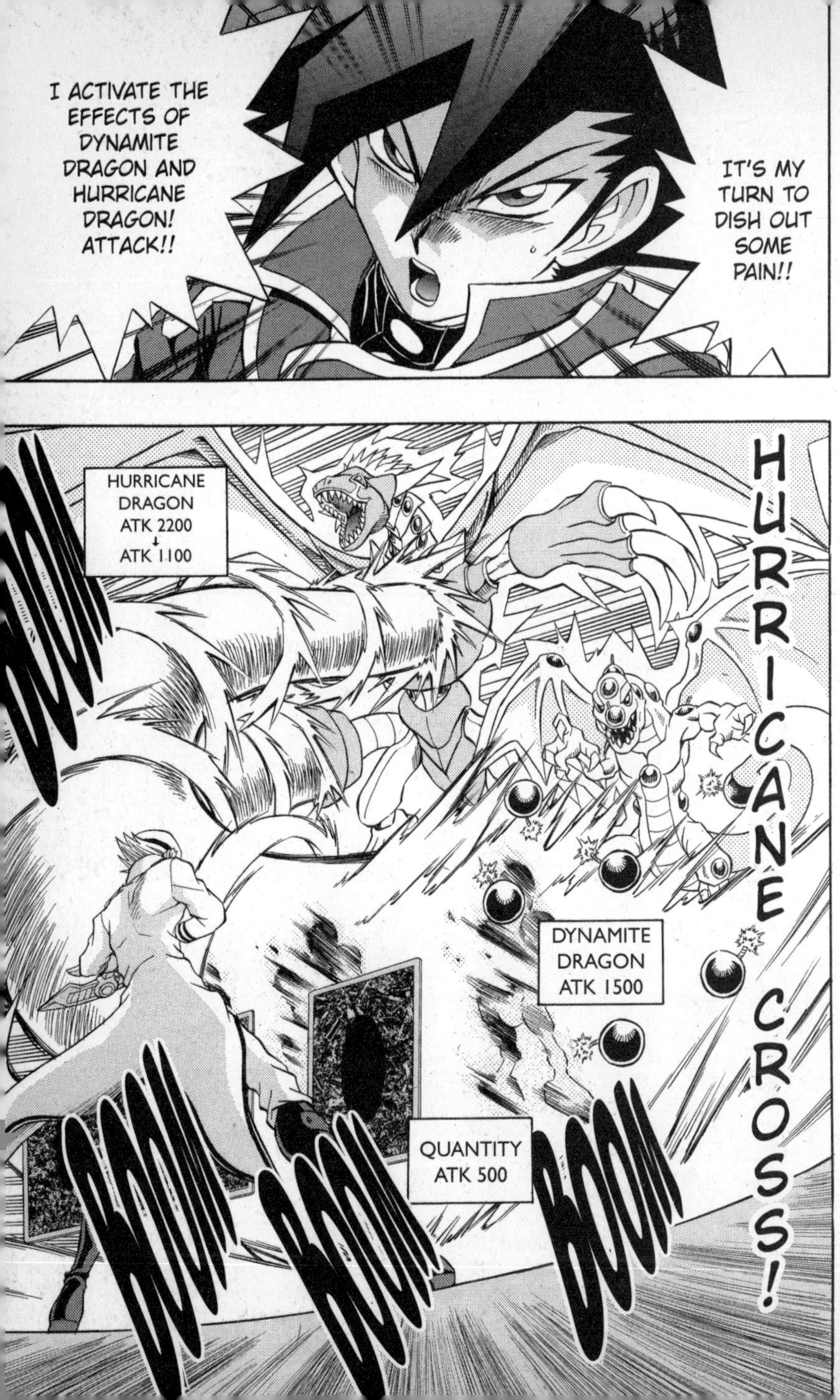
IT'S MY TURN TO DISH OUT SOME PAIN!!
I ACTIVATE THE EFFECTS OF DYNAMITE DRAGON AND HURRICANE DRAGON! ATTACK!!
HURRICANE CROSS!
HURRICANE DRAGON ATK 2200 ↓ ATK 1100
DYNAMITE DRAGON ATK 1500
QUANTITY ATK 500
BOOM
BOOM
BOOM

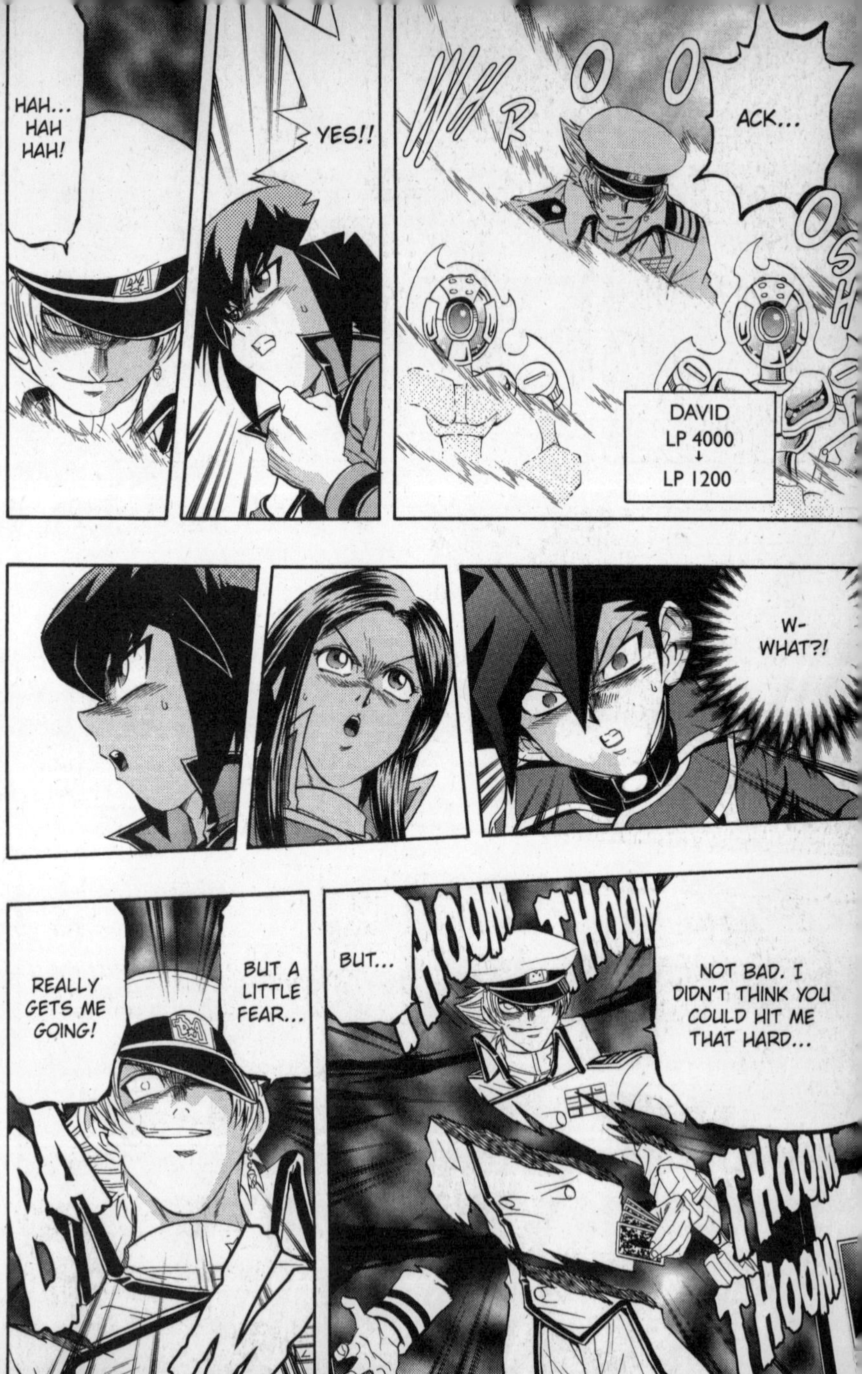
WHROOOOSH
ACK...
DAVID
LP 4000
↓
LP 1200
YES!!
HAH... HAH HAH!
W- WHAT?!
THOOM THOOM
NOT BAD. I DIDN'T THINK YOU COULD HIT ME THAT HARD...
BUT...
THOOM THOOM
BUT A LITTLE FEAR...
REALLY GETS ME GOING!
BAM

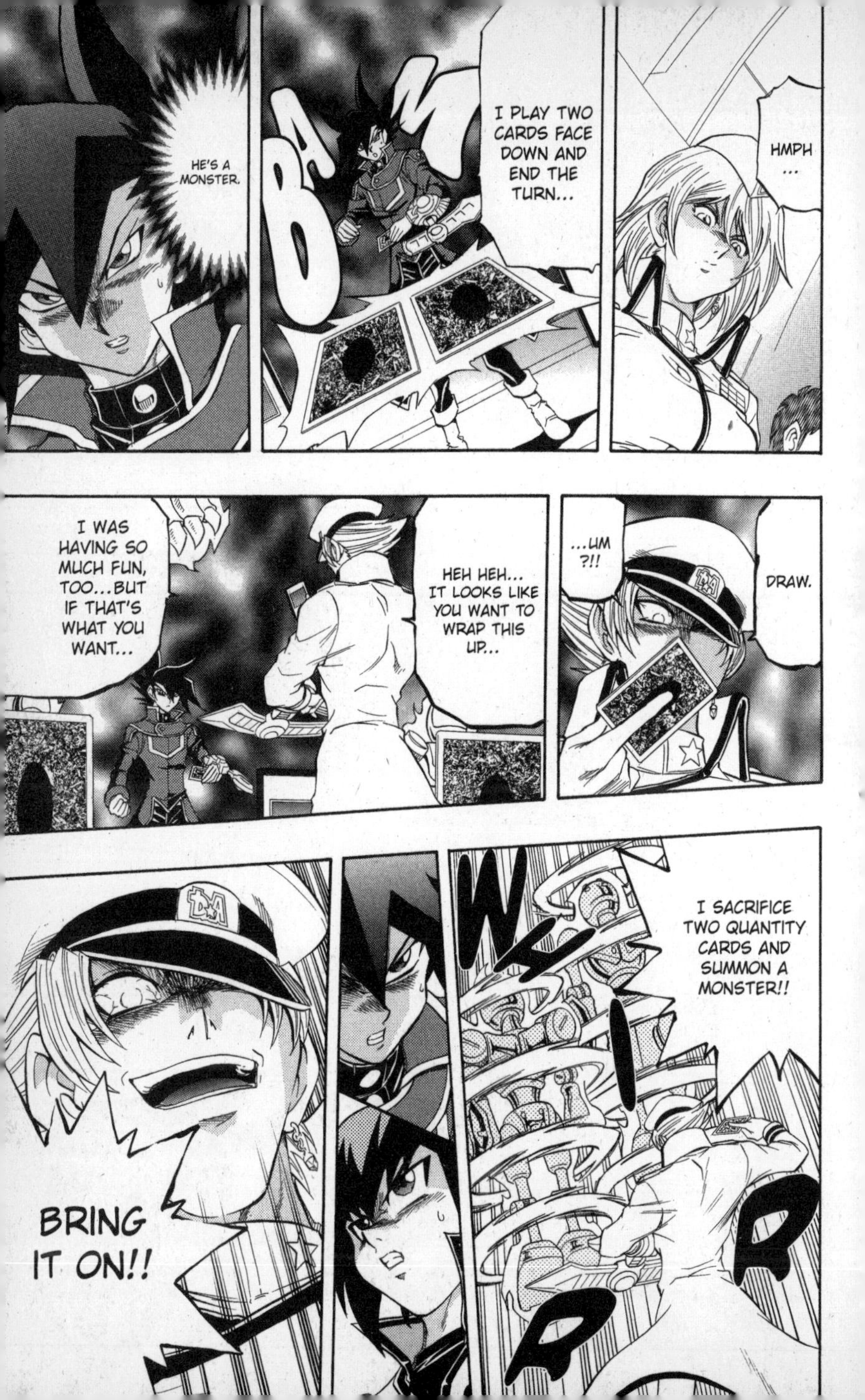
HMPH ...
I PLAY TWO CARDS FACE DOWN AND END THE TURN...
BAM
HE'S A MONSTER.
DRAW.
...UM ?!!
HEH HEH... IT LOOKS LIKE YOU WANT TO WRAP THIS UP...
I WAS HAVING SO MUCH FUN, TOO...BUT IF THAT'S WHAT YOU WANT...
I SACRIFICE TWO QUANTITY CARDS AND SUMMON A MONSTER!!
BRING IT ON!!

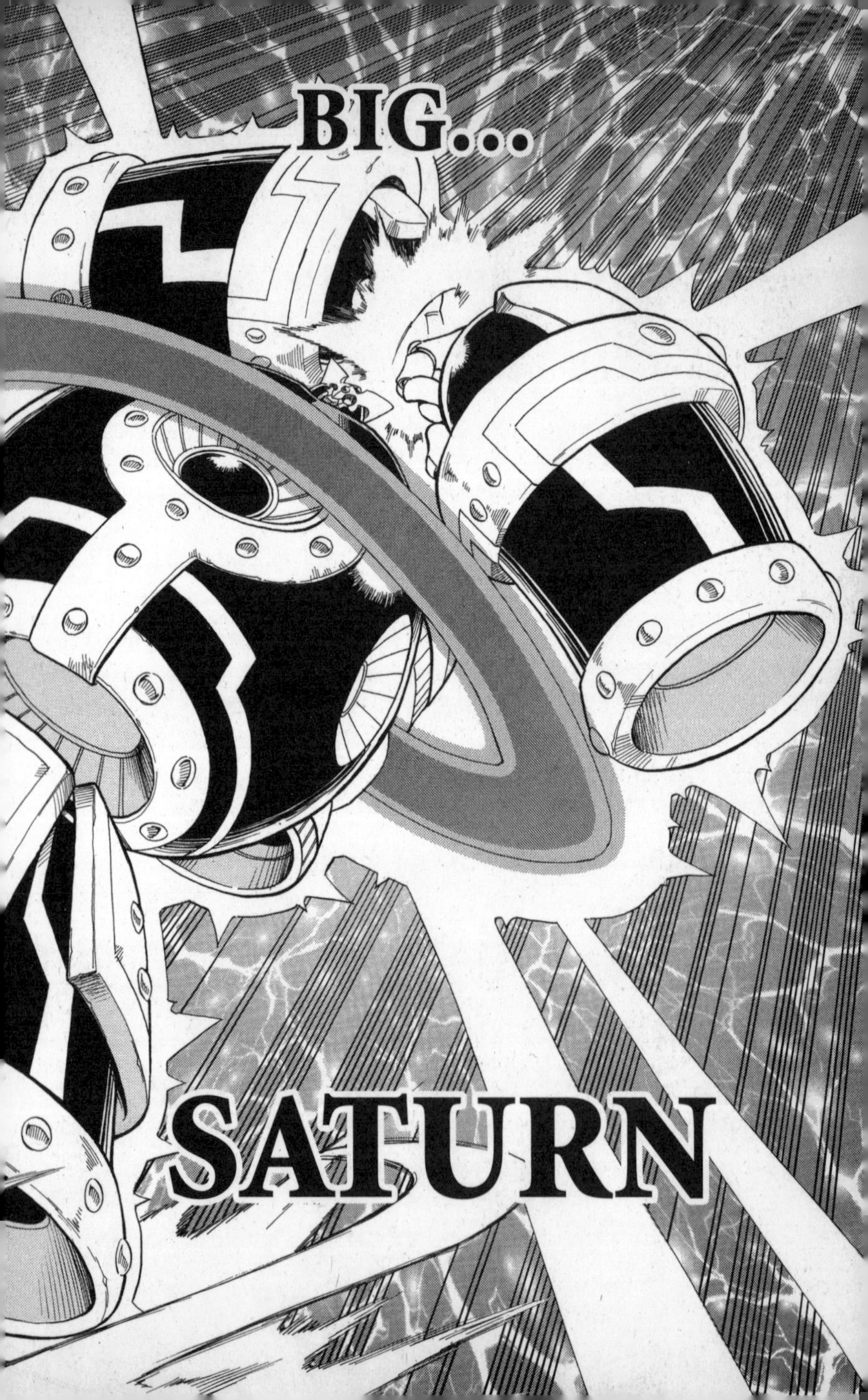
BIG...
SATURN

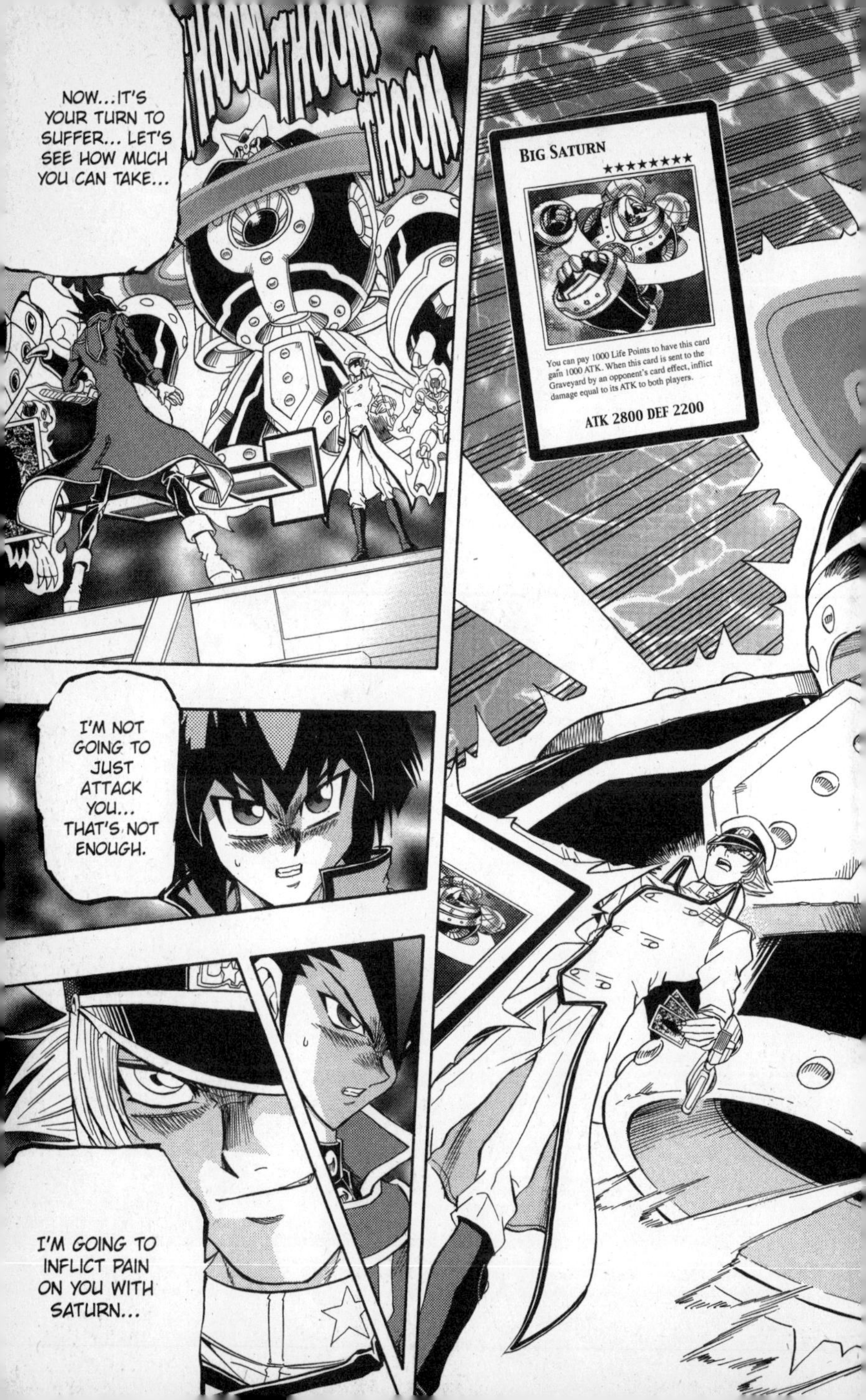
BIG SATURN
★★★★★★★★
You can pay 1000 Life Points to have this card gain 1000 ATK. When this card is sent to the Graveyard by an opponent's card effect, inflict damage equal to its ATK to both players.
ATK 2800 DEF 2200
THOOM THOOM THOOM
NOW...IT'S YOUR TURN TO SUFFER... LET'S SEE HOW MUCH YOU CAN TAKE...
I'M NOT GOING TO JUST ATTACK YOU... THAT'S NOT ENOUGH.
I'M GOING TO INFLICT PAIN ON YOU WITH SATURN...

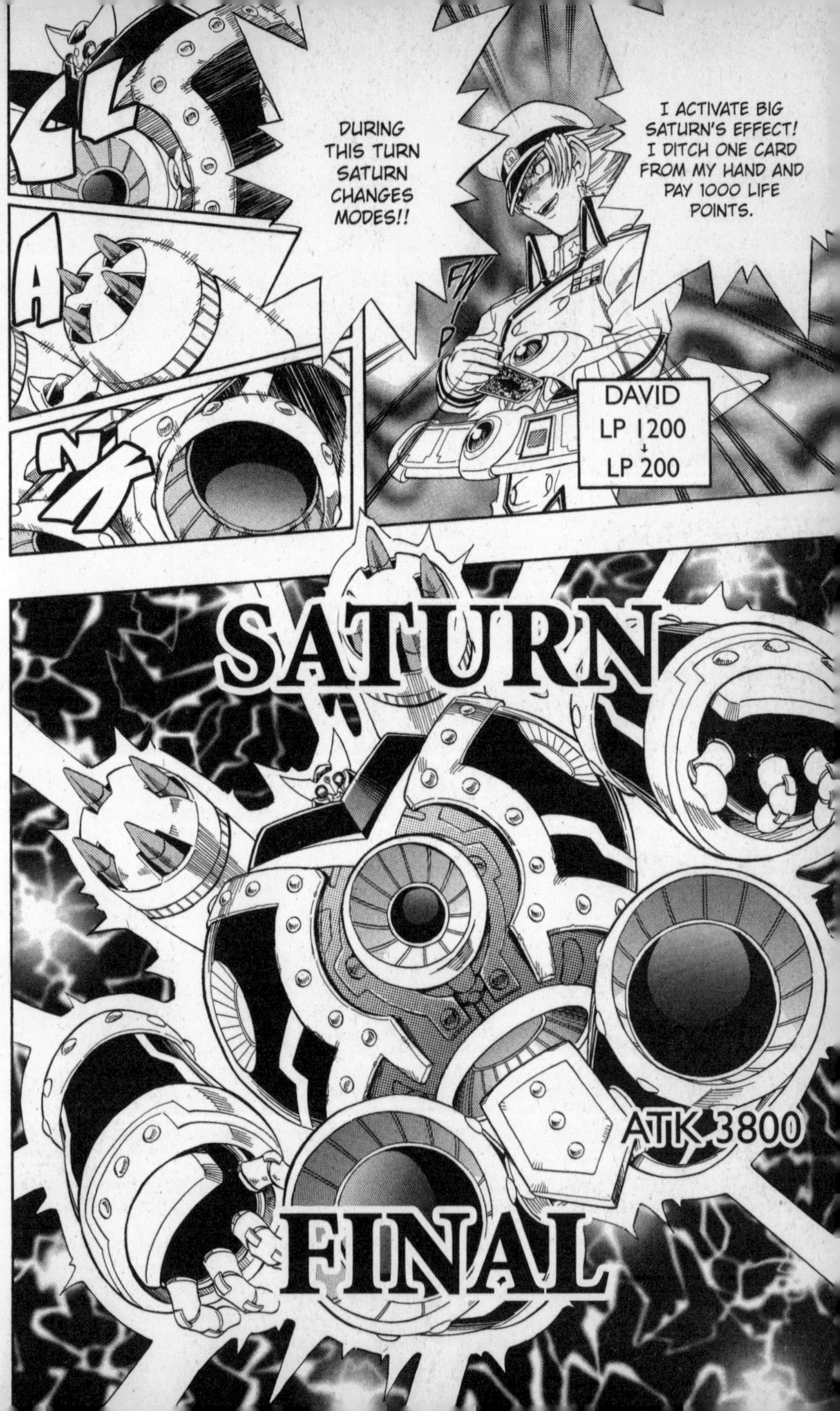
I ACTIVATE BIG SATURN'S EFFECT! I DITCH ONE CARD FROM MY HAND AND PAY 1000 LIFE POINTS.
DURING THIS TURN SATURN CHANGES MODES!!
DAVID LP 1200 → LP 200
CL
A
NK
SATURN
ATK 3800
FINAL

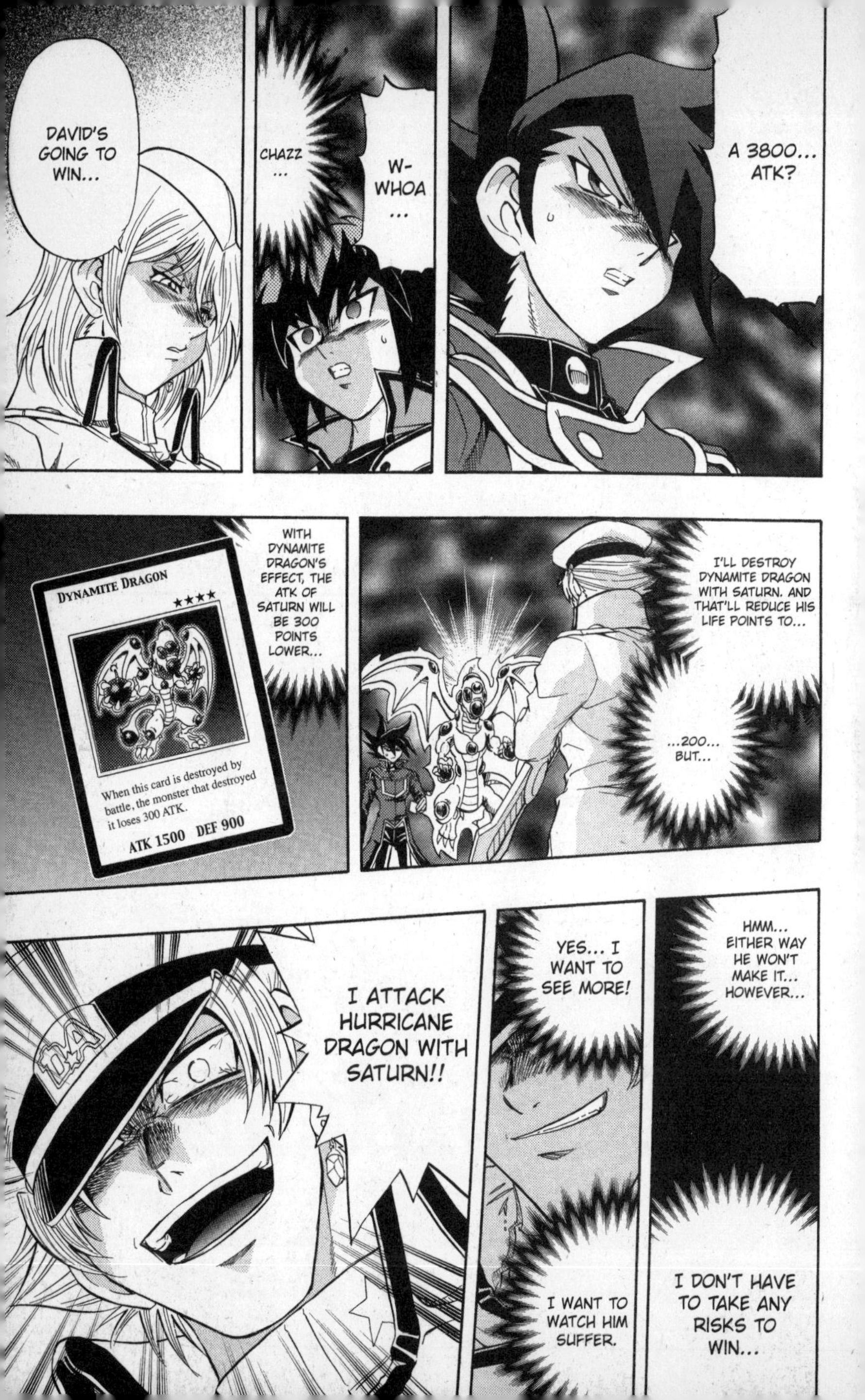
A 3800... ATK?
W-WHOA...
CHAZZ...
DAVID'S GOING TO WIN...
I'LL DESTROY DYNAMITE DRAGON WITH SATURN. AND THAT'LL REDUCE HIS LIFE POINTS TO...
...200... BUT...
WITH DYNAMITE DRAGON'S EFFECT, THE ATK OF SATURN WILL BE 300 POINTS LOWER...
DYNAMITE DRAGON
When this card is destroyed by battle, the monster that destroyed it loses 300 ATK.
ATK 1500 DEF 900
HMM... EITHER WAY HE WON'T MAKE IT... HOWEVER...
I DON'T HAVE TO TAKE ANY RISKS TO WIN...
YES... I WANT TO SEE MORE!
I WANT TO WATCH HIM SUFFER.
I ATTACK HURRICANE DRAGON WITH SATURN!!

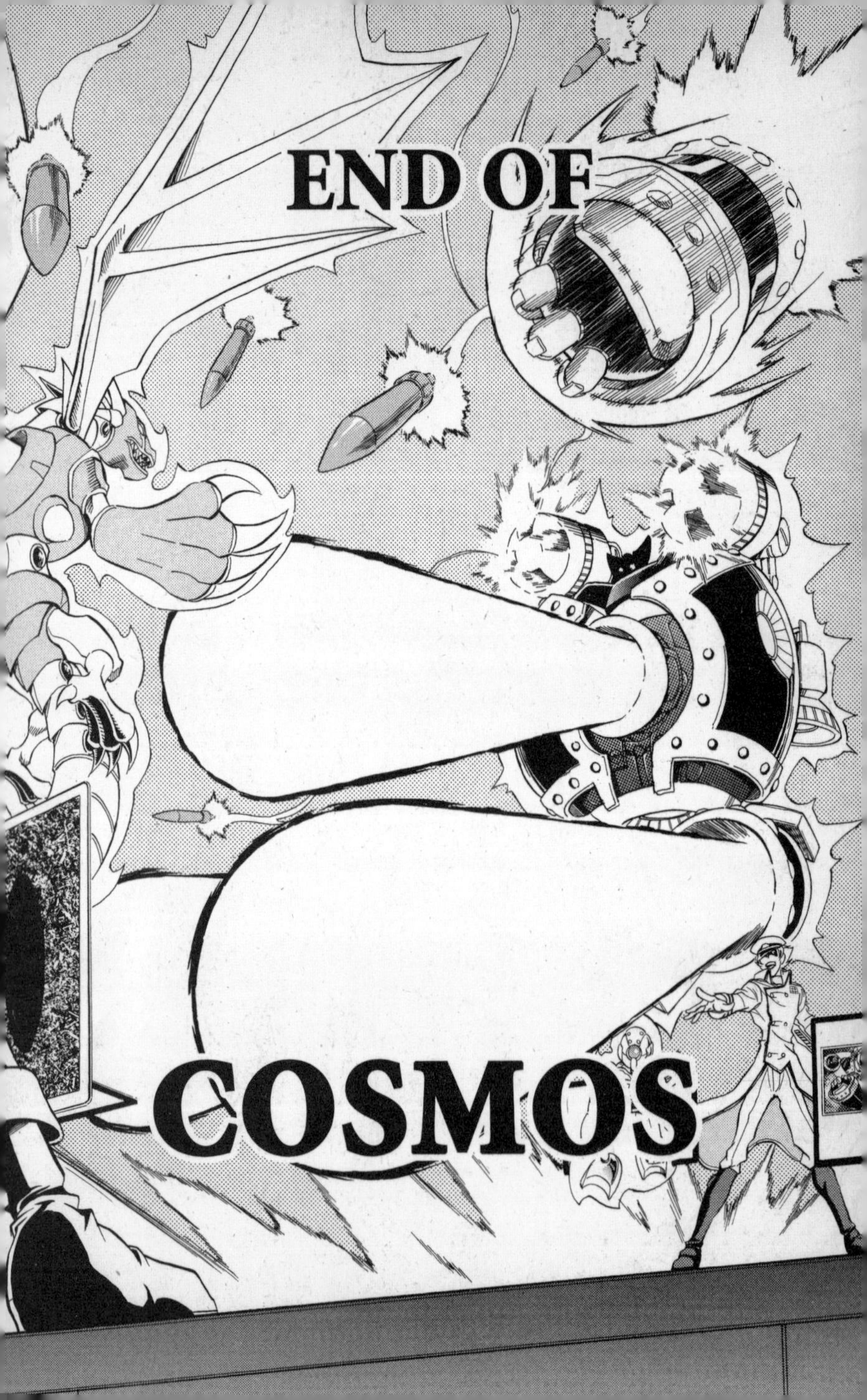
END OF
COSMOS

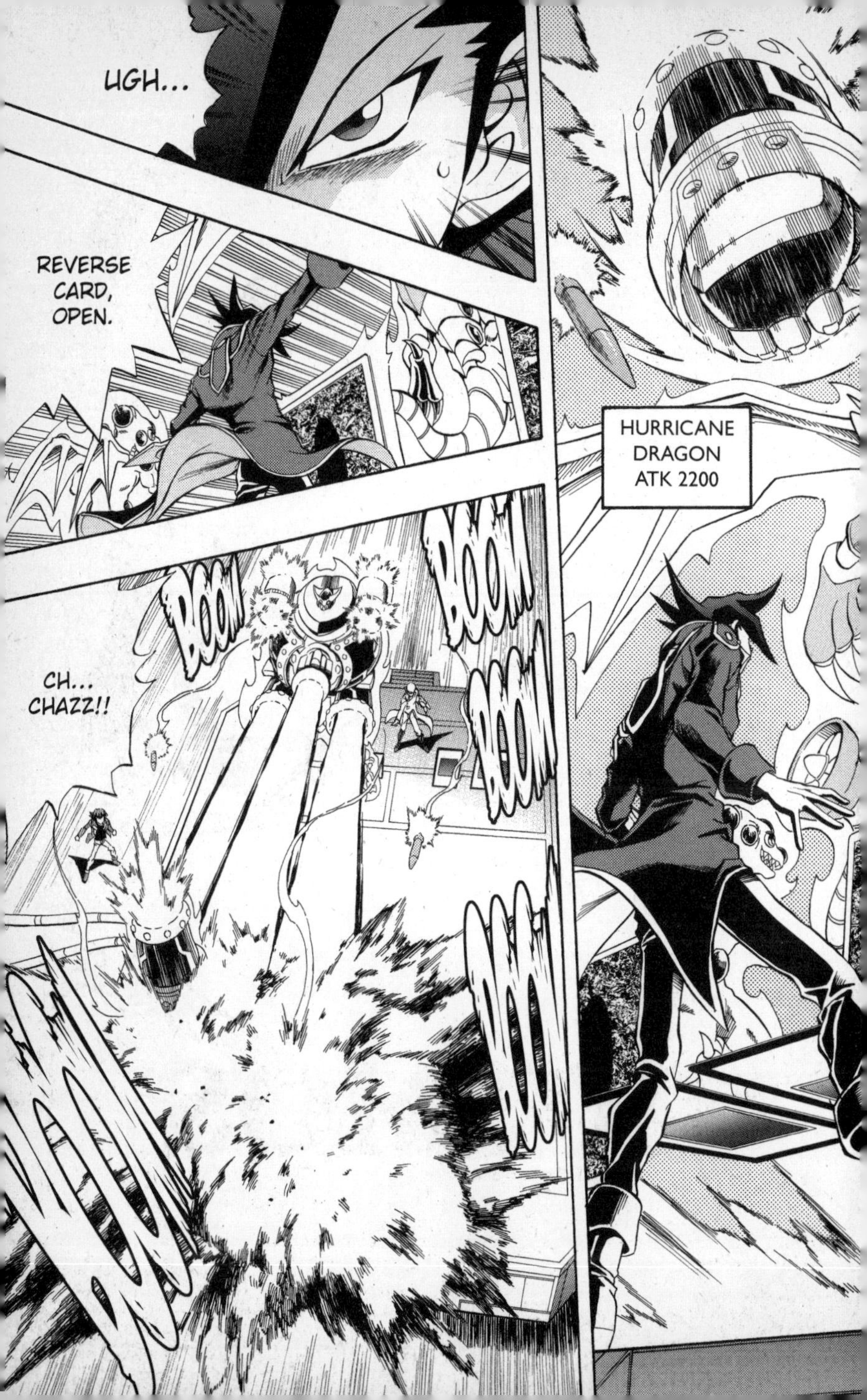
HURRICANE DRAGON ATK 2200
UGH...
REVERSE CARD, OPEN.
BOOM
BOOM
BOOM
CH... CHAZZ!!
BOOM

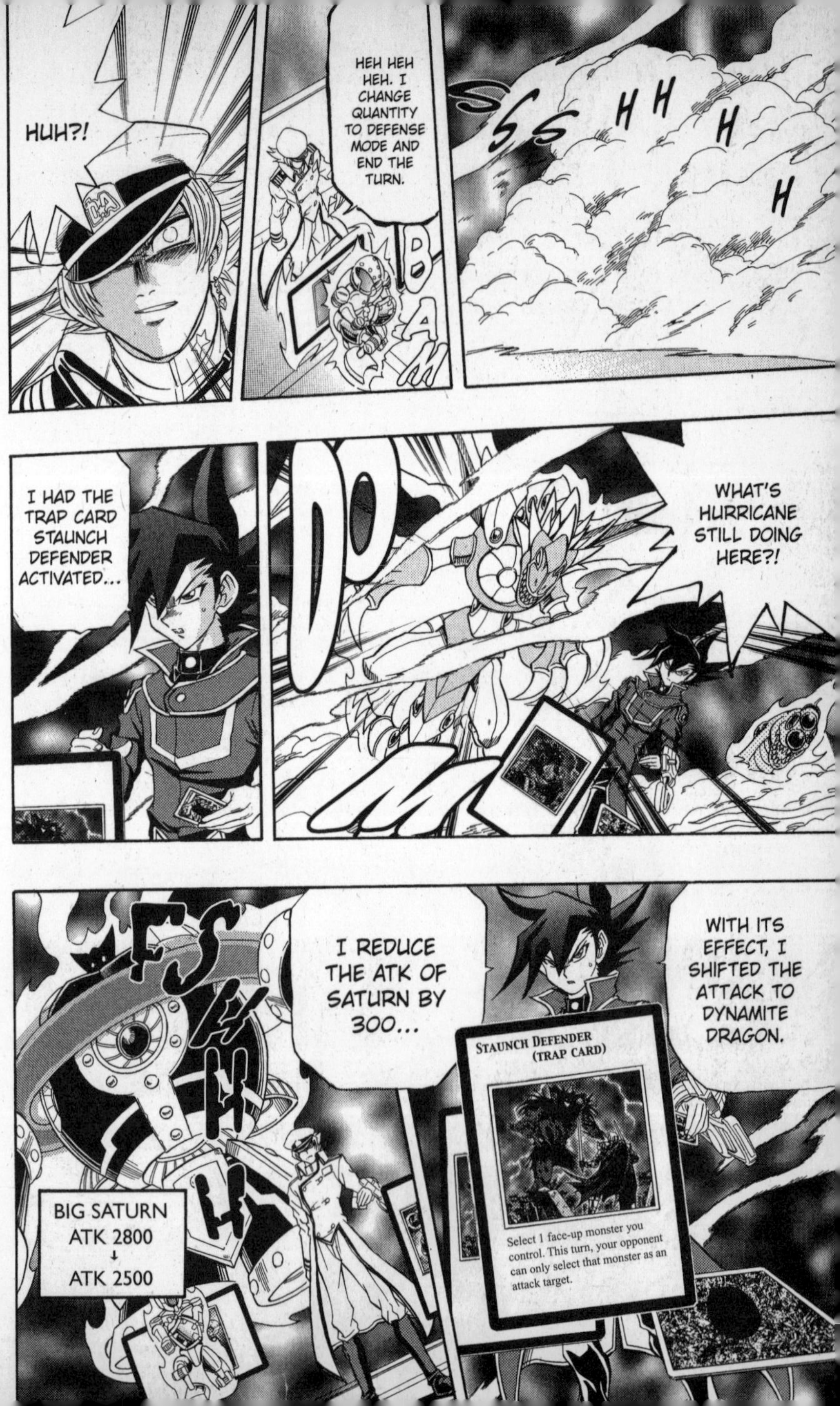
SSHHHH
HEH HEH HEH. I CHANGE QUANTITY TO DEFENSE MODE AND END THE TURN.
BAM
HUH?!
WHAT'S HURRICANE STILL DOING HERE?!
I HAD THE TRAP CARD STAUNCH DEFENDER ACTIVATED...
WITH ITS EFFECT, I SHIFTED THE ATTACK TO DYNAMITE DRAGON.
I REDUCE THE ATK OF SATURN BY 300...
STAUNCH DEFENDER (TRAP CARD)
Select 1 face-up monster you control. This turn, your opponent can only select that monster as an attack target.
FSHHH
BIG SATURN ATK 2800 ↓ ATK 2500

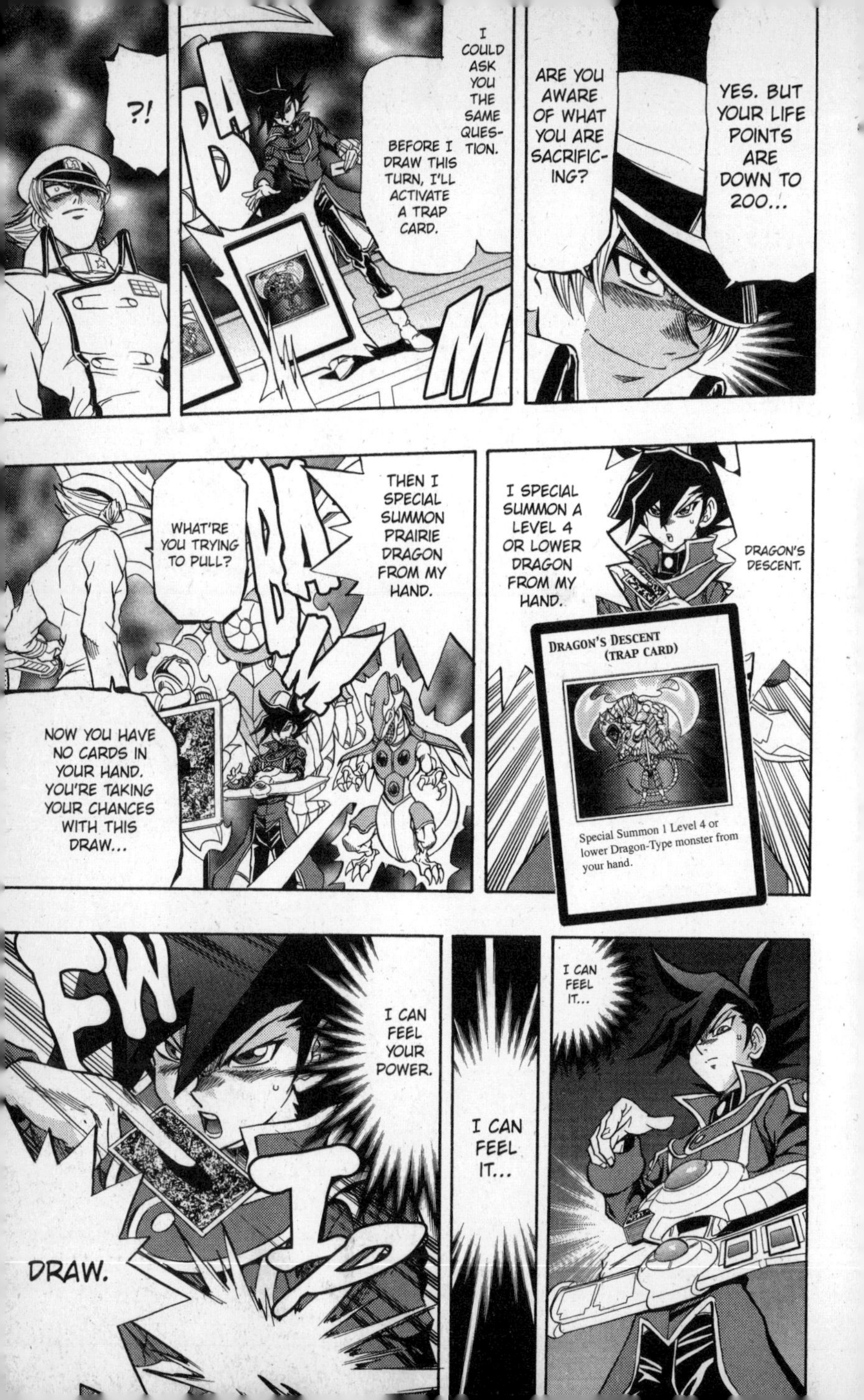
YES. BUT YOUR LIFE POINTS ARE DOWN TO 200...
ARE YOU AWARE OF WHAT YOU ARE SACRIFICING?
I COULD ASK YOU THE SAME QUESTION.
BEFORE I DRAW THIS TURN, I'LL ACTIVATE A TRAP CARD.
?!
DRAGON'S DESCENT.
I SPECIAL SUMMON A LEVEL 4 OR LOWER DRAGON FROM MY HAND.
DRAGON'S DESCENT (TRAP CARD)
Special Summon 1 Level 4 or lower Dragon-Type monster from your hand.
THEN I SPECIAL SUMMON PRAIRIE DRAGON FROM MY HAND.
WHAT'RE YOU TRYING TO PULL?
NOW YOU HAVE NO CARDS IN YOUR HAND. YOU'RE TAKING YOUR CHANCES WITH THIS DRAW...
I CAN FEEL IT...
I CAN FEEL IT...
I CAN FEEL YOUR POWER.
DRAW.

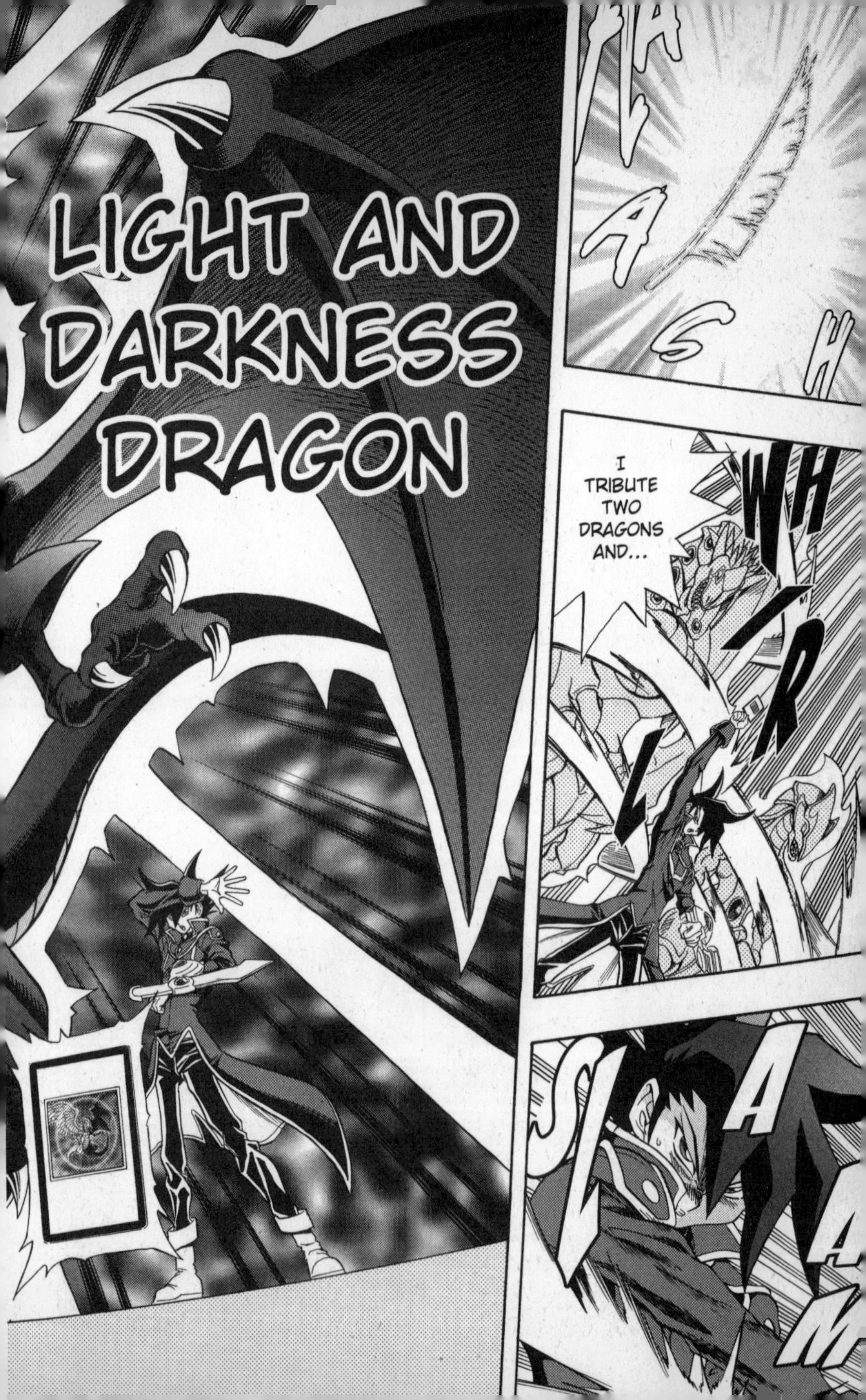
I TRIBUTE TWO DRAGONS AND...
LIGHT AND DARKNESS DRAGON

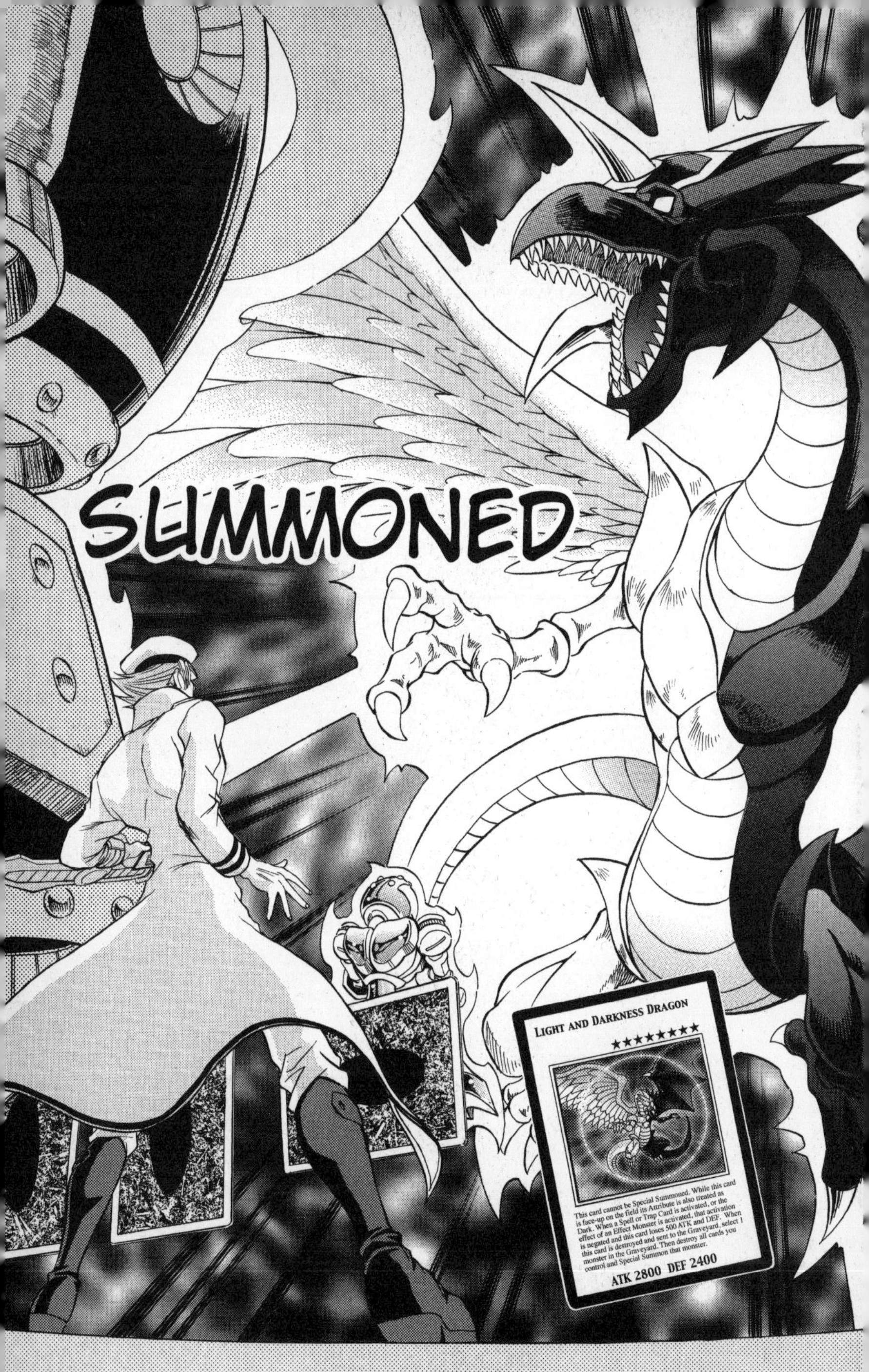
SUMMONED
LIGHT AND DARKNESS DRAGON
★★★★★★★★
This card cannot be Special Summoned. While this card is face-up on the field its Attribute is also treated as Dark. When a Spell or Trap Card is activated, or the effect of an Effect Monster is activated, that activation is negated and this card loses 500 ATK and DEF. When this card is destroyed and sent to the Graveyard, select 1 monster in the Graveyard. Then destroy all cards you control and Special Summon that monster.
ATK 2800 DEF 2400

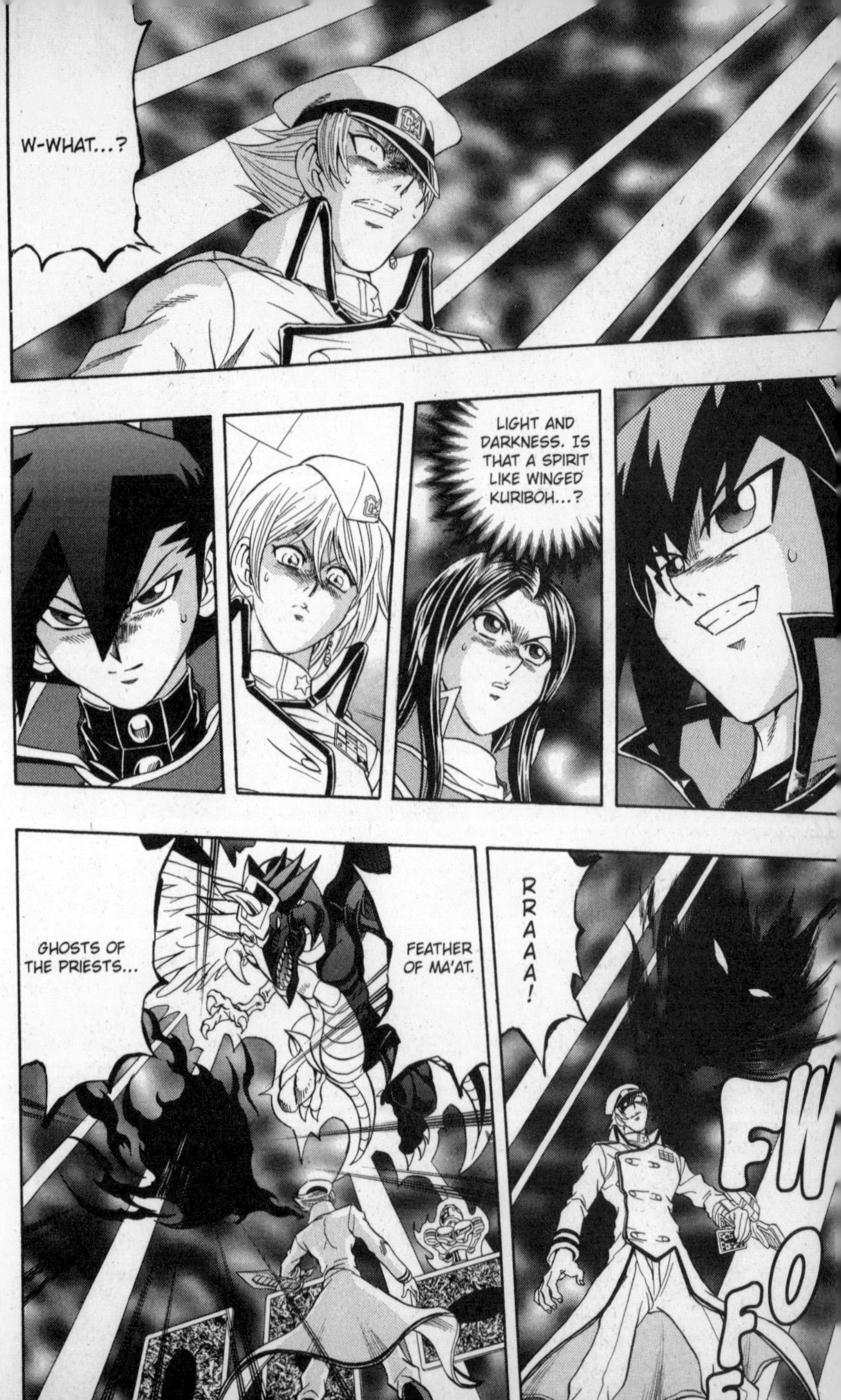
W-WHAT...?
LIGHT AND DARKNESS. IS THAT A SPIRIT LIKE WINGED KURIBOH...?
RRAAAA!
FEATHER OF MA'AT.
GHOSTS OF THE PRIESTS...

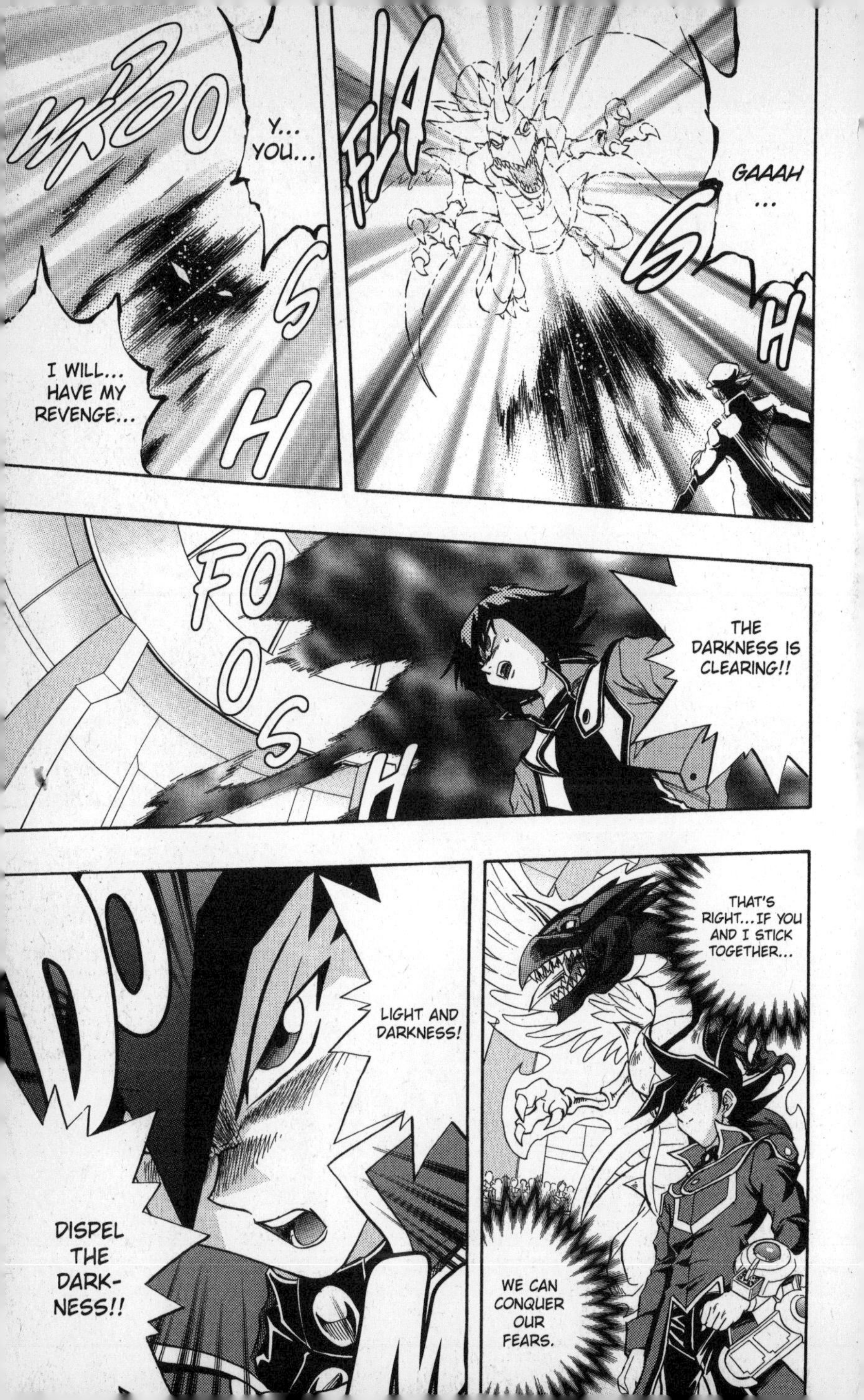
FLA
GAAAH ...
SH
WHOO
Y... YOU...
I WILL... HAVE MY REVENGE...
SH
FOOSH
THE DARKNESS IS CLEARING!!
THAT'S RIGHT...IF YOU AND I STICK TOGETHER...
WE CAN CONQUER OUR FEARS.
LIGHT AND DARKNESS!
DISPEL THE DARK-NESS!!

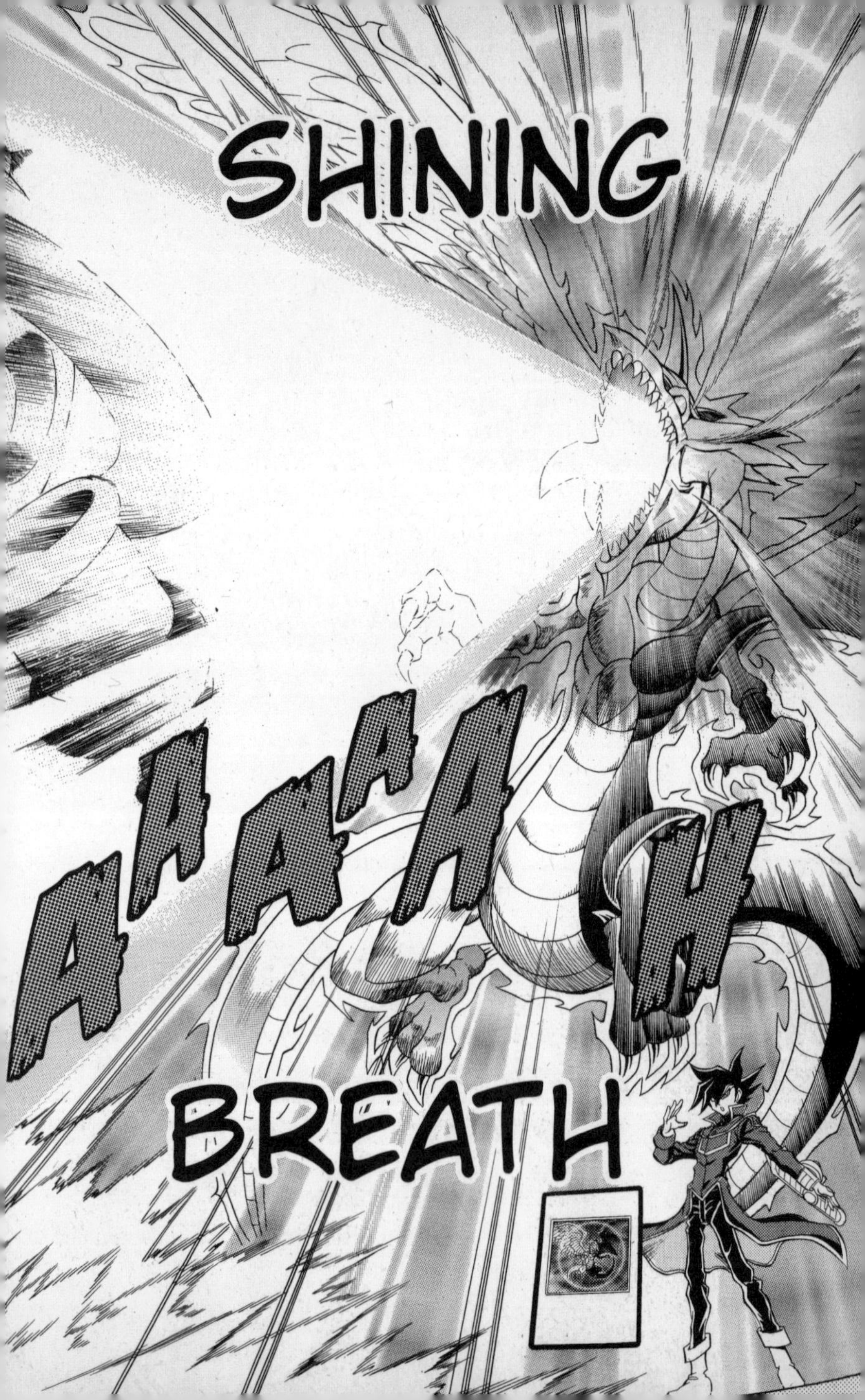
SHINING
AAAAAH
BREATH

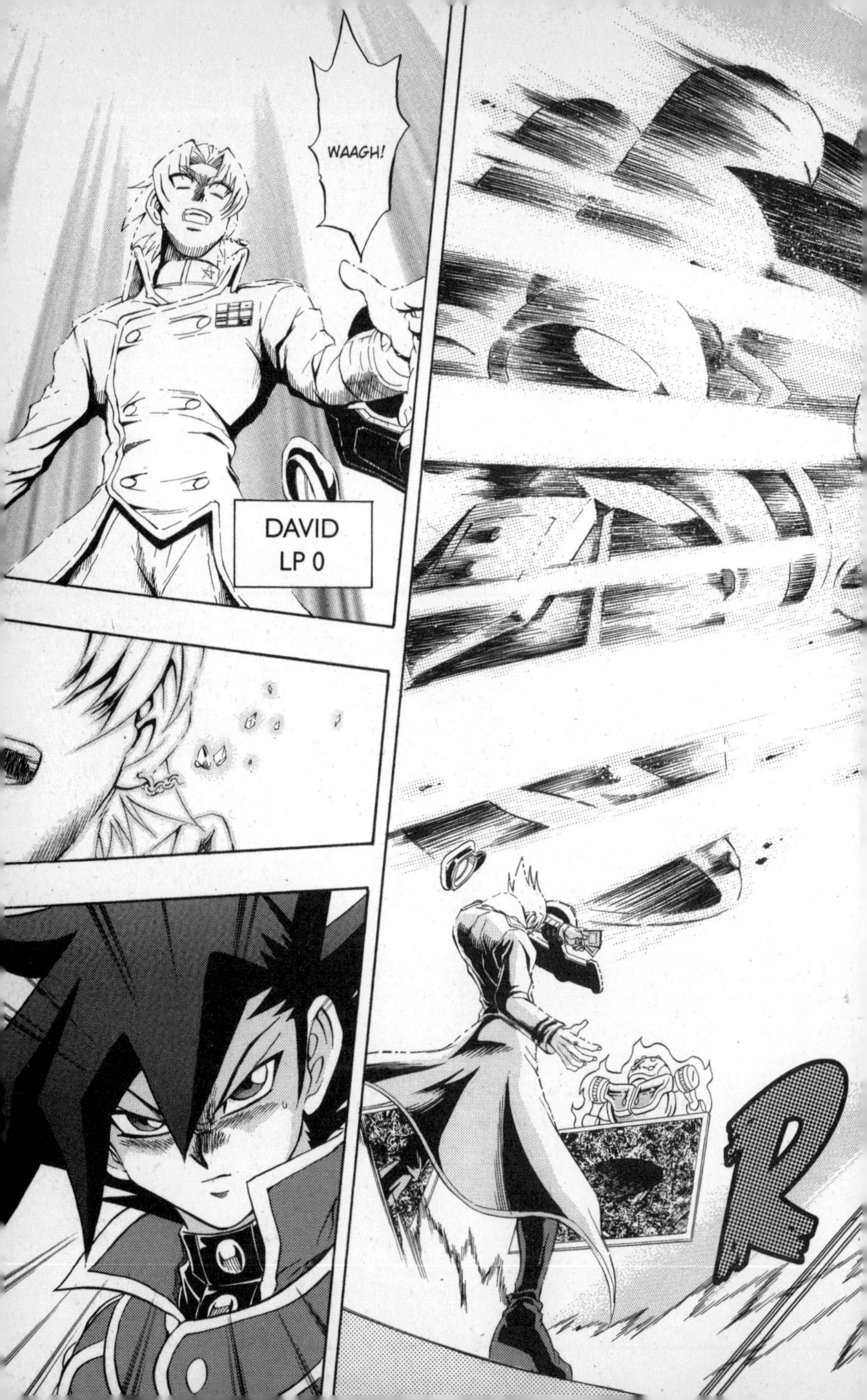
WAAGH!
DAVID
LP 0

DIGITAL WORK IS...
IN THE PAST, AFTER FINISHING ALL THE ILLUSTRATIONS FOR THE MONTH...
SEE YOU.
THANKS FOR THE WORK TODAY.
EXHAUSTED
...I WORKED ALONE...
...ON DIGITAL PROCESSING WORK AT THE STUDIO AFTER THE STAFF LEFT...
MAINLY CARD ILLUSTRATIONS...
A WHOLE DAY'S WORK.
GAH! IT FROZE UP!
AAAH! AND I DIDN'T SAVE!!
I HAVE TO START ALL OVER AGAIN...
NOW I ASK AKIRA-SAN TO COME ON THE LAST DAY...
...TO HANDLE THE DIGITAL PROCESSING WORK.

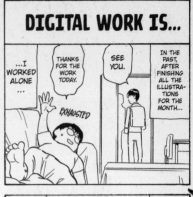

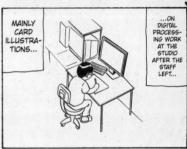

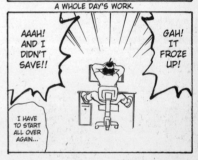

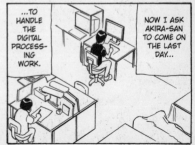

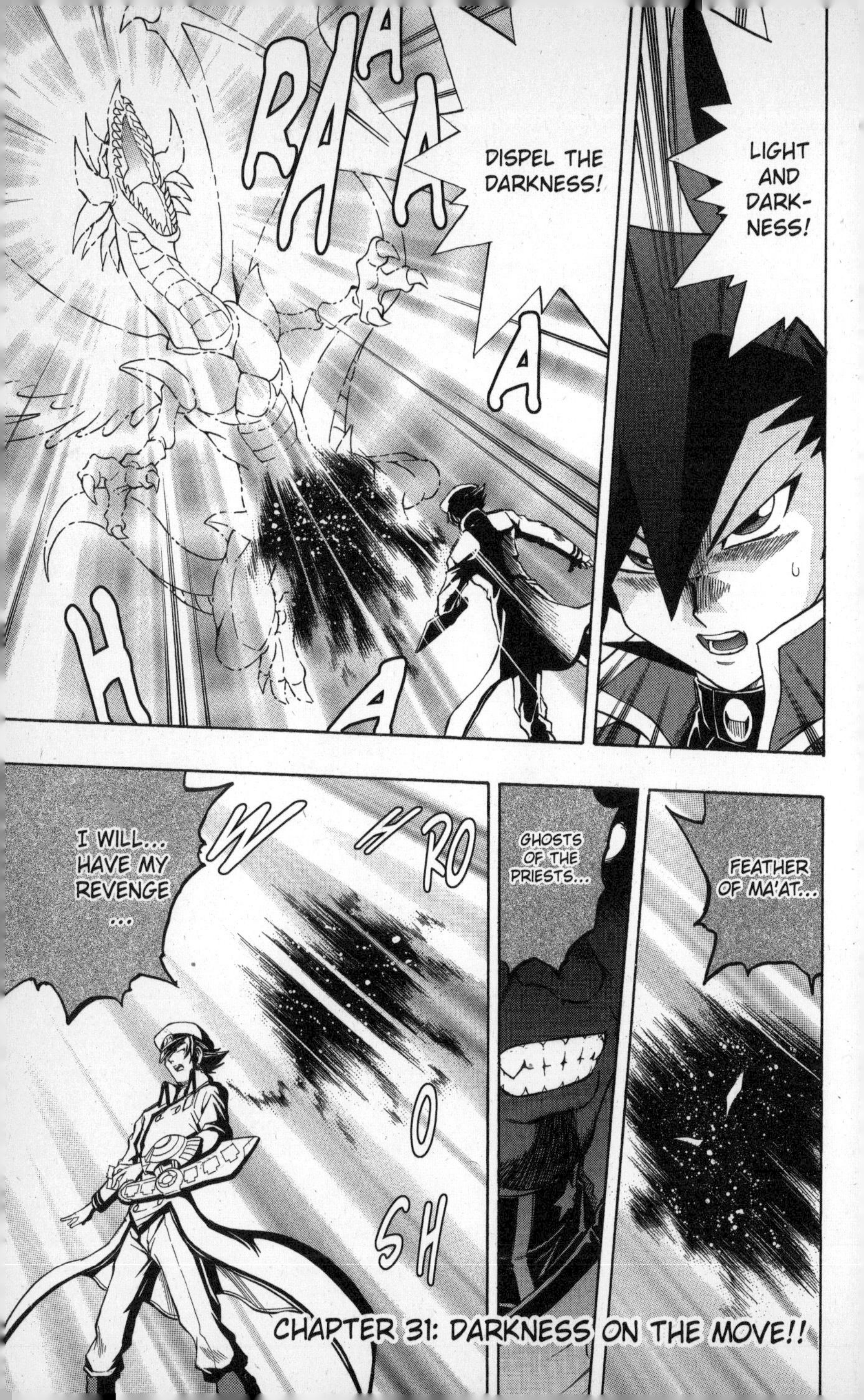
LIGHT AND DARKNESS!
DISPEL THE DARKNESS!
RAAAAAAH
FEATHER OF MA'AT...
GHOSTS OF THE PRIESTS...
I WILL... HAVE MY REVENGE ...
WHROOSH

CHAPTER 31: DARKNESS ON THE MOVE!!

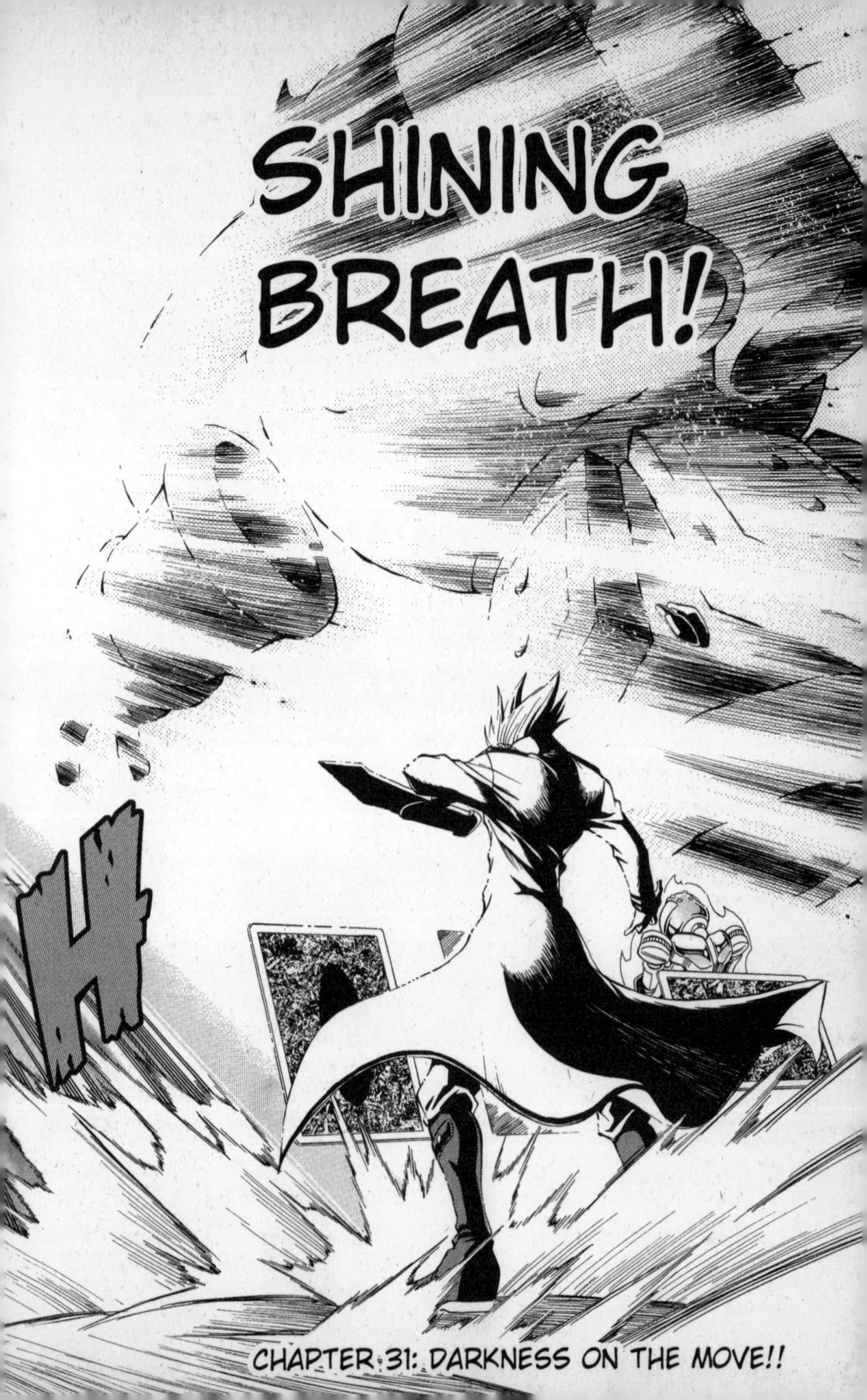
SHINING BREATH!
H
CHAPTER 31: DARKNESS ON THE MOVE!!

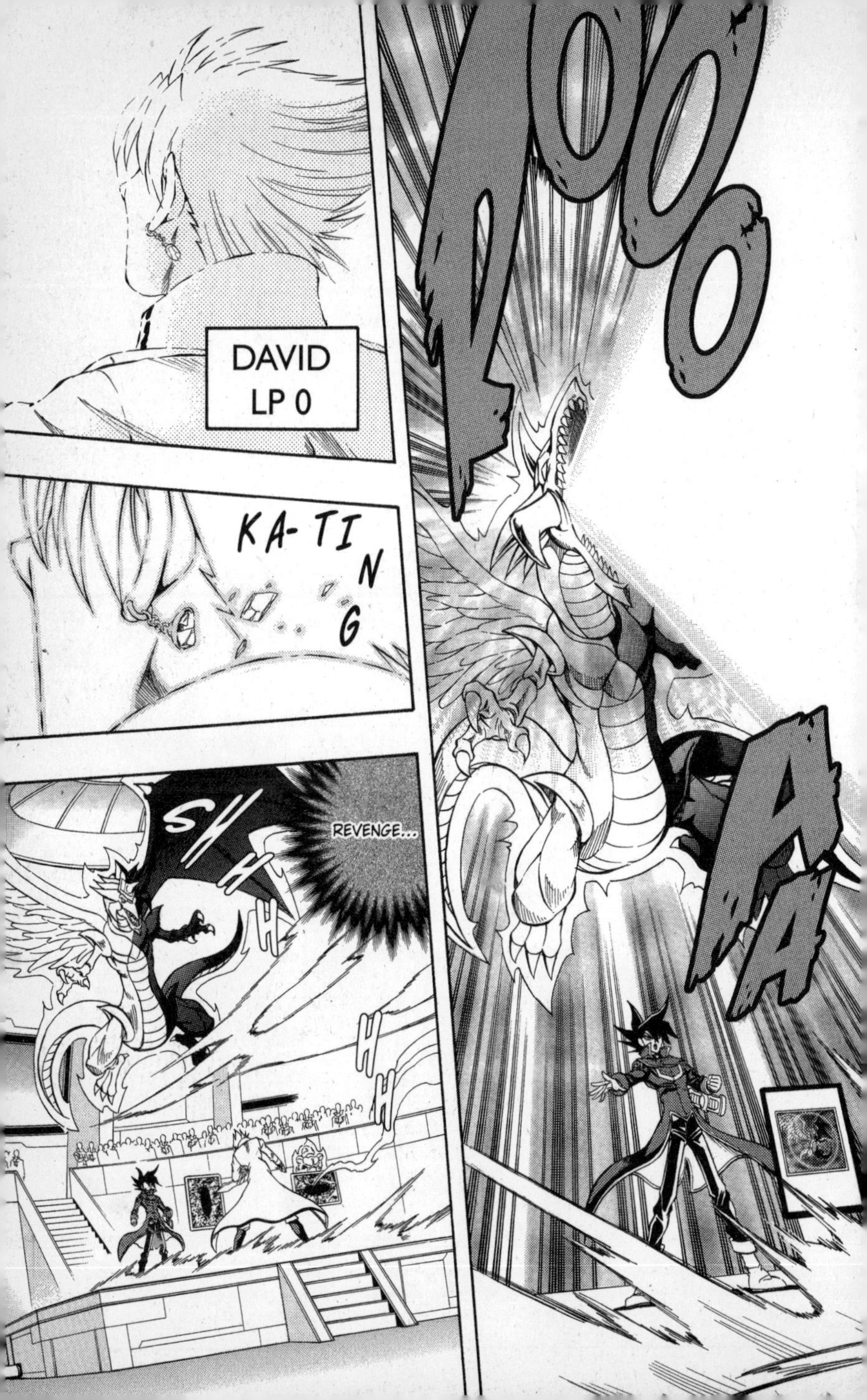
DAVID
LP 0
KA-TING
SHHHH
REVENGE...

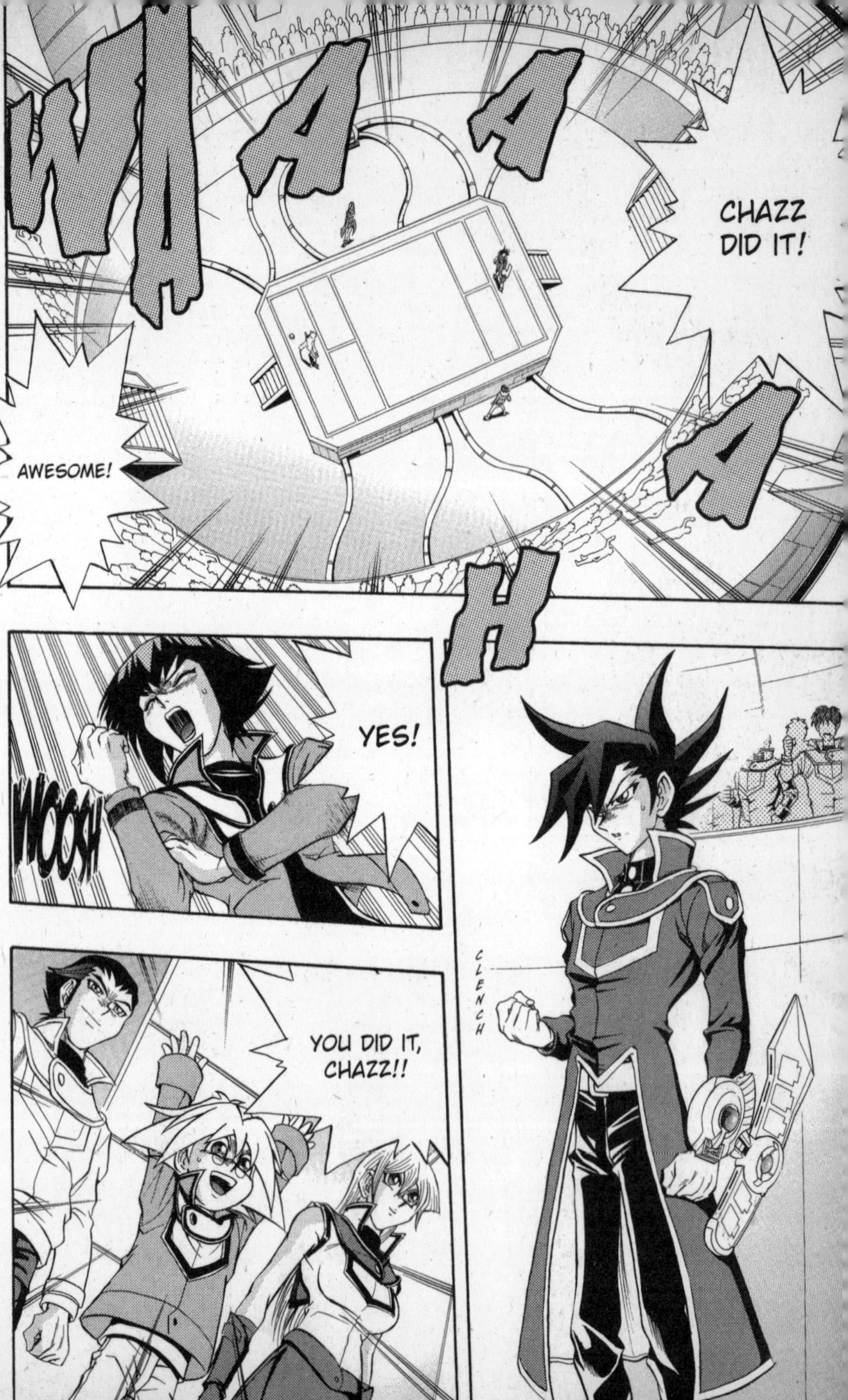
CHAZZ DID IT!
WAAAAH
AWESOME!
CLENCH
YES!
WOOSH
YOU DID IT, CHAZZ!!

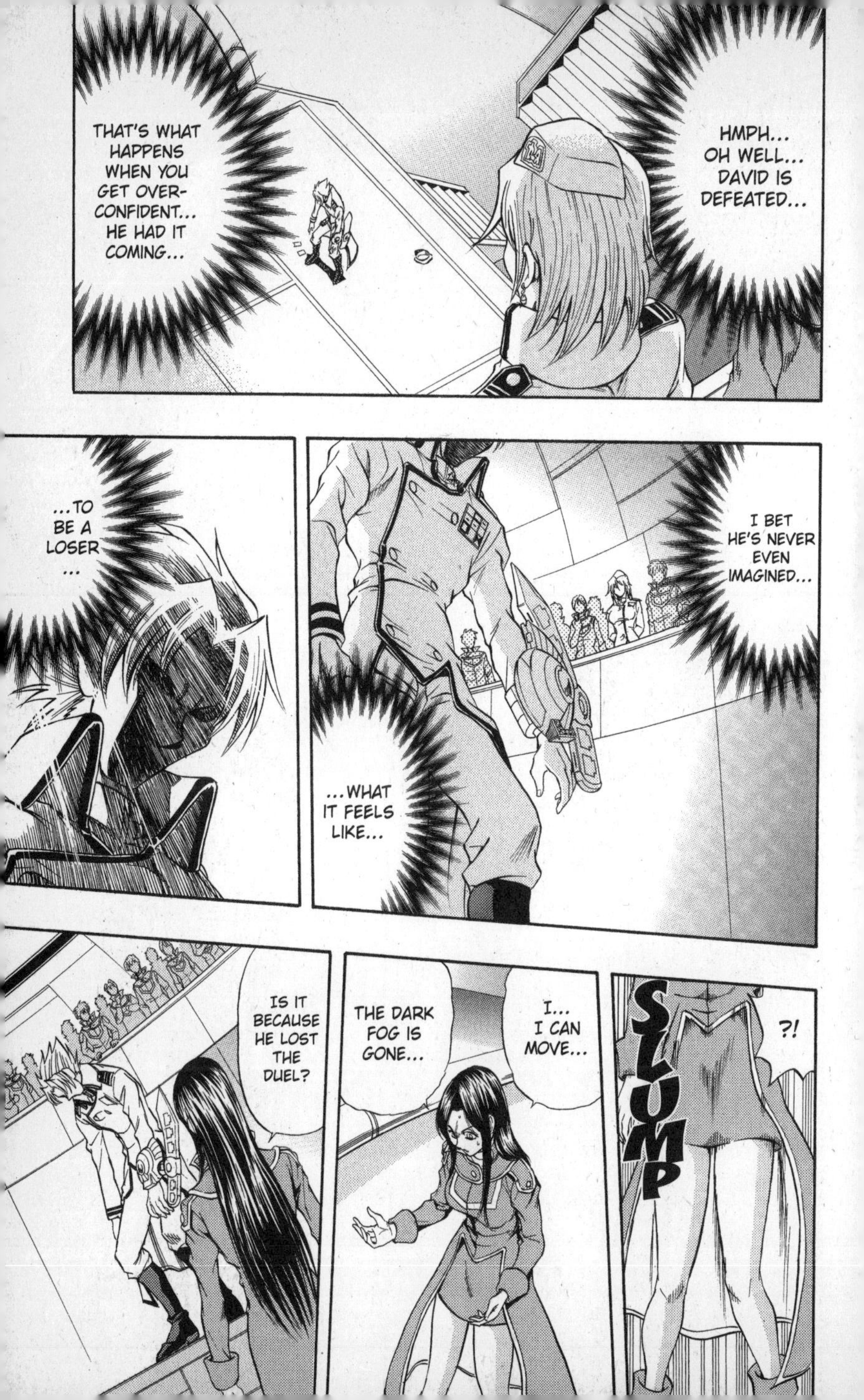
HMPH... OH WELL... DAVID IS DEFEATED...
THAT'S WHAT HAPPENS WHEN YOU GET OVER-CONFIDENT... HE HAD IT COMING...
I BET HE'S NEVER EVEN IMAGINED...
...WHAT IT FEELS LIKE...
...TO BE A LOSER ...
SLUMP
?!
I... I CAN MOVE...
THE DARK FOG IS GONE...
IS IT BECAUSE HE LOST THE DUEL?

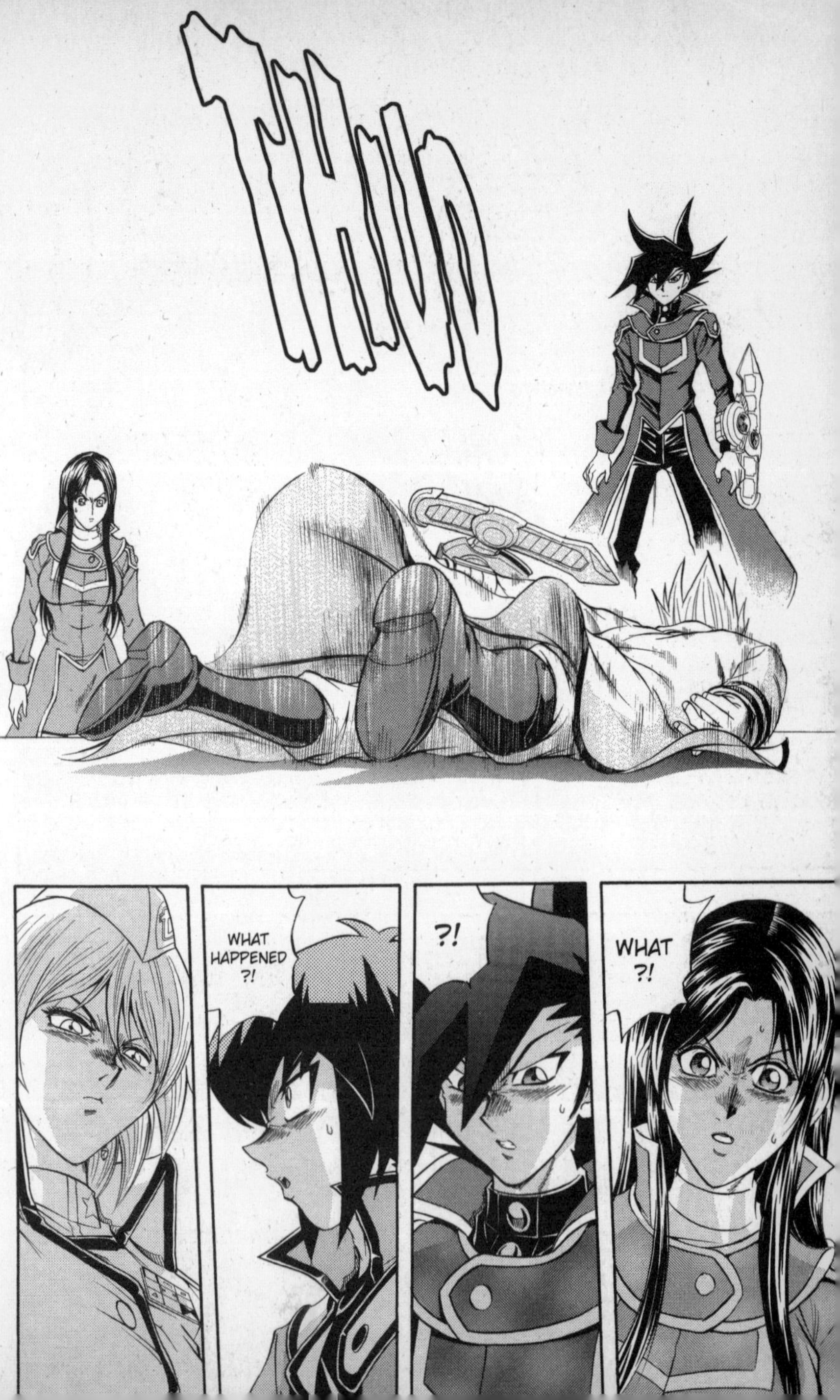
THUD
WHAT ?!
?!
WHAT HAPPENED ?!

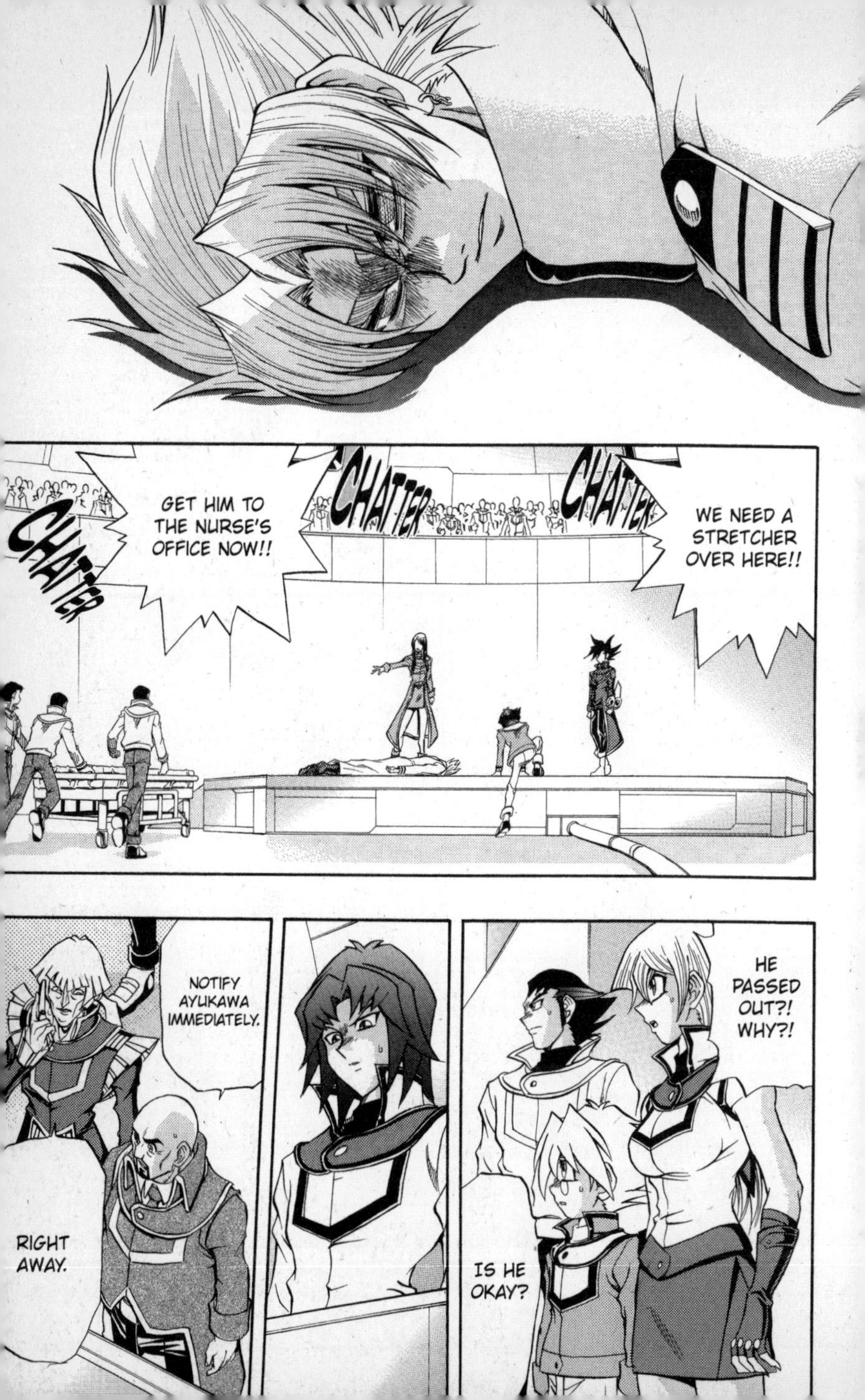
WE NEED A STRETCHER OVER HERE!!
CHATTER
CHATTER
GET HIM TO THE NURSE'S OFFICE NOW!!
CHATTER
HE PASSED OUT?! WHY?!
IS HE OKAY?
NOTIFY AYUKAWA IMMEDIATELY.
RIGHT AWAY.

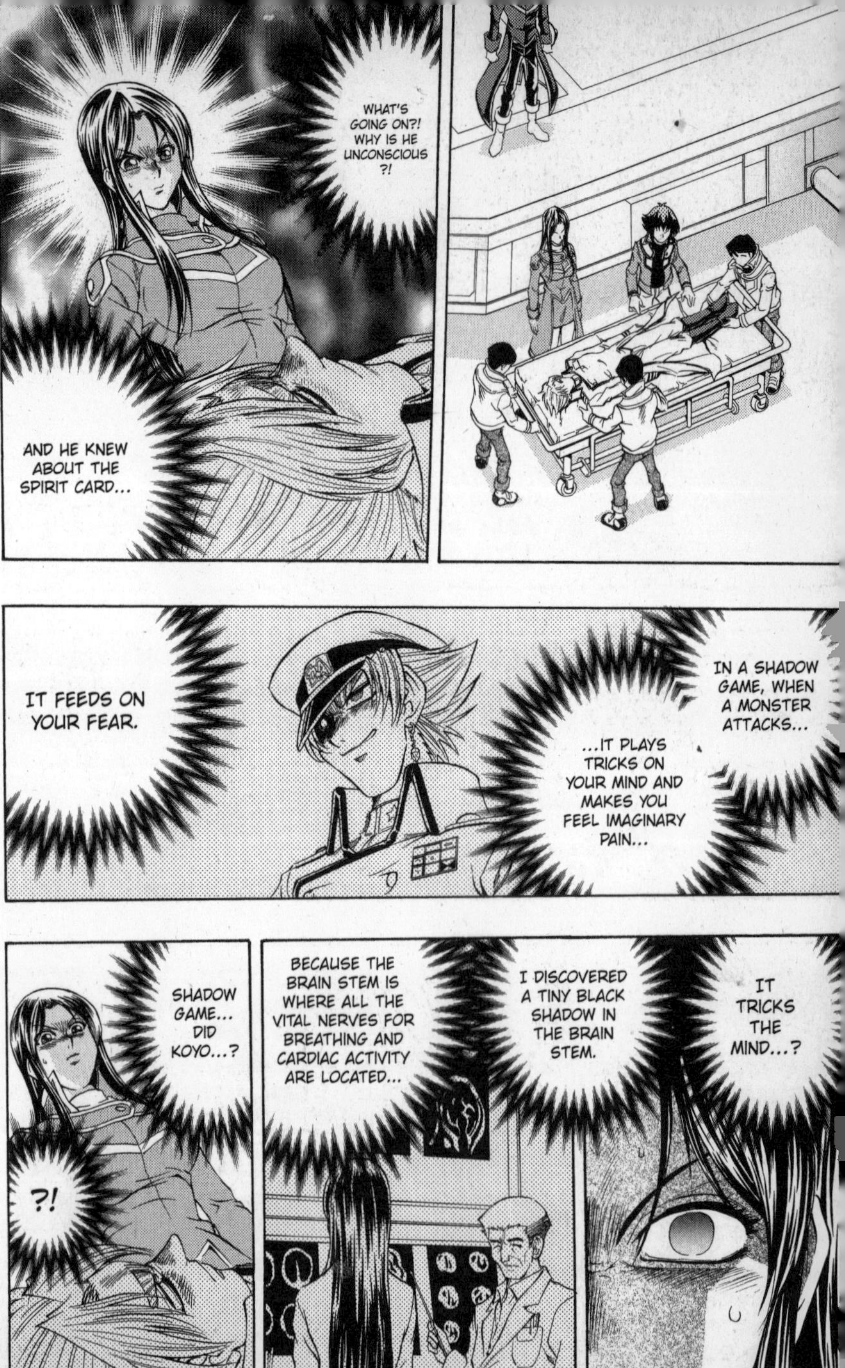
WHAT'S GOING ON?! WHY IS HE UNCONSCIOUS ?!
AND HE KNEW ABOUT THE SPIRIT CARD...
IN A SHADOW GAME, WHEN A MONSTER ATTACKS...
...IT PLAYS TRICKS ON YOUR MIND AND MAKES YOU FEEL IMAGINARY PAIN...
IT FEEDS ON YOUR FEAR.
IT TRICKS THE MIND...?
I DISCOVERED A TINY BLACK SHADOW IN THE BRAIN STEM.
BECAUSE THE BRAIN STEM IS WHERE ALL THE VITAL NERVES FOR BREATHING AND CARDIAC ACTIVITY ARE LOCATED...
SHADOW GAME... DID KOYO...?
?!

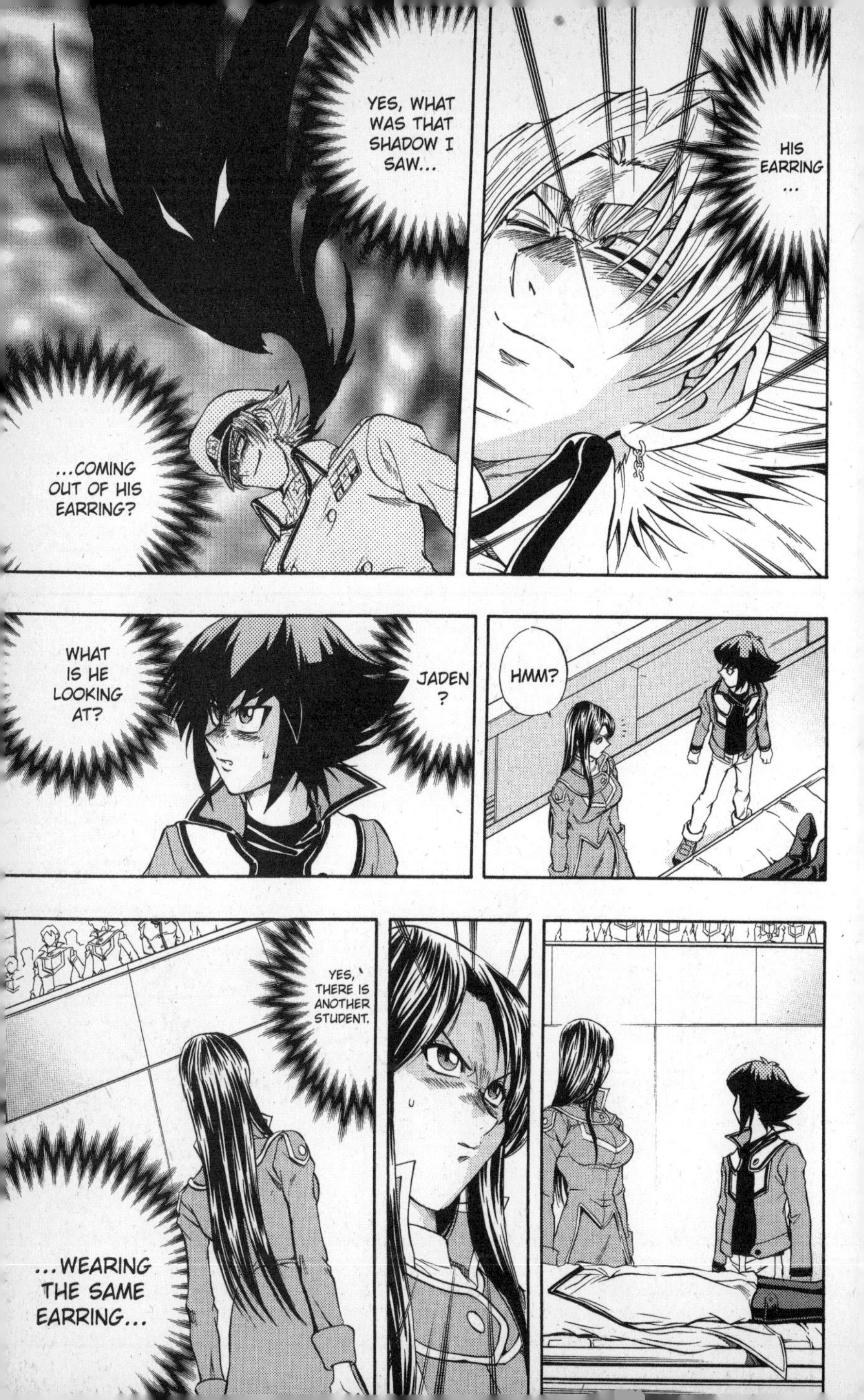
HIS EARRING ...
YES, WHAT WAS THAT SHADOW I SAW...
...COMING OUT OF HIS EARRING?
HMM?
JADEN ?
WHAT IS HE LOOKING AT?
YES, THERE IS ANOTHER STUDENT.
...WEARING THE SAME EARRING...

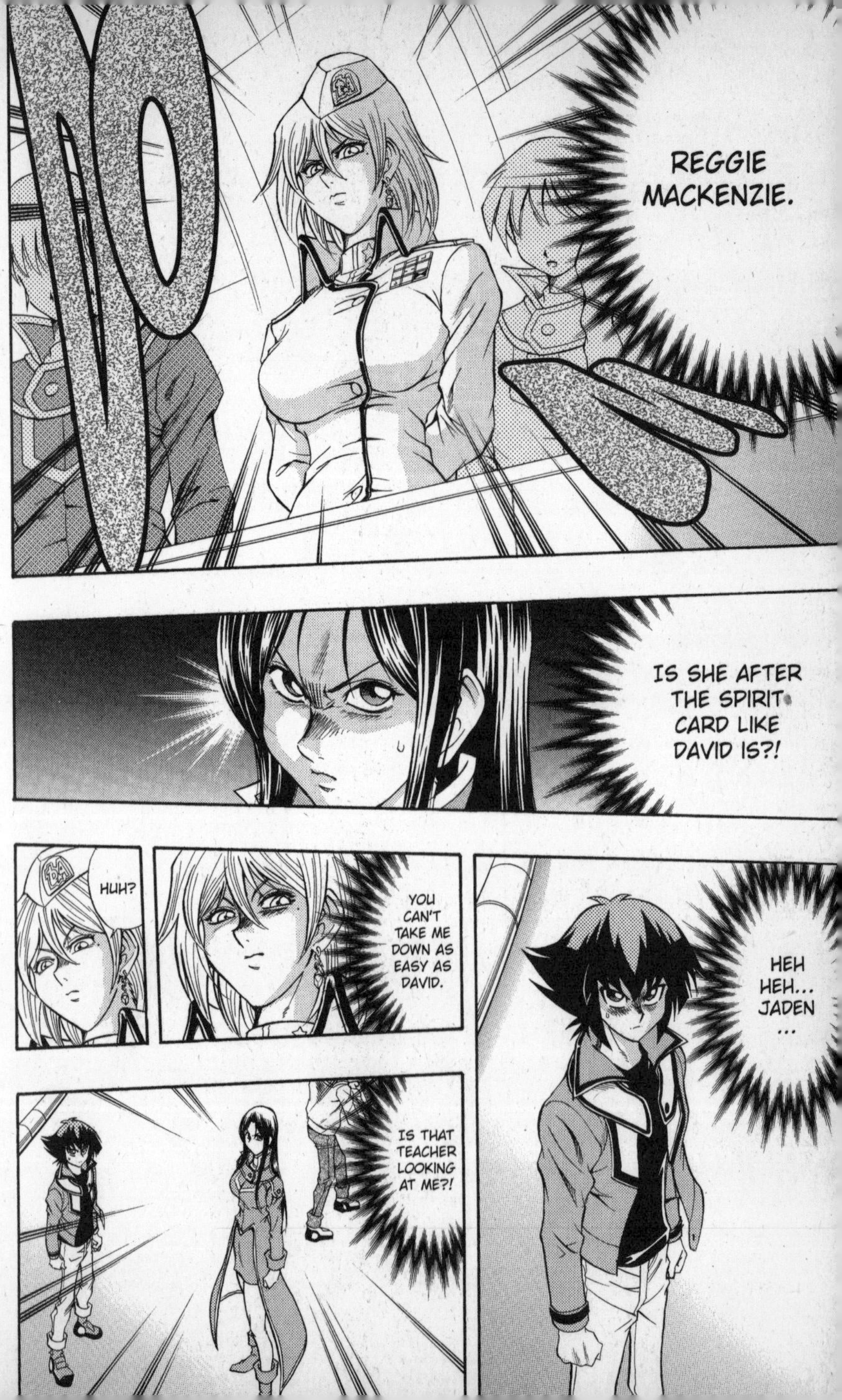
REGGIE MACKENZIE.
IS SHE AFTER THE SPIRIT CARD LIKE DAVID IS?!
HEH HEH... JADEN ...
YOU CAN'T TAKE ME DOWN AS EASY AS DAVID.
HUH?
IS THAT TEACHER LOOKING AT ME?!

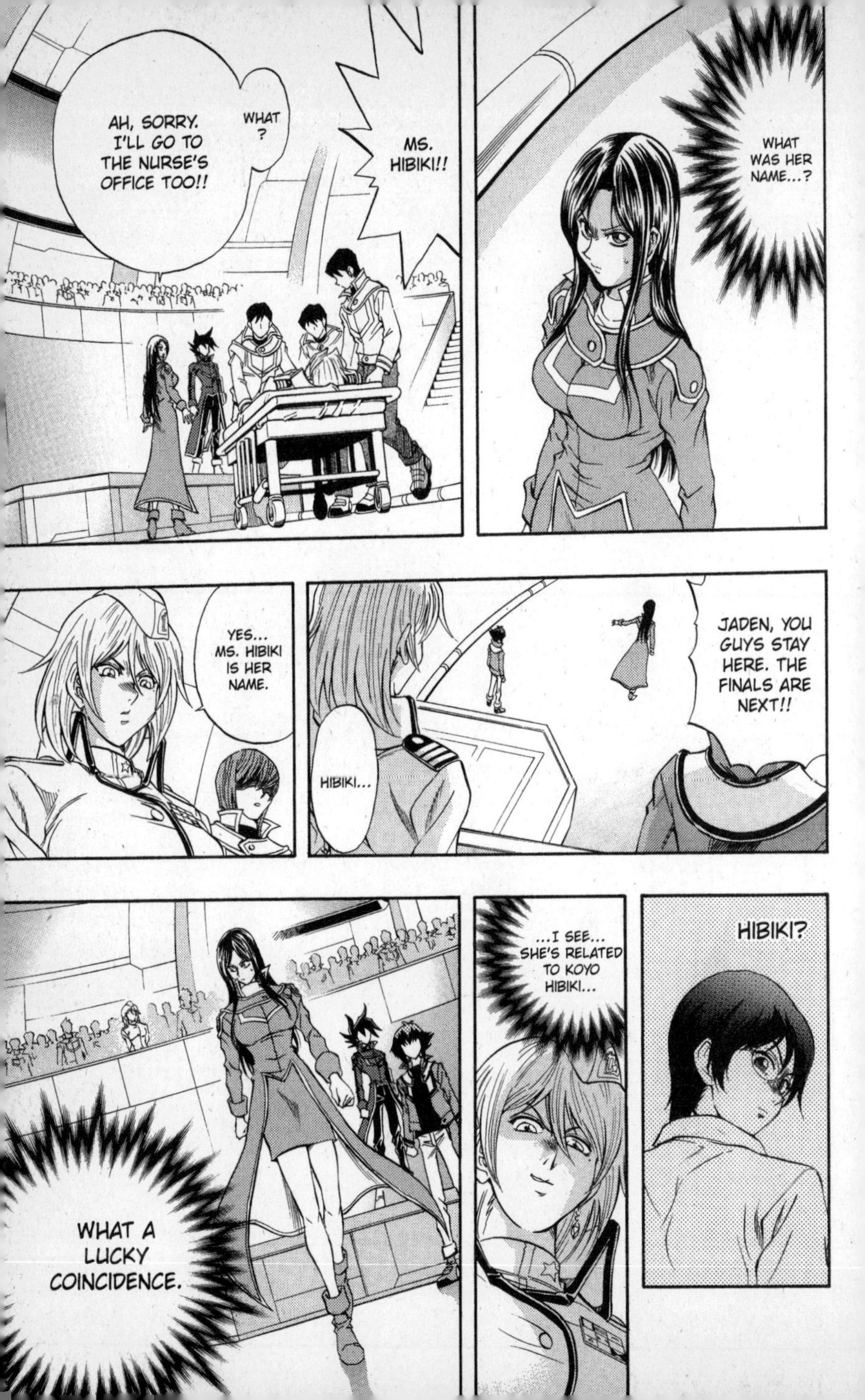
WHAT WAS HER NAME...?
MS. HIBIKI!!
WHAT ?
AH, SORRY. I'LL GO TO THE NURSE'S OFFICE TOO!!
JADEN, YOU GUYS STAY HERE. THE FINALS ARE NEXT!!
HIBIKI...
YES... MS. HIBIKI IS HER NAME.
HIBIKI?
...I SEE... SHE'S RELATED TO KOYO HIBIKI...
WHAT A LUCKY COINCIDENCE.

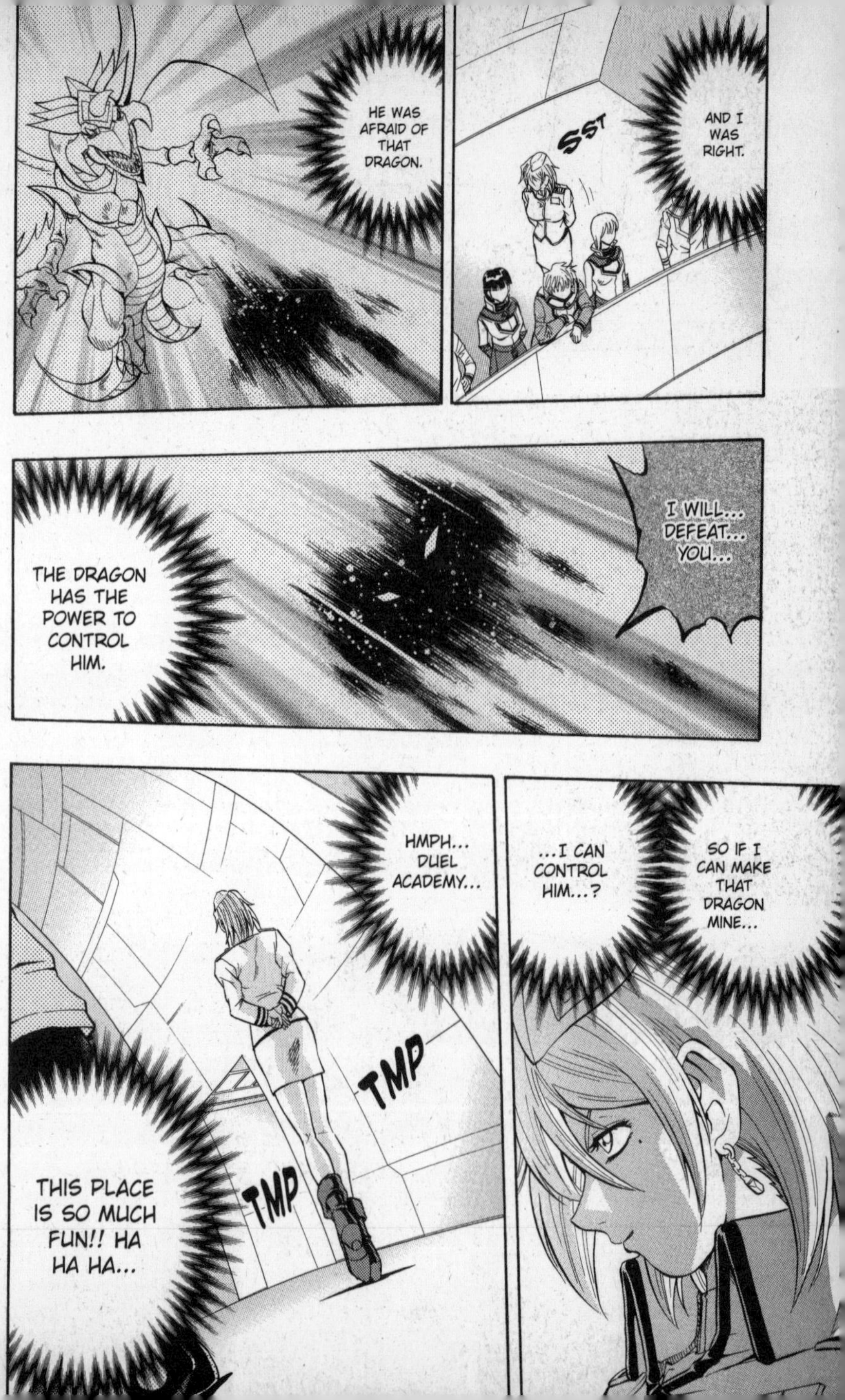
SST
AND I WAS RIGHT.
HE WAS AFRAID OF THAT DRAGON.
I WILL... DEFEAT... YOU...
THE DRAGON HAS THE POWER TO CONTROL HIM.
SO IF I CAN MAKE THAT DRAGON MINE...
...I CAN CONTROL HIM...?
HMPH... DUEL ACADEMY...
TMP
TMP
THIS PLACE IS SO MUCH FUN!! HA HA HA...

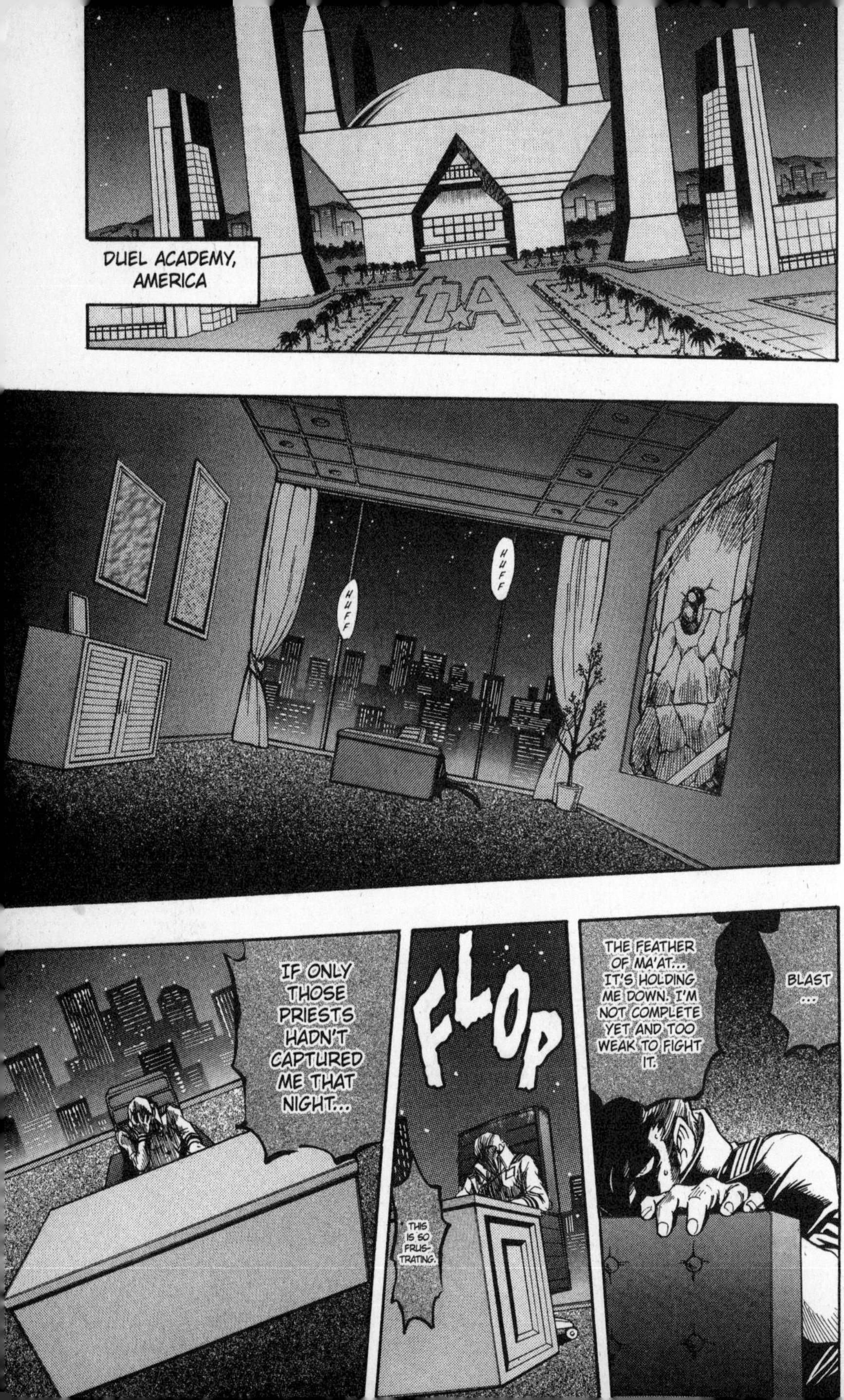
DUEL ACADEMY, AMERICA
HUFF
HUFF
BLAST...
THE FEATHER OF MA'AT... IT'S HOLDING ME DOWN. I'M NOT COMPLETE YET AND TOO WEAK TO FIGHT IT.
FLOP
THIS IS SO FRUS-TRATING.
IF ONLY THOSE PRIESTS HADN'T CAPTURED ME THAT NIGHT...

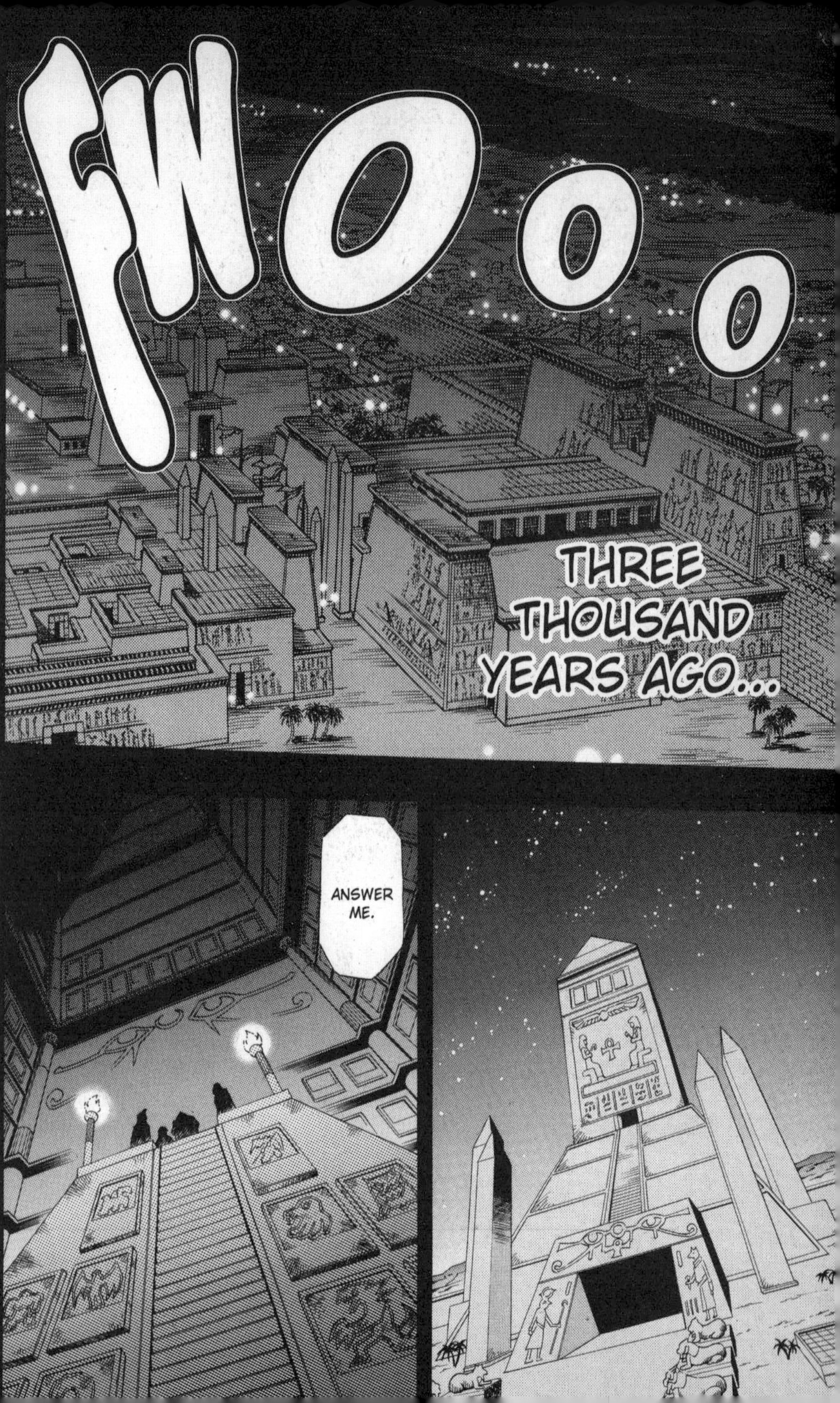
FWOOOO
THREE THOUSAND YEARS AGO...
ANSWER ME.

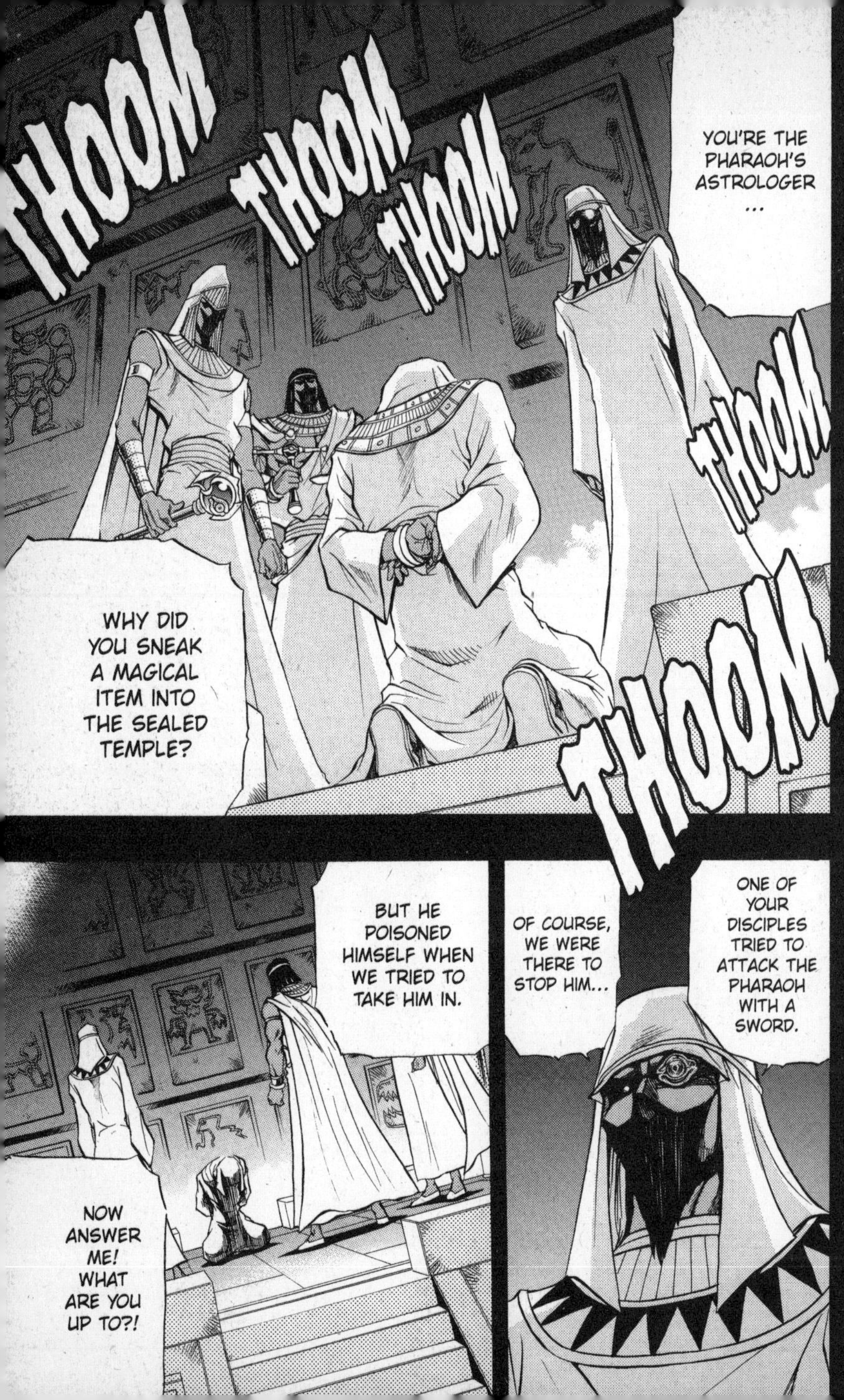
YOU'RE THE PHARAOH'S ASTROLOGER ...
THOOM
THOOM
THOOM
THOOM
THOOM
THOOM
WHY DID YOU SNEAK A MAGICAL ITEM INTO THE SEALED TEMPLE?
ONE OF YOUR DISCIPLES TRIED TO ATTACK THE PHARAOH WITH A SWORD.
OF COURSE, WE WERE THERE TO STOP HIM...
BUT HE POISONED HIMSELF WHEN WE TRIED TO TAKE HIM IN.
NOW ANSWER ME! WHAT ARE YOU UP TO?!

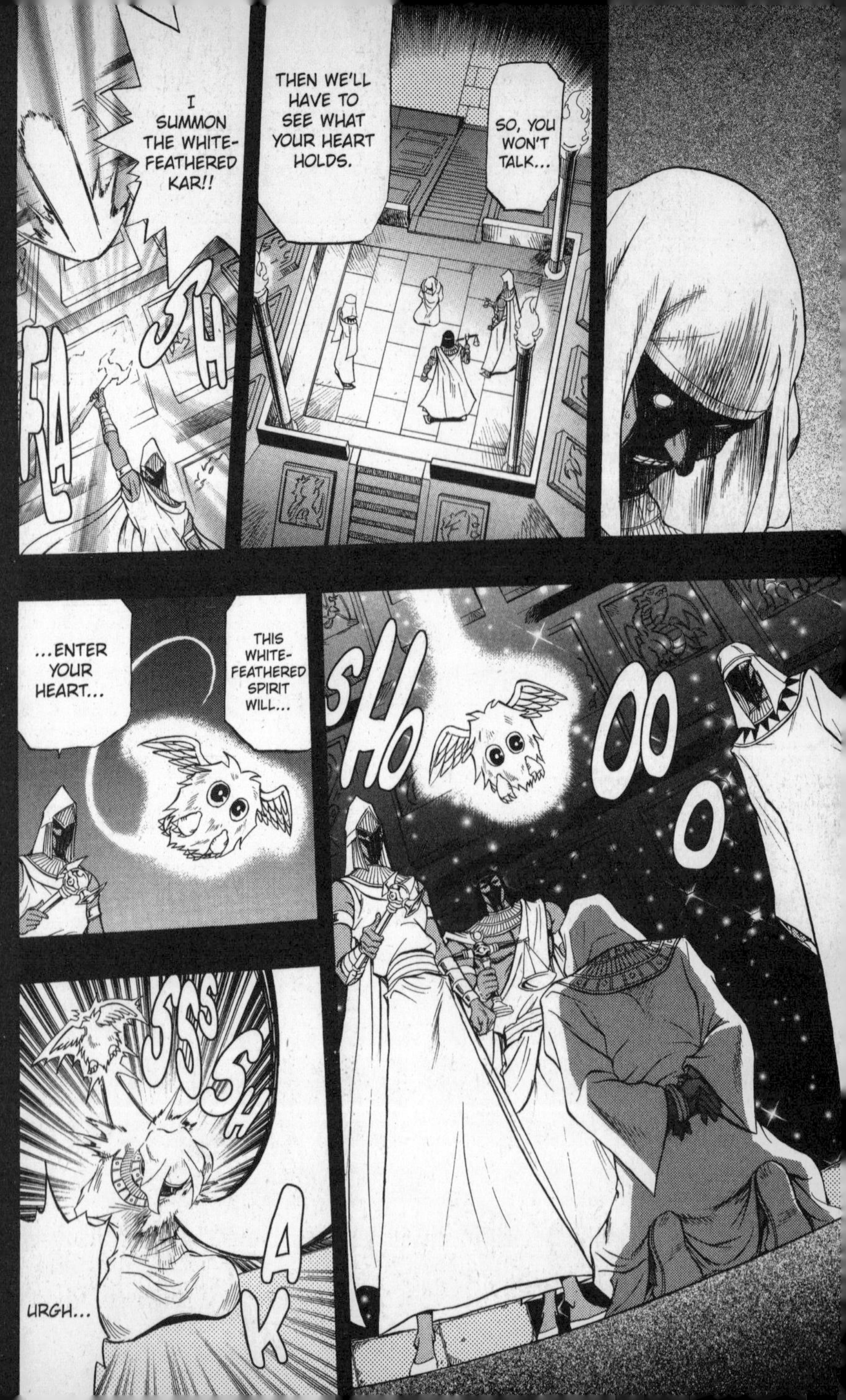
SO, YOU WON'T TALK...
THEN WE'LL HAVE TO SEE WHAT YOUR HEART HOLDS.
I SUMMON THE WHITE-FEATHERED KAR!!
FLASH
SHOOOO
THIS WHITE-FEATHERED SPIRIT WILL...
...ENTER YOUR HEART...
SSSSHAK
URGH...

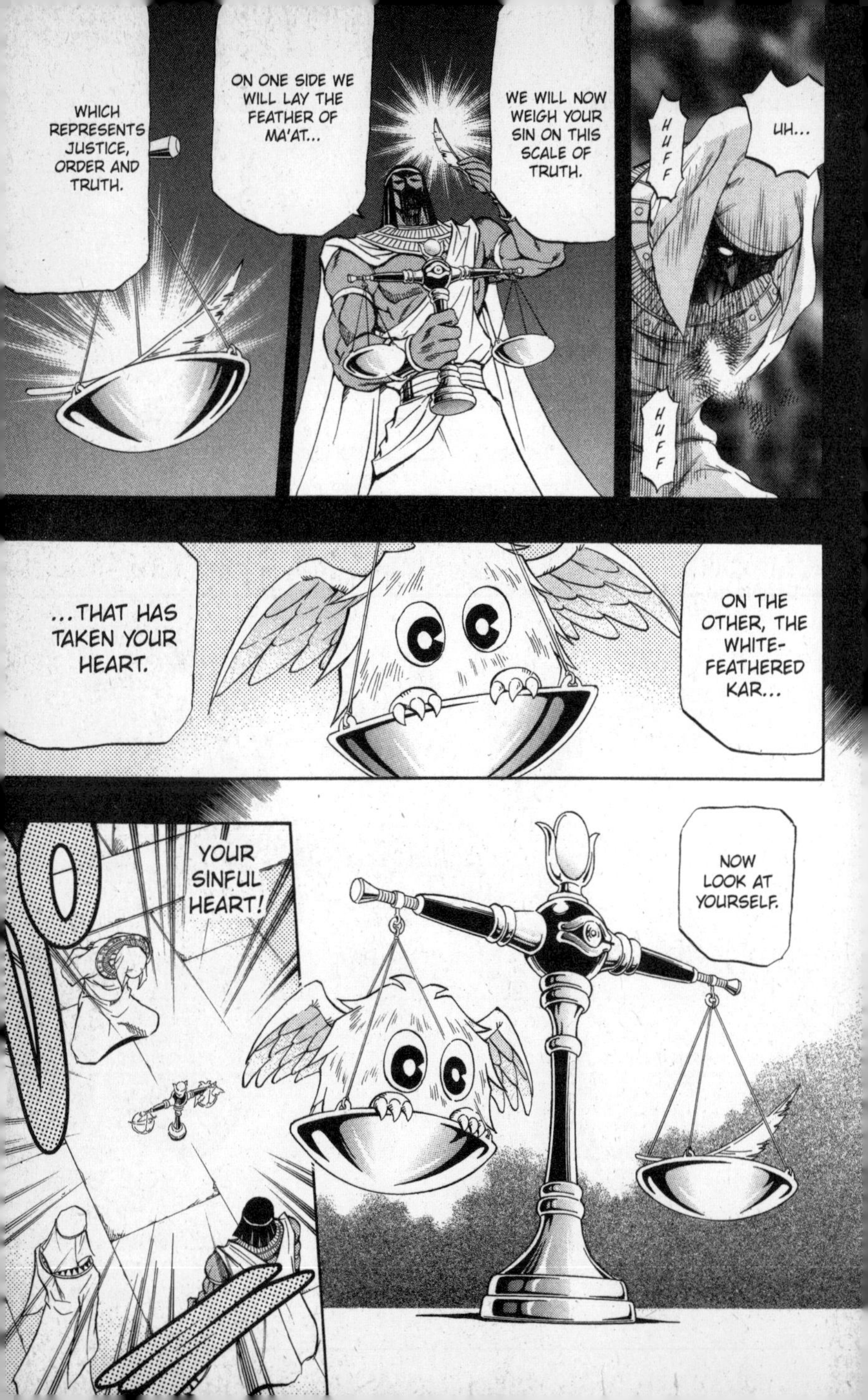
UH...
HUFF
HUFF
WE WILL NOW WEIGH YOUR SIN ON THIS SCALE OF TRUTH.
ON ONE SIDE WE WILL LAY THE FEATHER OF MA'AT...
WHICH REPRESENTS JUSTICE, ORDER AND TRUTH.
ON THE OTHER, THE WHITE-FEATHERED KAR...
...THAT HAS TAKEN YOUR HEART.
NOW LOOK AT YOURSELF.
YOUR SINFUL HEART!

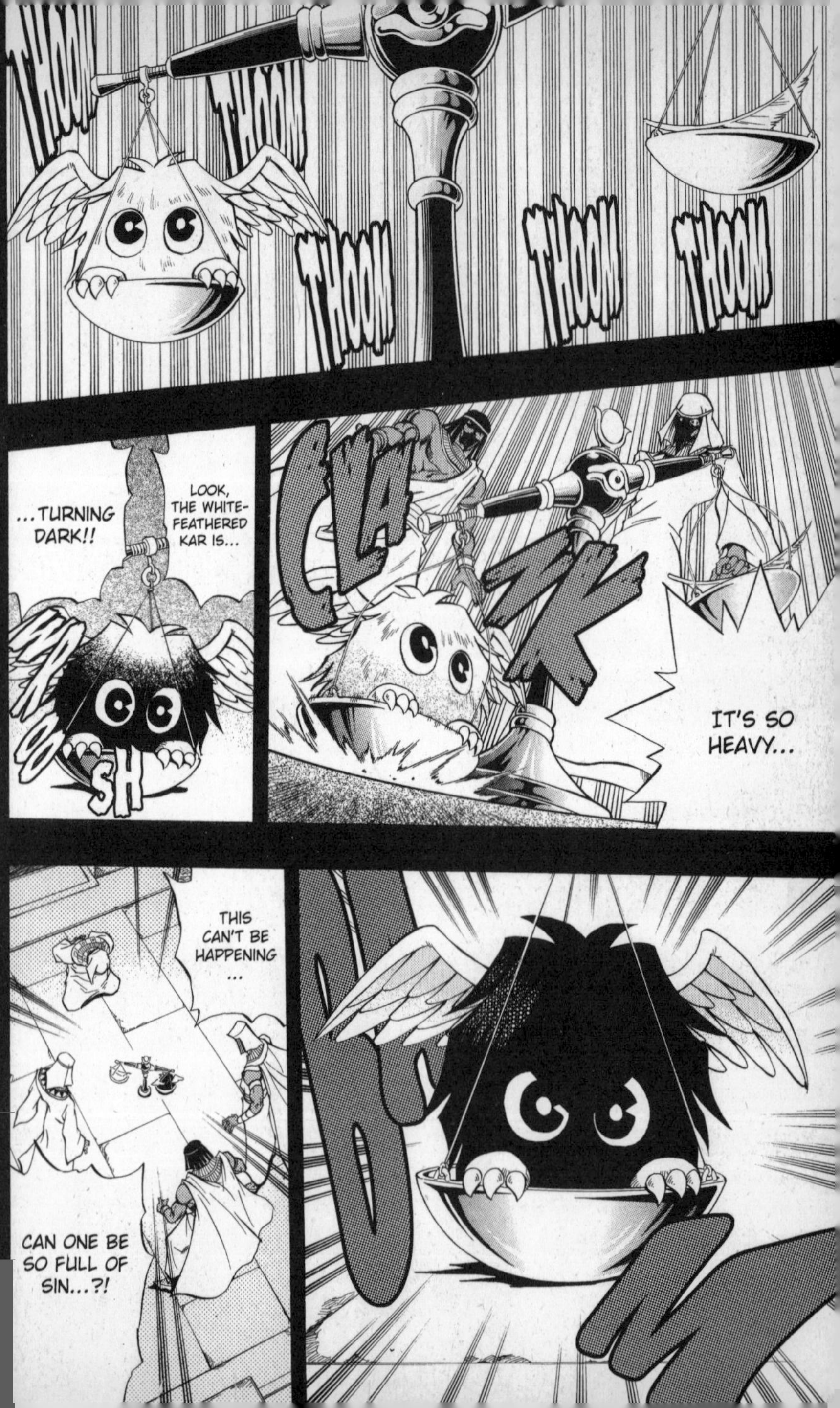
THOOM
THOOM
THOOM
THOOM
THOOM
CLANK
IT'S SO HEAVY...
LOOK, THE WHITE-FEATHERED KAR IS...
...TURNING DARK!!
WHOOSH
THIS CAN'T BE HAPPENING...
CAN ONE BE SO FULL OF SIN...?!

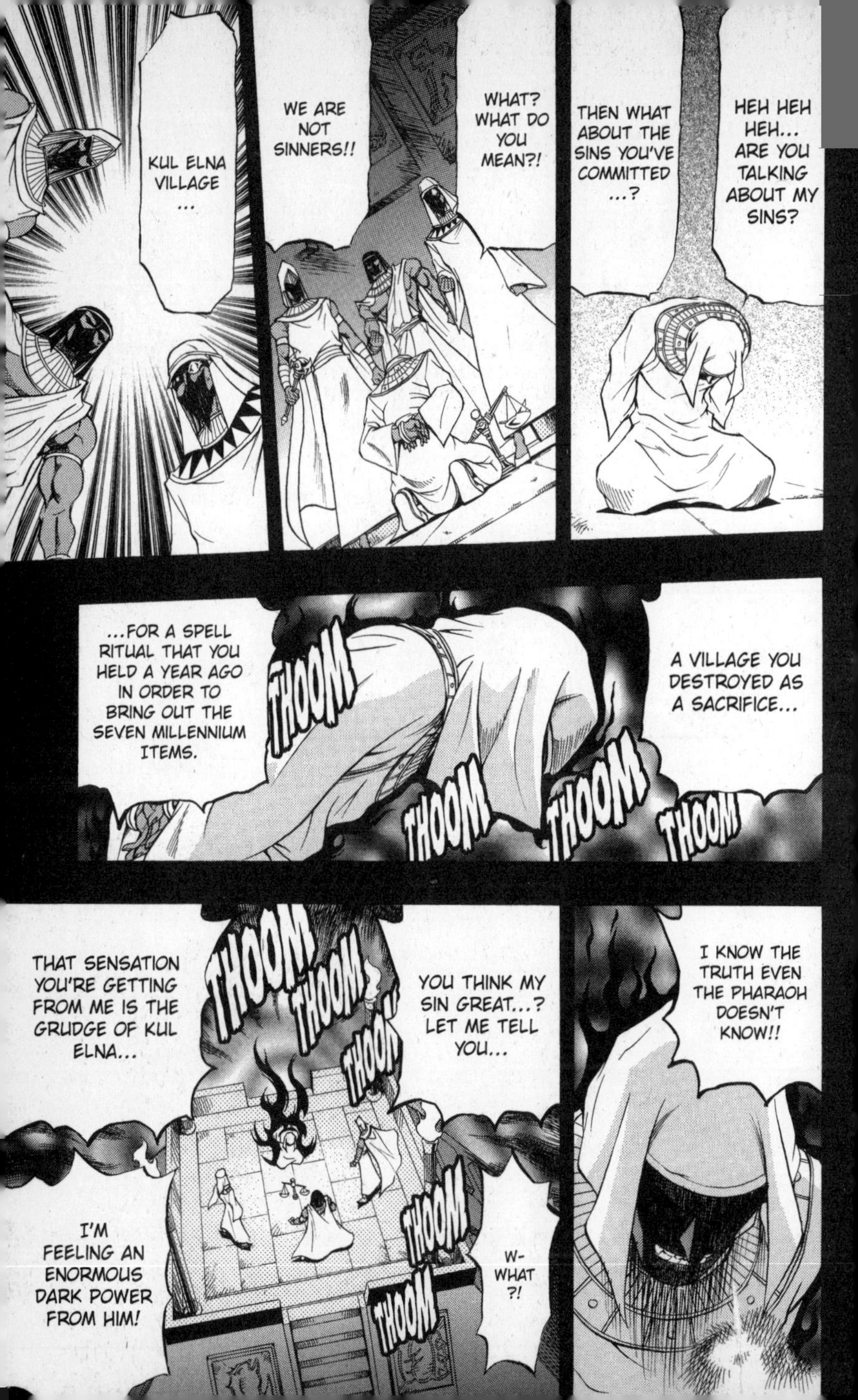
HEH HEH HEH... ARE YOU TALKING ABOUT MY SINS?
THEN WHAT ABOUT THE SINS YOU'VE COMMITTED ...?
WHAT? WHAT DO YOU MEAN?!
WE ARE NOT SINNERS!!
KUL ELNA VILLAGE ...
A VILLAGE YOU DESTROYED AS A SACRIFICE...
...FOR A SPELL RITUAL THAT YOU HELD A YEAR AGO IN ORDER TO BRING OUT THE SEVEN MILLENNIUM ITEMS.
THOOM
THOOM
THOOM
THOOM
I KNOW THE TRUTH EVEN THE PHARAOH DOESN'T KNOW!!
YOU THINK MY SIN GREAT...? LET ME TELL YOU...
THAT SENSATION YOU'RE GETTING FROM ME IS THE GRUDGE OF KUL ELNA...
THOOM
THOOM
THOOM
THOOM
THOOM
W- WHAT ?!
I'M FEELING AN ENORMOUS DARK POWER FROM HIM!

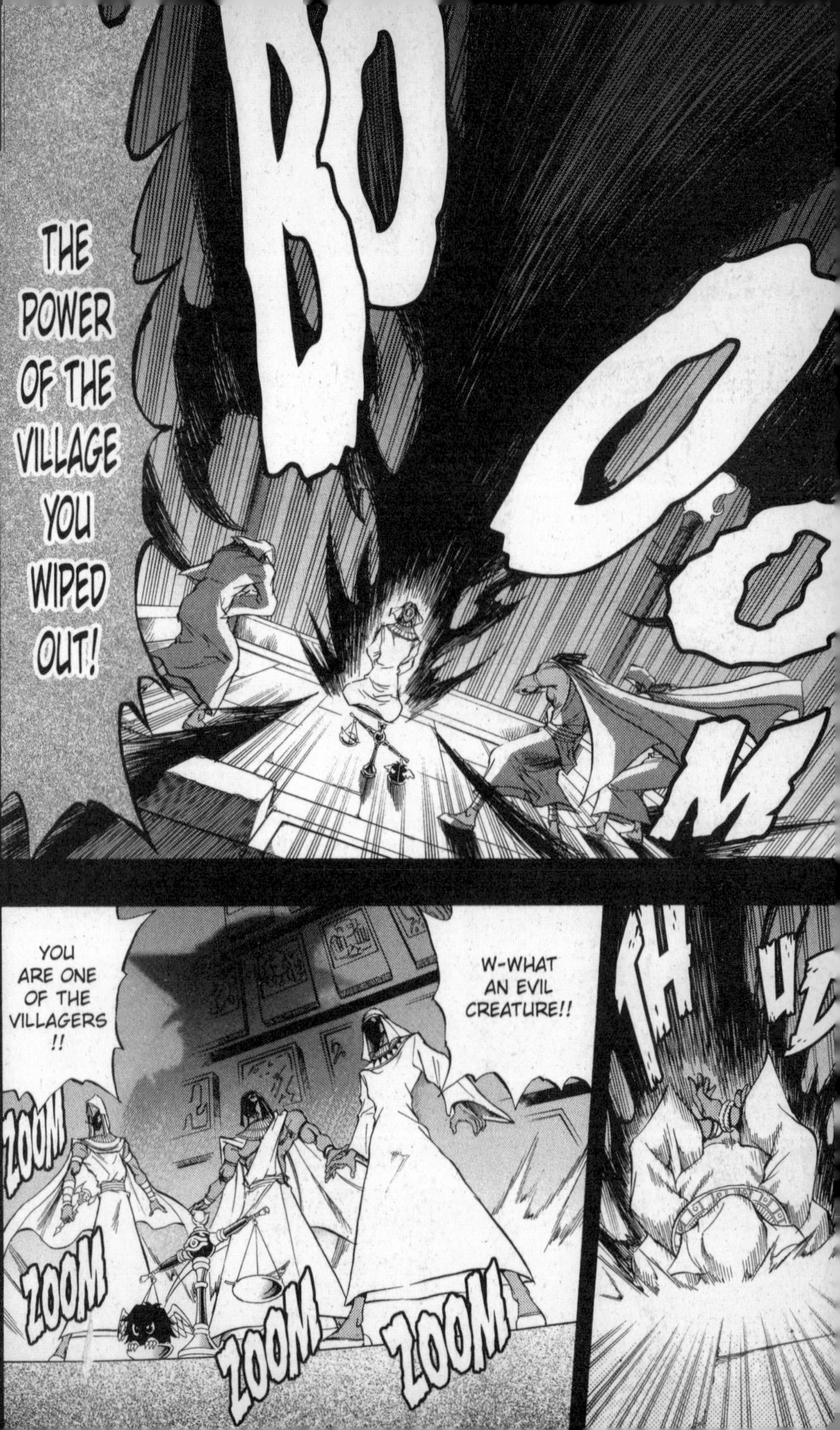
BOOM
THE POWER OF THE VILLAGE YOU WIPED OUT!
THU
W-WHAT AN EVIL CREATURE!!
YOU ARE ONE OF THE VILLAGERS!!
ZOOM
ZOOM
ZOOM
ZOOM

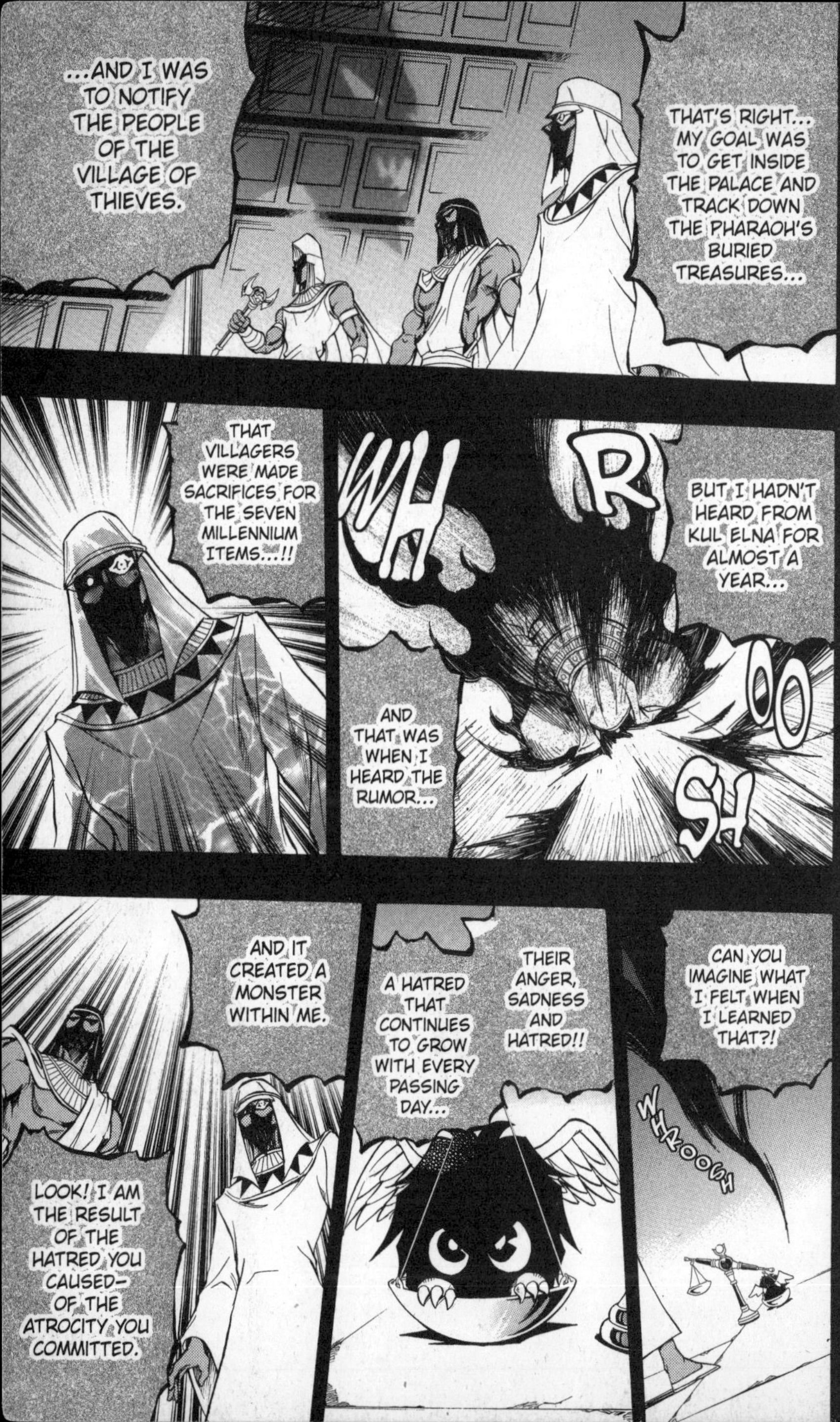
THAT'S RIGHT... MY GOAL WAS TO GET INSIDE THE PALACE AND TRACK DOWN THE PHARAOH'S BURIED TREASURES...
...AND I WAS TO NOTIFY THE PEOPLE OF THE VILLAGE OF THIEVES.
BUT I HADN'T HEARD FROM KUL ELNA FOR ALMOST A YEAR...
WHROOSH
AND THAT WAS WHEN I HEARD THE RUMOR...
THAT VILLAGERS WERE MADE SACRIFICES FOR THE SEVEN MILLENNIUM ITEMS...!!
CAN YOU IMAGINE WHAT I FELT WHEN I LEARNED THAT?!
WHAKOOSH
THEIR ANGER, SADNESS AND HATRED!!
A HATRED THAT CONTINUES TO GROW WITH EVERY PASSING DAY...
AND IT CREATED A MONSTER WITHIN ME.
LOOK! I AM THE RESULT OF THE HATRED YOU CAUSED— OF THE ATROCITY YOU COMMITTED.

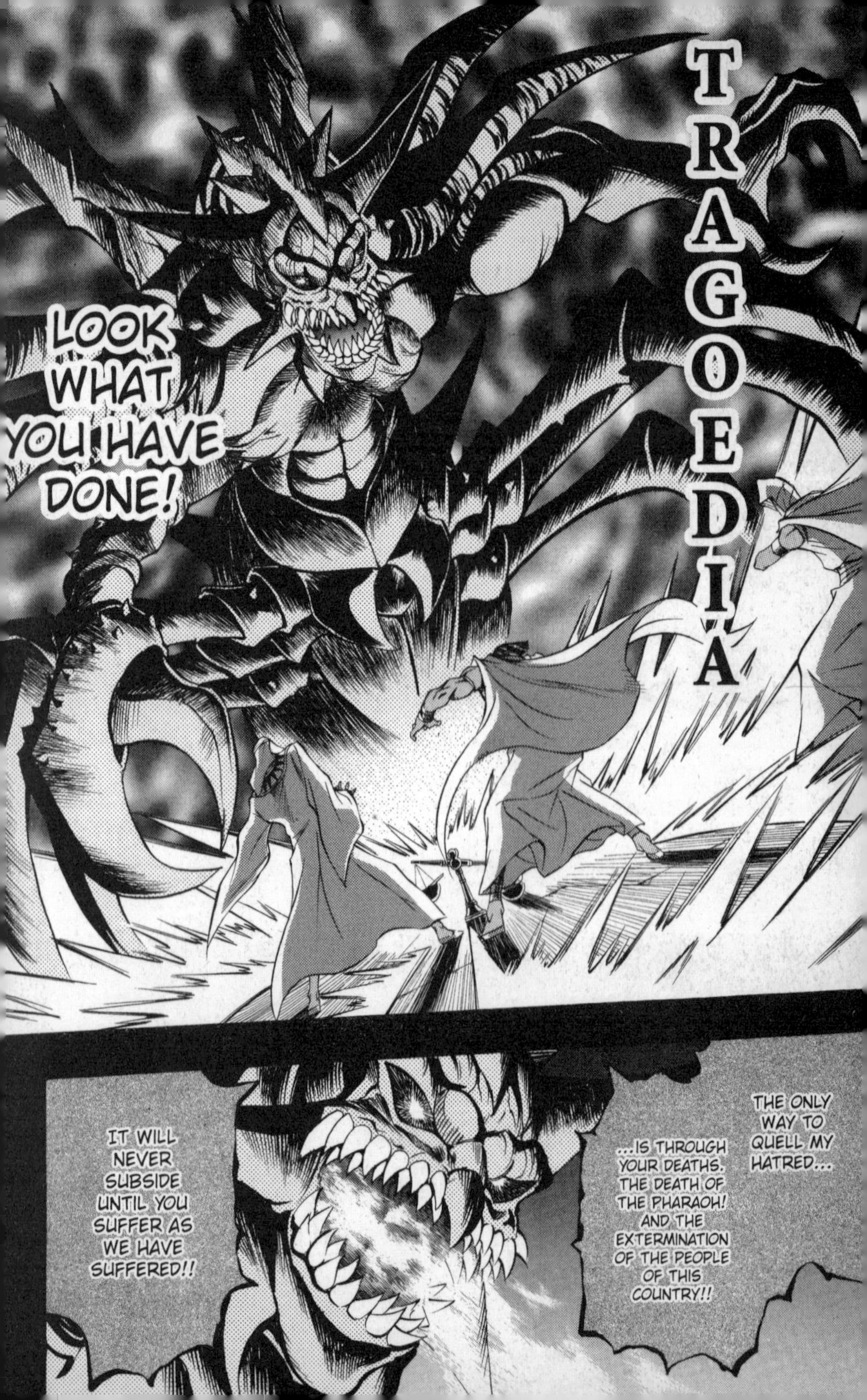
TRAGOEDIA
LOOK WHAT YOU HAVE DONE!
THE ONLY WAY TO QUELL MY HATRED...
...IS THROUGH YOUR DEATHS. THE DEATH OF THE PHARAOH! AND THE EXTERMINATION OF THE PEOPLE OF THIS COUNTRY!!
IT WILL NEVER SUBSIDE UNTIL YOU SUFFER AS WE HAVE SUFFERED!!

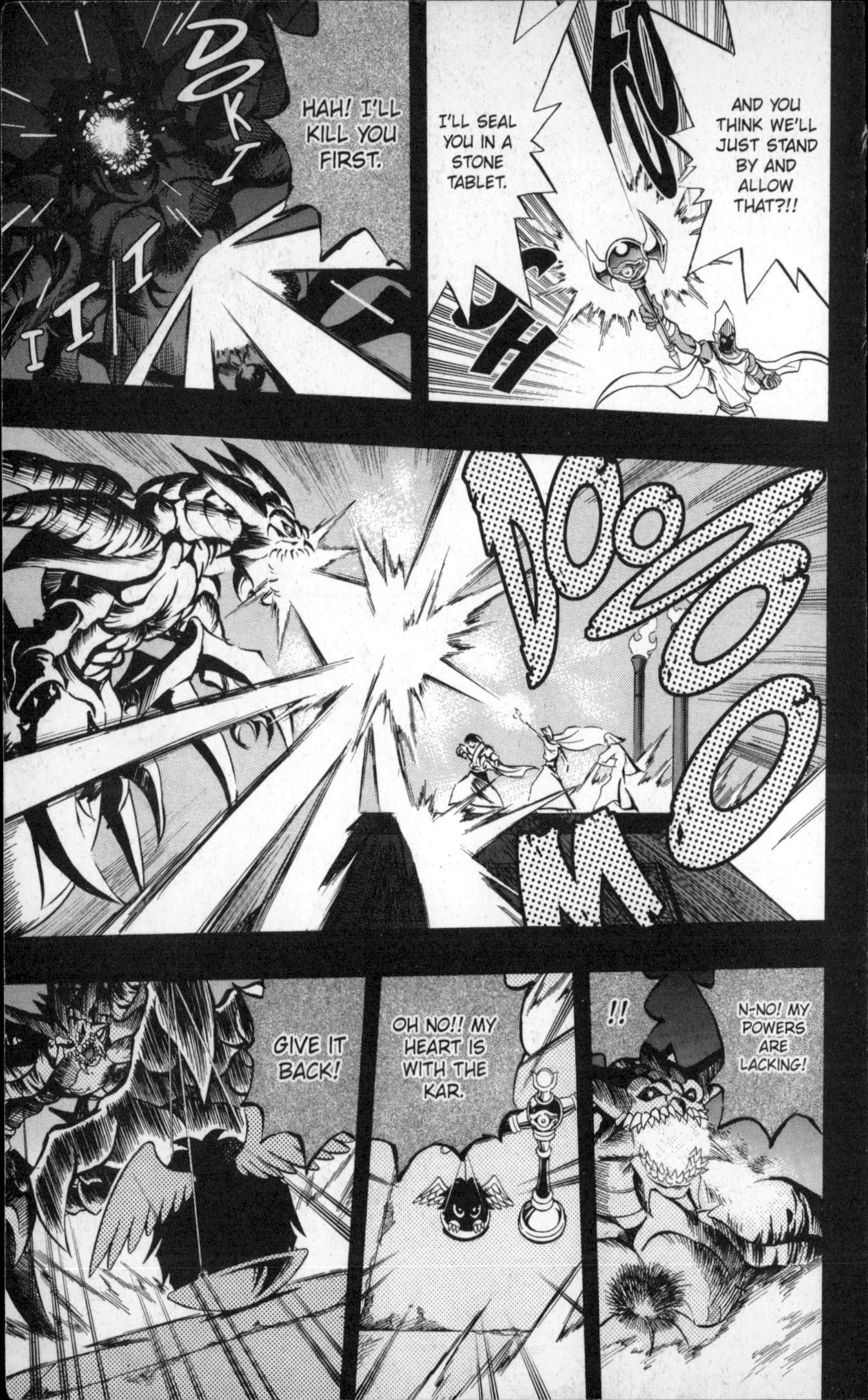
AND YOU THINK WE'LL JUST STAND BY AND ALLOW THAT?!!
I'LL SEAL YOU IN A STONE TABLET.
DOKI
HAH! I'LL KILL YOU FIRST.
DOOOOOM
N-NO! MY POWERS ARE LACKING!
!!
OH NO!! MY HEART IS WITH THE KAR.
GIVE IT BACK!

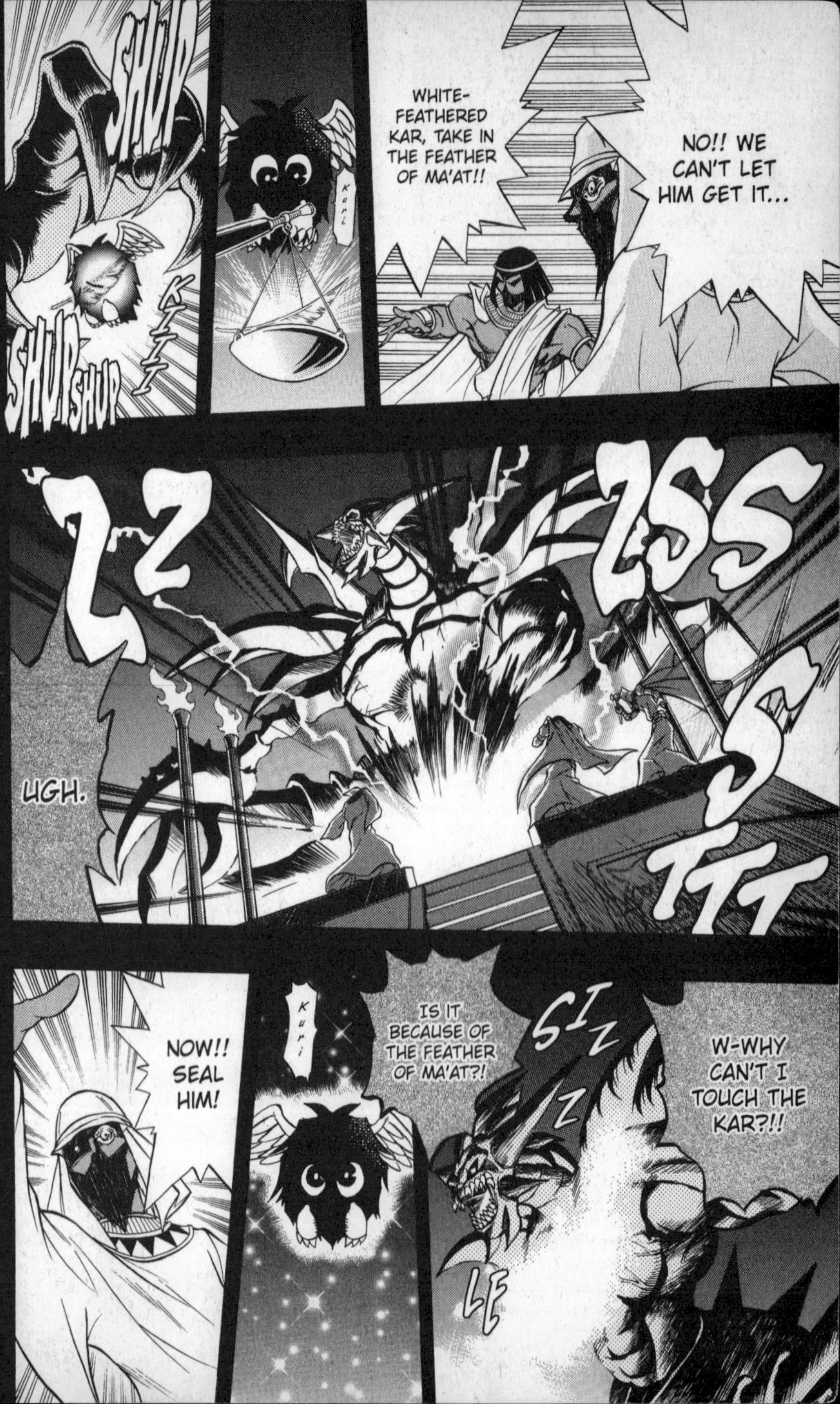
WHITE-FEATHERED KAR, TAKE IN THE FEATHER OF MA'AT!!
NO!! WE CAN'T LET HIM GET IT...
Kuri
SHUP
KITII
SHUP SHUP
ZSSSTTT
ZZ
UGH.
W-WHY CAN'T I TOUCH THE KAR?!!
SIZZLE
IS IT BECAUSE OF THE FEATHER OF MA'AT?!
Kuri
NOW!! SEAL HIM!

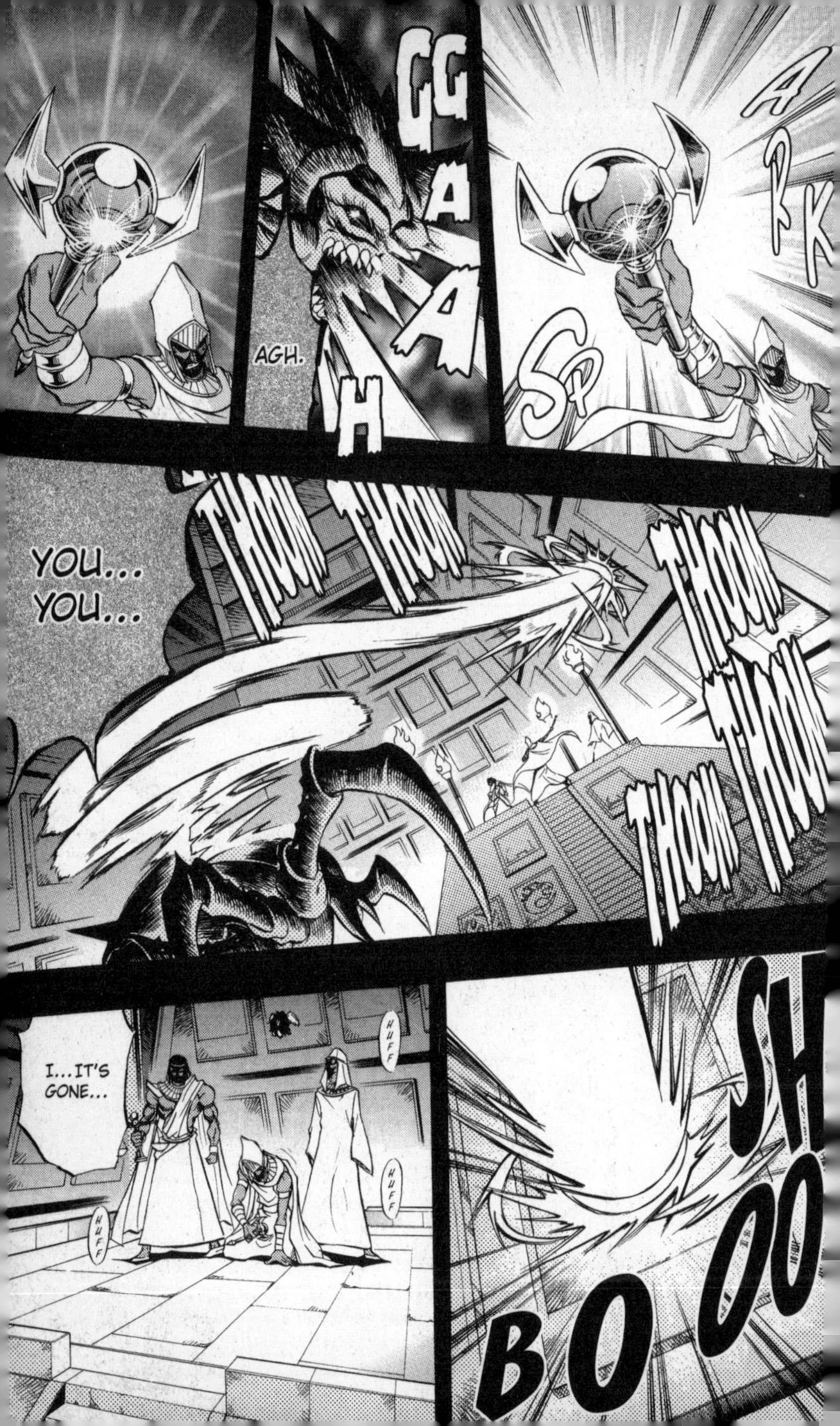

Sp
ARK
GGAAH
AGH.
THOOM
THOOM
THOOM
THOOM
THOOM
YOU...
YOU...
SH
BOOO
HUFF
HUFF
HUFF
I...IT'S GONE...

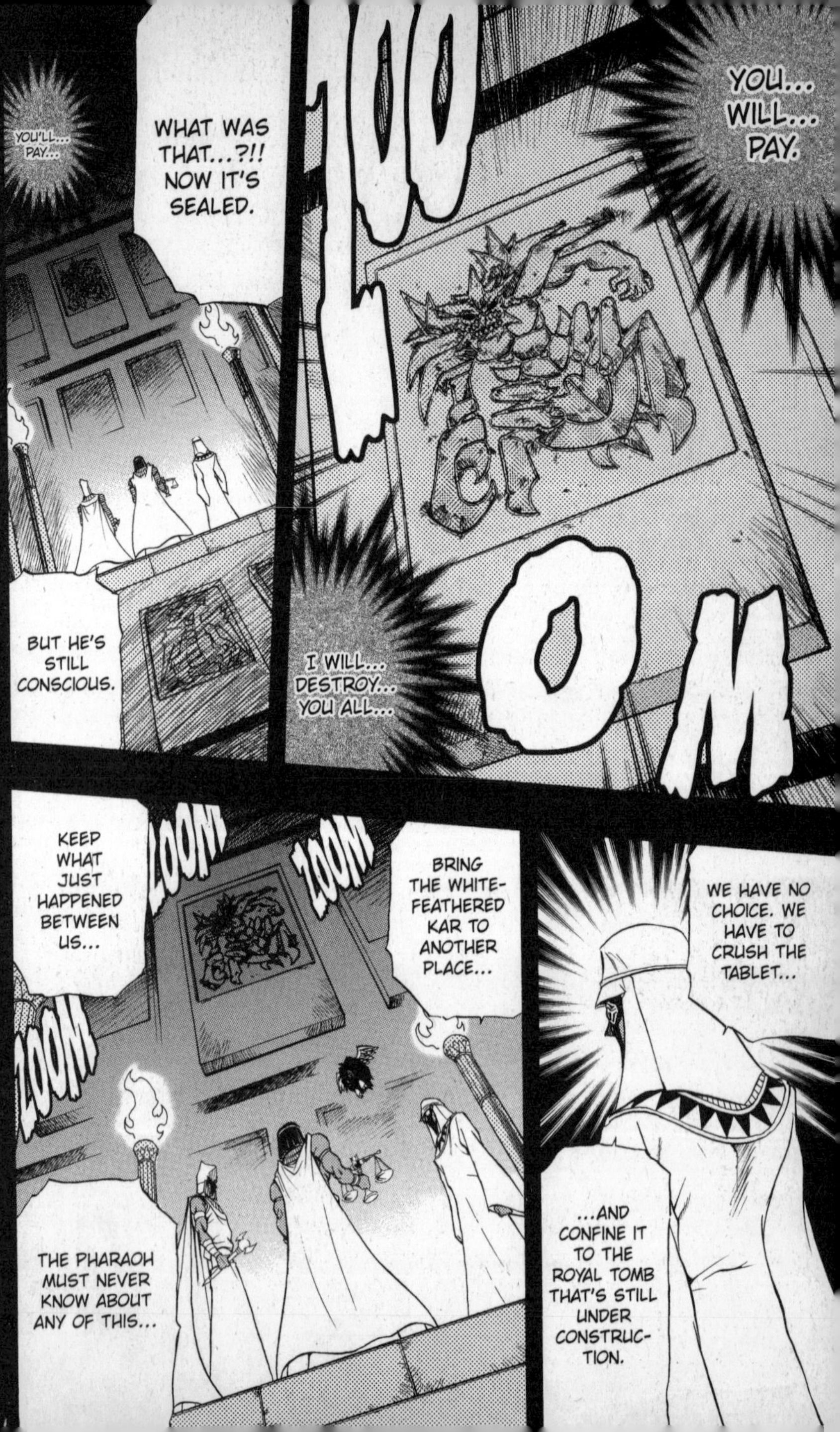
YOU... WILL... PAY.
I WILL... DESTROY... YOU ALL...
YOU'LL... PAY...
WHAT WAS THAT...?!! NOW IT'S SEALED.
BUT HE'S STILL CONSCIOUS.
WE HAVE NO CHOICE. WE HAVE TO CRUSH THE TABLET...
...AND CONFINE IT TO THE ROYAL TOMB THAT'S STILL UNDER CONSTRUC-TION.
BRING THE WHITE-FEATHERED KAR TO ANOTHER PLACE...
ZOOM
ZOOM
KEEP WHAT JUST HAPPENED BETWEEN US...
ZOOM
THE PHARAOH MUST NEVER KNOW ABOUT ANY OF THIS...

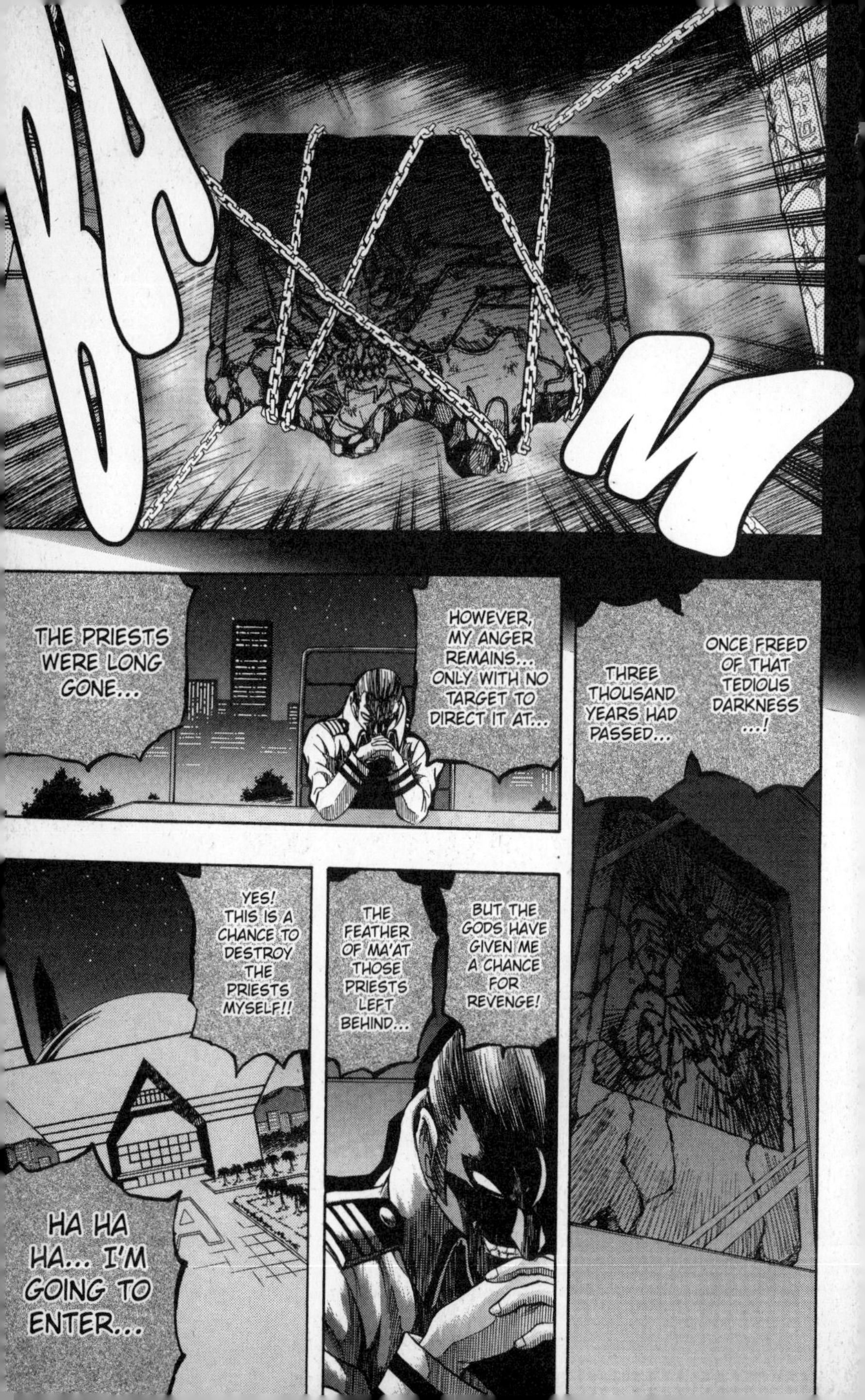
BAM
ONCE FREED OF THAT TEDIOUS DARKNESS ...!
THREE THOUSAND YEARS HAD PASSED...
HOWEVER, MY ANGER REMAINS... ONLY WITH NO TARGET TO DIRECT IT AT...
THE PRIESTS WERE LONG GONE...
BUT THE GODS HAVE GIVEN ME A CHANCE FOR REVENGE!
THE FEATHER OF MA'AT THOSE PRIESTS LEFT BEHIND...
YES! THIS IS A CHANCE TO DESTROY THE PRIESTS MYSELF!!
HA HA HA... I'M GOING TO ENTER...

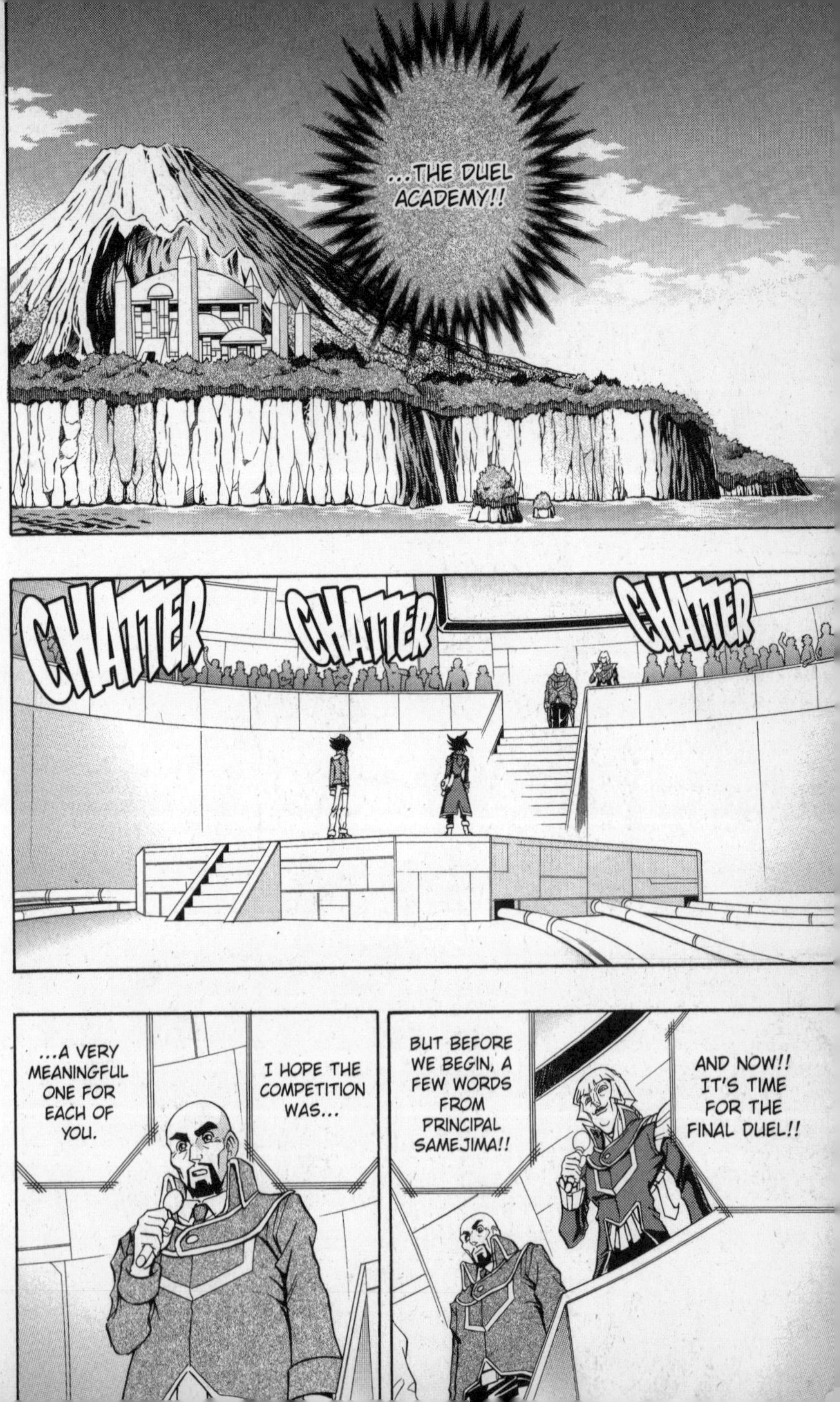
...THE DUEL ACADEMY!!
CHATTER
CHATTER
CHATTER
AND NOW!! IT'S TIME FOR THE FINAL DUEL!!
BUT BEFORE WE BEGIN, A FEW WORDS FROM PRINCIPAL SAMEJIMA!!
I HOPE THE COMPETITION WAS...
...A VERY MEANINGFUL ONE FOR EACH OF YOU.

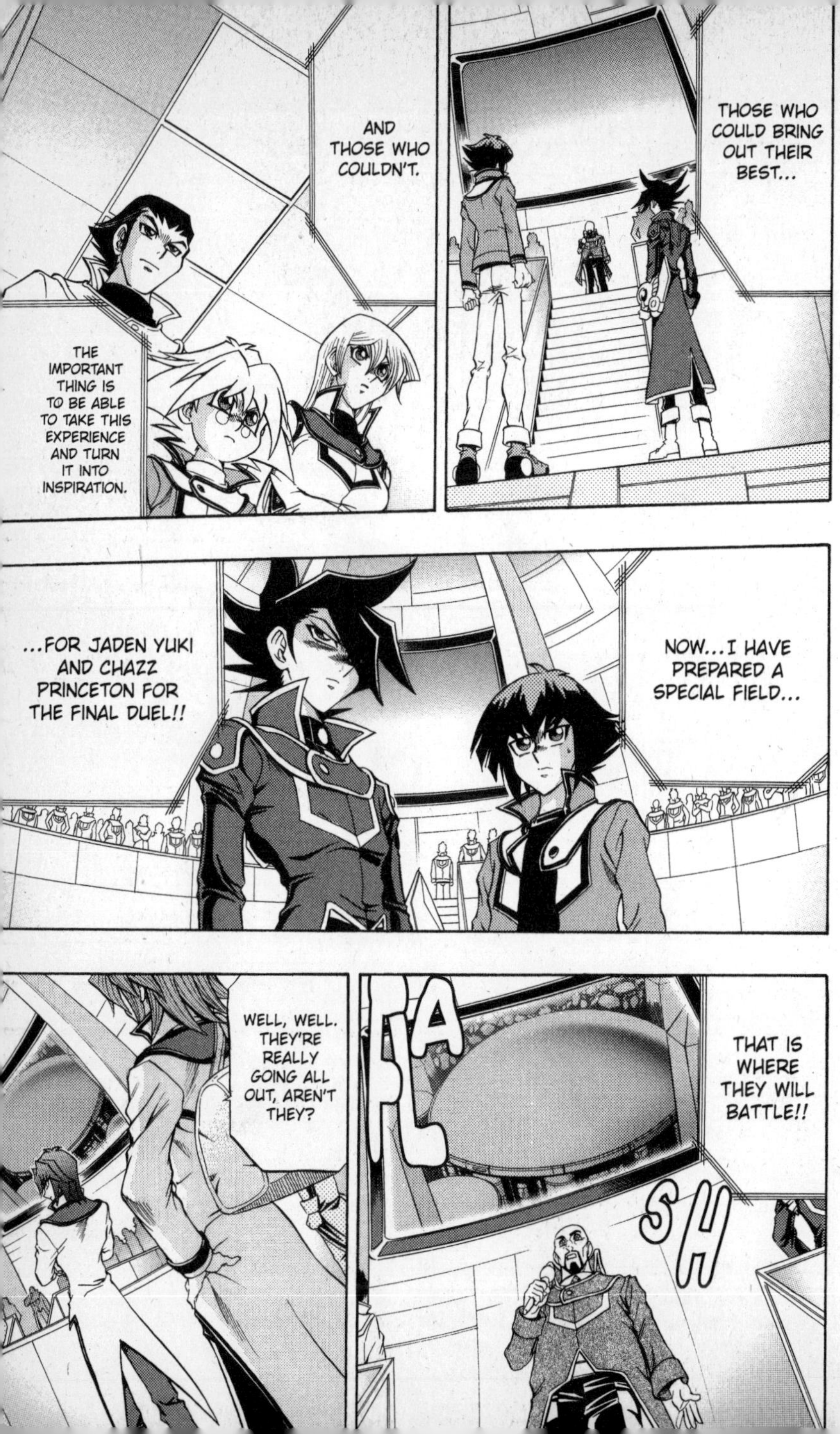
THOSE WHO COULD BRING OUT THEIR BEST...
AND THOSE WHO COULDN'T.
THE IMPORTANT THING IS TO BE ABLE TO TAKE THIS EXPERIENCE AND TURN IT INTO INSPIRATION.
NOW...I HAVE PREPARED A SPECIAL FIELD...
...FOR JADEN YUKI AND CHAZZ PRINCETON FOR THE FINAL DUEL!!
THAT IS WHERE THEY WILL BATTLE!!
FLASH
WELL, WELL. THEY'RE REALLY GOING ALL OUT, AREN'T THEY?

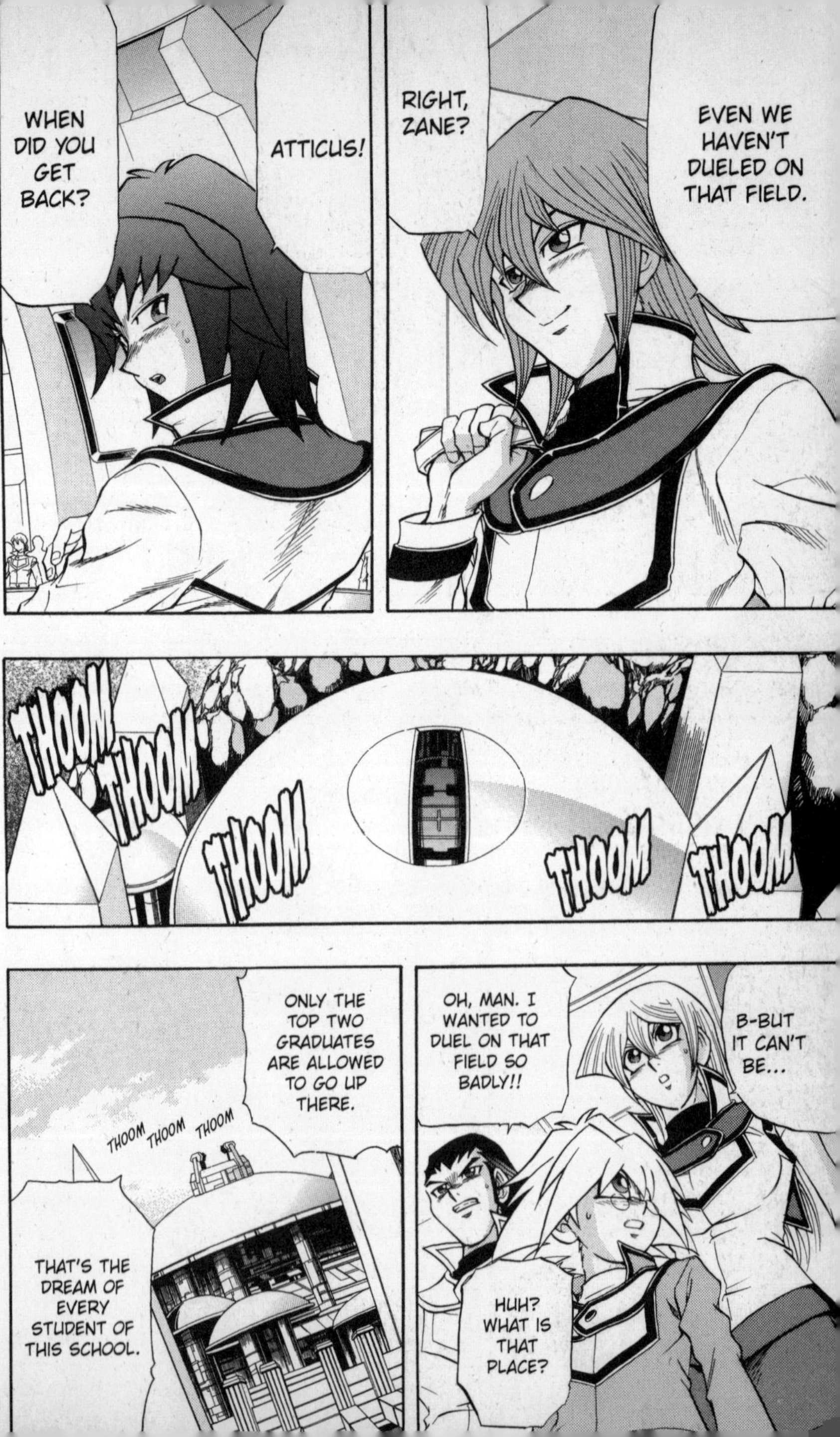
EVEN WE HAVEN'T DUELED ON THAT FIELD.
RIGHT, ZANE?
ATTICUS!
WHEN DID YOU GET BACK?
THOOM
THOOM
THOOM
THOOM
THOOM
B-BUT IT CAN'T BE...
OH, MAN. I WANTED TO DUEL ON THAT FIELD SO BADLY!!
HUH? WHAT IS THAT PLACE?
ONLY THE TOP TWO GRADUATES ARE ALLOWED TO GO UP THERE.
THOOM THOOM THOOM
THAT'S THE DREAM OF EVERY STUDENT OF THIS SCHOOL.

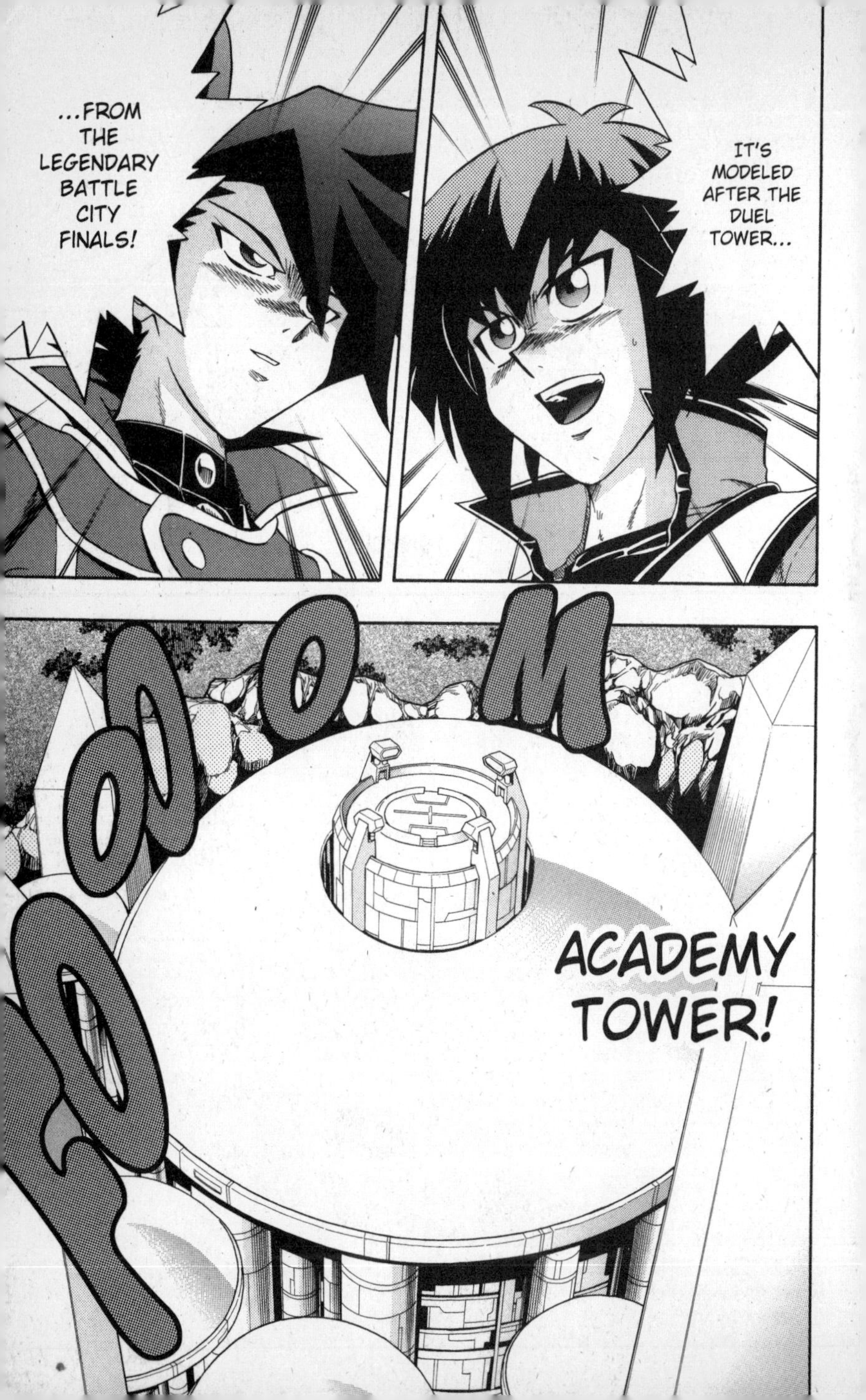
IT'S MODELED AFTER THE DUEL TOWER...
...FROM THE LEGENDARY BATTLE CITY FINALS!
ZOOOOM
ACADEMY TOWER!

HAVING DINNER WITH INU MAYUGE!
IN EARLY JUNE OF 2008 ...
...I HAD DINNER WITH ISHIZUKA-SAN.
Saito-san
Ishizuka-san
Terashi-san
Me
SHE HAS A WEALTH OF KNOWL-EDGE, SUCH AS...
HUH? IS THAT SO?!
YEAH. RIGHT.
...SECRET INFORMATION ABOUT *SHONEN JUMP*, CURRENT AFFAIRS, EVEN ABOUT CAVITIES, AND MUCH MORE...
Inu Mayu Expert
THIS NIGHT'S CONVERSATIONS URGED TERASHI-SAN TO GO TO THE DENTIST.
SHE SEEMED PRE-OCCUPIED WITH...
YOU MEAN... "YOU" OR "ME," AND STUFF, RIGHT?
THE ONE WHO TALKS LIKE, "YOU" OR "ME," RIGHT?
...CERTAIN EXPRES-SIONS IN *YU-GI-OH! GX*.
HAH, Y-YEAH... SORRY ABOUT THAT...
SHE DREW ISHIZUKA'S VERSION OF THE CHAZZ VS. DAVID STORY...
...IN A GIVEAWAY *V-JUMP* BOOKLET...

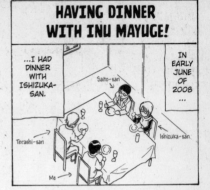

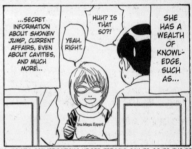

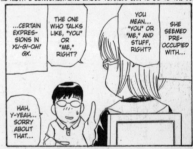

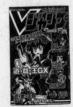

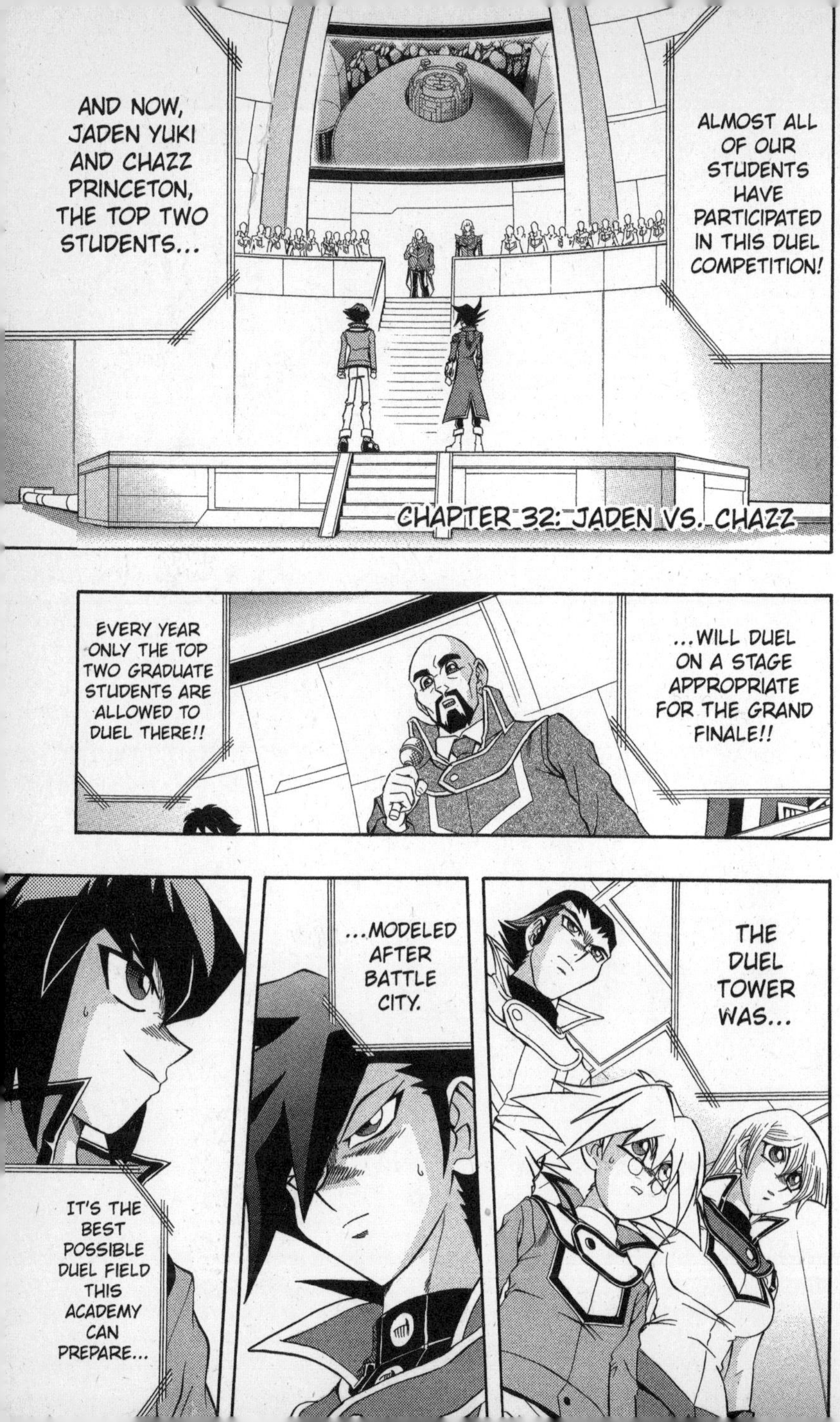
ALMOST ALL OF OUR STUDENTS HAVE PARTICIPATED IN THIS DUEL COMPETITION!
AND NOW, JADEN YUKI AND CHAZZ PRINCETON, THE TOP TWO STUDENTS...
CHAPTER 32: JADEN VS. CHAZZ
...WILL DUEL ON A STAGE APPROPRIATE FOR THE GRAND FINALE!!
EVERY YEAR ONLY THE TOP TWO GRADUATE STUDENTS ARE ALLOWED TO DUEL THERE!!
THE DUEL TOWER WAS...
...MODELED AFTER BATTLE CITY.
IT'S THE BEST POSSIBLE DUEL FIELD THIS ACADEMY CAN PREPARE...

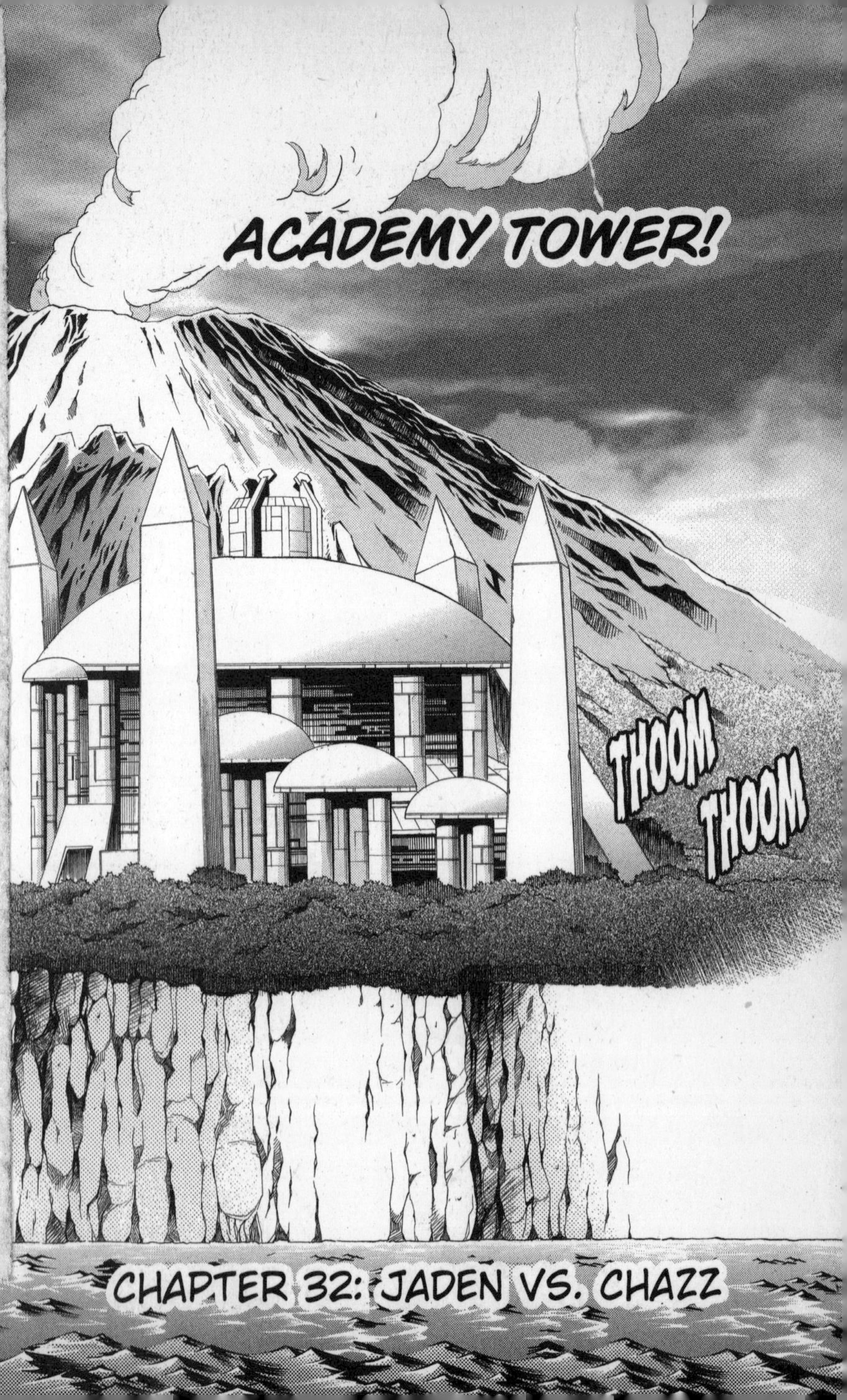
ACADEMY TOWER!
THOOM
THOOM
CHAPTER 32: JADEN VS. CHAZZ

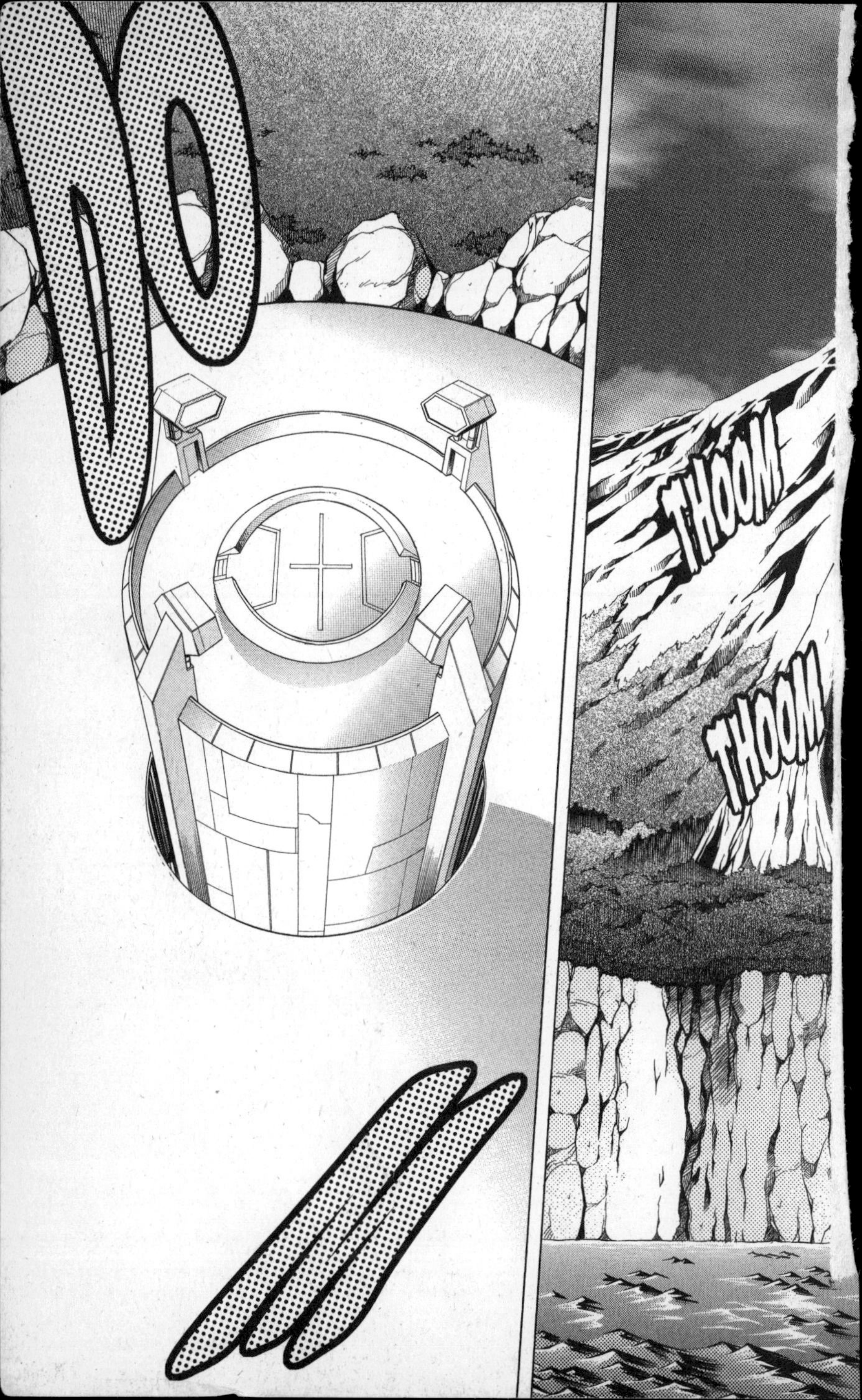
THOOM
THOOM

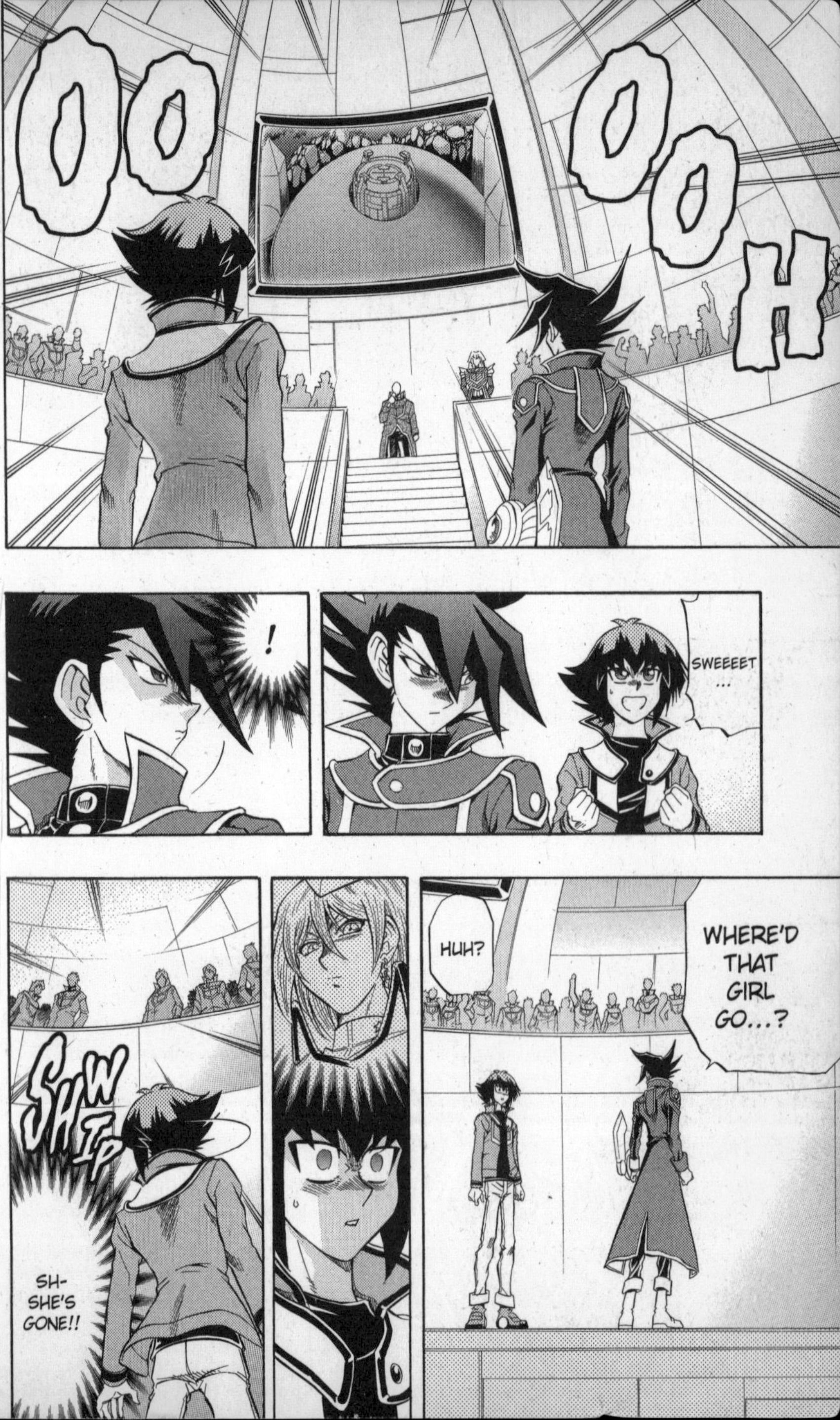
OOOOOH
SWEEEET...
!
WHERE'D THAT GIRL GO...?
HUH?
SHWIP
SH- SHE'S GONE!!

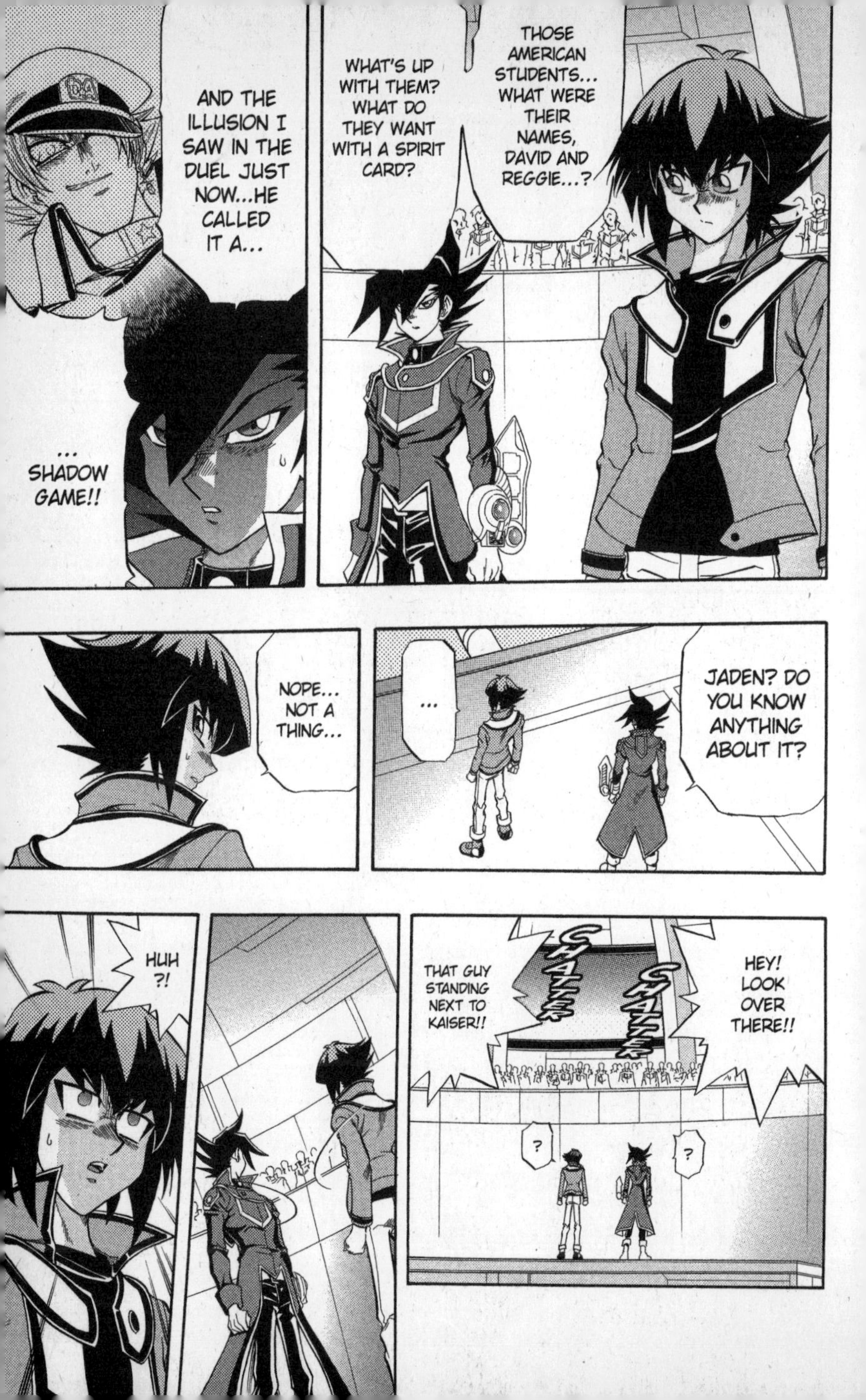
THOSE AMERICAN STUDENTS... WHAT WERE THEIR NAMES, DAVID AND REGGIE...?
WHAT'S UP WITH THEM? WHAT DO THEY WANT WITH A SPIRIT CARD?
AND THE ILLUSION I SAW IN THE DUEL JUST NOW...HE CALLED IT A...
... SHADOW GAME!!
JADEN? DO YOU KNOW ANYTHING ABOUT IT?
...
NOPE... NOT A THING...
HEY! LOOK OVER THERE!!
CHATTER
CHATTER
THAT GUY STANDING NEXT TO KAISER!!
?
?
HUH ?!

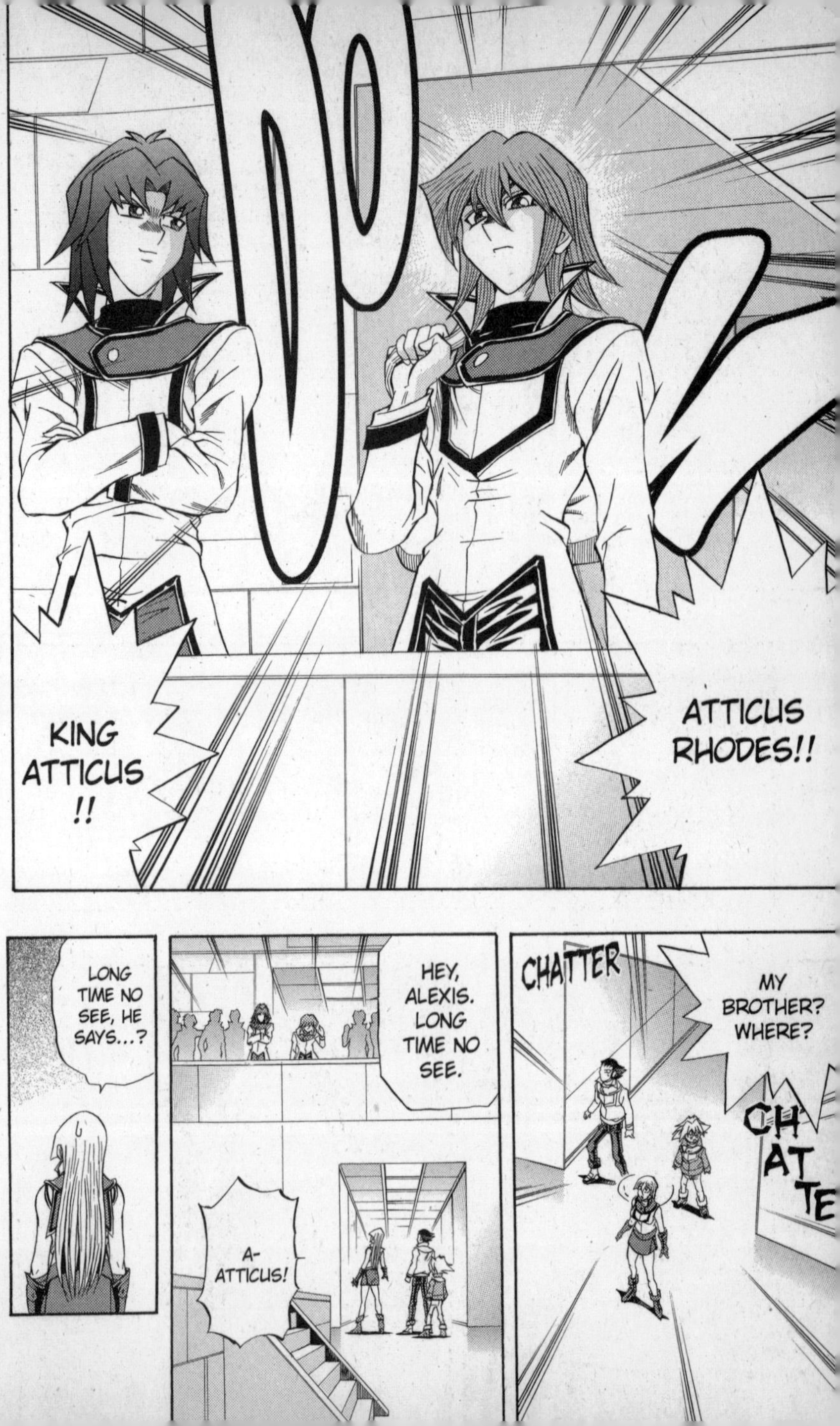
ATTICUS RHODES!!
KING ATTICUS !!
CHATTER
MY BROTHER? WHERE?
HEY, ALEXIS. LONG TIME NO SEE.
A- ATTICUS!
LONG TIME NO SEE, HE SAYS...?

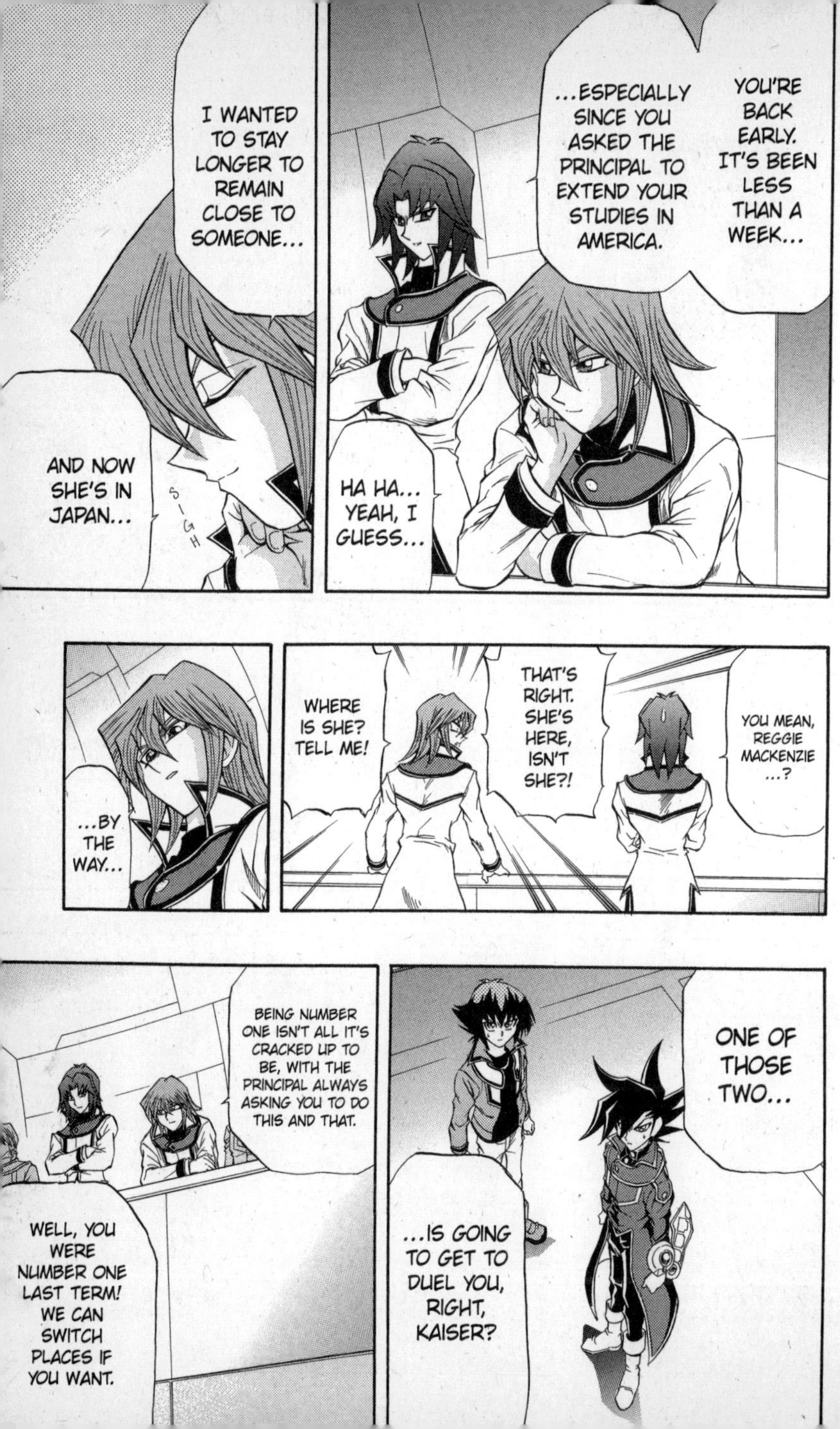
YOU'RE BACK EARLY. IT'S BEEN LESS THAN A WEEK...
...ESPECIALLY SINCE YOU ASKED THE PRINCIPAL TO EXTEND YOUR STUDIES IN AMERICA.
HA HA... YEAH, I GUESS...
I WANTED TO STAY LONGER TO REMAIN CLOSE TO SOMEONE...
AND NOW SHE'S IN JAPAN...
SIGH
YOU MEAN, REGGIE MACKENZIE ...?
THAT'S RIGHT. SHE'S HERE, ISN'T SHE?!
WHERE IS SHE? TELL ME!
...BY THE WAY...
ONE OF THOSE TWO...
...IS GOING TO GET TO DUEL YOU, RIGHT, KAISER?
BEING NUMBER ONE ISN'T ALL IT'S CRACKED UP TO BE, WITH THE PRINCIPAL ALWAYS ASKING YOU TO DO THIS AND THAT.
WELL, YOU WERE NUMBER ONE LAST TERM! WE CAN SWITCH PLACES IF YOU WANT.

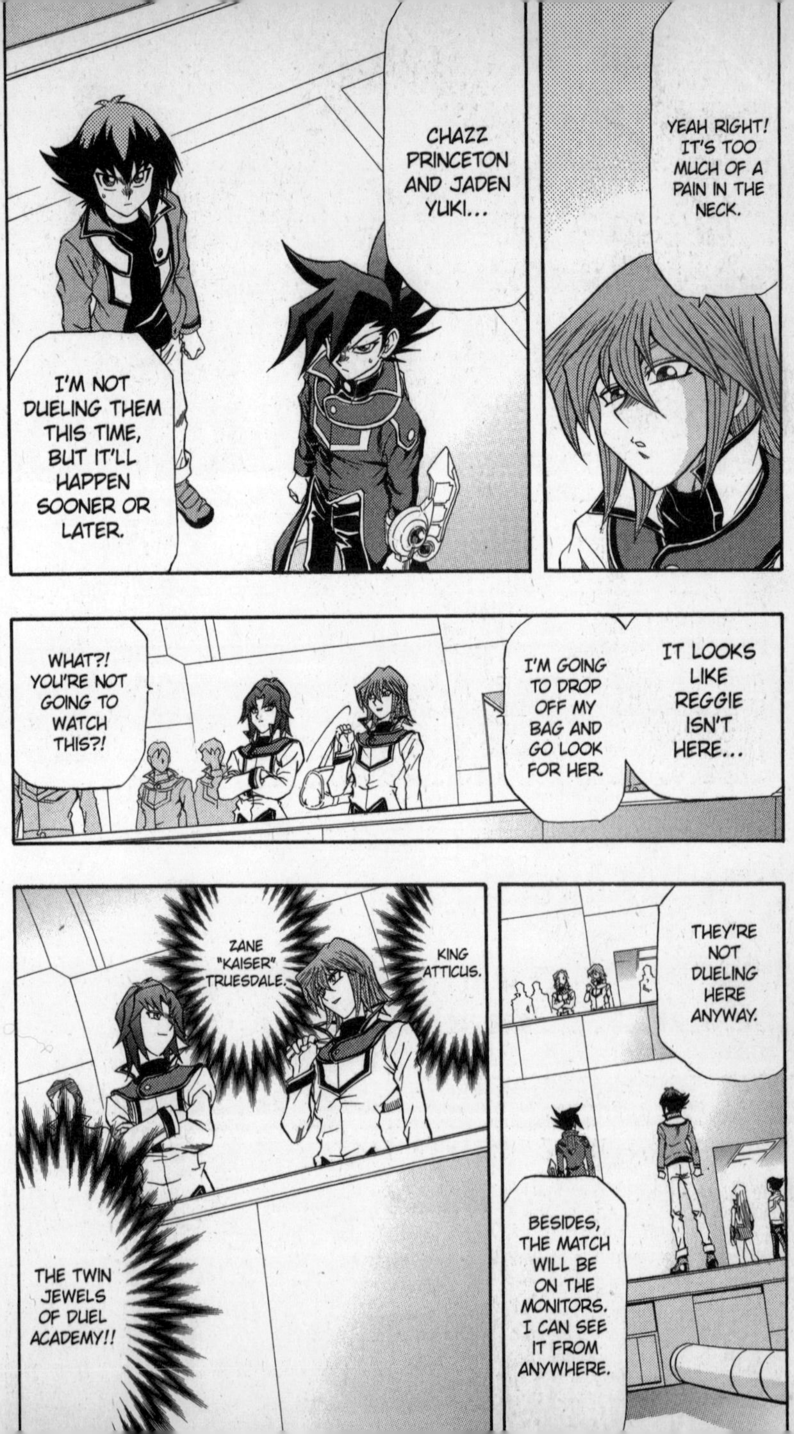
YEAH RIGHT! IT'S TOO MUCH OF A PAIN IN THE NECK.
CHAZZ PRINCETON AND JADEN YUKI...
I'M NOT DUELING THEM THIS TIME, BUT IT'LL HAPPEN SOONER OR LATER.
IT LOOKS LIKE REGGIE ISN'T HERE...
I'M GOING TO DROP OFF MY BAG AND GO LOOK FOR HER.
WHAT?! YOU'RE NOT GOING TO WATCH THIS?!
THEY'RE NOT DUELING HERE ANYWAY.
BESIDES, THE MATCH WILL BE ON THE MONITORS. I CAN SEE IT FROM ANYWHERE.
KING ATTICUS.
ZANE "KAISER" TRUESDALE.
THE TWIN JEWELS OF DUEL ACADEMY!!

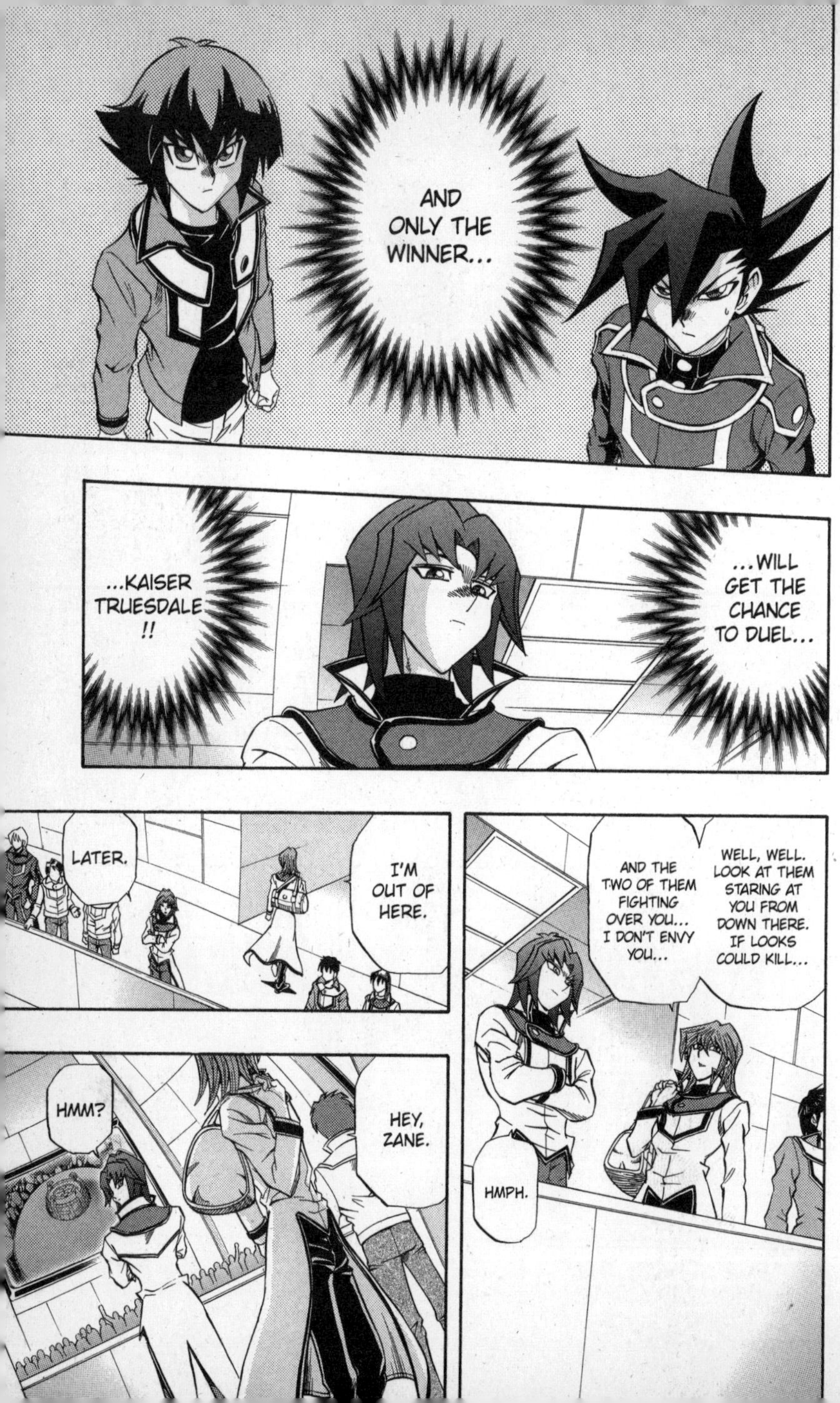
AND ONLY THE WINNER...
...WILL GET THE CHANCE TO DUEL...
...KAISER TRUESDALE !!
WELL, WELL. LOOK AT THEM STARING AT YOU FROM DOWN THERE. IF LOOKS COULD KILL...
AND THE TWO OF THEM FIGHTING OVER YOU... I DON'T ENVY YOU...
HMPH.
I'M OUT OF HERE.
LATER.
HEY, ZANE.
HMM?

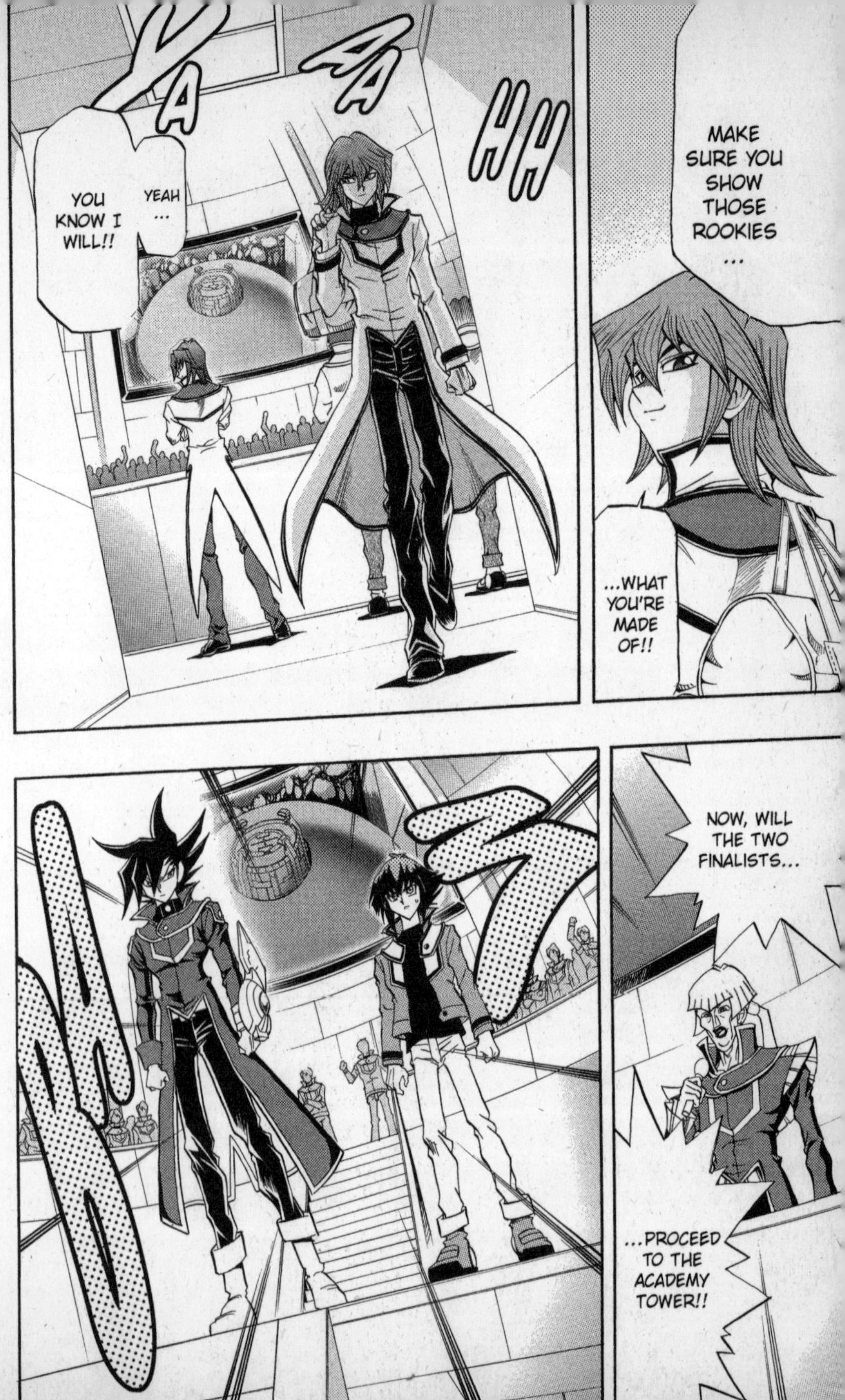
MAKE SURE YOU SHOW THOSE ROOKIES ...
...WHAT YOU'RE MADE OF!!
YAAAHH
YEAH ...
YOU KNOW I WILL!!
NOW, WILL THE TWO FINALISTS...
...PROCEED TO THE ACADEMY TOWER!!

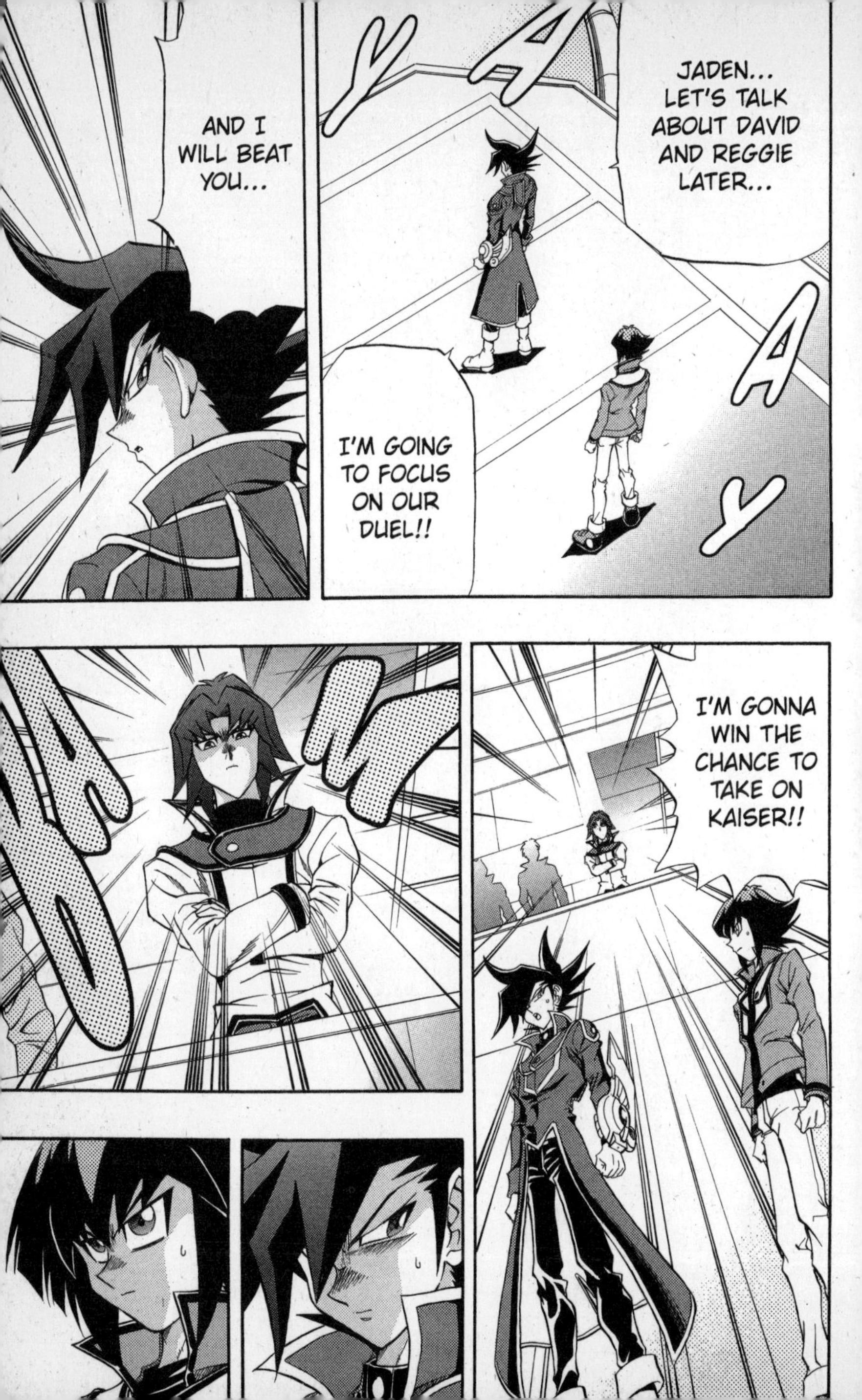
JADEN... LET'S TALK ABOUT DAVID AND REGGIE LATER...
I'M GOING TO FOCUS ON OUR DUEL!!
AND I WILL BEAT YOU...
I'M GONNA WIN THE CHANCE TO TAKE ON KAISER!!

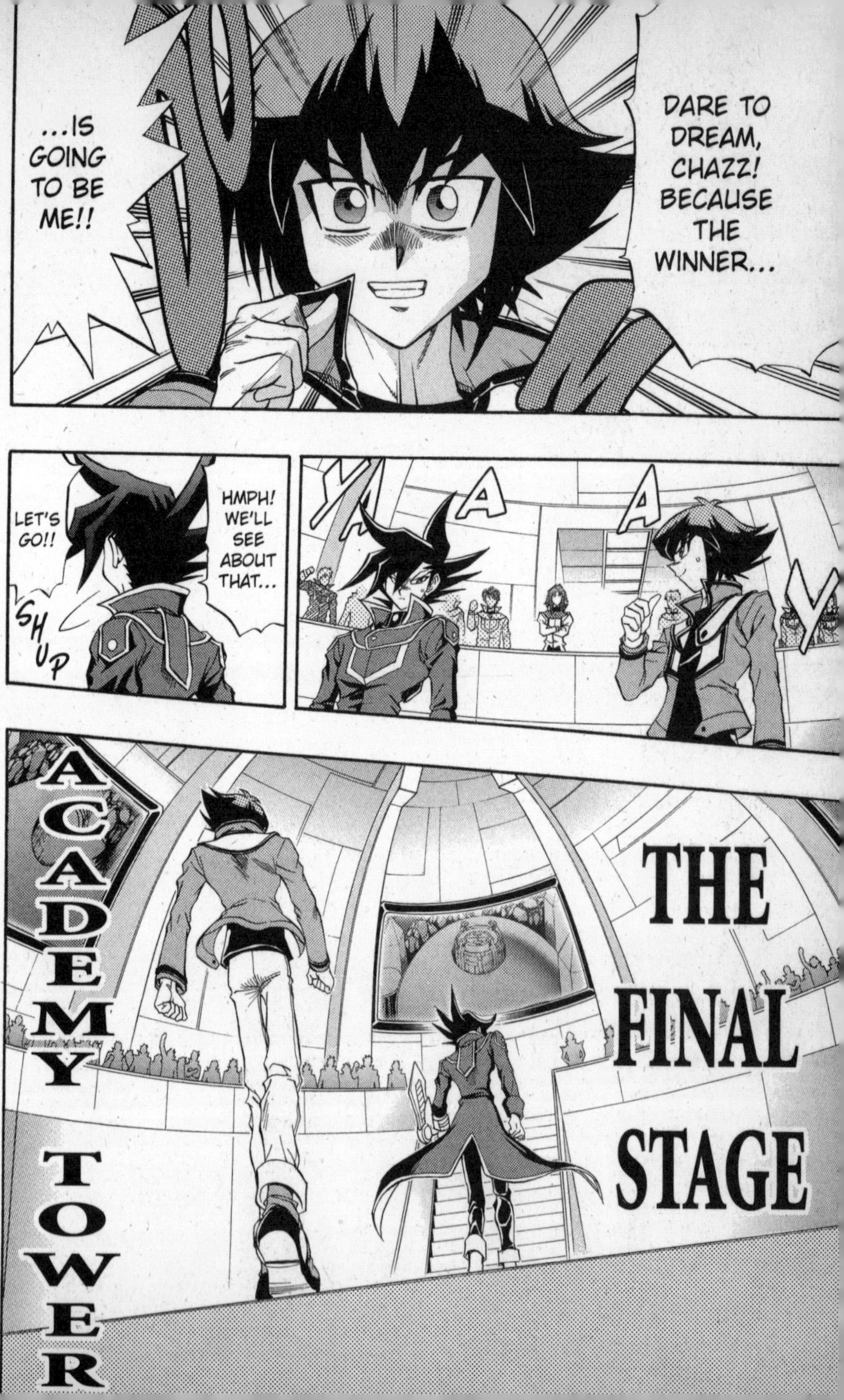
DARE TO DREAM, CHAZZ! BECAUSE THE WINNER...
...IS GOING TO BE ME!!
YAAAY
HMPH! WE'LL SEE ABOUT THAT...
LET'S GO!!
SHUP
THE FINAL STAGE
ACADEMY TOWER

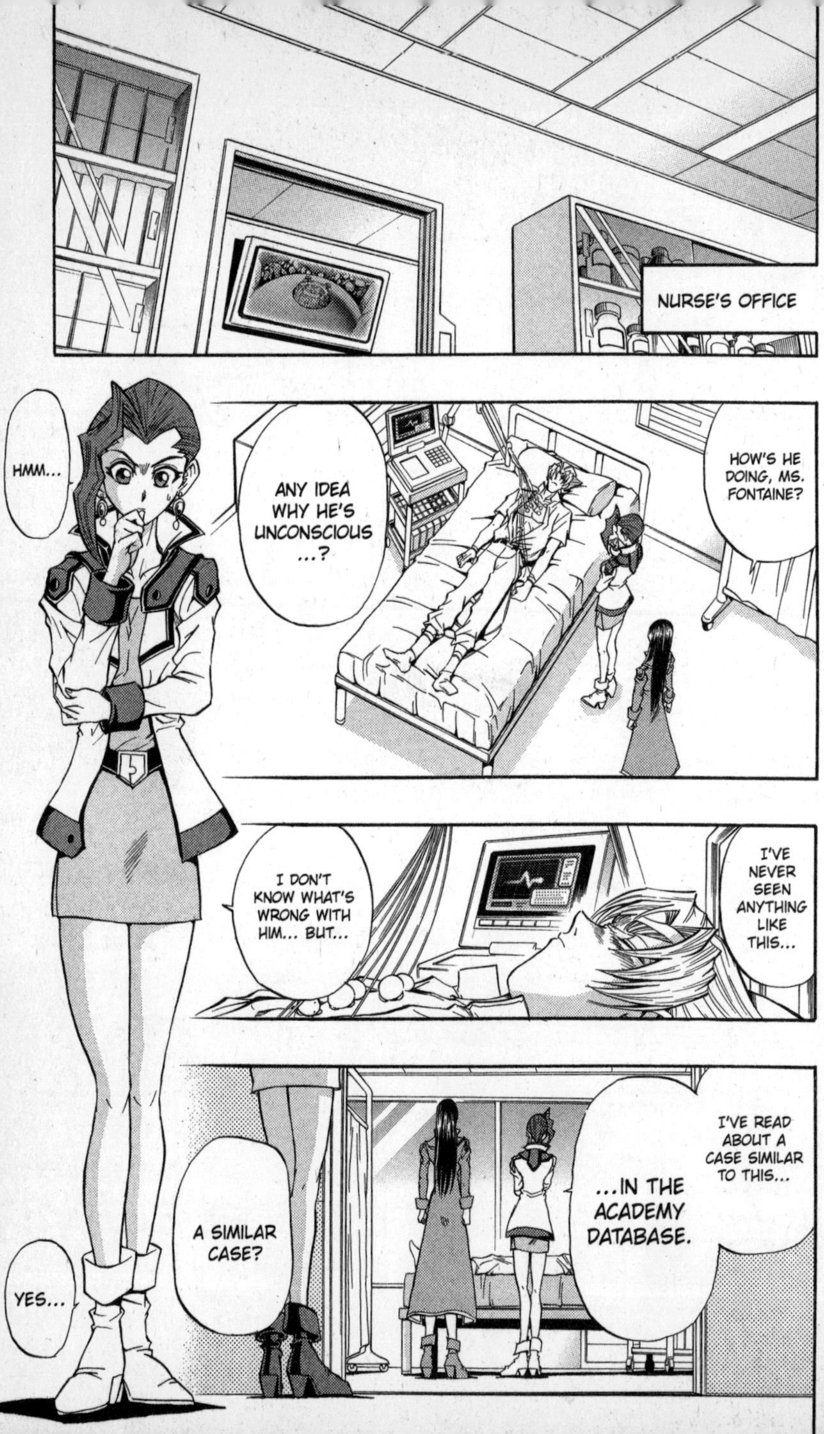
NURSE'S OFFICE
HOW'S HE DOING, MS. FONTAINE?
ANY IDEA WHY HE'S UNCONSCIOUS ...?
I'VE NEVER SEEN ANYTHING LIKE THIS...
I DON'T KNOW WHAT'S WRONG WITH HIM... BUT...
I'VE READ ABOUT A CASE SIMILAR TO THIS...
...IN THE ACADEMY DATABASE.
A SIMILAR CASE?
HMM...
YES...

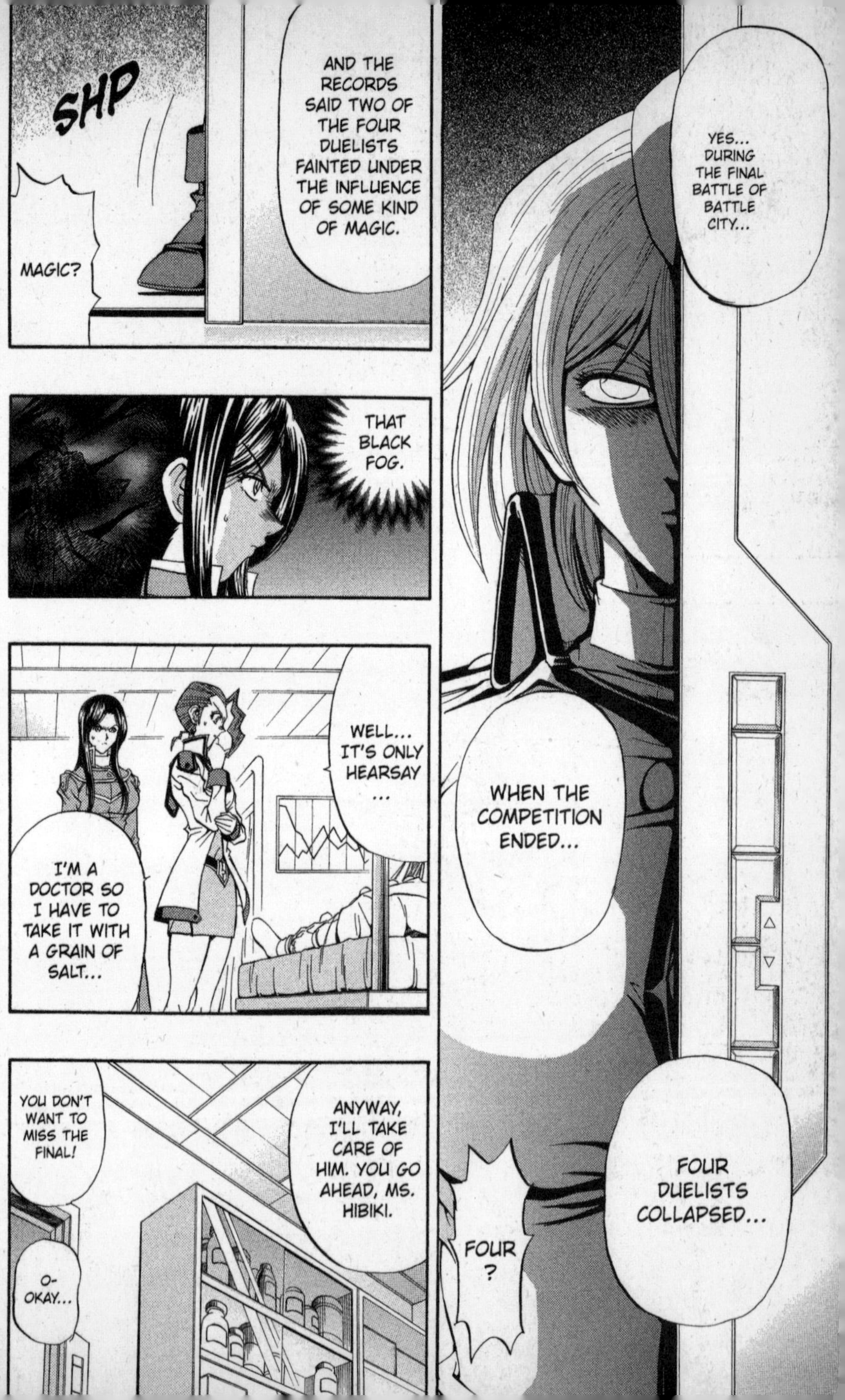
YES... DURING THE FINAL BATTLE OF BATTLE CITY...
WHEN THE COMPETITION ENDED...
FOUR DUELISTS COLLAPSED...
FOUR?
AND THE RECORDS SAID TWO OF THE FOUR DUELISTS FAINTED UNDER THE INFLUENCE OF SOME KIND OF MAGIC.
SHP
MAGIC?
THAT BLACK FOG.
WELL... IT'S ONLY HEARSAY ...
I'M A DOCTOR SO I HAVE TO TAKE IT WITH A GRAIN OF SALT...
ANYWAY, I'LL TAKE CARE OF HIM. YOU GO AHEAD, MS. HIBIKI.
YOU DON'T WANT TO MISS THE FINAL!
O-OKAY...

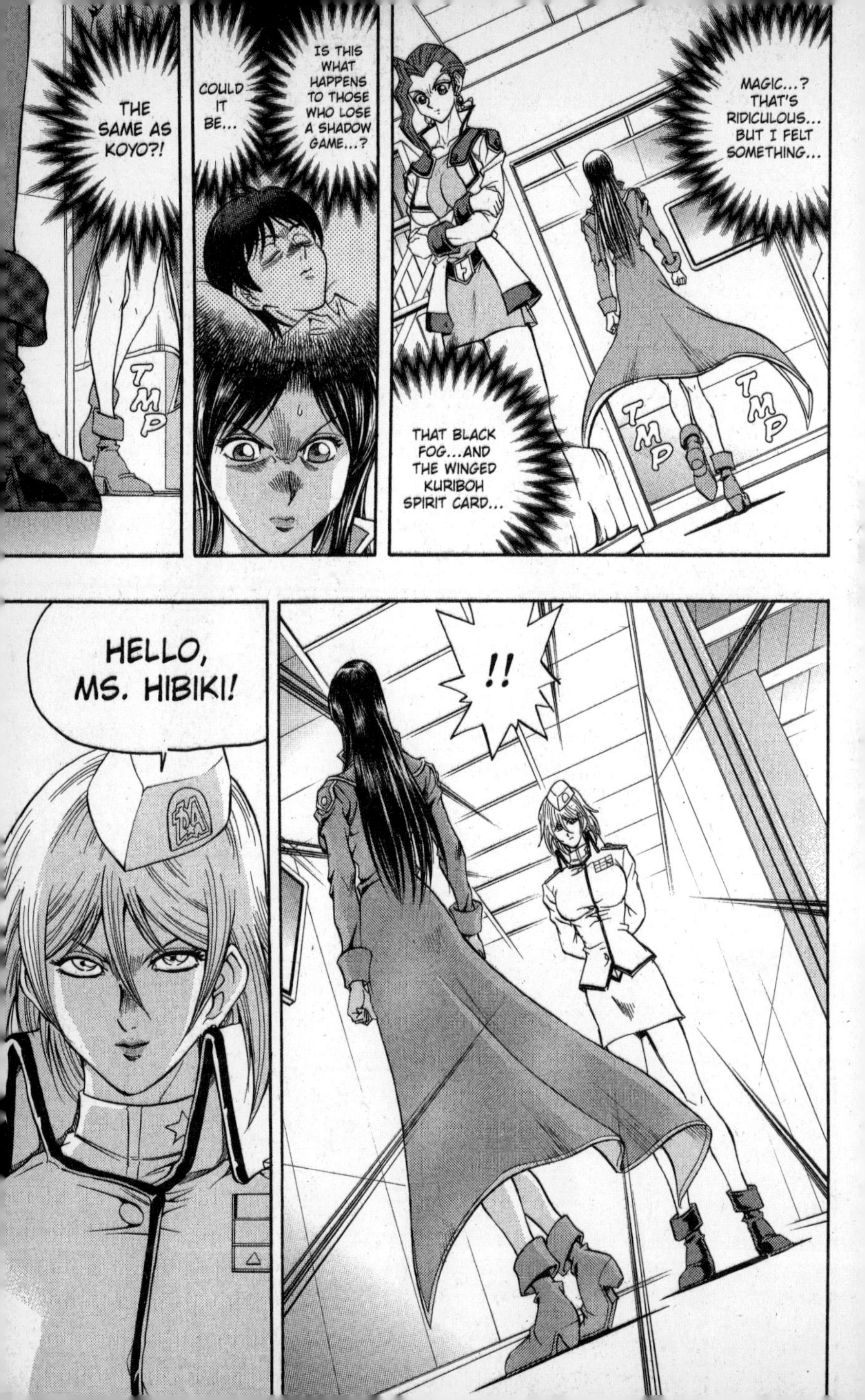
MAGIC...? THAT'S RIDICULOUS... BUT I FELT SOMETHING...
TMP
TMP
THAT BLACK FOG...AND THE WINGED KURIBOH SPIRIT CARD...
IS THIS WHAT HAPPENS TO THOSE WHO LOSE A SHADOW GAME...?
COULD IT BE...
THE SAME AS KOYO?!
TMP
!!
HELLO, MS. HIBIKI!

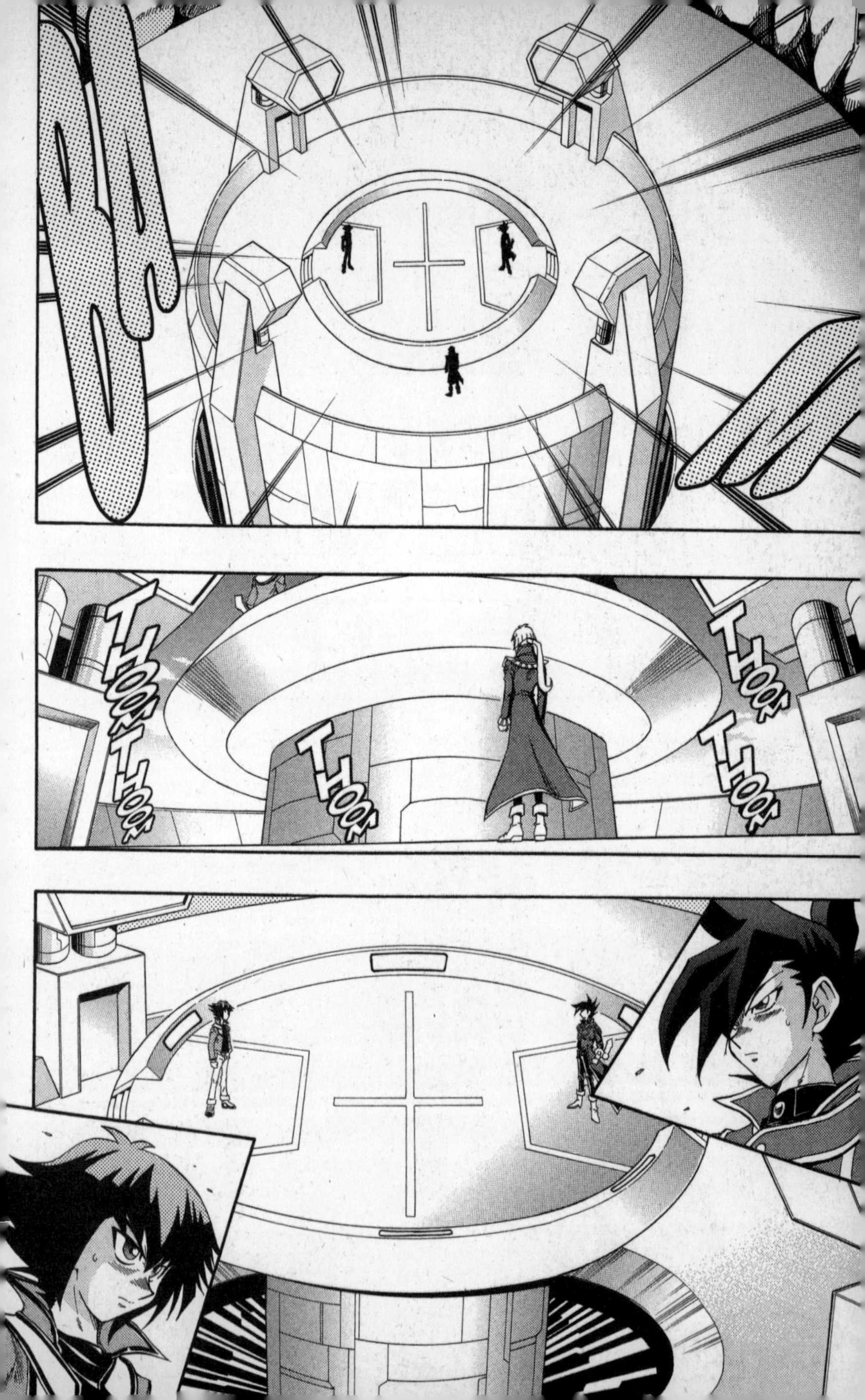
THOOM
THOOM
THOOM
THOOM THOOM

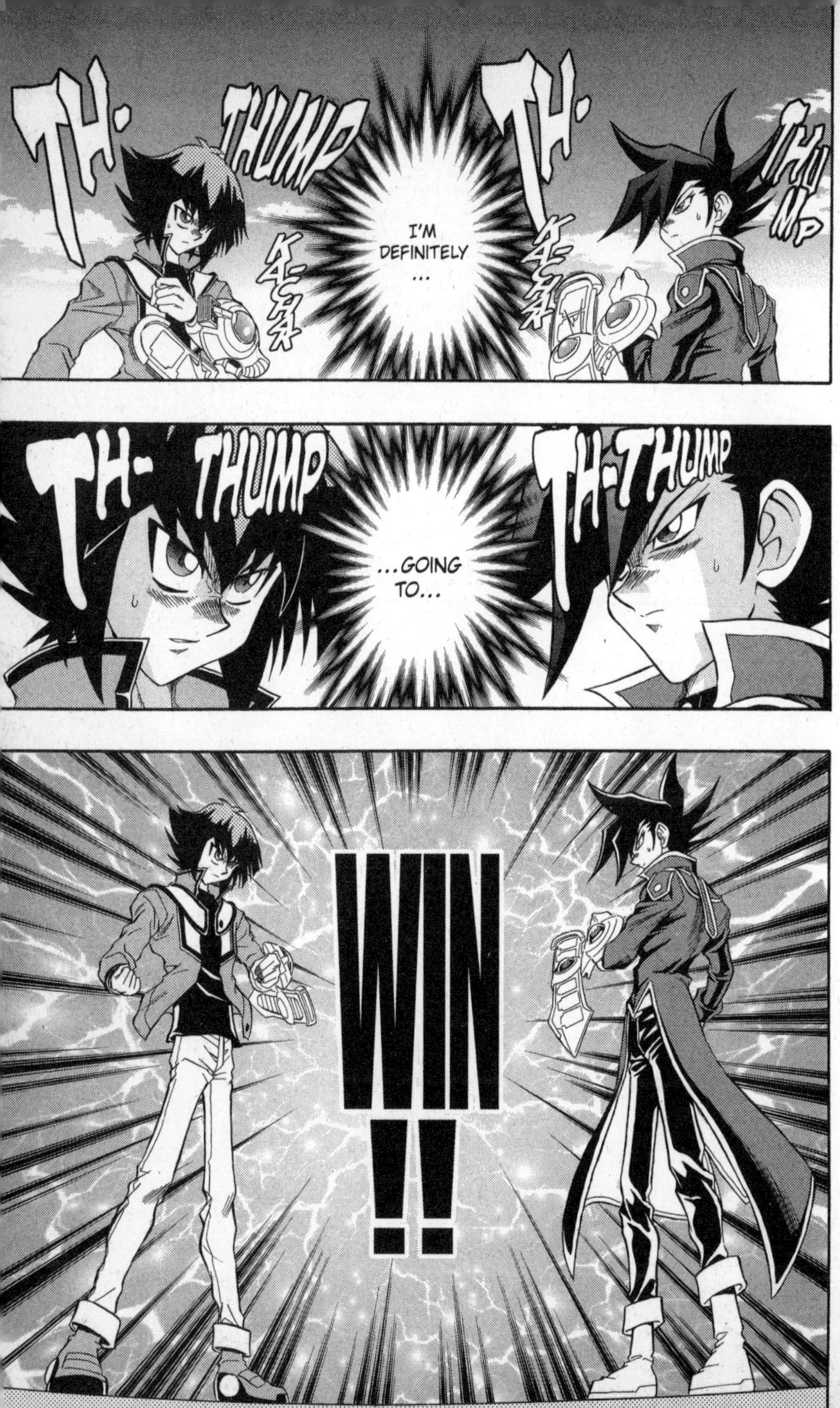
TH-THUMP
KA-CHAK
I'M DEFINITELY ...
TH-THUMP
KA-CHAK
TH-THUMP
...GOING TO...
TH-THUMP
WIN!!

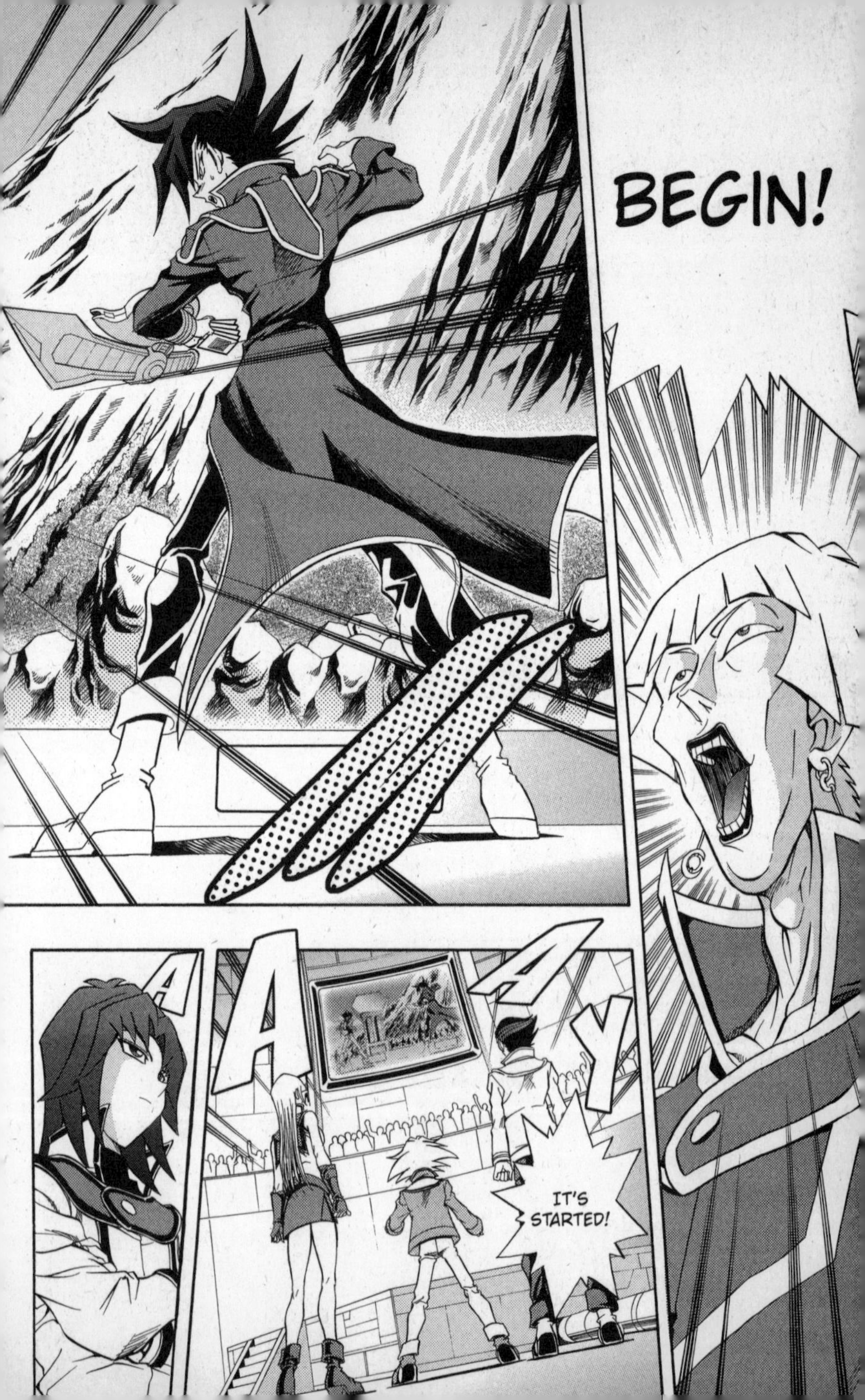
BEGIN!
AAAY
IT'S STARTED!

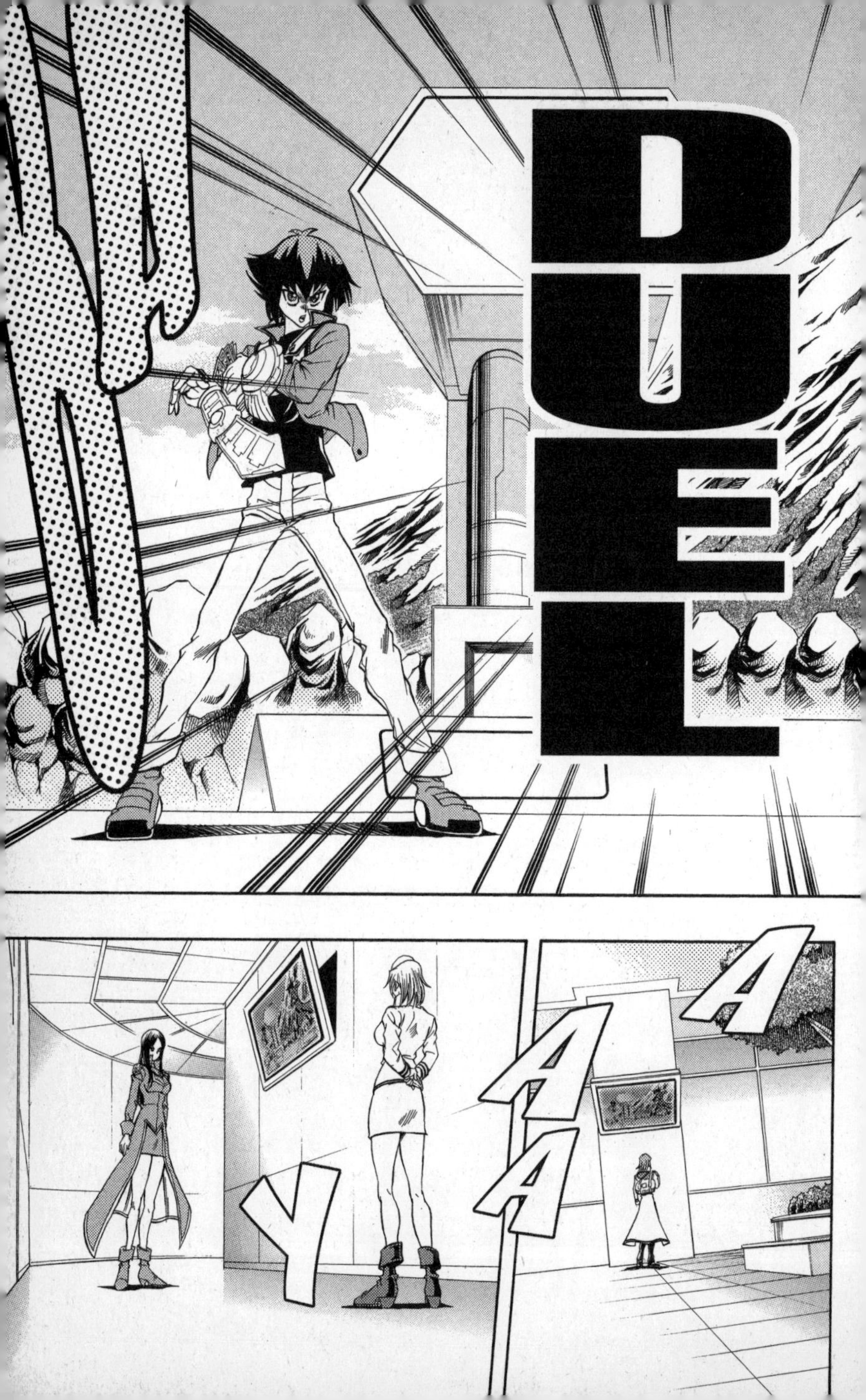
DUEL
YAAA

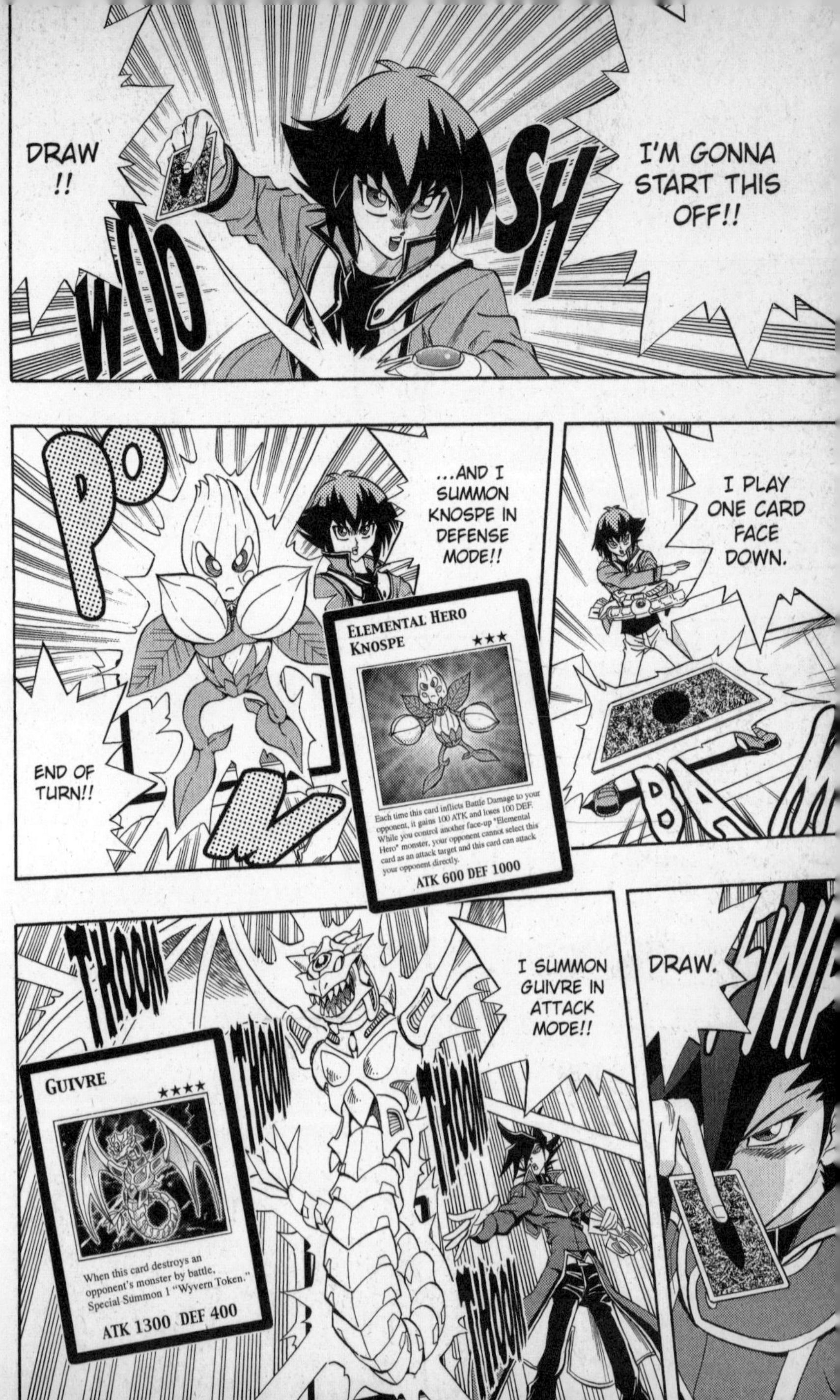
I'M GONNA START THIS OFF!!
DRAW !!
WOOSH
I PLAY ONE CARD FACE DOWN.
...AND I SUMMON KNOSPE IN DEFENSE MODE!!
POW
ELEMENTAL HERO KNOSPE
Each time this card inflicts Battle Damage to your opponent, it gains 100 ATK and loses 100 DEF. While you control another face-up "Elemental Hero" monster, your opponent cannot select this card as an attack target and this card can attack your opponent directly.
ATK 600 DEF 1000
END OF TURN!!
DRAW.
I SUMMON GUIVRE IN ATTACK MODE!!
THOOM
THOOM
THOOM
THOOM
GUIVRE
When this card destroys an opponent's monster by battle, Special Summon 1 "Wyvern Token."
ATK 1300 DEF 400

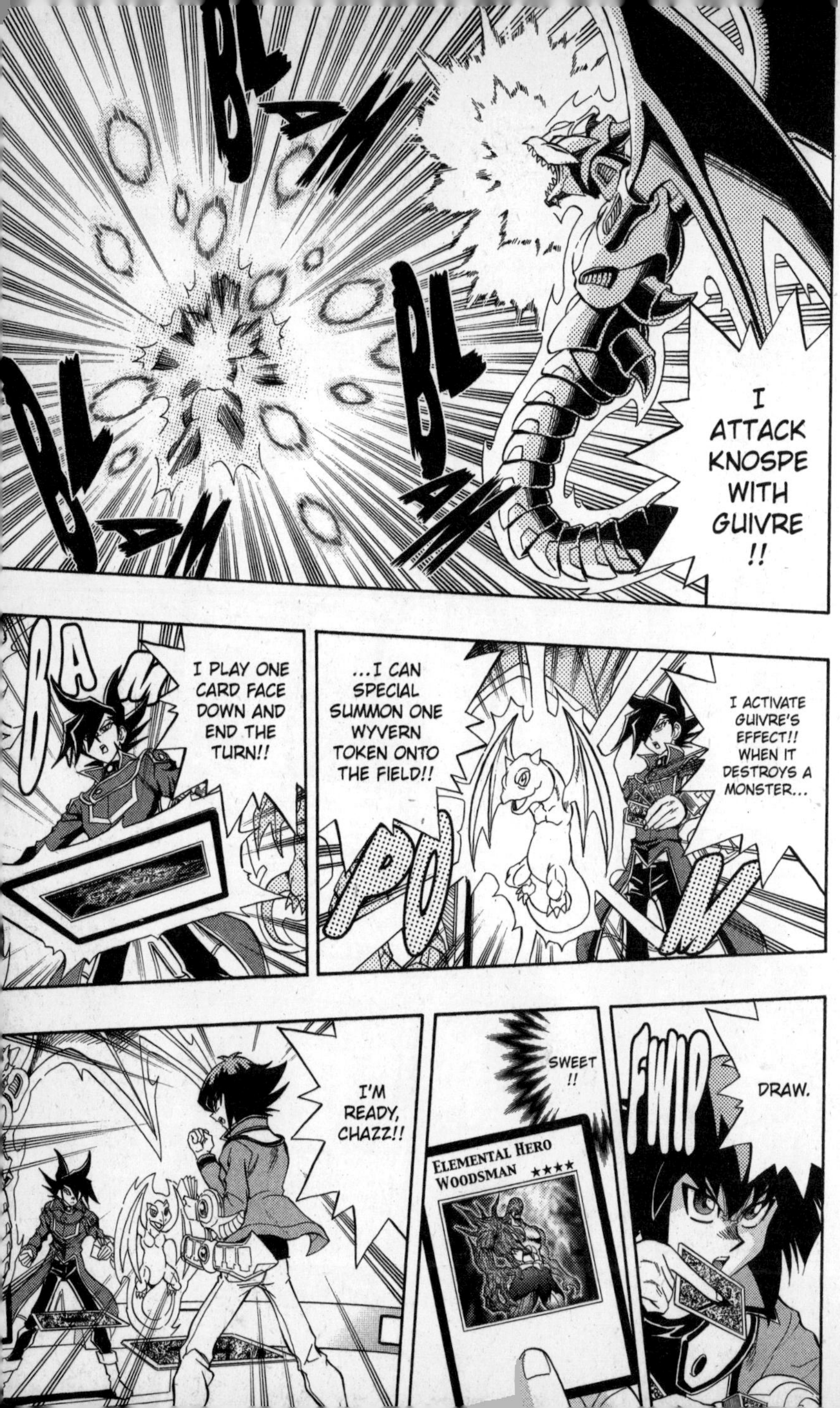

BLAM
BLAM
BLAM
I ATTACK KNOSPE WITH GUIVRE!!
I ACTIVATE GUIVRE'S EFFECT!! WHEN IT DESTROYS A MONSTER...
...I CAN SPECIAL SUMMON ONE WYVERN TOKEN ONTO THE FIELD!!
POW
BAM
I PLAY ONE CARD FACE DOWN AND END THE TURN!!
FWIP
DRAW.
SWEET!!
ELEMENTAL HERO WOODSMAN ★★★★
I'M READY, CHAZZ!!

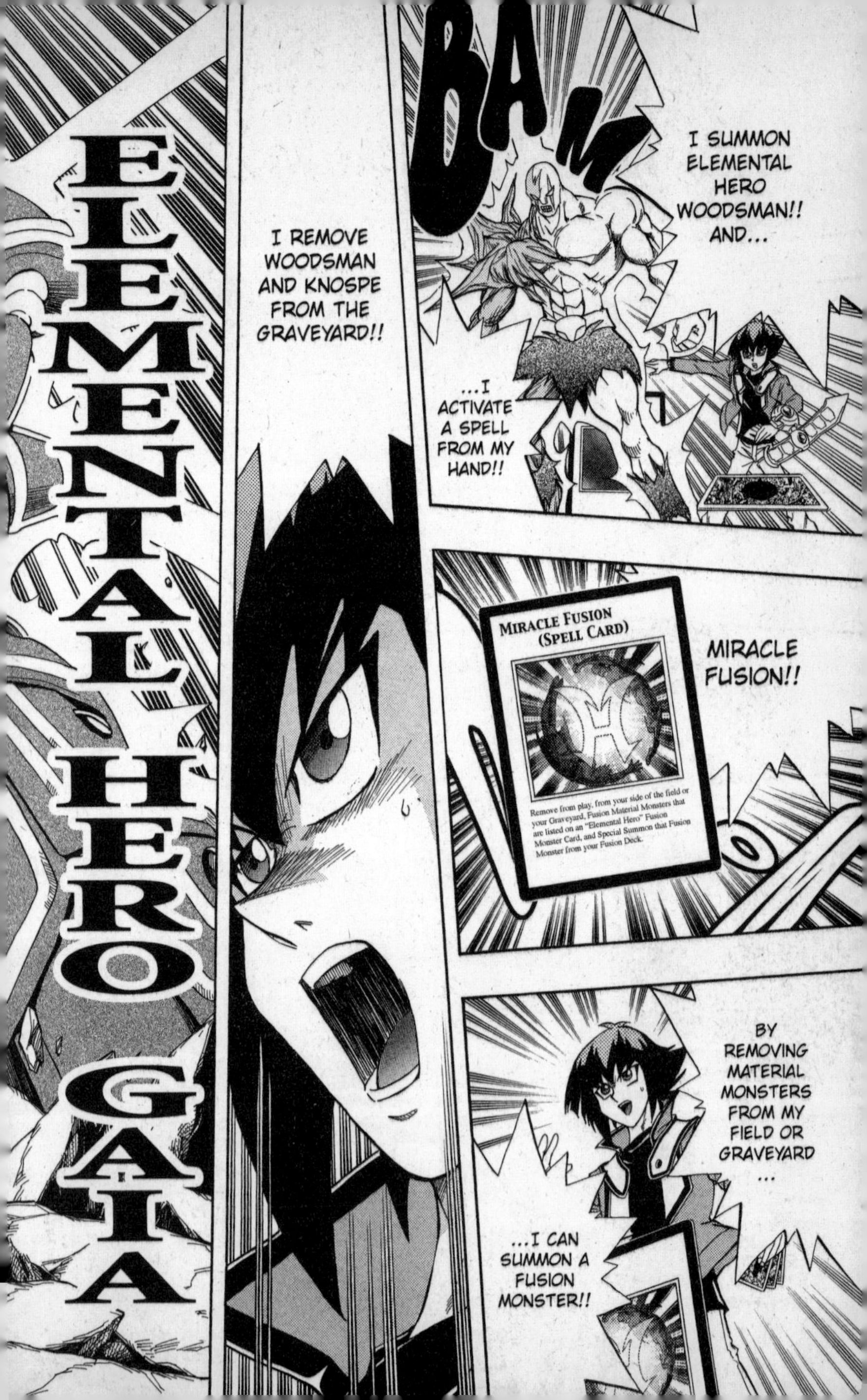
BAM
I SUMMON ELEMENTAL HERO WOODSMAN!! AND...
...I ACTIVATE A SPELL FROM MY HAND!!
MIRACLE FUSION (SPELL CARD)
Remove from play, from your side of the field or your Graveyard, Fusion Material Monsters that are listed on an "Elemental Hero" Fusion Monster Card, and Special Summon that Fusion Monster from your Fusion Deck.
MIRACLE FUSION!!
BY REMOVING MATERIAL MONSTERS FROM MY FIELD OR GRAVEYARD ...
...I CAN SUMMON A FUSION MONSTER!!
I REMOVE WOODSMAN AND KNOSPE FROM THE GRAVEYARD!!
ELEMENTAL HERO GAIA

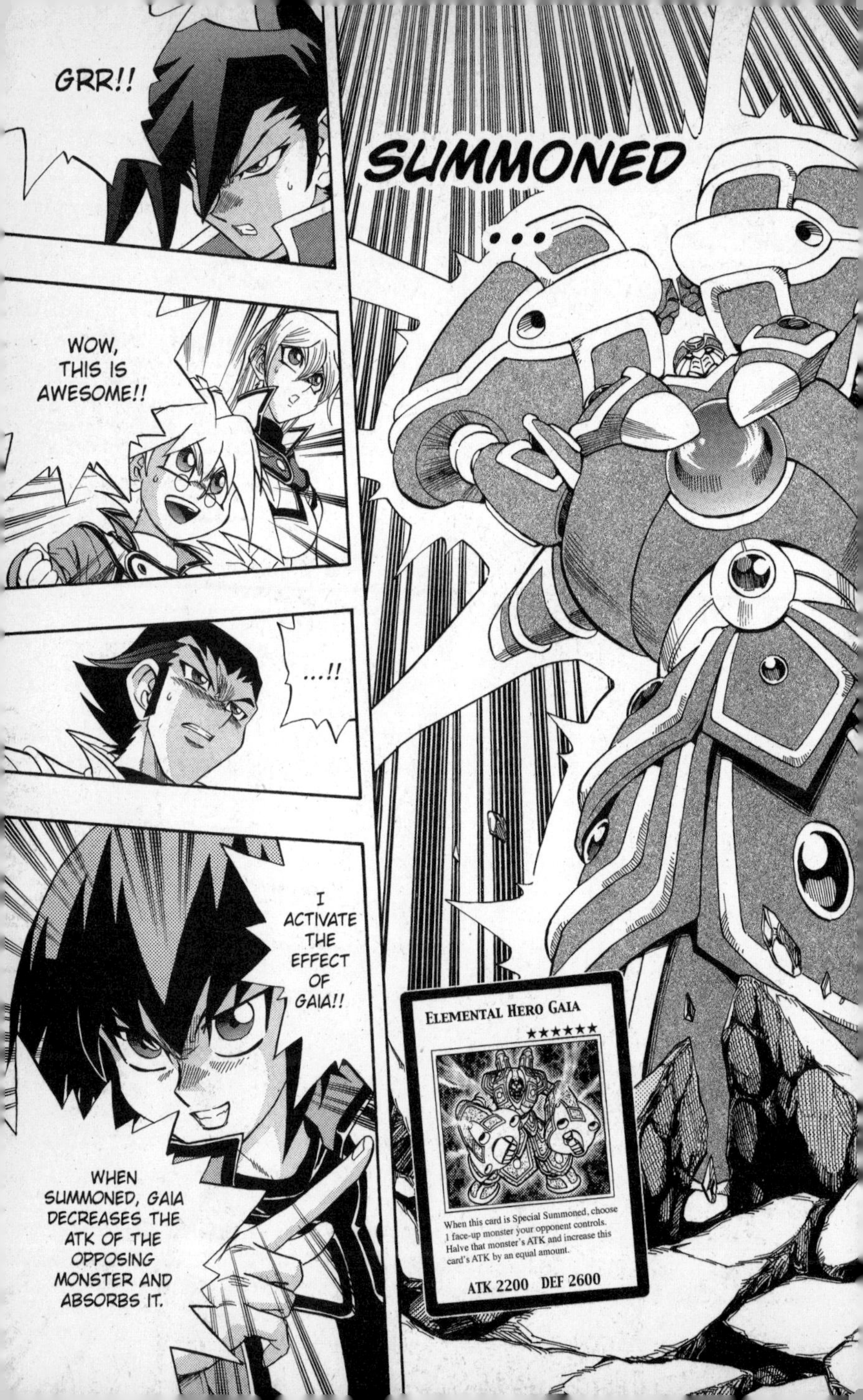
SUMMONED
...
ELEMENTAL HERO GAIA
★★★★★★
When this card is Special Summoned, choose 1 face-up monster your opponent controls. Halve that monster's ATK and increase this card's ATK by an equal amount.
ATK 2200 DEF 2600
GRR!!
WOW, THIS IS AWESOME!!
...!!
I ACTIVATE THE EFFECT OF GAIA!!
WHEN SUMMONED, GAIA DECREASES THE ATK OF THE OPPOSING MONSTER AND ABSORBS IT.

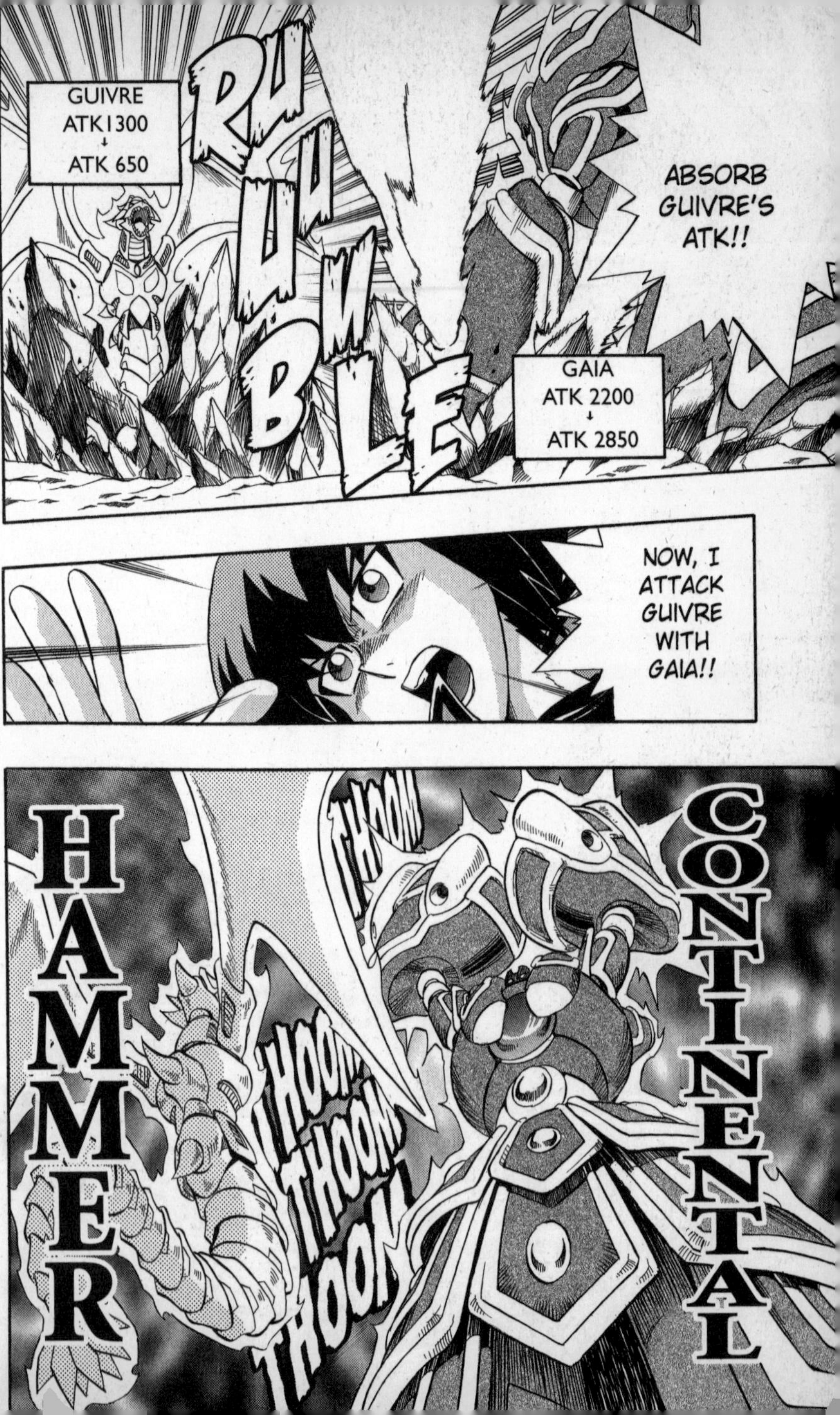
ABSORB GUIVRE'S ATK!!
GAIA ATK 2200 ↓ ATK 2850
RUMBLE
GUIVRE ATK1300 ↓ ATK 650
NOW, I ATTACK GUIVRE WITH GAIA!!
CONTINENTAL
THOOM
THOOM
THOOM
THOOM
HAMMER

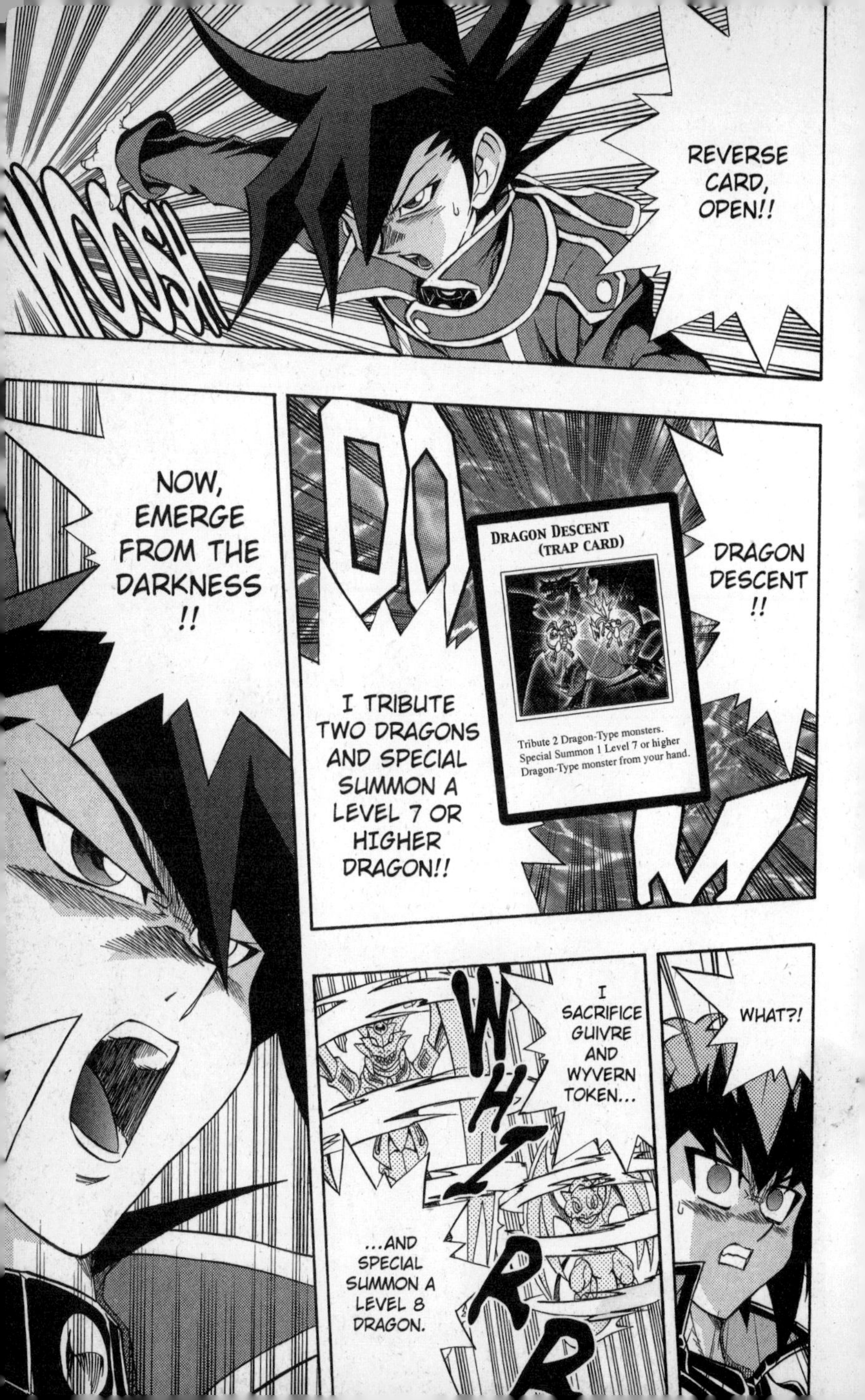
REVERSE CARD, OPEN!!
WOOSH!
DRAGON DESCENT!!
DRAGON DESCENT (TRAP CARD)
Tribute 2 Dragon-Type monsters. Special Summon 1 Level 7 or higher Dragon-Type monster from your hand.
I TRIBUTE TWO DRAGONS AND SPECIAL SUMMON A LEVEL 7 OR HIGHER DRAGON!!
WHAT?!
I SACRIFICE GUIVRE AND WYVERN TOKEN...
...AND SPECIAL SUMMON A LEVEL 8 DRAGON.
WHIRR
NOW, EMERGE FROM THE DARKNESS!!

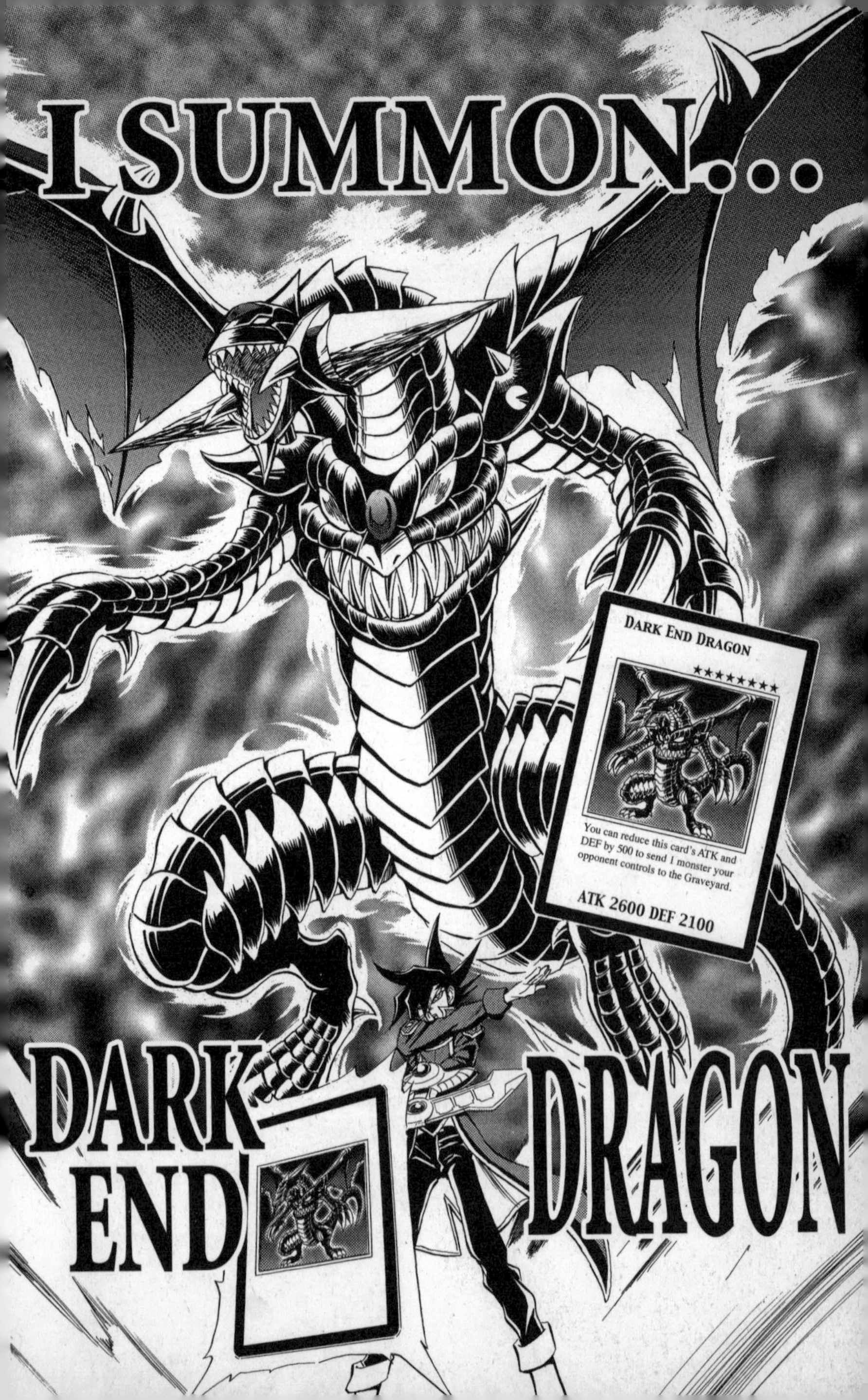
I SUMMON...
DARK END DRAGON
DARK END DRAGON
You can reduce this card's ATK and DEF by 500 to send 1 monster your opponent controls to the Graveyard.
ATK 2600 DEF 2100
DARK END
DRAGON

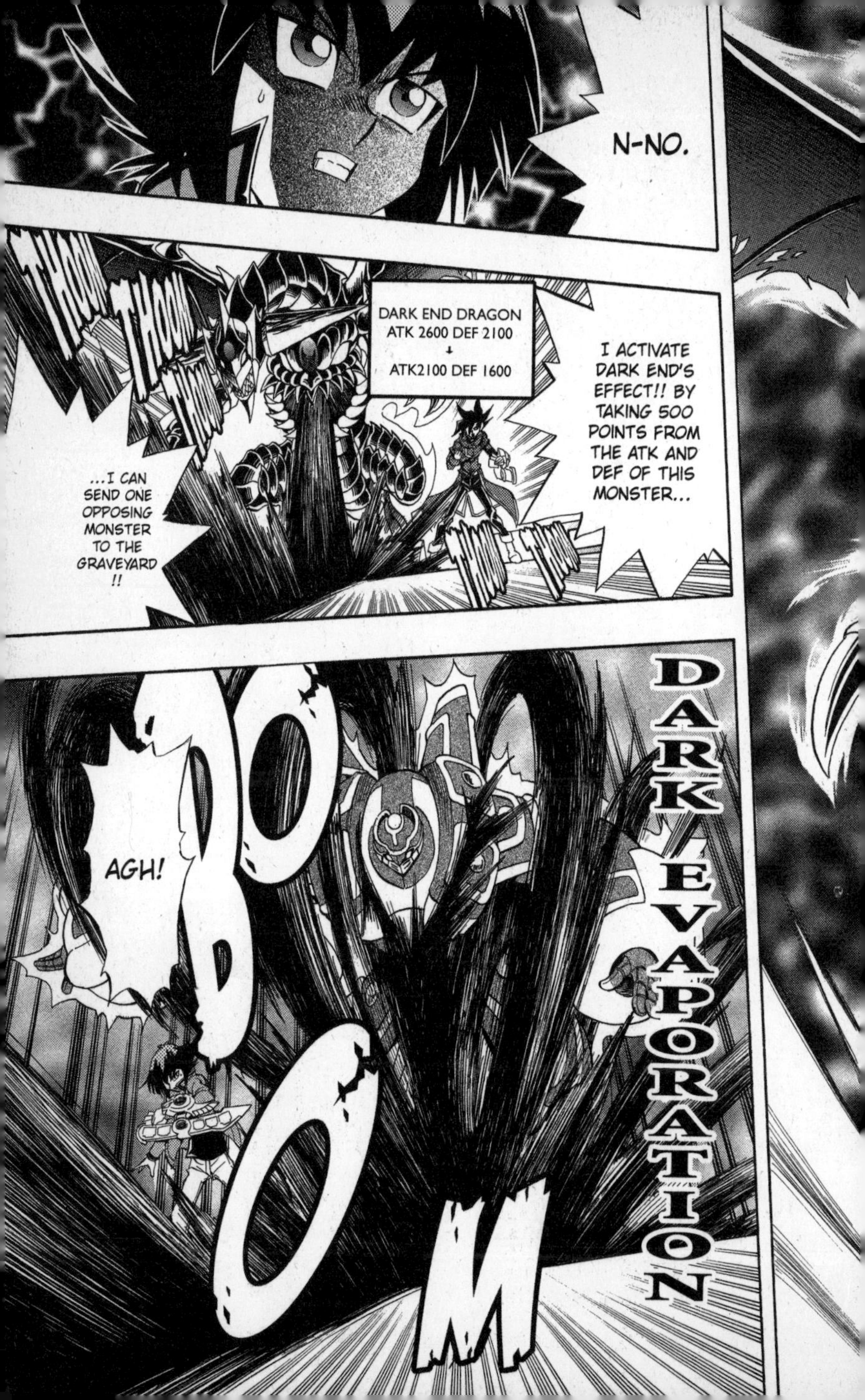
N-NO.
I ACTIVATE DARK END'S EFFECT!! BY TAKING 500 POINTS FROM THE ATK AND DEF OF THIS MONSTER...
DARK END DRAGON
ATK 2600 DEF 2100
↓
ATK2100 DEF 1600
THOOM THOOM
...I CAN SEND ONE OPPOSING MONSTER TO THE GRAVEYARD !!
DARK EVAPORATION
AGH!

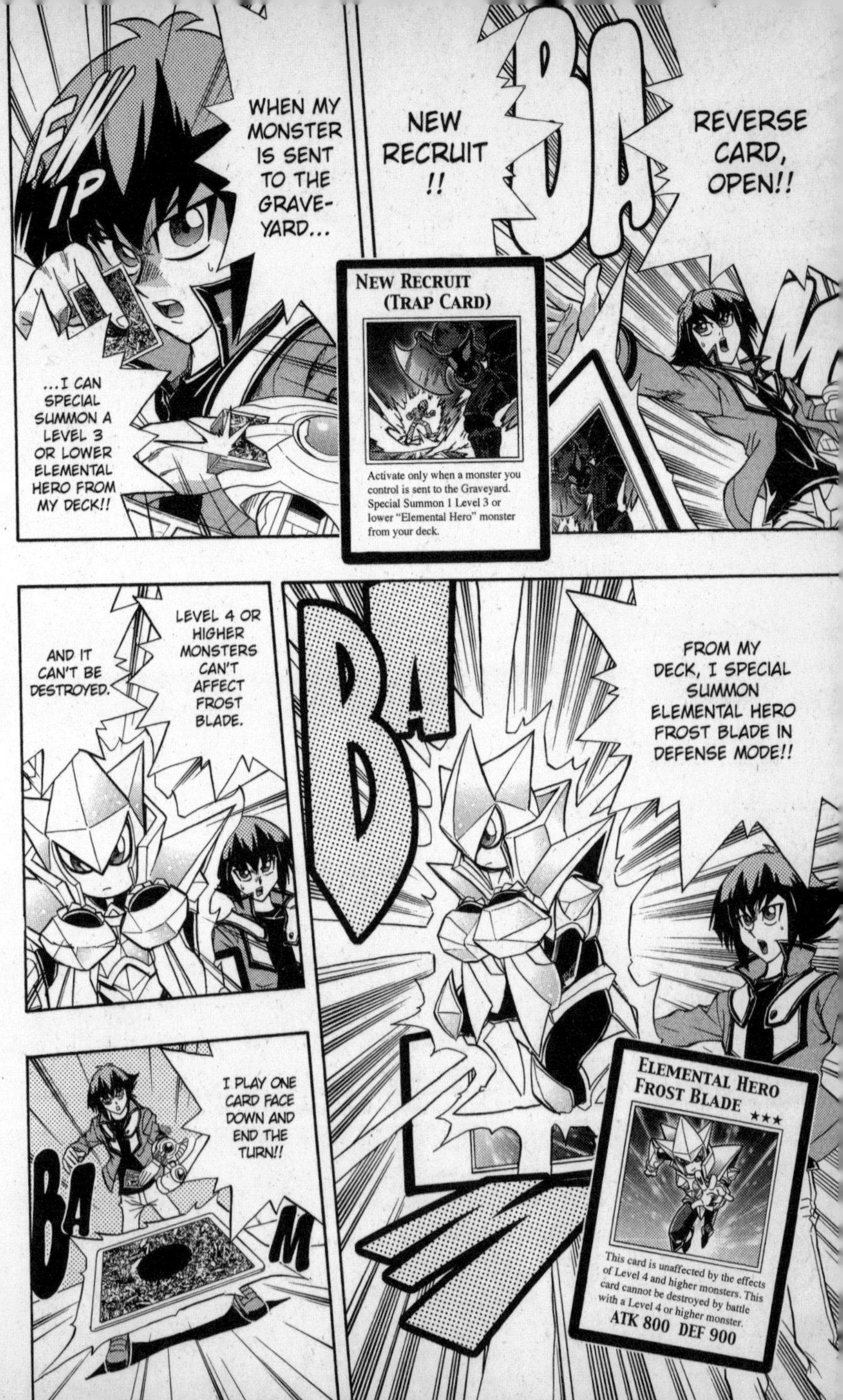
BAM
REVERSE CARD, OPEN!!
NEW RECRUIT!!
New Recruit (Trap Card)
Activate only when a monster you control is sent to the Graveyard. Special Summon 1 Level 3 or lower "Elemental Hero" monster from your deck.
FWIP
WHEN MY MONSTER IS SENT TO THE GRAVEYARD...
...I CAN SPECIAL SUMMON A LEVEL 3 OR LOWER ELEMENTAL HERO FROM MY DECK!!
FROM MY DECK, I SPECIAL SUMMON ELEMENTAL HERO FROST BLADE IN DEFENSE MODE!!
BA
Elemental Hero Frost Blade ★★★
This card is unaffected by the effects of Level 4 and higher monsters. This card cannot be destroyed by battle with a Level 4 or higher monster.
ATK 800 DEF 900
LEVEL 4 OR HIGHER MONSTERS CAN'T AFFECT FROST BLADE.
AND IT CAN'T BE DESTROYED.
I PLAY ONE CARD FACE DOWN AND END THE TURN!!
BAM

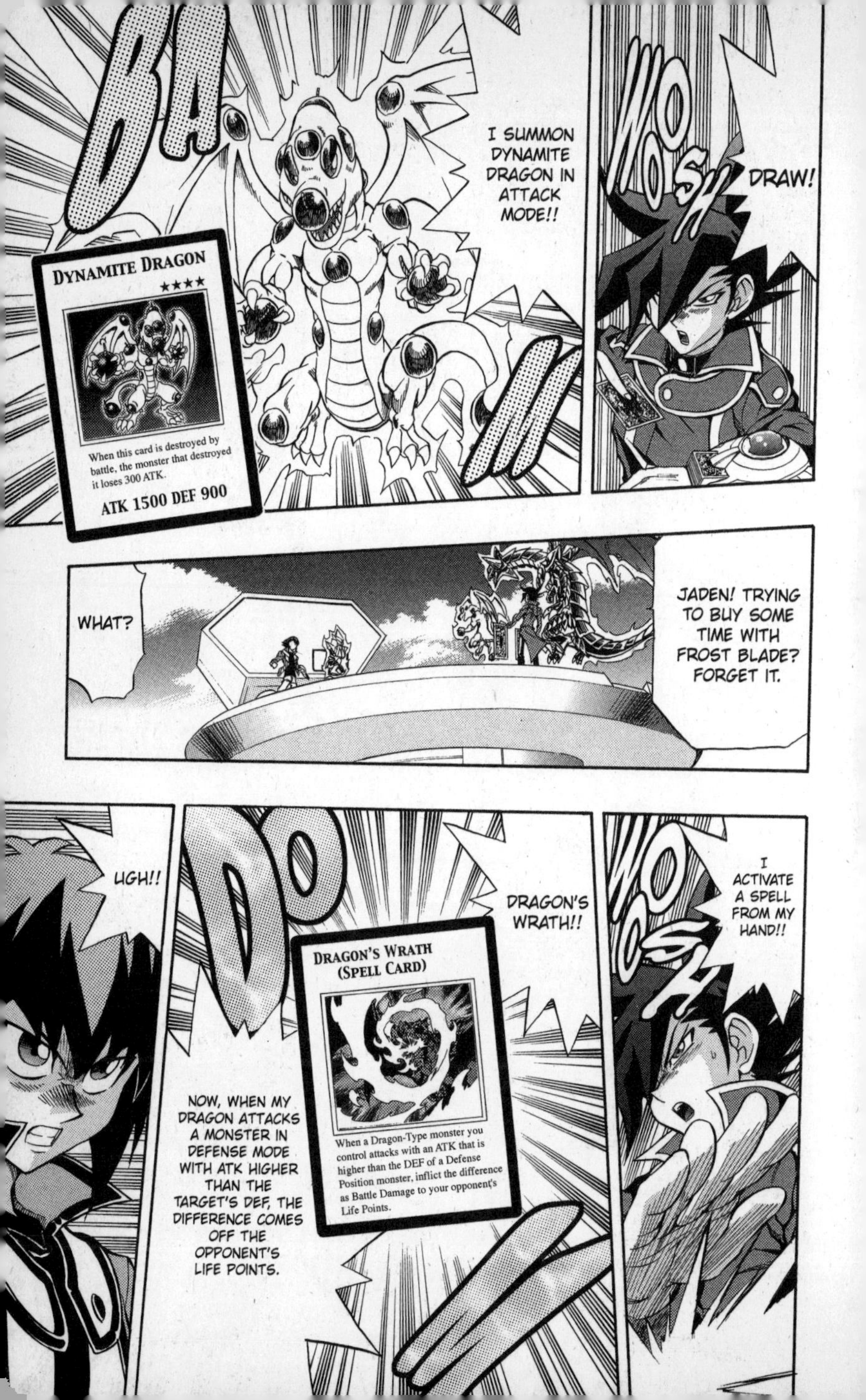
DRAW!
I SUMMON DYNAMITE DRAGON IN ATTACK MODE!!
BA
DYNAMITE DRAGON
★★★★
When this card is destroyed by battle, the monster that destroyed it loses 300 ATK.
ATK 1500 DEF 900
JADEN! TRYING TO BUY SOME TIME WITH FROST BLADE? FORGET IT.
WHAT?
I ACTIVATE A SPELL FROM MY HAND!!
DRAGON'S WRATH!!
DRAGON'S WRATH (SPELL CARD)
When a Dragon-Type monster you control attacks with an ATK that is higher than the DEF of a Defense Position monster, inflict the difference as Battle Damage to your opponent's Life Points.
DO
NOW, WHEN MY DRAGON ATTACKS A MONSTER IN DEFENSE MODE WITH ATK HIGHER THAN THE TARGET'S DEF, THE DIFFERENCE COMES OFF THE OPPONENT'S LIFE POINTS.
UGH!!

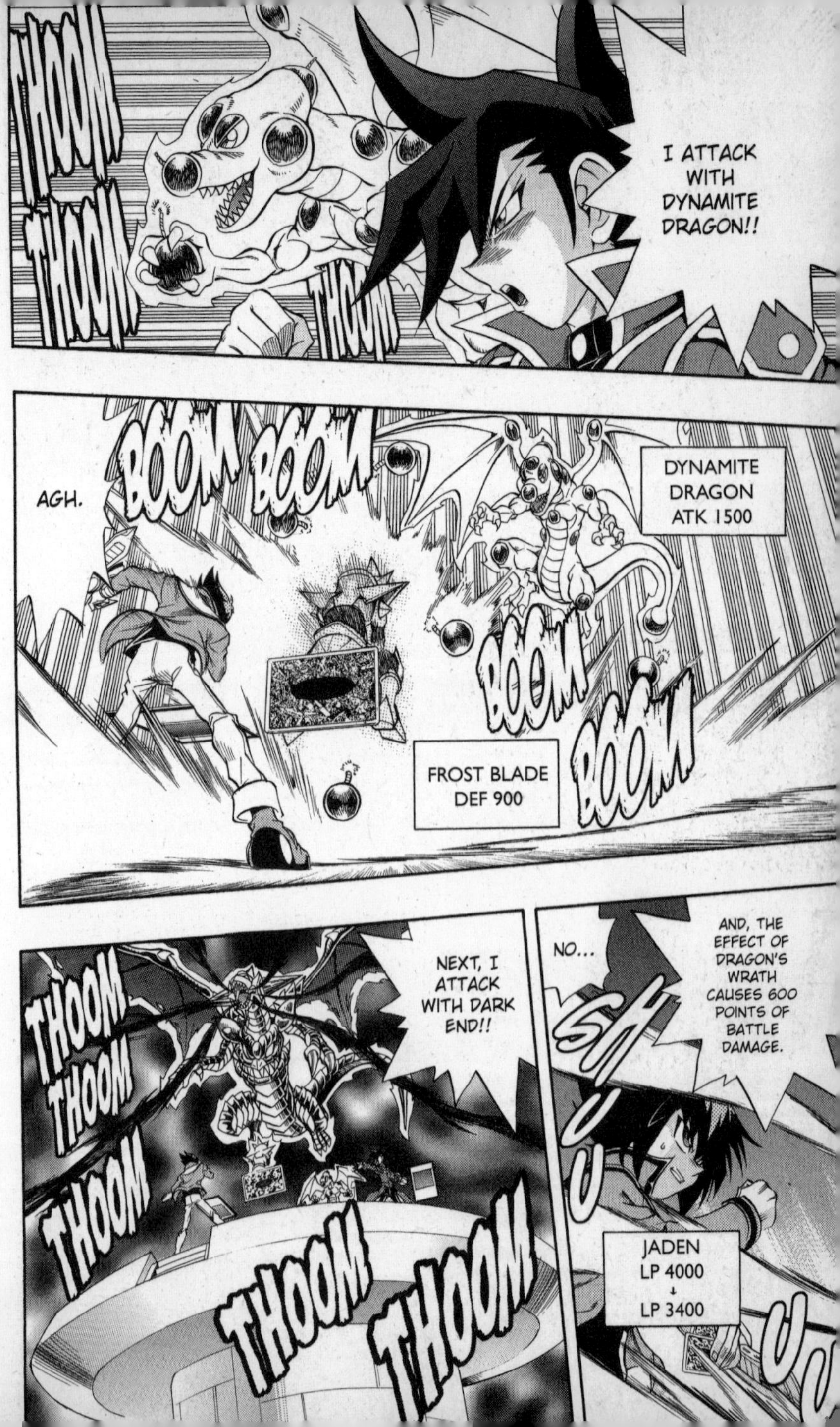
I ATTACK WITH DYNAMITE DRAGON!!
THOOM
THOOM
THOOM
THOOM
DYNAMITE DRAGON ATK 1500
BOOM BOOM
AGH.
BOOM
BOOM
FROST BLADE DEF 900
AND, THE EFFECT OF DRAGON'S WRATH CAUSES 600 POINTS OF BATTLE DAMAGE.
NO...
SH
JADEN LP 4000 ↓ LP 3400
NEXT, I ATTACK WITH DARK END!!
THOOM
THOOM
THOOM
THOOM
THOOM

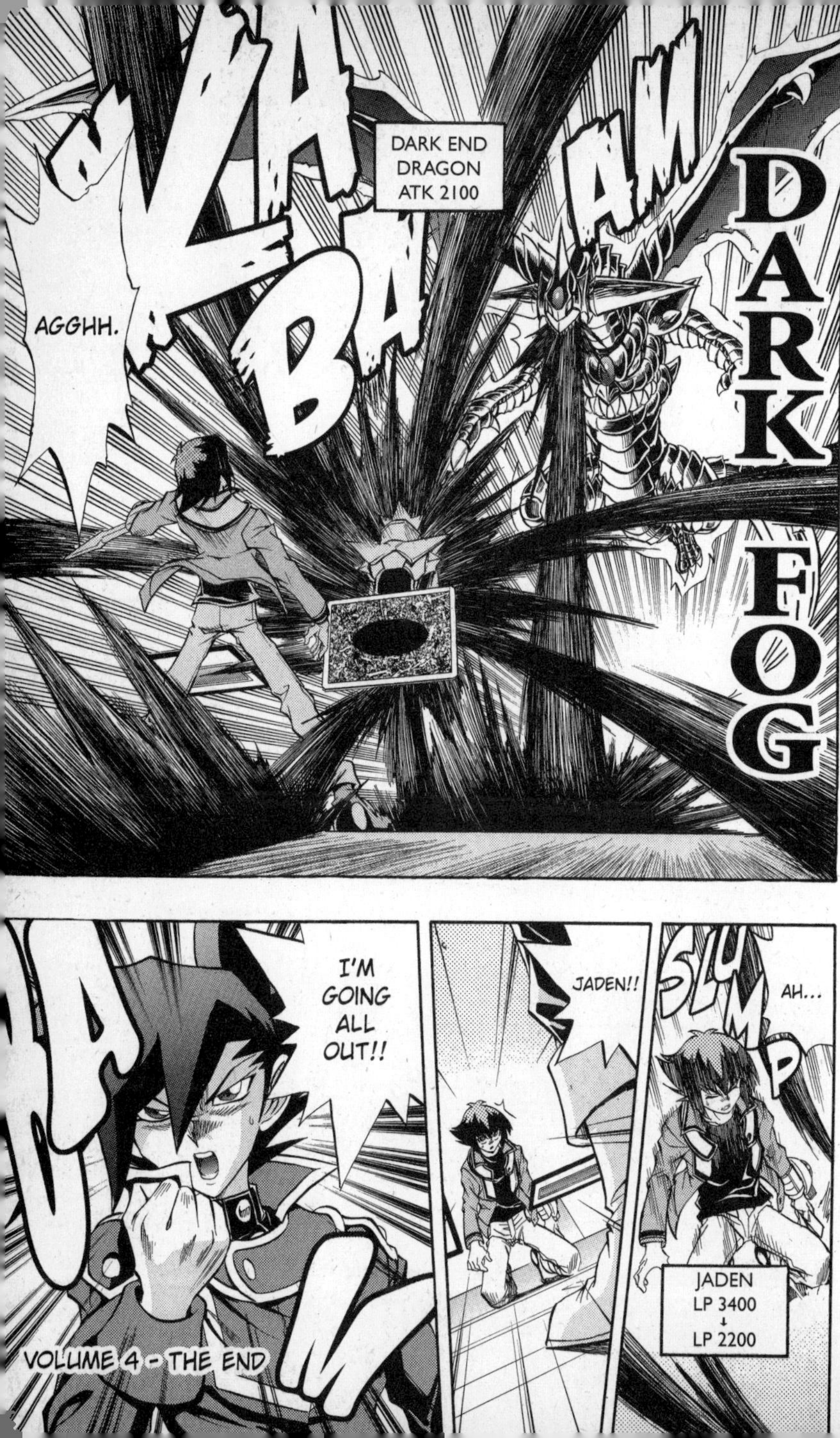
DARK FOG
DARK END DRAGON ATK 2100
AGGHH.
SLUMP
AH...
JADEN LP 3400 ↓ LP 2200
JADEN!!
I'M GOING ALL OUT!!
VOLUME 4 - THE END

STAFF

MASAFUMI SATO
AKIHIRO TOMONAGA
AKIRA ITO

DUEL CONFIGURATION COOPERATION

MASAHIRO UCHIDA

COLORING

NABETARO

EDITOR

DAISUKE TERASHI

MASTER OF THE CARDS

Jaden Yuki and the rest of the next generation of Duelists have introduced their own cards into the *Yu-Gi-Oh!* TCG, which also make their first appearance here in the fourth volume of the *Yu-Gi-Oh!: GX* manga! As with all original *Yu-Gi-Oh!* cards, names can differ slightly between the Japanese and English versions, so we're showing you both for reference. Plus, we show you the card even if the card itself doesn't show up in the manga but the monster or trap does! And some cards you may have already seen in the original *Yu-Gi-Oh!*, but we still note them the first time they appear in this volume anyway!

First Appearance in This Volume	Japanese Card Name	English Card Name <<!>> = Not yet available in the TCG.
p.7	Dragon of Light and Darkness 光と闇の竜	Light and Darkness Dragon
p.7	Winged Kuriboh ハネクリボー	Winged Kuriboh
p.7	*Elemental Hero The Earth* E・HERO ジ・アース	Elemental Hero Terra Firma
p.18	*Mezuki* 馬頭鬼	Mezuki
p.19	*Polymerization* 融合	Polymerization
p.19	*Elemental Hero Forestman* E・HERO フォレストマン	Elemental Hero Woodsman
p.20	*Onnen no Kodachi* 怨念の小太刀	Saber of Malice <<!>>
p.22	*Zoen* 増援	Reinforcement of the Army

p.22	*Senshi no Zeikan* 戦士の生還	The Warrior Returning Alive
p.24	Narukami no Takitsubo ナルカミの滝壺	Narukami Waterfall <<!>>
p.27	*Eiyu no Kikan* 英雄の帰還	Hero's Return <<!>>
p.27	*Onmoraki* 陰魔羅鬼	Onmoraki <<!>>
p.29	*Elemental Hero Ocean* **E・HERO** オーシャン	Elemental Hero Ocean
p.31	*Shiranui no Yurameki* 不知火の揺らめき	Fires of Shiranui <<!>>
p.34	*Enma no Sabaki* 閻魔の裁き	Enma's Judgment <<!>>
p.34	*Akaoni* 赤鬼	Red Ogre <<!>>
p.35	*Tamashii no Kikan* 魂の帰還	Soul Return <<!>>
p.36	*Gozuki* 牛頭鬼	Gozuki <<!>>
p.44	*Library of the Magician* 魔術師の書庫	Magician's Library <<!>>
p.47	*Fusion Birth* フュジョン　バース	Fusion Birth <<!>>
p.54	*Ghost Reinforcements* 妖魔の援軍	Ghostly Reinforcements <<!>>
p.56	*Fire Wagon* 火車	Fire Wagon <<!>>

p.61	*Elemental Hero Knospe* **E・HERO クノスペ**	Elemental Hero Knospe
p.61	*Gift from the Weak* 弱者の贈り物	Gift of the Weak <<!>>
p.61	*Soul Release* 魂の解放	Soul Release
p.61	*Parallel World Fusion* 平行世界融合	Parallel World Fusion <<!>>
p.64	*Elemental Hero Gaia* **E・HERO ガイア**	Elemental Hero Gaia <<!>>
p.86	*Quantity* クオンティティ	Quantity <<!>>
p.87	*Shine Dragon* シャイン　ドラゴン	Shining Dragon <<!>>
p.88	*Scrap Okiba* スクラップ置き場	Scrap Storage <<!>>
p.89	*Quality* クオリティー	Quality <<!>>
p.91	*Genesis Dragon* 創世龍	Genesis Dragon <<!>>
p.93	*Special Coating Body* スペシャル　コーティング ボディ	Indestructible Armor Plating <<!>>
p.94	*Sniper Mode* スナイパー　モード	Long-Range Strike <<!>>
p.115	*Bomb Dragon* ボム　ドラゴン	Dynamite Dragon <<!>>
p.115	*Dragon Evolution* ドラゴン　エヴォリューション	Dragon Evolution <<!>>

p.116	*Hurricane Dragon* ハリケイン　ドラゴン	Hurricane Dragon <<!>>
p.120	*The Big Saturn* ザ　ビッグ　サターン	Big Saturn <<!>>
p.126	*Staunch Defender* 立ちはだる強敵	Staunch Defender <<!>>
p.127	*Descending Dragon* 舞い降りる龍	Dragon's Descent <<!>>
p.127	*Prairie Dragon* プレアリー　ドラゴン	Prairie Dragon <<!>>
p.156	*Toragoedia* トラゴエディア	Tragoedia <<!>>
p.186	*Giburu* ギーブル	Guivre <<!>>
p.188	*Miracle Fusion* ミラクル フュジョン	Miracle Fusion
p.191	*Dragon Switch* ドラゴン スウィッチ	Dragon Descent <<!>>
p.192	*Dark End Dragon* ダークエンド　ドラゴン	Dark End Dragon <<!>>
p.194	*Rookie Fight* ルーキー ファイト	New Recruit <<!>>
p.194	*Elemental Hero Ice Edge* **E・HERO** アイス エッジ	Elemental Hero Frost Blade <<!>>
p.195	*Dragonic Enrage* ドラゴニク エンレジ	Dragon's Wrath <<!>>

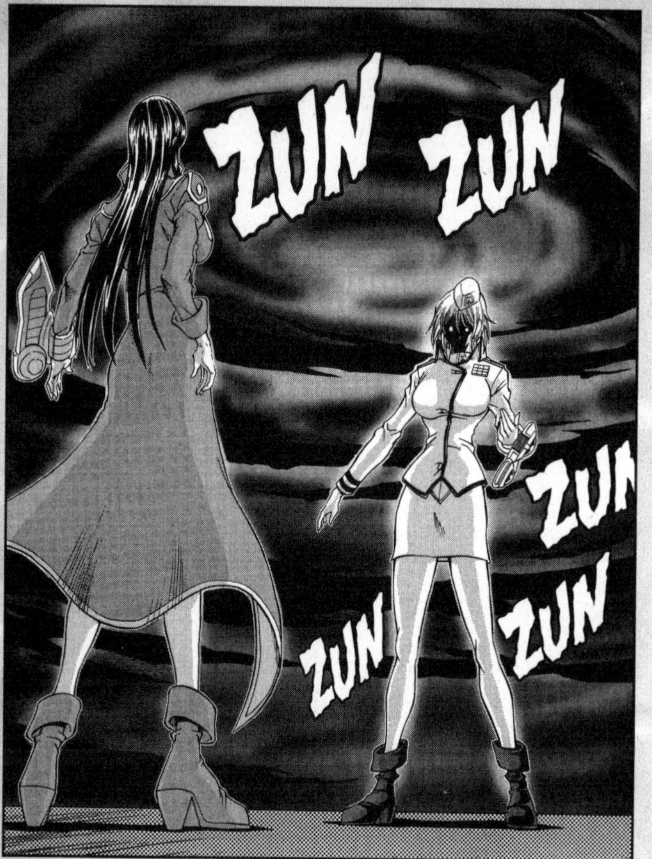
ZUN ZUN
ZUN
ZUN ZUN

IN THE NEXT VOLUME...

The ultimate hero vs. the ultimate dragon! Jaden and Chazz go head to head in the semifinals for the right to fight Kaiser—and to prove once and for all who is the better Duelist! Meanwhile, Ms. Hibiki confronts Reggie about the mysterious "spirit cards," her brother's condition, and Reggie's real reason for coming to Duel Academy. In response, Reggie challenges Ms. Hibiki to a secret Shadow Game...in an abandoned corner of the Academy, where no one can hear you scream!

COMING OCTOBER 2010!

SAVE 50% OFF
THE COVER PRICE!

IT'S LIKE GETTING 6 ISSUES
FREE!

OVER 350+ PAGES PER ISSUE

THE WORLD'S MOST POPULAR MANGA

This monthly magazine contains 7 of the coolest manga available in the U.S., PLUS anime news, and info about video & card games, toys AND more!

❏ **I want 12 HUGE issues of SHONEN JUMP for only $29.95*!**

NAME

ADDRESS

CITY/STATE/ZIP

EMAIL ADDRESS   **DATE OF BIRTH**

❏ YES, send me via email information, advertising, offers, and promotions related to VIZ Media, SHONEN JUMP, and/or their business partners.

❏ **CHECK ENCLOSED** (payable to SHONEN JUMP)   ❏ **BILL ME LATER**

CREDIT CARD: ❏ **Visa** ❏ **Mastercard**

ACCOUNT NUMBER   **EXP. DATE**

SIGNATURE

CLIP&MAIL TO:

3 1901 04365 3973   ept.

Mount Morris, IL 61054-0515

P9GNC1

* Canada price: $41.95 USD, including GST, HST, and QST. US/CAN orders only. Allow 6-8 weeks for delivery. ONE PIECE © 1997 by Eiichiro Oda/SHUEISHA Inc. BLEACH © 2001 by Tite Kubo/SHUEISHA Inc. NARUTO © 1999 by Masashi Kishimoto/SHUEISHA Inc.

ratings.viz.com   www.viz.com